THE LIBRARY OF HOLOCAUST TESTIMONIES

# *Through Blood and Tears*

Henry Skorr

3.19.06

# The Library of Holocaust Testimonies

Editors: Antony Polonsky, Martin Gilbert CBE, Aubrey Newman,
Raphael F. Scharf, Ben Helfgott MBE

Under the auspices of the Yad Vashem Committee of the Board of
Deputies of British Jews and the Centre for Holocaust Studies,
University of Leicester

SPECIAL OFFER
Books in the Library of Holocaust testimoies series may be bought in groups at a
discount of 25% For furthur details contact Toby Harris toby.harris@vmbooks.com
Tel.: 020 8952 9526 Fax.: 020 8952 9242

# Through Blood and Tears

## Surviving Hitler and Stalin

### HENRY SKORR

with
Ivan Sokolov

VALLENTINE MITCHELL
LONDON • PORTLAND, OR

First published in 2006 in Great Britain by
VALLENTINE MITCHELL
Suite 314, Premier House
Edgware, Middlesex HA8 7BJ

and in the United States of America by
VALLENTINE MITCHELL
c/o ISBS, 920 NE 58th Avenue, Suite 300
Portland, Oregon 97213-3786

Website: www.vmbooks.com

British Library Cataloguing in Publication Data

A catalogue record has been applied for


ISBN 0 85303 477 X



Library of Congress Cataloging-in-Publication Data

A catalogue record has been applied for

Printed by MPG Books Ltd, Bodmin, Cornwall

# Contents

# List of Plates

Photo captions prepared by Henry Skorr and Ann Weiss

# The Library of Holocaust Testimonies

Ten years have passed since Frank Cass launched his Library of Holocaust Testimonies. It was greatly to his credit that this was done, and even more remarkable that it has continued and flourished. The memoirs of each survivor throw new light and cast new perspectives on the fate of the Jews of Europe during the Holocaust. No voice is too small or humble to be heard, no story so familiar that it fails to tell the reader something new, something hitherto unnoticed, something previously unknown.

Each new memoir adds to our knowledge not only of the Holocaust, but also of many aspects of the human condition that are universal and timeless: the power of evil and the courage of the oppressed; the cruelty of the bystanders and the heroism of those who sought to help, despite the risks; the part played by family and community; the question of who knew what and when; the responsibility of the wider world for the destructive behaviour of tyrants and their henchmen.

Fifty memoirs are already in print in the Library of Holocaust Testimonies, and several more are being published each year. In this way anyone interested in the Holocaust will be able to draw upon a rich seam of eyewitness accounts. They can also use another Vallentine Mitchell publication, the multi-volume *Holocaust Memoir Digest*, edited by Esther Goldberg, to explore the contents of survivor memoirs in a way that makes them particularly accessible to teachers and students alike.

**Sir Martin Gilbert**
London, April 2005

*To my sweet Shelly, who shared with me*
*this tumultuous life*

# Acknowledgements

For their indispensable roles in bringing this memoir to publication, Henry extends his heartfelt appreciation to Professor Arthur Shostak, who first heard the story and helped to move it on its way, to Professor Daniel Gillis, who believed in me, to Ivan Sokolov, my dear friend and co-author, who spent so much effort to translate my story into readable English, and to Ann Weiss, my beloved friend and helper – my diamond polisher of words – who spent so much time and effort in helping me with the captions and everything else I needed.

Henry would also like to thank his friends: Mike Brown and Robert Higgins, from Smith Barney, who advise him with capability and with heart; Slava Kulikov and Sue Duberstein from the Jewish Federation Family and Children's Service of Greater Philadelphia, for their efforts to help his wife and him; Kelly Brown, the wonderful caretaker of his sick wife Shelly, who has become a valuable part of our family; Mrs Sandy Stouffer, owner of the Bakery House in Bryn Mawr, Pennsylvania, and her wonderful staff, for helping him to distribute leftover, delicious baked goods to needy people; Stephanie Yocum, Director of the Adult Day Center in Bryn Mawr, and her wonderful staff for helping Shelly, to Ludington Library for their deep interest in his life and excitement about his forthcoming book – especially Margaret Hall, Head Librarian, Marcia Bass, Head of Reference, Betty Stueblebine, Library Secretary and the whole wonderful staff; and to their wonderful neighbors, who make his life a little easier and who punctuate his walks through the neighborhood with their cheerful hellos.

Henry also gives special thanks to his daughter Esther Skorr Bleier and his son-in-law Henry Robert Bleier, to his younger brother Moishe and dear cousin Shlomo, the last of the brothers Boms, to his two nephews, Nuchem and Josh Salzberg and their families in Israel, to dear friends Seymour Shapiro and Lee Waters, to Julius, of blessed memory, and Dorka Lefkowitz, without whom the Skorr family would not have come to the United States, and to his best friend from Kalisz, Shaya Kawe, known as 'Die Geileir' ('the redhead'), who died in October 2005, just as this book was going to press, and Shaya's wife Esther. When Shaya was in the Gulag, Henry sent his friend a photo of himself as the fire chief, with the inscription: 'So long as you have life, you must have hope' – an inscription which, Shaya said, helped him hang onto life (see Plate 20).

Henry also wishes to recognize the memory of his wife Shelly's heroic Aunt Ziska, who was active in the valiant prisoner revolt at Treblinka, and her husband Jacques, the former leader of the Jewish partisans in France. He also acknowledges the holy souls of his extended family who disappeared in the hell of the Holocaust without a trace, and the blessed memory of all those victims from Kalisz and from across Europe.

Finally Henry thanks the youngest branches of the Skorr family tree, his grandchildren Joshua, Benjamin and Sarah, and his great grandchildren, Kayla and Joseph Bleier, who carry the flame of the future.

For their support and guidance throughout, Ivan would like to thank his family, especially Marion and Jason Sokolov, and friends Adrian Healey and Eleanor Emerson, Phil Simon, Doug Scheer, Dr Rivers Cuomo, Matthew Carberry, Jared Dietch, Brandon Volbright, Haverford College, Steadman Bass, Aaron Yeater, Seth Lambert, Zac Woolfitt, Jonathan Gurrie, John Willard, Nicholas Tyner, Claire Reardon, Max, Harvey and Tina Crosby, Eric and Emily Giza, Kurt and Ali Gaugler, Joshua Gallu, Sarah C. Kim and Anja Menger.

Henry and Ivan want to acknowledge deep appreciation for the dedication and commitment to memory of the staff of Valentine-Mitchell: publisher Frank Cass and editors Mark Anstee and Sian Mills – their task was a challenging one and they handled it in a professional and supportive way. Finally Henry wants to thank Sir Martin Gilbert for his invaluable help and for being the keeper of the flame, and for knowing how important it is to immortalize the victims of Nazi barbarism – and help them live forever in the pages of this book.

# Preface

During the war, as youngsters we saw weekly newsreels of aerial dogfights, battleships' guns blazing, torpedoed ships sliding under the waves, dive bombers strafing, infantry using flame-throwers, tank battles, bombsights over German cities, house-to-house fighting. We knew that war was a serious business, and that we were going to win it, but nothing prepared us for the films from liberated concentration camps in the spring of 1945. I speak for my generation when I say that they left an indelible mark on our brains: skeletal forms in striped suits or rags, with dark piercing eyes staring at the camera, scarcely recognizable as human beings; and worse, stacks of emaciated corpses being bulldozed into pits. We had nightmares.

Five years later, during my first visit to New York City, I was surprised to see so many adults walking around in short sleeves with tattooed numbers on their arms. I know exactly what that meant. They were now healthy, handsome people purposefully building new lives in the United States, focused on the present and the future. Perhaps they wanted New Yorkers to see their numbers and remember. But had any one of these good people spoken to me, I would not have known what to say.

That was a time when few wanted to talk about the Holocaust. A total of 50 New York publishers rejected Anne Frank's *Diary* before Doubleday published it in 1952. It did not become a force until the Hacketts' play (1955) and film based on it a year later. The Eichmann trial in Jerusalem stirred up painful memories in 1961. But we had to wait three more decades before a recognizable field of Holocaust Studies was in place, before the United States Holocaust Memorial Museum was opened to unexpected and astonishing success, and before our universities offered doctoral programs in this discipline.

In the autumn of 1993 I gave the first Holocaust course at Haverford College. I was dismayed at how little my students knew about it. The day after the last class, on 8 December, Steven Spielberg was interviewed on public radio about his forthcoming film *Schindler's List*. He said he expected to lose money on the film because interest in the topic was so limited. The worldwide triumph of his film, and its own Academy Award shortly thereafter, no doubt surprised him. In his acceptance speech he pleaded eloquently with historians not to let the Holocaust become 'a footnote to history'.

There is not much chance of that now. As the 50th anniversary of the liberation of the camps approached, important books began to appear, continuing to this day. Eyewitness accounts and personal memoirs form a major part of this growing bibliography. After decades of silence elderly Holocaust survivors, realizing that the hour was late, found the strength to give us their legacy. A series of books probing the trauma of Holocaust memory itself has added new weight to the discourse, and a generation of authors born after the war began producing Holocaust novels at the highest artistic level. Largely through the efforts of Edgar M. Bronfman, president of the World Jewish Congress, and his brilliant attorney Neil Levin, tragically killed in the bombing of the World Trade Center on 11 September 2001, an unprecedented US$1.25 billion settlement for Holocaust survivors was effected, against the will of collaborationist Swiss banks.

In spring 1995, when I gave my second Holocaust course, we had available only one book of Jewish sufferings in wartime Russia, *The Holocaust in the Soviet Union*,[1] and one memoir of a Jewish family, *Sixteen Years in Siberia*.[2] The collapse of communism and the breakup of the Soviet Union had not yielded much new information; the communist governments of eastern Europe, more or less in denial, or perhaps for their cynical contemporary purposes, had firmly discouraged research on this theme. Once they were gone, however, the situation did not markedly improve.

Henry Skorr's memoir will help. Like most of the famous Holocaust memoirists, Henry was a teenager when his Polish–Jewish world, already battered by Polish anti-Semitism after 1918, fell apart when Hitler attacked his country. A sharp, inquisitive mind enabled him to observe and recall everything, without exaggeration or sentimentality. A complex sociology of Jewish domestic and civil life, set against the backdrop of ingrained Polish anti-Semitism, emerges from the 1939–41 horrors he witnessed; and once his family had fled to Russia, the Jewish community's struggle for survival under siege in a certifiably insane system makes for gripping reading.

A central image recurs in Henry's pages, the Jewish cemetery as symbol of linkage to family and ancestors, of hope, of petition and consolation. He may not admit it, but he has given us a deeply religious book, one with an overpowering sense of the Jewish family as it faced systematic annihilation. He ends his second chapter thus:

> But the love in our community far outshone the specter of tragedy. As Jews, we knew we were surrounded by enemies and in danger of losing our way of life, yet we clung passionately to our provincial ways. We lived, in many ways, as they did centuries ago: simply and independently. Those of us who survived have never seen a community like it; and so 60 years later we remain refugees.

And 60 years later we have little beyond fatuous apologies from High Church sources. Make no mistake: the murderers of Jews in the Holocaust were Catholics and Protestants. We carry a heavy burden of guilt, and it will not go away.

**Daniel Gillis**
*Haverford College, Haverford, PA*

*Notes*

1.  Lucjan Dobroszycki and Jeffrey S. Gurock, eds, *The Holocaust in the Soviet Union: Studies and Sources on the Destruction of the Jews in the Nazi-occupied Territories of the USSR, 1941–1945* (Armonk, NY: M.E. Sharpe, 1993).
2.  Rachel and Israel Rachlin, *Sixteen Years in Siberia* (Tuscaloosa, AL: University of Alabama Press, 1988).

# Foreword: Henry Skorr, A Man for All Seasons

Henry Skorr is a presence that no one can ignore and no one can forget: no one is quite the same afterward.

I first met Henry when I was launching my own then newly published book.* In the crowd of several hundred people, Henry stood out – not only because of his long, thick white hair, which fell over his forehead as he spoke. No, it was something else.

In the course of doing Holocaust research for the last 18 years, I have had the privilege of hearing many hundreds of memorable stories from many hundreds of memorable people. And yet Henry and his words were quite unique – not the story alone, but the man behind the story.

During a book tour, especially a first book tour, a new author is often overwhelmed with strangers wanting more intimacy than circumstances allow. Henry Skorr has a presence that makes it impossible not to want more – not because he is pushy, but because he is sincere; not because he is demanding, but because he is earnest and compelling, all at once. He is also one of the kindest, most other-directed people one can imagine. Resourceful, enterprising, determined and kind.

Late every afternoon, Henry makes his rounds of bakeries and bagel shops, collecting what they have not sold. Early every morning, after he takes his wife to her Center, he distributes the bagels, scones, muffins and loaves of bread to people in the area – workers at the public library, the senior citizen center, and a host of other places. Why? 'Why should it go to waste? And why shouldn't I try to help?' And so it goes, Henry on his path of philanthropy, one bagel at a time.

I began to collaborate with Henry on the captions for this book, and I made a decision: I wanted Henry's voice to prevail in each caption. Together with the identification of a photo or a document, the reader will get a sense of Henry.

Despite his European accent, Henry Skorr, born Heniek Skorupa, is one of the most articulate speakers I have had the privilege to know. When we were interviewed on National Public Radio on the popular show *Morning Edition* with host Bob Edwards, Henry commented on the photos in my traveling photo exhibition and book, which feature beautiful pre-war Jewish images brought to Auschwitz-Birkenau in 1943:

> This town is all our towns, all our synagogues and all our youth groups. These pictures show our schools and our sports clubs and all the people that I remember. Ann Weiss shows the world who we were, not when we were dying, but when we were living. And where did she find these photos of life? Where? In Auschwitz, the citadel of death!

So, too, does Henry's simple account of a life lived in times both exceptional and ordinary open for us a window on to a world we would not otherwise know. Although there have been many Holocaust and wartime accounts, there have been few tellers who have the heart and vision of Henry. I regret that you cannot hear Henry telling the story himself, because it is only when you look into his dancing eyes, and hear the playful twists of phrases, that you truly get a sense of the man and the storyteller.

He once commented to me, describing his teenage love, that he 'envied the sidewalk because she walked on it'. In truth, although I have heard many descriptions of adoration, few have rivaled the simple eloquence of this one.

As he speaks, Henry pushes back the soft wisps of hair, using his fingers like a comb. His dark eyes – at once magnetic and probing, yet soft with kindness – often flash with a sense of playfulness that makes each conversation deeply memorable and yet fun. Henry tends to focus intently on every word spoken. And he has a smile that erupts often, an irrepressible smile that has the power to warm hearts. Is it obvious that I admire and love him? I couldn't hide it if I tried. And I wouldn't try.

Because I wish to introduce Henry to you in the most authentic way I know, I've chosen a story or two that stand as testimony of who is Henry Skorr. When possible, I have used Henry's words directly, edited only slightly for meaning and syntax, so his unique phraseology and authentic voice is evident. I did not write this book with Henry. I only had the privilege of writing the photo and document captions with him, and in those captions I have attempted to give not only relevant details (perhaps more than you've read in any other captions), but also the sound of Henry Skorr.

Although the totality of Henry's memories and the people and places he brings to life are the strength of this book, there are several stories that are so powerful that my thoughts come to rest on them again and again. In abbreviated form, I will share them with you now, in Henry's words, to give you a *forspize* (appetizer) of what is to come.

### BEATING MY BROTHER

After work as a slave laborer, Henry returned to the barrack with the other prisoners. For extra 'fun' the Nazis would beat the Jews at night.

> I was always getting double beated up. They were doing beating for sport. Then they got a new idea: Why should *they* beat us up? *We* should beat each other up. And they forced the people, whoever you were standing near, to beat up your friend. Or what? We didn't know what would happen if you refused. We thought we'd be killed, probably.
>
> My little brother was standing near me, like he always did. So they tried to force me to beat him up. No one before us refused their order, and two by two, the people fought. Now it was our turn, my brother and me.
>
> I decided at that moment, I will not pick up my hand.

I told the gendarme that this is my brother. I will not beat him up. No one had *ever* said such a thing. Everyone was watching to see what would happen. And I prepared to die.

I was wearing a leather jacket and with his whip, he cut into my skin like knives. My jacket, with each whip, was cut into strips like noodles. I covered my face, so he could not see my tears. Between my fingers, I could still see his pistol on his belt. So long as he didn't reach for the pistol, I could endure the beating.

And so it continued, story after story of decency, courage and unimaginable strength – not just the strength to endure beatings and the horror, but the even greater challenge of finding a way to remain human in a world devoid of humanity.

After his defiance and the beating that almost ended his life, his friends (who had complied with the Nazi order to beat up each other), criticized Henry, because they feared that his defiance would put them in jeopardy. Yet he continued to live by his principles.


THE BREAD LINE

During another time, when the people in his building needed bread, Henry gathered up their ration cards, and stood in the bread line for hours. There were special stores for each items – bread in the bread store, meat in the meat store. In order to have a chance to receive bread, Henry left at 3 a.m. and began to walk the distance through the sometimes impenetrable mounds of snow to reach the bread store. In telling the story, Henry made a gesture, high up on his chest, to show me the depth of the snow. Then he described the frigid temperatures, how desperate the situation was, and what happened when the bread store opened.

You had to be careful to calculate where to stand. The first time, I didn't know and felt so happy that I was in the front right beside the door. But when they opened the door, the force of the unruly crowd pushed so hard that I was trapped behind the door, and couldn't get in. I didn't get any bread that day – worst of all, the people I was trying to help got nothing.

Afterward, I learned to stand a little further back so that the power of the crowd – instead of pushing me out – succeeded in pushing me into the store. Here there was no policeman. Usually a policeman would be present to discipline the line and keep it in order. But not this time. The policemen knew that the girls in the shop would hide some bread for them and their friends. Here in the line, even the young boys – maybe 10 or 12 years old – were climbing over our heads to get to the front.

When I stood in line, and the snow was up to here [he motioned to just below his neck], I thought of all the people asleep and warm in their beds. [Here I was expecting a feeling of resentment, or at least envy; but instead Henry thought of them and said, 'I felt high!']

When I finally succeeded to get into the store and there was still some bread left [because the bread supply ran out after a few minutes], I then had the problem of how to get these five or six loaves home intact. I had to hide it in my clothing so the boys wouldn't steal it from me. I was hiding the bread behind my *foofaikah* [a *foofaikah* is a cotton shirt tied with a belt, both my hands free], so I could fight them off.

On the way back, I was flying, like on the wings of success. I was running to bring the bread back to the people – mostly women and children who no longer had their husbands and fathers to help. When I passed the little Jewish cemetery in our town, I would stop for a minute to say an improvised prayer of thanksgiving to G-d. In Yiddish, I would say: 'Thank you, my dear G-d, that you helped me to succeed to help the people.'

Although the outside temperature was 45 below zero, I felt warm from happiness.

When Henry thought of the people, asleep and warm in their

beds, and described his feelings, he felt happy, 'high' is the way he has always put it. His words, his actions, have inspired me, every time I think of them – or him – as I suspect they will inspire you.

This is Henry Skorr. A man of courage, a man of heart, a man of profound goodness.

Despite the sorrows he has known, the losses he has suffered and the health challenges he faces even now, he remains an optimist, with, admittedly, a bit of a mischievous edge. Every day, he buys a lottery ticket for his daughter, Esther, and for me. When I gently tried to tell him not to waste his money, at least on me, because the lottery was so hopeless, he said in his inimitable style, 'If you don't try, you have no chance.'

And so it is with life. You have to try, and try again, and yet again, to stay in the game. And, if need be, keep on trying until the challenges have been faced and met. Henry has succeeded in not just staying in the game, but playing the game well by rules that are strictly his own.

There are times when life demands more of us than we think we can bear. At these times, some choose to go inward, focusing only on their own or their family's welfare; some surrender to despair, giving up altogether. And some, those who can muster the strength and the will to do so, some choose to fight – not only with weapons of destruction (in most cases, Jews had no physical weapons) but with weapons of the soul, perhaps the most powerful weapons of all.

At times of such overwhelming inhumanity, as during the Nazi era of the Second World War, some rare few even found the strength to become more human. Henry Skorr is one.

I have been privileged to hear Henry's stories, not only how he coped in brutalizing times but how – despite everything – he managed to retain his humanity intact, and in fact, to set, as far as I'm concerned, a new standard for what it means to be human. Though tortured by the Nazis for helping others, he continued, and still continues, to help others. Though heartbroken by friends who abandoned and treated him badly, Henry chose to act with decency in an indecent world. His lifelong examples serve as an homage to the past, an example to the present, and an inspiration to the future.

I envy you your first 'meeting' with Henry. It is my wish that he will teach you precious lessons about life, as he has done for so many others, and that your life will be enriched by the experience of 'knowing' Henry, as has been mine.

I must stop now. I can already anticipate Henry's pained face as he reads these words. Humble to a fault, he would probably say, 'Stop, it's too mushy.' And so I will stop.

**Ann Weiss**
Bryn Mawr, PA
September 2004

*Ann Weiss, *The Last Album: Eyes from the Ashes of Auschwitz-Birkenau* (New York: W.W. Norton, 2001). Ann Weiss is the founder and director of the Eyes from the Ashes Educational Foundation (www.thelastalbum.org), a documentary filmmaker and a curator of a traveling photographic exhibition, based on *The Last Album*. Since its inception, she has served on the Second Generation Advisory Committee of the United States Holocaust Memorial Museum in Washington, DC. She has been a member of the Transcending Trauma Research Team at University of Pennsylvania since 1988.

# Introduction

The words 'Democratic Socialism' stood out boldly on my T-shirt, emblazoned, as they were, over a bright red rose and a clenched fist. In the deli department of the local supermarket I heard a comment, not quite *sotto voce*: 'not too good under socialism'. I looked up at the man behind the counter, his eyes peering at me from under a weathered peaked-cap. His nametag read 'Henry'.

Slightly startled by the mild rebuke, I countered, 'Under Stalinism, you mean. Nothing was too good under Stalinism.'

'I should know. I cut trees for him in that bleak Russian forest.'

I thanked him for his assistance and returned to my wife already waiting in the checkout line. I told her about our exchange and we quickly concluded that he must have been a Gulag survivor, one of the few. I felt a need to learn more of this man's story. I went back to the deli department and handed Henry my card with my home number scribbled on its back, telling him that if he ever wanted to let me know more of his story, I would love to hear it. Not a half-hour after we returned home, Henry and I were having a conversation.

Off and on for the next four years, Henry and I met for an hour each week and tape-recorded our conversations. While transcriptions of these sessions contain priceless moments, it became clear that the scope of Henry's experiences, coupled with a need to further explore the philosophical and spiritual struggles he had undergone, required another step before Henry's story was put in print.

The trouble was time. As a full professor I had precious little of it, and Henry had had much to do at home taking care of his wife Shelly who was in poor health. It seemed as if we were never going to find the time to finish what we had started in the manner we felt the material deserved. Then, in the summer of 1999, a young man offered to help.

I gratefully handed all of the material I had gathered to Ivan and asked that he do his best to compile a more lucid, flowing memoir. Instead of working with the existing transcriptions, Ivan and Henry began anew. For the sake of continuity and in the hope of bringing every memory from those days back into the fold, the two talked for hours at a time, several times a week, until they had transcriptions from over 50 hours of discussions.

From these transcriptions Henry and Ivan put together *Through Blood and Tears: Surviving Hitler and Stalin*. This triumphant memoir, which began with an off-hand comment directed at a T-shirt, is not only a study in oral history, but a unique and inspiring lesson in cooperation.

**Arthur B. Shostak**
*Emeritus Professor, Drexel University, Philadelphia, PA*

*Part I
The Way It Was*

# 1 Kalisz life

Initially in Kalisz the laws forbade a Jew to rent a house in a Christian neighborhood. As a result there was a collection of streets called the Jewish streets, governed by special laws. It was a small but old and important Jewish ghetto. Later, when the laws were relaxed, the Jewish people started to expand outside the ghetto and some gentiles moved in (they too spoke Yiddish). But in my time, though it was not required, most still lived in the original neighborhood. In these streets, we Jewish people of Kalisz were living our own life … and we were happy. This was all that we knew.

The main street was called the Jewish Street. We had a very famous synagogue and a concentration of Jewish buildings: a hospital, an old-people's home, a nursery school and an orphanage. We also had many small synagogues and kosher butcher shops set in unique storefronts which had been standing since the Middle Ages. It was a great concentration of Jewish people. This old city was so beautiful to my eyes, especially on Friday nights when I walked to the *mikvah* (the ritual baths) and saw the candles gently lighting the windows of houses. With each step I sensed the coming of the sabbath and I felt the holiness descending onto the city – it was so beautiful and so peaceful.

We made our living selling our merchandise at fairs and markets. Jews had to follow strict laws and could only perform trades that did not compete with the Polish guilds. It was forbidden to carry goods from one town to another, except certain merchandise for which a license was required. There were *rogatki* (customs checkpoints) in the corners of the cities, where tradesmen had to pay a Jewish tax for bringing in these commodities. There was an organization called the *Kleinhandeler Verein*, which dealt with the problems Jewish tradesmen had with the Polish guilds. They would offer protection from looters and pogroms, grant loans without interest (often on a weekly basis) and provide a unified voice in dealings with the guilds and the Polish government.

The whole industry in Kalisz was either Jewish or German. On the street next to our home there was the Mueller textile factory, a German factory big enough to have its own fire department. Nearby was the Pfiebeger piano factory, famous throughout Europe. Neither hired Jews. The factories took up whole blocks and exported their wares throughout Europe, Russia and China. From our house we would sit and watch the Mueller factory firemen do safety exercises, or in the night watch the swallows circle around the big steam chimney. There was a very big Jewish embroidery industry in Kalisz. It was Jewish-owned, only the masters working on the machines were either Belgian or German because they were always bringing in new, automated machinery from the west. I remember strikes protesting against the introduction of this new machinery, which resulted in the factories not needing so much manual labour.

The name of our street was Ciasna Strasse, Narrow Street. It started from the bridge at the Prosna River and went all the way to the new market, the *Dekerta*. The street was made of cobblestones and lined with old buildings. It had no drainage system or canalization, so to clean the street, janitors would throw down white disinfectant and push it along with water. There were grocery stores, three bakeries, Helfgott, Szmlewitcz and Gumbprich (always in competition with each other) and a cinema. The films we saw were silent, but there was a live orchestra to play the score. There was a man who came on a bike at night and lit the gas lamps, returning the next morning to extinguish the flames. Such a narrow street with these lights was very beautiful.

The streets were always alive and bustling, filled with Jewish men standing around and talking politics. These men always used to congregate on the corner of Jewish and Ciasna streets, especially when it was a holiday or a Sunday when Jewish people were officially not allowed to trade. Someone would buy a newspaper for 4 or 5 cents (this was very expensive) and read it before handing it on to someone else. Not everybody was able to read, so meeting in the street was an important forum for communication.

The women would sit in front of their houses, which was against the law, and tell stories while the children ran around and played in the street. If they saw a policeman they would have to take in the chairs and run to the backyard. We, the children, would shout false alarms to the women, 'A policeman is coming!' and everybody would run, affording us much merriment. Also on Sundays, small groceries would be sold illegally from a back door. In the same way, a beggar would stand guard at the front to warn them if a policeman was coming. If this was the case they would immediately close and disperse because everybody was afraid of punishment.

Every Sunday soldiers came to the movie house from the *kesernes,* the army bases, wearing hobnailed boots and emitting a distinctive smell, possibly from cabbage. It was wonderfully exciting for the children because we were in love with these soldiers. To us they were so brave and impressive, beautifully dressed, with bayonets on their sides. Jews had to enlist, like Polish citizens, but there was discrimination in the army. During holidays, we would invite the Jewish soldiers into our houses to celebrate and eat with us.

There were four bases around Kalisz, including a base for the *ulani,* Poland's famous cavalrymen. It was the cream of the crop – a very elite group made up only of boys of a specific height and build. As a boy, I loved to go to the fields to watch them train, to see them expertly swing their sabers while galloping through obstacle courses.

We had all kinds of people on my street. We had people we called *nar,* stupid people, and we had people we called *misiganah,* crazy people. There was a man, Moishe-nar, who came on the street to report who had just died. He worked for our burial society and this was his only job. Our neighbor, Krocl, a small grocery owner, had a boy who went crazy. On hot days he would walk around the streets and climb on the telegraph poles. His mother would lure him down, offering him pieces of bread. She would have to tell the other children

5

to stop laughing. We had *misiganah* gentile people, like Crazy Olszewski. He fought Jews and cursed Jews, but to us he was harmless. We would tease him and laugh while he chased dogs.

There was a daughter of the famous Voler Rabbi who went crazy. They told me she had been in love with somebody but it did not work out because his family was not religious enough – she had to marry a rabbi. She once took a child and ran away. For weeks the people and police searched for her until they found her deep in the forest. Another time she took a knife and cut her own throat. They called on my father because he was so strong. He had to immobilize her, tying her hands with a wire so others could take her to the hospital. Her end was tragic: she jumped from the second floor to the street and killed herself.

At the end of our street was the house of the famous Dr Dresher. He kept beautiful horses he used when visiting sick people. He was particularly special to the Jews of Kalisz because in 1918, during the pogrom celebrating Polish independence, he was the only one to open the gates of his estate so that Jews could escape the mob. My Aunt Figah, who looked like a gentile, stood in the street secretly telling Jews to run to his home. His funeral was the biggest I ever saw, such was our admiration.

On that bustling street there were big wagons with horses carrying coal for the factories, wood for the bakeries and bringing sugar beets to the processing plant. A gang of gentile boys would steal from the wagons. One boy would climb up on the wagon and throw down coal, wood, or sugar beets to a group of boys behind him. The driver was afraid of them, so he just whipped his horse and kept going. Later, they would sell these things very cheaply. Sometimes a policeman would come, walking in those days, but he could not catch the boys because they ran underneath a bridge and hid along the gas lines coming out of a factory.

From the time of my birth in 1921 until we moved in 1934 my family lived in a building with over 100 tenants. It was our home and social center. There was a big gate with an entrance in front that locked at night, and a series of smaller buildings in the backyard. Our one building was like a small town. We had so many different types there: shoemakers, tailors, a boy scout organization, two bakeries, two Jewish organizations, a monument maker, the famous Voler Rabbi with a Yeshiva school, and many others. Mostly Jews populated the building, but there was a gentile tenant, a Polish man named Szczepan with a decent Polish mustache. He and his children also spoke Yiddish.

That backyard was our social laboratory. It was filled with groups of children, usually separated by age groups. One neighbor, Szmulek Rotsztein, had a horse-drawn carriage. Every Friday the children went with him to the river to wash the horses. It was a very good time for us, as were most days. Often we would be having so much fun we would refuse to go to our homes to eat, shouting up to my grandmother instead, begging her to throw down some bread with butter and sugar.

There were always activities in the evening, starting when the grown-ups returned from work. There we could see traveling acrobats, like gypsies and their bears. At times the men would compete to see who was the strongest and my father always won. I remember we had a big piece of iron from a factory that nobody could pick up, except my father who did it easily. I was so proud of him, I felt like he was a king!

There was a public toilet, because there were no toilets in the house. In the morning you could see people with their night pots going to throw away the dirty water. There was also a garbage dump infested with so many rats that the policemen in the neighborhood would sometimes come to our backyard for shooting practice. It was emptied once or twice a year, and then the Polish peasants would come and take away what was left to fertilize their fields.

We had a pump in the backyard, a well, which was a central point. Mostly it was the center of fighting, arguments over who took too much water. There were plenty of boys living at the Yeshiva and getting water from the well. At the same time a Polish man, who was working for one of the bakeries and probably an anti-Semite, would come to take water. He would start to pick on them, the Yeshiva boys, but there were a few boys who were not afraid. Soon they would hear the commotion and come to the well, then a fight ensued.

We lived on the fourth floor with no water, no electricity and no toilet. Everything had to be done by hand and we accepted this as a normal life. My father, I remember, was always carrying up two buckets of fresh water in the morning and taking down the dirty water the next day. Later two tenants, Rifkah-nar and Moishe-nar, started to bring us water. You would pay them by throwing a nickel in the buckets. The Voler rabbi occupied a whole floor. Rifkah-nar and Moishe-nar would take out his night pots because the rabbi did not use the outside toilet – it was beneath his station. Later the Rabbi married Rifkah-nar and Moishe-nar, it was a *mitzvah*.

My mother and my grandmother kept a great kitchen. Everything hung on the walls, all the dishes and all the pots. The meals were cooked over coal, which I thought made the kitchen smell wonderful. I loved to watch my mother when she made bread or noodles. At that time nothing came ready-made, you did it all yourself. She always baked a lot of cakes on Friday because on Saturday it was forbidden to make a fire so everything had to be prepared beforehand.

We were very close to our neighbors in that building. I remember third-floor tenants with whom we were very friendly, the Kawe family. The father was a very religious man and the monument maker for the Jewish cemetery. We would play on the stones he was carving in the backyard. His boy, Shaya Kawe, was like a brother to me. In our house there was also my uncle, Shloime Gerszin (really my mother's cousin) who, as well as being a shoemaker, was the leader of the illegal Communist Party in Kalisz and, perhaps more famously, a great practical joker. When it rained he would take little pieces of glass, used for cleaning the soles of shoes, and throw them into the street so people would believe that coins were falling.

We had plenty of crazy people in our house. There was one woman, Misigina Sheidle, who would sit in the attic above us and make all kinds of noises. We were terribly afraid of her, she had such green, glowing eyes. In the summer time she would go out to the river, take off her clothes and walk naked along the banks, back and forth. Once she took my younger brother and tried to throw him in the river!

Our house had long wooden steps and in the night the stairway was pitch black. There were supposed to have been little kerosene lights, only they were not refueled very often. We were so afraid to go up and down in the dark, especially with Misigina Sheidle, so we would play all day in the backyard and wait for the adults to come home and take us upstairs. My father would carry us like bundles under his arms.

At ten o'clock at night, the gates would close and you could not get in. You would have to ring a special bell for the janitor to come out, and then you had to give him 10 *grosze*. You had to pay him, and he was fanatically anti-Semitic. Letting the tenants in gave him control and also allowed him to know who was going in and who was going out. The janitor was like an agent for the police, telling them what was going on in the house, what was legal and what was not legal. He had more power than the landlord, who was Jewish, because he knew more and he was a gentile. You could be the richest of the Jews, the most educated of the Jews, but you were already lower than the janitor was. A Jew could not be a janitor, it was one of the professions that had an association barring Jews.

In our apartment lived my parents, my maternal grandmother, my older sister Henya, my younger brother Nuchem and later my youngest brother Moishe. My mother was like the sun, always surrounded by a warm glow. She was so good that everybody, all the tenants, would cling to her – on the sabbath our house was filled with guests. She had such a warm heart. One Friday there was a crisis when people had no money, and the Jewish landlords became callous and started evicting tenants, throwing them out on the street. My mother ran round to all the tenants, through the entire building, collecting money and negotiating with the landlord to let the people stay for a week. Other times she would collect bread for the poor people – there were so many poor people suffering from hunger. She was the heart and the soul of our family. I adored her and I remember as a boy loving the way she smelled.

My father was a kosher butcher, strong enough to kill a cow with his fist. He was so brave and so big in my eyes, he was my hero. At home his word was law. My mother, I would say, was smarter than my father was, but she stayed half a step behind him, always doing whatever he was doing. He was a true perfectionist, they say you could shave with his knives. Orders used to come from across the city for special cuts of meat from him, such was his reputation. He was well known in the community, and when we went walking along the river I could hear the people say, 'There goes Josef with his son.' I was so proud.

My grandmother was a wonderful homemaker and cook, always singing old Jewish folk songs to us. She was a clever shopper, going throughout the town to get cheaper sugar and better water. She even brought her own bags so the weight on the scales would be less! She did not hear so well but she wanted to know everything that was going on. My father would settle her in a chair and he would yell out what was in the newspaper. We were just children, so this was so funny to us and we always laughed. My father would say, 'Don't you laugh at your grandmother!' He loved her deeply. My father had a temper sometimes, and she was the only person not afraid of him. If he started to come after us, she would stand between us like a rooster and say, 'I want to see what you'll do to them!' And he would yell, 'Go away grandmother, go away!' until he started to laugh. She was terribly thin because she had an illness which caused her to vomit after she ate something or if she became excited. Sometimes we had to massage her head over a basin.

My older sister Henya was like all the children in that house, running around and playing constantly. Once, my father came home from the slaughterhouse with an ax – we had never seen such a big and sharp ax – which he put behind the door in the entrance of the house. The girls were playing hide and seek and Henya hid behind the door and accidentally cut her leg to the bone! She was taken to hospital and had that scar for the rest of her life. My father was desperately upset.

My younger brother Nuchem was a sweet and talented boy. He was very slender but good-looking and he was very gifted with his hands. When we were older and in school, we could see that he excelled in both the girls' and the boys' traditional work – carpentry, shoemaking, sewing and darning – plus he was very good with electricity. He made a box for my coin collection in which, if you pressed the Poland button, a light would shine on the Polish coin. I was two years his senior, but we were very close.

I remember when my youngest brother Moishe was born. We were staying in my Uncle Shloime Gerszin's apartment, and I did not know why. He woke me up and told me I had a brother, and I remember thinking, 'Where did I get a brother from?' He took us home and I saw many small children from the *kheder*, the Jewish preschool, praying near my mother. It was a tradition that children pray for the health of the mother, and she was not in good health. Both my sister and my mother were overweight and my mother's lungs were very weak. For a short time after that pregnancy she was very ill.

Moishe was born partially blind and a little slow. We did not know this at first, but my grandmother discovered it. He was very sickly. He had sores on his head that would form pus and scab, so we had to apply fish oil given to us by the Jewish health organization. He was always accidentally getting into trouble. He would try to climb trees and he would fall because he could not see. Sometimes when it would rain, the janitor would lift the cover off the drain in the backyard to increase the drainage. Poor Moishe walked into it and almost drowned. We always had to keep an eye on him.

Throughout Kalisz we had many relatives: cousins, aunts and uncles. My father's side was very religious. His mother, my grandmother Liebe Rivkah, carried a prayer book for women and wore the traditional *szeitle* (a wig), pearls and a Turkish shawl. When I was three she brought me to the *kheder*. I remember being terrified and offended by the rabbi's beard, which smelled of snuff and was dirty with tobacco. My grandmother was thrilled to see the other children dance around me, putting candy and nuts on my head. This was a traditional ritual, and she was very proud.

My paternal grandfather Henrik, my namesake, was a dairy farmer in Warta and a strong man, like a typical Polish peasant.

He was killed in a riot against the Jews when my father was a small boy. He tried to beat off the Poles with the shaft of his carriage, but somebody knocked him down from behind and the rioters caught up with him and beat him to death.

My father had three sisters living in Kalisz: Blima, Chaya Sura and Figah. He had another, Polcha, living in the small village of Sieradz. My mother had two brothers, Shloime and Herschel. Shloime moved to Brazil to be with his rich second wife, but Herschel was always around. His wife Rifka was so kosher that she would not visit us in our house, we were not religious enough. She was not keen to allow her children to visit us either, she thought they would be influenced by our behavior. My parents had cousins coming and going in Kalisz, and I had plenty of my own. There was a wonderful feeling of family on those streets.

My father, like most men in Kalisz, was strongly political. At that time, with German fascism on one side, Russian communism on the other and the Polish government becoming less tolerant of Jews, it was important that we were all aware of politics. Every part of our lives was touched somehow by our political affiliations. In Kalisz the Jews had four political parties: the Bund (Polish socialists); the Poalei Zion (labor Zionists); the Aguda (orthodox Jewry); and the illegal Communist Party. My father was a member of the Poalei Zion. All but the communists maintained their own schools and youth groups in Kalisz and fought intensely for seats in the *kehila*, a committee of Jews separate from the city council but sanctioned by the government.

The Bund believed in Poland, that it was the fatherland and they would someday build a socialist government with the Polish people. It was born out of the Socialist Democratic Party before the Russian Revolution and was made up of Jews from Poland, Russia and Lithuania. In 1897, at the Conference of Socialist Parties in Czarist Russia, the Bund split with Lenin and the Bolsheviks (the majority party) and joined Martoff and the Mensheviks (the minority party). As a result, neither the Bund nor the Polish Socialist Party (PPS), their Polish brother-organization, looked towards Russia as a model. The

Poalei Zion party was socialist but also Zionist, believing in the creation of a Jewish state, today's Israel. Within the Poalei Zion there were different groups – left, right, center – my father was from the left. The parties were very similar in many respects, but their differences emerged most during elections and on May Day (1 May) the traditional workers' holidays.

In line with his political beliefs, my father was planning to move the family to Palestine in the mid-1920s. We had our passports ready, but we never received a certificate of permission from the British government. They only issued a certain number, which would be given to the party leadership who would then divide them among the competing members. Since we were not rich industrialists or rabbis, we never received our permission.

The Bund's newspaper was called *Die Volkszeitung* (the People's Paper) and the Poalei Zion's was called *Die Arbeiterzeitung* (the Workers' Paper). They were filled with election babble and jabs directed towards the other parties. There was a Poalei Zion joke about the corruption in Bund campaigns:

> *Bund candidate: Yankel, what do you want from*
> *this election?*
> *Voter: A two-room apartment.*
> *Bund candidate: Chaim! Put him down for a*
> *two-roomer.*

The rhetoric was strongest on 1 May, when demonstrations covered many parts of the city. The Jewish streets were filled with great debates. Kalisz was an important city in national politics and many speakers would come from Warsaw for the demonstrations. This was a real holiday! The politicos would sing ferocious songs that day, and looking back, I would say the songs were mostly bloodthirsty, a lot of singing about killing. The famous *International*, the official song of the Communist Party, was especially so:

> *If the flag is red, it is from the blood of the workers!*
> *We will be the judges and cut down the capitalists!*

13

The Communist Party was not allowed to organize demonstrations so they perfected a technique called a *masuwka*, a lightning-quick political rally and speech that always ended with a red flag being left behind to mark their presence. My cousin Moszka, the son of Shloime Gerszin, was spotted by a Polish informer and was arrested for making such a speech but managed to escape to Spain. We had a few of our people elected to the city council in Kalisz to protect the Jewish interests. These elections were also very fiercely fought. In national Polish elections, Jews could vote for congressmen in the lower house, the *Sejm*, but not for the *Senat*, the upper house. To vote for this you had to be a businessman or have a higher education. The Aguda had a deputy in the *Sejm*, a congressman named Greenberg.

The youth groups were much like the boy scouts in the United States. The children had to go through all kinds of routines: wearing uniforms, chanting their slogans (*chazak, vometz!* – strong and ready!), performing daily exercises and receiving political guidance. These groups were the basis for most of our friendships, the basis for our social and religious development – like an extension of the family.

By the time I was 10 years old, my parents had four children, my father was thinking about going into business for himself and the landlord was about to charge the tenants a fee to install electricity. My mother saw all this and helped convince my father to take a look at new apartments. A widow of a gentile butcher told him that there was a nice apartment to rent on Niecala Street near a park. It was not in the old city but Jewish people did live over there, so my father and mother went to see the place. They fell in love with that apartment, with that house and with that neighborhood. Plus, Polish landlords liked to have Jewish tenants because they were decent and quiet people.

The new house already had electricity and a sewage system – you did not have to carry the dirty water downstairs! The house was at No. 14 Niecala Street, which later became Piernackiego Street with the Polanization of street names, and our apartment was on the second floor. It was a small street, a very nice street, which ran from Kilnickiego Plaza to the city park. Almost everything was in good condition, including the water pump and the backyard, and it had big windows that looked out onto a small river that flowed into the Prosna. We even had a balcony from which we could see the suburbs of Kalisz.

The backyard had a number of trees under which I loved to sit, reading my books and imagining that I wandered through all kinds of countries. There was a small stable where we sometimes kept a cow for a month or two, preparing it for slaughter. I loved to cook potatoes and other things, then feed the cow. I adored its warmth and its beautiful, stupid eyes. I even learned to milk her. Bartosz, the son of the landlord, helped me. He had another brother, Emanuel, who was violently anti-Semitic. Once, during a riot against Jews in the park, he was badly beaten up by my father. Imagine his surprise when we moved in! Thereafter he avoided my father.

Niecala Street was less of a Jewish center, but it was very interesting. The Shreier toy factory was on our street, a big, beautiful Jewish toy factory that occupied almost half the block. Next to that was the office of the dentist Schmegelsky, then a villa also owned by Mr Shreier. The German minority had their church in a beautiful house filled with plants next to the Shreiers' villa. The pastor was a nice, fair-haired man, but the porter who took care of the church had two sons who were always fighting. One of his sons once threw a stone that split my head open. On the other side of the street was a small, beautiful Russian church next to an unemployment office. I remember people coming to register for work at the office, and sometimes police fighting the rioters because there was no work. Also on that street was an old music hall, an enterprising auditorium where orchestras played and choral groups sang. Directly opposite our house was a famous photographer of the time, his name was Engel.

From our balcony we could see the old prison, which was built like a fortress. Sometimes we saw prisoners wearing distinctive gray clothing emerge with the guards to buy things in the city. The prison had a political section where they held Communists who were serving long sentences.

From time to time these political prisoners went on hunger strike, demanding to wear their own clothing, not the same attire as the criminal prisoners, and the right to read literature and newspapers.

One of our neighbors was a Polish tenant named Staszek, a shoemaker who was extremely anti-Semitic and was forever cursing and fighting us. We were involved in many battles with him. We had six or seven strong Jewish boys living in that house, such as the brothers Szivek, sons of the blacksmith, who were always fighting – with or without Staszek.

The Szivek sons made clothing for others to sell at markets in other towns. This family was very musically inclined, playing on fiddles and on their piano. They were the first people we knew to have a radio. One night, Mr Szivek called in all the Jewish tenants to hear the famous Joseph Schmidt, a cantor and movie star from Austria, sing in a Jewish concert. We listened with great pleasure and, following the performance, Mr Szivek's sons played on fiddles and other instruments. It was wonderful.

Below us on the first floor lived the Zelver family, part owners of the Jewish bus service. They loved to sing beautiful Jewish songs. On the bottom floor lived a particular anomaly, a Polish policeman living with the Lenczitskys, a Jewish family. The policeman was a nice, old man called Ferdunos who was building a villa in Vinjary, a suburb of Kalisz. He had three daughters. The middle daughter was Wanda, a real anti-Semite. She was a leader in the girl scouts and she moved so stiffly that we joked she must have swallowed a stick. When she saw a Jew she would turn her head away or spit on the floor.

The whole Lenczitsky family was communist and all had been imprisoned. They said that one son was an informer for the police. They found him 'swimming' one day in the river, dead. His legs and hands were bound with wire.

The Kopel family lived on the top floor of the house. We were very close to them, as we were to the Kawe family on Ciasna Street. They had four nice children: Lola (my age, or a year older), Fela, Israel and Lolek the baby. Mr Kopel made his living by buying merchandise in other towns and bringing it to Kalisz to sell.

In our apartment, in her own section, lived a Polish maid who had been there with the former tenant, a Polish pastor. She was very quiet and kept to herself, so much so that I have hardly any memories of her at all. Later, when the Nazi government kicked out their Jews of Polish descent, we had another woman and her daughter living with us. It was a case of my mother doing anything she could to help.

We loved our new apartment, though we missed our old neighborhood very much. We were like birds remembering the place where they were hatched. We visited frequently but soon grew accustomed to our new place and could not have been happier.

# 2 My family: such warm memories

On Saturdays my father would order a big siphon of seltzer water from Cohen's factory, along with some ice. This was the best thing. There was a cellar in the same building as the *kheder*, where peasants brought huge chunks of ice they had cut from the river in the winter to be sold in the summer. People paid to put their food on ice for the sabbath and on holidays, to keep it from spoiling. A boy would deliver the seltzer to us with the ice in wooden barrels. Friends and guests would come over and we had a great celebration.

The extended family came to our house because of my mother's warm-heartedness. Uncle Hershel would come on Saturday with his boys, while Aunt Rifka stayed home with their girls – lest we should influence them. He liked to sit down and read a book because he could not do this in his own home – he was very much a book person. My father's cousin Nuchem would come about once a month. He did not live in Kalisz, but when he did join us he just sat in the corner and said nothing. We, the children, would play with our cousins and friends or walk along the riverbanks in the park. Different kinds of people would end up at our house, either by chance or through my mother's generosity. There was always something new.

My sister eventually got work as a seamstress through which she acquired an ethnic German friend, Else. She was the daughter of the pastor of the German church near our house, a beautiful building with ivy growing on the walls. She said she liked to come to Jewish houses on Friday nights when the table was covered with white, the candles were lit and the electric light was on, she liked the atmosphere very much. She especially liked to come over when a particular guest came to our table, an old man we called Moishe

Papierosnik – Moishe the cigarette maker.

At that time people rarely bought cigarettes in the stores, they made their own. It was a special profession to make cigarettes for clients. Moishe bought all kinds of tobaccos, Turkish and Kurdish for example, mixing them together with a little liquid and using a special instrument to roll the cigarettes. He made approximately 200 cigarettes a week for my father, who was a heavy smoker, something which caused my mother some concern.

Amazingly, Else liked to flirt with Moishe, that old Jewish man! He had a beard, a red nose and always smelled of tobacco. He would talk to her in Yiddish, she would answer in German and they had a good laugh in which we all joined.

After those wonderful Saturdays, it was hard for us to go back to our daily lives. I remember when I was older and an apprentice, I used to start worrying and moaning about work the next week on Friday night!

My father would not go to work on Sundays but to the *rav* of Kalisz, the very famous head rabbi, to take part in the *vikuchim*, the discussions about kosher laws. This was a dynamic topic and the debate was always heated. Under kosher law, the animals had to be killed by the *szoscshet*, a designated executioner who performed the ritual slaughters. In Kalisz, the *kehila* employed the *szoscshet*. The slightest thing which contradicated kosher law would cause him to declare the meat *traif*, not kosher, and this would demoralize the butcher. The conduct of the butchers was discussed since a kosher butcher had to be very pious. If, by mistake, my father took off his hat on Saturday just for a moment, the rabbi would admonish him, saying, 'Rab Josef, a kosher butcher without a hat on a Saturday?' As his son, I was not allowed to go to school on Saturdays, this would have counted against him. When I was going to a Polish school that met on Saturdays, I would have to spend all day Sunday rushing to catch up on my work.

There was a modern slaughterhouse in Kalisz where my father would take his cows to the *szoscshet*. Mostly the cows were declared kosher, but from time to time they were not. My mother could tell by the sound of his steps coming up to the apartment whether he was upset. If he was, it meant that his cow had been declared *traif* and he had no meat to sell, plus he had to sell the cow to a gentile butcher at half the usual price. She would say, 'Children, you have to be quiet. Your father is upset.' If we were drinking tea, we could not even make a noise with our teaspoons, we were that afraid of him.

In that time, a tradesman started as an apprentice, then a *gazelle*[1] and eventually a master. After my parents married, my father became a *gazelle*, later a master. When I was a small boy my father was a *gazelle* working in the Butchers Union. I remember lying in bed hearing fighting, cursing voices coming from the kitchen – they were organizing the union. I heard these voices, I smelled their cigarettes and I was scared, so I started to cry. My father said, 'Be quiet!' But the more he told me to be quiet, the more I cried until I interrupted them. He came into my room and I remember him asking me, 'Why are you crying?' I replied, 'I'm afraid. The room is very dark and somebody is standing over there.' He calmed me down by putting his big heavy hand very gently on my head and saying, 'Everything will be okay, don't be afraid.' He went out to the others and said, 'Now *you* be quiet because you're scaring my son.' Eventually my father went to work for himself.

Of course, one had to buy cows to be a butcher. Sometimes people would come to the butcher shop to sell a cow, bringing the cow's *metrica*, birth certificate, but mostly my father went to the countryside. In a quiet way my father was training me to become a butcher, taking me with him to buy cattle. It was an intricate process that mystified and impressed me; it was an adventure. We would walk the length of the city, down Michovska Street, named after the owner of the Michov estate, and into the fields. My father prepared for the trip by putting a knife in one boot, his money in the other and an oak cane in his hand. It was not safe for Jews to walk into some villages. The country roads were dotted with crosses and icons of the Virgin Mary. My father told me, 'If you see a Pole who does not take off his hat or cross himself at the icon, you know he's a dangerous person, he's a killer. If he's not religious, he can't be trusted.' He would give me instructions:

'If somebody invites me inside a barn to look over a cow or for something else, don't come in with me, just stay outside. You have to keep watch.'

The peasant would not know if my father was a butcher or just someone sent to buy a cow. There were retired butchers who made money by buying cows for other people. It was a dangerous business, especially for older butchers. There was the tragic slaying of Shloime Zelmud, a retired butcher who had gone out to buy cows. A peasant invited him into his barn, Shloime Zelmud began taking out his money and the peasant hit him from behind and killed him. After taking his money he buried him. All the Jewish butchers searched for him, not relying on the police until they had found the evidence. When they had found the body and the police had arrested the peasant, my father gave the policeman 5 zlotys to hit the criminal, which he did, and that murderer almost lost his head.

We would enter a village, usually one I had never seen before, and my father would start to sing: 'I'm buying calves!' '*Krowki jalufki kupuye!*' He would go around the streets singing, and he would say to me, 'You say it too!' I was embarrassed, but I would also sing: '*Krowki jalufki kupuye!*' The peasants would hear us and one would emerge.

My father would approach the peasant saying, '*Szczesz Boze*', 'God bless you', and take off his hat. The peasant would say, '*Boze Zaplac*', 'God keeps you'. He would invite him in with pleasantries and then the whole procedure would start. There were many things my father had to determine, most importantly the weight, value and probability of its being kosher. My father would grab the cow behind the neck, under the haunch, along the back, and he could tell you to the kilogram how much it weighed. He could also tell by touch if it was a fatty cow or a lean cow; at that time it was more desirable to get a fatty cow, people did not like lean meat. There was no way to tell if the cow was kosher before it was slain, but my father always preferred to buy from simple peasants rather than big ranches that sometimes dropped nails into the potatoes that they fed to the cows.[2]

After my father had inspected the cow and decided he

wanted to buy it, the two would negotiate a price. The market for cows was always fluctuating, so weight and quality were not the only factors. The peasant would be the first to name a price. He would say, '100 zlotys,' and hold out his hand. My father would say, '80 zlotys,' and slap the peasant's hand. They would do this until they agreed on a price: *slap* – 100 zlotys! *slap* – 80 zlotys! *slap* – 90 zlotys!, haggling together until they would shake on a figure. My father would never take out the money in front of the peasant, because he could be killed. Instead he would go to the toilet out back, remove the money from his boot and return to pay the peasant. For these trips my father always took paper money because it could be hidden.

We would load the cow into the cart – no easy task – and bring the cow back to Kalisz. The peasant would have to give my father the *metrica*, which had to be shown to the health inspector before the cow was slaughtered. Sometimes we would keep a cow at our apartment and sometimes the cows would be put out in a peasant's field, for which my father would pay.

I helped my father in many ways, mostly in cleaning the shop and feeding the cows. On Sundays, when the shop was closed, I used a special scraper on the butcher's block and covered it with a wet towel. I then went down to the basement and checked to see that the skins were in good condition. I knew being a butcher was not for me; however, after I went to the slaughterhouse for the first time, I witnessed the killing of a cow, I smelled the blood and I fainted.

There were other factors that kept me away from butchery. My father had his shop in an old medieval building alongside many other butchers. Only three or four were Jewish, the rest were Polish. The relationships that developed there were indicative of so much of Poland. My father would address the other butchers politely with 'Mr' and 'Sir', while they would call him 'Josek', a diminutive of his first name. There was a *Volksdeutscher*, an ethnic German, named Stark who always spoke harshly and sarcastically to my father. I could not take this, yet to my father it seemed normal.

I did not like this, I did not like the killing and I did not like the smell of blood. I saw how the gentile butchers put live pigs in boiling water to take off the hair, and I heard their horrible squeals. I saw the kosher butchers with knives in their mouths like devils, slaughtering cows. When my father bound the legs of a slain cow and tossed it across the cutting table, with its blood gushing, I was sure that I was in hell, it was like Dante's Inferno.

Sometimes I would deliver one of my father's famous filet mignons across the city to a gentile bar, a bar for hunters. The owner would come to the shop with a cigar and say, 'Josek, make me one of your special cuts.' I would put the meat inside a long, wooden carrying case with a cover, strap it on my back and deliver it. The bar was filled with smells alien to me, Christian smells. It was the odor of cigars, different alcohol and gentile men. I would present the cut to the owner with my hat in my hand, waiting for him to inspect and accept it. This was the tradition, but for me it went against the grain – he was up there and I was down here. My father did not know that this was a problem for me, we never discussed it. When it came time for me to study a trade, my mother helped me avoid upsetting my father by somehow explaining to him that butchery was not for me, which helped me a great deal.

My parents' generosity extended not only to our family and friends in Kalisz, but also to those in surrounding cities and villages. My father's sister, Aunt Polcha, lived with her husband Feter Schmul in Sieradz, an old town like Kalisz, and the town where my mother was raised, not too far away. They had four or five daughters, all very beautiful and strong like real peasant girls. You did not see such powerful yet feminine girls in the city. Aunt Polcha sent them to live with us in Kalisz, hoping they would eventually find some household work. There was a woman who made a profession of finding work for Jewish girls from the villages, and my mother had many discussions with her about her nieces.

One daughter, Michka, worked in the household of a man who owned a fancy, imported food store. She was very strong, yet when she hugged me I could feel that she had the hands of a woman. We went over to that house and she gave us all kinds of food that we had never seen at home: lox, different kinds of salami, watermelon and bananas. She dated a Jewish soldier, so my mother warned her, 'Don't go out with a Jewish soldier. A Jewish soldier is not a serious man, he goes with you because he's here in the army.' I was a young boy at the time and did not understand what she meant. Still, Michka was happy, always smiling, showing her beautiful teeth.

With such a large family there was bound to be tragedy. My mother's cousin Sura and her husband Josef Stackman lived on Ciasna Street in a basement apartment with their four children. They were very poor so my mother was constantly giving them help. I would go with her sometimes to visit or to bring extra food or money. As you walked down the steps to that basement a smell of dampness emanated from the walls, a smell I equated with poverty for many years. The floor was covered with sand, an old Polish housecleaning tradition.[3] The windows were at street level so as a small child watching people pass by I used to think the feet were walking on their own. I asked my mother where the rest of the people had gone, and this made them laugh.

My mother was always talking to Sura; she felt that she needed to give her help, not only materially, but also just to talk to her. She was such a depressed woman, always clutching a peasant's shawl tight to her chest. Her face was gaunt, her eyes sunken and she had no teeth. Despite my mother's invitation, she rarely came to our house; it was too lively and full of light. Her depression was compounded by their poverty. Josef was a glazier, but he was not very prosperous. He would carry glass, a frame and his diamond cutter around to the outlying villages, fixing broken windows. Rarely did he return with enough money to support his family. This poverty caused Sura to worry constantly about finding husbands for their daughters because there would be no dowry.

They had such nice, quiet children. My mother arranged for one of the daughters, Chayale, to come to our house every day to eat while she was learning to be a seamstress. She asked us to behave less boisterously, to make Chayale feel more comfortable. Both my mother and my grandmother would talk to her in a special way, trying to make her feel at home. She would come and sit quietly like a bird, and I could see that she did not feel comfortable. They would ply her with questions, which she would answer tersely, as if she were hurt or offended.

When I was older and learning how to make the upper parts of shoes, I was able to get an unpaid job for my cousin Gerszen, Chayale's younger brother. I convinced the master to accept him without money and without a contract, just so he could be around the trade, hopefully learning something while he was there. He would run errands for us and come to eat with my family.

The other two children were the baby, Esther, and the oldest, Dovora. Sura was obsessed that Dovora should be married. Somehow they made a *shiduch*, an arrangement for marriage, with Sura's brother, Herschmendle from Sieradz. I remember there was a huge *vicooach*, a debate within the family whether she could marry her uncle by Jewish law. The rabbi said it was okay. The wedding was held in our house, and she went to live with him in Sieradz where he was working as a tailor and playing soccer – he was a great soccer player.

Temporarily Sura was satisfied, but not for long. Soon she was depressed again and ultimately she killed herself, jumping into the river. It was a tragedy.

But the love in our community far outshone the specter of tragedy. As Jews, we knew we were surrounded by enemies and in danger of losing our way of life, yet we clung passionately to our provincial ways. We lived, in many ways, as they did centuries ago: simply and independently. Those of us who survived have never seen a community like it; and so 60 years later we remain refugees.

*Notes*

1. *Gazelle* is a German term, widely used before the war, to connote an artisan who had already finished his apprenticeship. He had passed the government test, regulated by the Industrial Laws of the land. The roots of these Industrial Laws, with the requirements stipulated for each of the artisan specialties (such as shoemakers, carpenters, bakers, butchers, etc.) had their derivation in medieval times, when the newly qualified artisan had to wander from town to town for three years before he was considered ready to begin his own business. By the 1930s this three-year wandering period was no longer required.

2.  To be a kosher butcher you could only sell the front part of the cow because the back held the milk. To check to see if the front part was kosher you had to open the stomach and inspect what the cow had eaten. If it had eaten a piece of wood or a nail, if there was a scratch or a damaged organ, the *szoscshet* could declare the meat *traif*, and the front part would have to be sold to a gentile butcher very cheaply.
3.  Merchants would walk through the streets yelling, 'White Vistula Sand!'

# 3 Growing up, standing tall

I was a student at the *kheder* for three years, until I was six. Regardless of the family's political alignment, all the Jewish children in Kalisz attended a *kheder*; it was the initial Jewish education. If the family was wealthy, their children attended a better *kheder* with better teachers. My *kheder* was like most in Kalisz, named after a rabbi and very primitive – one big table with two benches in a sparse room. We learned Hebrew and studied the lessons of the Torah, which we did not yet understand. I was a good student, reporting to my father what we had learned throughout the week. When guests came over on Saturday, he would show off by asking me to recite these lessons.

I attended kindergarten and elementary school at the Borchoff school, an establishment of the Poalei Zion party named after a famous Socialist/Zionist. We were told at an early age that our destiny was to emigrate to Palestine where we would work for a Jewish state. The other schools were also affiliated with political parties or religious institutions. The Bund party's school was called the Medem; the Aguda party maintained the Aguda School; and there was the Talmud Torah, sponsored by the *kehila*, where poor children received food and clothing as well as an education. The wealthier families sent their children to the Tarbut school, the best school in the city. Tarbut means 'education' in Hebrew.

The Borchoff school was like a continuation of the home; its main focus was on social development and Jewish community development. We learned Yiddish and Hebrew and read the great Jewish authors like Shalom Aleichem, Peretz, and Mendele. We were treated to all kinds of exhibitions from Jerusalem and Palestine. I remember seeing miniature models of the Temple in Israel and watching the movie *Springtime in*

*Palestine.* The teachers taught us how to interact with our parents, with each other, and how to survive in Jewish society. Political indoctrination was a major part of our education, and we were always aware of the upcoming elections as well as sometimes being part of the campaign organization.

I was a very good student, reading Yiddish very well by the second grade. Again my father would like to show off with me, but this time it was a joke. The newspapers ran serials at that time, excerpts from novels printed in parts over a number of weeks. My father had me reading aloud various embarrassing love stories to the whole family, but I had no idea what I was reading!

When I was eight, the Bund's Medem School collapsed through lack of funding and their students joined us at the Borchoff School. Two years later the Borchoff school collapsed in the same way and we were forced to continue our education in the Polish public school system. This was a terrible shock for us because the Borchoff had not prepared us for Polish society at all. We were cut off from the Polish world, unable to speak the Polish language and taught that there was nothing but hatred for Jews on the Polish streets. We never heard of the positive side of the Poles, although in the end there was a positive aspect. Still, we were thrown in the deep end without being able to swim.

I was enrolled at a school called Mikolai Reja, located in a converted embroidery factory on the other side of town. For the most part, schools in Poland were neglected and dilapidated buildings, converted structures left over from various industrial ventures. Poland's poverty was never more prevalent than in its school system. We had too many students for the space provided, so we were schooled in shifts: eight o'clock in the morning until two o'clock in the afternoon and two o'clock in the afternoon until eight o'clock in the evening.

I enjoyed studying and was a good student at the Borchoff School, but because we had very little exposure to Polish, I failed the entrance exam and was forced to repeat the third grade. This was a tragedy for my parents because they valued education so highly and believed that I was a good student. I saw how much this upset them and I forced myself to learn

Polish and become a good student again. By the following year I was the best student in my class and later I became the best student in the school.

The Polish education system was very different from our Jewish education. In many ways it was better. Since most students attended school only until they were 14 years old the system was geared towards practical knowledge, designed to prepare us for life. We were taught how to write official letters, the system of taxation, proper table manners, proper posture, even how to wash our hands after going to the toilet. Only a few went on to study at a *gymnasium*, (a grammar school) and fewer still to university. At the age of 14 we were supposed to be active and capable members of society.

Mikolai Reja was for me a mirror of Polish society, with all its pros and cons. There were plenty of ethnic Germans, Jews, and Russian émigrés in our classes, a result of the Russian occupation of Kalisz until 1914 and our proximity to the German border. Initially we were mistreated because of our poor Polish and strong accents and we had to work hard to adjusts. The teachers were divided, some were anti-Semites and some were progressives; some were motherly and some were very strict; some were friendly to me and some were hostile.

Mikolai Reja was filled with personalities, none more authoritative than the anti-Semitic janitor, Pan Yavoiszny. Being a janitor was a government job, something a Jew could not do, so in the eyes of the citizens he was a big shot. In the school the teachers respected him. He had a difficult job since his duties not only included cleaning the building but making sure it stayed intact – it was a very old building.

I formed special relationships with some of my teachers. Pani Ottinovska taught me literature – my favorite subject. She was very fond of me and often praised me in front of the other students. If I gave a report using a word unfamiliar to my classmates, she would tell them that I understood its meaning and could explain it to the class. We covered a different work of Polish literature every month, which pleased me because I was becoming a Polish patriot. I learned that for most of the history of Polish literature Jews were ignored or

29

simply called *kykes*, but I discovered a period when their presence was shown in a positive light. This was so uplifting for me. I read an epic poem by Miskeyvitch with a sympathetic Jewish innkeeper, Yankel, and it made me feel like this was also my Poland. I was falling in love with Poland.

My geography teacher was an elderly woman named Pani Sikorska. She lived on New World Street with Pani Ottinovska and was also very kind to me. I was very impressed with her because she had been a follower of Pialsufsky, the great Polish hero, and had been an active member of the illegal PPS under the czar before the war. She was arrested as a political prisoner and exiled to Siberia. She told us stories of the poor treatment she received from the soldiers, the forced marches through the snow wearing irons and her eventual release at the time of the revolution. She described the peasants of Russia, the poverty, the types of food they ate, and the conditions in which they lived. To her it may have been tragic, but for us it was very exotic. I was interested in geography mainly because I read so much Polish history at the time. Sometimes Pani Sikorska would sit back and let me lead the class. When I did I always gave a lesson that was very patriotic and praised the women fighters against the czar.

The maps for the geography and history lessons were kept in the school director's office, Pan Browislaw Mjorkowski. I would go to his office to collect these materials and he would talk to me in a friendly way. He was very progressive and seemed to be interested in me, probably because I was Jewish. We came from two different worlds but we respected each other very much. He took good care of me and once even saved me from being expelled.

I was a flag bearer during a holiday celebration in honor of three divisions of Polish soldiers stationed in our region. At one point during the gathering we were meant to kneel towards a field altar the soldiers had created, but I would not kneel. It was against my upbringing. I had never attended church, so why should I kneel? When we returned from the ceremony there was a big uproar, I had offended and shown disrespect for the school. Pan Mjorkowski defended me: he explained that it was against my religion to kneel down and therefore I was upholding one of the covenants of the school, respect for religion. He was very good to me.

Unfortunately there were no Jewish teachers at Mikolai Reja, they were forbidden to teach in public schools, as it was a government job. It was rare to find Jewish teachers, since the teachers' university in Vilna only accepted a small number of Jews, usually the very wealthy. The closest universities were in Warsaw and Poznan, both famous for anti-Semitic student groups. There were rumors that students would cut the faces of Jews with blades as an initiation. Ironically, Jewish money and the Jewish community helped set up the first university in Poland.

Lack of exposure to Poles and the ingrained antiSemitism of Poland made life for the Jewish students somewhat difficult. It was normal for me to be beaten up during recess or on my way to and from school. Kids would wait behind trees in the park with stones, ready to hurl them at the Jews walking home. When I missed two weeks of school because a stone had split my head open, the ethnic German teacher, Elza Ebenhaut, asked me why I had not attended class. I told her I had been hit with a stone because I was a Jew. The class remained quiet – this was acceptable to them. It was at times a very anti-Jewish environment, even our uniformed hats were four-pointed resembling a cross, which did not please our rabbi.

I did not have schoolbooks, these you had to buy. Instead I would go to friends' houses to do my homework. Before every school year there was a book exchange on the Jewish street. My mother offered to buy my books but I told her it was not necessary, I knew how little money we had. In going to different houses and being a good scholar, I was able to make myself useful to the other students. Later, especially after I started to meet the girls, the other students would bring their books over to my house. Even a *Volksdeutscher* named Zelzer, who later worked for the Gestapo, came to my house to study.

Outside school, I tried to read whatever I could get my hands on. My head was filled with books: travel books, history books, political books, the popular American novels (*Gone with the Wind*). I read all the serials in the newspaper and picked up books at the penny library in the Jewish section. Later, my sister and I would go to the city library to find new books to read. This was not such a simple thing. The librarian had the power to accept or deny someone's application to be a member. I remember kissing her hand and politely answering her questions regarding my interests. She not only accepted us, but she prepared lessons for us, laying out a number of books from the same genre to be read in a certain order. I remember she gave me a whole series of Tarzan books, which I loved. I was so involved in these stories that I would sit in the tree outside our balcony and pretend I was in Tarzan's nest. Later came sections on American Indians, books like *The Last of the Mohicans* by J.F. Cooper, and of course Polish history. She was not very close to my sister and me, but she was a liberal woman and enjoyed educating us. She even sent us to the museum below the city hall, instructing us to study the contract of Kalisz among other things.

I was becoming a personality at the school. There was a European competition of airplane pilots at that time and the Polish team of Zwirko and Wigura took first place. Shortly after their triumph they were killed in an accident. We had a memorial celebration at the school to honor these two national heroes and I was chosen to read a poem in the auditorium. I remember I said that Zwirko and Wigura were not dead, simply lost in the stars; mortals were capable of death, but not these two. Despite the occasion, the Polish girls still stuck their tongues out at me; such was the balance.

Reluctantly, the treasurer of the school, an antiSemitic priest, called on my mother to tell her that I was entitled to a scholarship to attend the *gymnasium*. She was so happy, especially since Henya had been unable to go. She was not accepted despite the fact that she was very intelligent, they only admitted a certain number of Jews and we had no money. Even with the scholarship, however, I knew that the *gymnasium* would offer me nothing for the future and cost my family a lot of money. You needed proper clothing and the means to buy books, and I would have to be fed during those years instead of bringing in some money myself. Even if I finished the school without too many problems, what was there for me to do in Poland? I would still be a poor Jew, unable to attend university, forced to pick up a trade that I should have started learning years before. I explained to my mother that I did not want to attend. It would be better for me to learn a trade, and so I did.

My first job was very characteristic. I signed a contract to be an apprentice shoemaker. I was learning how to make the leather, upper parts of shoes; this was in itself a profession. The master had me come to his house, set up a table in his kitchen and work hunched over for 12 hours a day by the light of a kerosene lamp. My back hurt constantly and I did not like the work or the atmosphere at all. The master and his wife Yetka were continually fighting, yelling at each other all day while their two children cried at the commotion. He said he was a compulsive moviegoer, he had to see a movie on Saturdays. She did not believe him, she assumed he was seeing another woman. On Sundays, when we resumed our work, it was the worst day of the week. This was not good for me.

Compounding my misery, Yetka often asked me to do domestic work in addition to the shoemaking. I took care of the baby, constantly trying to get the child to sleep. Yetka sent me food shopping from time to time, never with any money. I always had trouble with the grocer who never wanted to give me anything on credit because the couple's ever-increasing tab was an issue.

There was a crazy man named Alexander who would come up to their apartment from time to time asking for money. The master would invite him in and ask him about the Polish prostitutes that he was fond of visiting. Alexander would explain how clever he had been to barter a good price, proudly stating that he had 'done the job'. The master would then give him a nickel. It was very demoralizing, I knew I had to get out of my contract.

I tried to transfer my apprenticeship to a better-quality shoemaker, but the Jewish Guild forced me to go back. I had signed a contract and I was expected to fulfill my obligation. I could not bear to go back so I broke our agreement and lost some money.

I had to decide which trade to pursue next and somehow

avoid joining my father at the butcher shop. My friend Chaim Katz worked for a carpenter, one of the best in town. He explained to me how Polish carpentry was an art, a thing of beauty more than a trade. Most furniture built in Poland was put together without nails but with plugs, dowels, and glue, yet lasted for hundreds of years. In discussing this with him, I began to see the beauty of carpentry and I wanted to learn.

I explained to my mother that I had made a mistake with shoemaking and I had ended my training. My mother was very upset, and I was upset. She asked me what I really wanted to do, and I told her I wanted to be a carpenter, which delighted her, this was a very nice profession. In our old house on Ciasna Street there was a carpenter named David Gelbert, a friend of my parents. Although he did not need an apprentice, my mother persuaded him to take me on. I was a strong boy and he was happy to oblige.

I learned quickly that Master Gelbert was very skillful, that he made his own tools and was capable of doing the most elaborate work. He was once commissioned to replace the head of a wooden Russian eagle adorning a famous synagogue, transforming it into a Polish eagle. His skill impressed and inspired me. From the beginning I enjoyed working with him and with wood. I was fascinated with the French polish, so intricately created and applied. I enjoyed the gluing days, when we had to keep the big pots heated and the entire shop hot until the clamps were in place. I remember the first time we used machinery to cut the wood – it amazed me. I began working as a carpenter's apprentice in 1937, and this was my profession until the outbreak of the Second World War.

Meanwhile my social life became more involved as I grew older. Despite the fact that the Borchoff School had closed long ago, the Poalei Zion's youth group, the *Yutzenka*, was still an integral part of my life. Most everyone belonged to a youth group affiliated with one political party or another. At times these groups resembled gangs, but mostly they provided us with a place to meet our friends and to grow up together. The Bund's youth group was called the *Stern* (the star) and we were in constant competition with them, though we were allied together against any Polish group we might have encountered. When Jewish boys fought each other, I was never beaten up because I was a good student, for which there was an underlying respect. We had very little contact with the religious groups, the Yeshiva boys from the Aguda. All youth groups, however, had small units of communists within their ranks. Although it was illegal to be a communist, we sympathized with them and we read their literature with open minds.

We were young Zionists who had come out of the Borchoff School, proud to be who we were and not afraid to fight other youth groups or the Polish kids. We had headquarters, a *lokal* on the second floor of a factory building in the Jewish section. There was a meeting hall, a library, a small podium and, of course, a ping-pong table. We were all ping-pong maniacs at that time. The electricity was connected to a meter, so we would begin our meetings by passing around a collection plate, hoping to scrounge enough change to keep the *lokal* lit while we were there. From time to time we had shows or speakers at our meetings, but mostly we went there to be with each other, to discuss politics and other things. There was a nice library filled with good Jewish books, which I took to my father, in addition to magazines and newspapers.

Every Friday I came home from work, washed myself in a basin and walked down the main streets to the *lokal*. I enjoyed looking at the storefronts lit with electric lights as I made my way to the old factory. On the way home I took Babina Street through the Jewish part because it was like a walk through history for me. The section would be half-asleep by the time I would leave. Still, tiny kerosene lamps would burn dimly through some of the windows, peacefully reminiscent of centuries past. I carried a heavy stick for protection made of oak from the carpenter's shop because people were sometimes attacked at night.

On Babina Street there was an office of an antiSemitic political party called the Endeki. Its leader was Roman Dmovski, nicknamed the Polish Hitler. The party was organized to fight Jews. According to the Endeki, all of Poland's problems stemmed from the Jews who, after being invited by the churches out of pity to enter Poland, swore to destroy the Polish state. Their business was mainly propaganda. They created and circulated antiSemitic church hymns and two newspapers, and strung placards and banners all over Kalisz. The papers, *The Messenger* and *The Stock*, regularly put out lists of gentile alternatives to Jewish businesses. The banners read: 'The Jews are the source of unhappiness in Poland! Endeki: for a Kalisz without Jews.' I walked past the office defiantly, seething with anger.

One night I was on a real high, not caring who crossed my path or what happened to me. I stood outside the Endeki office, noticed I was alone and started ripping down all their placards and breaking their windows. I felt like Hercules, almost wanting someone to catch me so I could fight. If I was to be outnumbered, I could have run to the old market where a band of hoodlums would have come to my aid. Nobody saw me, which was probably for the best. There were times, however, when I did have to fight.

On warmer Saturdays we took trips to the city stadium to play soccer for a few hours or we went to the river to swim. Sometimes we took trips to Vinjare, a very anti-Semitic village where many Polish policemen built homes, like our neighbor Ferdunos. It was adventurous and dangerous, yet we felt strong in our group. Sometimes Polish gangs and dogs attacked us, but we always held our own. My friend Michael Jusofovitch looked for fights. He developed a technique of fighting, grabbing the collar of his assailant and head-butting his chin. As tough as he seemed to us, he was terrified of his father. Still, he was one of the few Jews that instilled fear in the gentile boys.

Market days in Kalisz were Tuesdays and Fridays and the Endeki somehow had divided the crowd into two sections: Jew and gentile. They forbade Poles from buying products from Jews, which was detrimental to the Jewish economy. The air of antagonism during market days often led to fights, sometimes serious, between youth groups – not unlike gang fights. A Polish group affiliated with the Endeki often terrorized us. We fought back, mainly with the help of the Betar, the Polish youth group from the PPS. Tragically, one of our members, a carpenter's apprentice named Kronenberg, was killed on the street during one of these fights, stabbed through the heart with a knife. Initially we responded by making plans – nothing written down – to retaliate. Our better judgment prevailed, however, and we did not retaliate. After Kristallnacht, the supposed result of one man's violence, who knows what would have happened if our hands had caused bloodshed. The Endeki and the Church had groomed the Polish youth to kill Jews – all they needed was an excuse.

Our discussions at the *lokal* and in the park became more and more political as Polish nationalism became increasingly anti-Semitic. The treatment of the Jews had worsened steadily under the government of the colonels. Protesting *kehila* members were dismissed and replaced by government-appointed stooges. Storefronts were required to display the owner's name, making Jewish-owned stores an easy target for vandals and anti-Semites. A central industrial center (COC) built in a triangle between three rivers for the production of defense equipment was to be potentially *Judenrein* – free of Jews. The *Sejm*, the lower house of the legislature, busied itself with laws contesting kosher slaughtering – this as Hitler waltzed through Austria. It was clear to us that we were facing a serious situation.

We were under suspicion from the police and from our elders that we were flirting with communism and, in fact, we were. We were given pamphlets written in Yiddish on very thin paper, like cigarette paper, smuggled out of Russia. A very religious boy, the son of one of the teachers at the Aguda, brought this literature to us and tried to convert us to communism. It was obvious we were leaning left, our library was moving further away from the *Arbeiterzeitung*. A detective began following us and inspecting the *lokal* periodically, hoping to catch us involved in illegal activity. Some of us became active in the Communist Party, including my sister.

After being rejected from studying at the *gymnasium*, Henya, under the influence of Uncle Shloime Gerszin, joined the Communist Youth of Kalisz against our parents' wishes. She and a friend were putting up illegal placards and foolishly tried to post one on the gates of an army base when the gate opened and the two girls were arrested. They were led through the city to the Kalisz jail. Soon detectives came to our house with a search warrant trying to find some evidence that we were also involved with the communists. My mother and father were horror-struck. I tried to defend my sister's actions, explaining how we were all moving left, towards social justice, but this only angered my father. He clipped me with his hand, crashing me against a wall where I wet myself and fainted. It was the only time he ever hit me.

My sister was put on trial. We were promised help from the Moper, an international communist organization that provided lawyers for political trials. They came to us and said they would help, but they never returned for the trial. Henya was sentenced to seven years in the 'halls of education'. We went to the court of appeal, but we had to pay 200 zlotys for a lawyer. The trial was in Poznan and the lawyer convinced the judge to suspend the sentence until Henya was 21 years old. From then on, I was more inclined to sympathize with the communists.

We lived in a time when most of our neighbors wanted to see our destruction, yet it was also our time of glory. Relationships between boys and girls held so much beauty then. A girl was placed on a pedestal, deserving of the utmost respect and devotion. The boys who had girlfriends changed their clothing, acted so politely, so delicately, and developed a spiritual bond with the girls. It was so beautiful and it was so good; we were on a moral high. Every person became a pearl and every girl was a diamond. We were filled with pride and a thirst for adventure, but with the shadow of the Nazis closing in on Poland, we saw signs that our lives were going to change for the worse.

# 4 Something unfamiliar, something horrible

We felt that something horrible and unfamiliar was approaching. We knew repression and expulsion, it had been normal in Europe for hundreds of years, but this was different. This was more politically radical, a threat to our physical existence. As we read the Jewish newspapers, we grew more fearful. The bad news continued: Hitler occupied Austria and Czechoslovakia without firing a bullet; *Mein Kampf* outlined Hitler's plans and his opinion of the Jews; Il Duce gassed the helpless Ethiopians; huge rallies took place in Germany with hundreds of thousands screaming 'Heil Hitler'; Franco championed Christianity over Bolshevism in Spain; and Russia was silent. Europe was in turmoil and Poland was in turmoil, somehow we knew that the Jews would suffer.

In Great Poland anti-Semitism sharpened as the economy faltered. The American Depression sent shock waves throughout Europe, and Poland was not spared. The blame fell on the Jews who, as a result, were virtually pushed out of economic relations with the rest of Poland. The shoemakers, for instance, could not sell their shoe uppers to gentile solemakers; there was a new boycott of many Jewish products. Signs adorned storefronts: 'Jewish store!'; 'Don't buy from a Jew!'; 'Jews to Palestine!'; 'Poles buy only from Poles!' The prime minister of Poland at the time, Sladkovski, implored Polish citizens to refrain from hitting the Jews physically, but to hit them economically.[1] It was a disastrous time.

The irony was that the Jewish minority, as opposed to the German, Lithuanian, Ukrainian, or Russian minorities, was intricately tied to the Polish economy. The Polish and Jewish systems of trade were codependent. The other minorities worked for themselves, had their own interests and pined for their territory to be reclaimed by their mother nations.

They had not been with Poland from the beginning of its history, but had arrived with conquering armies. Later it was clear that many ethnic Germans were part of Hitler's fifth column, steadily planning a German conquest of Poland. Unfortunately, they were trusted as loyal citizens and were entitled to hold any government job, no matter how high-ranking. Kalisz was about 30 per cent *Volksdeutsch*.

Hitler expelled all the Polish Jews from Germany, claiming they lacked citizenship and were thus illegal residents. Many were brought to the Polish border, but the Poles did not want to let them in. The Jewish community was very organized and active at that time and helped many refugees find homes in Kalisz. My family took in a mother and her daughter, the Liebeskinds. It was amazing, Hitler had thrown them out yet they remained staunchly pro-German. I remember the little girl would say on a nice day, 'This is really Führer weather!' There was a rumor that the mother was a German spy. We never knew if this was true, but when the Germans occupied our section of Poland, she disappeared.

Hitler started to demand territory from Poland, specifically a corridor stretching through Danzig to East Prussia and the Baltic coast. It was another piece of Germany's *Lebensraum*, living space the Nazis claimed was rightfully theirs. The push eastward was called *Drang nach Osten*, Germany's manifest destiny, a recurring theme for thousands of years. To these demands the Polish General Rich Smigila replied, 'We will not give one button', and we believed him. In our eyes the Polish army was very strong, if not invincible.

Poland's historic enemy had always been Germany. There was ingrained contempt for Germany within the Polish psyche, but there was also tremendous admiration. Poles sang anti-German songs in school about carrying their guns to the Wartar river, still celebrating the famous victory over the Teutons on the Grumwald in 1412. Yet the government leaned towards fascism, even building their concentration camps for communists on the German model. The Polish government was more concerned with Trotsky's appeal for a worldwide communist revolution, massing troops along the Russian border while patrolling the German border only with police.

A non-aggression pact between Germany and Poland had been signed, but Hitler's demands weakened its worth. The secretary of state could not come to terms with Germany over a retooling of the pact, despite being a strict pro-German. Talk of an invasion ensued and Poland began to prepare itself for attack.

The ethnic Germans, the *Volksdeutschen,* started to become very active, even forming a branch of the Hitler Youth. On Sundays they would come from surrounding cities and villages and march in Kalisz, brandishing uniforms and flags adorned with swastikas. The Jewish and PPS youth groups wanted desperately to fight, but these demonstrations were protected by the police, many of whom were ethnic Germans.

The fifth column was in place, laying the groundwork for an invasion. We knew that in normal life the *Volksdeutschen* organized private concerts, kept their own factories and maintained their own fire department. What we did not know was that they were also doing the preliminary work for the Gestapo. They had lists of Jews in prominent and influential positions and helped the Nazis in any way they could.

The older Jewish people thought this was a temporary situation, that we younger adults were over-reacting, that we should stay quiet. Even my father could not be convinced that this wave of anti-Semitism and despotism was not temporary, but a momentum-gathering threat to our survival. The youth was not so confident. We became more militant, preparing ourselves for a coming fight and planning our potential escape and our resistance. The Jewish organizations recognized the potential danger and helped prepare Kalisz's Jews for future hardships. I trained even harder by myself. Sometimes I would not eat for a whole day to get used to the feeling of hunger. Sometimes I would prick myself to get used to pain. I did not share this with anyone.

In my naiveté, I believed that a war might be a good thing because undoubtedly the Russians would enter the conflict, set the Germans straight, and open up Poland to the social equality I had read about in Soviet Russia. It was not the first time I thirsted for action. I tried to fight in Spain for the Republican Army and prepared myself by reading the

Spanish vocabulary lists in the paper and following the success of the Polish regiments (filled with Jews and members of the PPS) with excitement. I longed to fight but was not allowed to go to Spain because I was too young to be a soldier.

The Polish government quietly started a civil defense league. We worked to help Poland stall Germany's perceived advances and learned how to increase our chances of survival in the event of an attack. We were told to line the inside of our windows with paper to protect us from flying glass if there was an explosion. In the basement of the city hall we were taught the proper use of a gas mask. We were mobilized to dig trenches. Everyone helped, even the rabbis.

On the way to dig trenches the Jewish organizations would march carrying flags, proud of their beliefs and proud to serve Poland. They divided us into groups, each responsible for a section. My section was near the slaughterhouse, not far from a Jewish bakery. We dug the trench in a zigzag under the supervision of an anti-Semitic Polish engineer. He was calling a rabbi *Judki*, a diminutive and derogatory nickname for a Jew. I could not stand the disrespect – this rabbi was about 70 years old. I wanted to swing my shovel and hit the engineer on the head. To this day it still angers me, that insult to our humanity.

Secretly, as if Poland were calling the Germans' bluff, troops started to accumulate around Kalisz and the German border. At the river I saw many soldiers, all dressed in such beautiful clothing and boots. I was sure they were invincible, that they would destroy the Germans if there were an attack. Also I felt that we, the Jews of Kalisz, would make a valiant stand against the Germans.

My friends and I would sit by the bridge, not far from a band of strong-armed Jews called the *Cherna Ronczka*, the Black Hands. They were, I would say, hoodlums, but respected by the community nevertheless. We looked up to them and saw them as another line of defense against a Nazi invasion. In short, they were the Jewish justices, hired to right the wrongs that the Polish police would not touch.

At that time people had to make a living in any way they could. Many embroidery factories had shut down after the

Russian and European markets disappeared, causing massive unemployment. People were selling tea, coffee, American lottery tickets (quarter-tickets, half-tickets and so on) and anything else they could to bring in a little money. There were porters, porters with carriages, and porters with carriages and horses. Begging was a profession. One man would come to a door, mostly on Fridays, and hold up five fingers, meaning he was representing five beggars. Thieves and con-artists rounded out the work force. With such activity, it was only natural that the Black Hands came into being – could a con-artist with a table and cards really go to the police for help? They would sit by the bridge and wait for people to come to them, mostly with collection problems.

We had a relative in the Black Hands, my mother's cousin Lazar Kaminsky. By profession he was a glazier but this did not support his family. Instead he kept a knife in one pocket, brass knuckles in the other, and waited by the bridge for work. He was very friendly and very playful. He always tried to wrestle my father, who was stronger but less of a fighter. My father was on the borderline, more of a professional than a Black Hand. Still, sometimes he would join Lazar in beating up the gentiles.

Once Lazar was sitting near Uncle Shloime Gerszin when somebody said a gentile had beaten up a Jew. He jumped up and beat the guy until he was covered in blood. He ran up to our apartment and asked my mother for water to wash up. He had lost his hat in the fight, so my mother went downstairs and retrieved it. Another time, my Aunt Rifkah had a shawl stolen and Lazar Kaminsky followed the robber to ten different towns before he caught him.

They had nicknames like 'Cut Machine' and 'Iron Life', and they were like an inspiration to us. The police knew about them but did not touch them. They were doing the police work in the Jewish section, keeping the streets clean because they were so feared. They also escorted the street peddlers and the bus services to the surrounding cities and villages since attacks on the roads had become more frequent.

Sitting by that bridge seeing the strong soldiers and the Black Hands, I felt that nothing could conquer our Poland. But when the Nazis did come, both groups proved inadequate. I was so horribly disappointed with the Black Hands. I was sure they would do something, but they disappeared. Lazar had gone to Belgium to work in a coal mine and then to Palestine to fight for its independence. The Black Hands offered no resistance to the Germans and in my rebellious heart I felt terribly bitter.

The city was in a state of unrest; echoes of 1914 rang through the air. People started to take precautions. Rumors said that Kalisz would be the first city destroyed. It seemed a good idea to remove our valuables from our homes and bring them to surrounding cities, so I volunteered to help. I saw it as a chance for adventure, something as exciting as the books I spent hours reading.

Uncle Szama had horses and a wagon. We collected clothing and valuables from all our relatives and put them under tarpaulins, then we went out on the highway in the direction of Lusk. Why Lusk, I do not know. It was such a small, offbeat town near Lodz, maybe they thought it was too inconsequential a town to be touched by the Nazis. The carriage ride was the longest I had ever taken, an entire day and an entire night. My only other rides were from Kalisz to the summer retreats, only 30 minutes outside town. The sense of adventure overwhelmed me.

As we rode through the forest at night we were suddenly halted by a band of Polish hoodlums carrying axes. I had never been so frightened, I really thought we had met our end. One of the Poles said, 'Szama, is that you?' and my Uncle Szama said that it was. They let us through without doing anything. I was shocked. Apparently my Uncle Szama was also on the edges of something like the Black Hands. Plenty of people were on that kind of borderline.

We came to my mother's hometown of Sieradz, a town as ancient as our city – an emissary from Sieradz had witnessed the signing of the Contract of Kalisz. We stopped to rest a little and to make contact with our relatives. In Sieradz lived Aunt Polcha and Uncle Feta Szmul along with two of their daughters (the others were working in households in Kalisz). Feta Szmul looked like Topol in *Fiddler on the Roof*: similar clothing, similar build – a real peasant! He spoke Yiddish with such a

Polish accent, like an American hillbilly. They lived near the Warta river in a house set into the ground, lower than the land. They gave us breakfast, that big, black farmer's bread with peasant cheese. My uncle would not let me eat without my head covered or before we washed and said the blessing. They were very religious and so humble, like trees from the ground, really God's people.

The Sieradz peasants seemed very different to my eyes. In Poland every section had different clothing and in Sieradz it was very, very colorful. I thought I was seeing the same group of people running back and forth, but there were hundreds of peasants mobilized for defense work, all wearing the same outfit. The Sieradz prison loomed behind them. Its size dwarfed the Kalisz prison and it housed mainly communists.

I remembered the tales my mother told me about her childhood in Sieradz, about the flooding Warta and how they would sit in the wooden clothes-washing basin and float as if in a raft. She had one Polish neighbor named Kazik who was blind but had perfect pitch. He came to Kalisz to work in the Fuverger piano factory as a piano-tuner, and when my mother met him he sometimes recognized her voice saying, 'Hinda, is that you?' The Fuverger piano factory did not employ Jews, so this friendship between my mother and the Polish piano-tuner was exceptional. But, then again, it was not so unusual for my mother, who was friends with everyone. I had a lot of relatives in that town including Uncle Shloime Gerszin's mother. She sold greens in the market and we paid a quick visit to her too.

We continued to travel through more forest and more small towns and I could feel that something was in the air. In Polish poetry they say you can see danger in the sway of the trees, and I imagined I could. In every village, people were mobilized for defense work and moving uneasily. We finally came to Lusk and put everything in the basement of somebody's house. I tried to separate our things from those of our relatives, but there was too much. I never understood the logic of bringing our belongings there, especially since we did not know these people.

We headed back to Kalisz on the same route, sensing

increasing tension as we neared our home. We returned to find our city in a hyper-state of readiness and fear. There was a system of code words for radio broadcasters to alert citizens and the militia of any urgent developments. Soldiers buzzed back and forth in trucks from one station or another. My old shoemaking boss loved it, he was a good shooter and wore a marksman's sash, and he planned to be a hero.

War was in the air. The Polish government put up propaganda placards in the streets. One showed a German cockroach wearing a swastika facing the bayonet of a Polish soldier which read, 'Go back you cockroach because we will repeat Grumwald, 1412.' I remember walking with my father when I saw this and he pointed out that the Polish soldier had only a bayonet while the cockroach held a grenade. He was not very impressed with that poster, or the Polish government, or their army.

The Poles started seeking out members of the fifth column. Outside the Jewish-owned Shreier toy factory there was a posting of four employees' names, *Volksdeutschen* captured spying for the Third Reich and sentenced to death. The workers were part of the German underground and, we were told, shot to death in Kalisz.

Already people started to hoard food, which was absurd in Poland. There was plenty of food, it was a very agrarian nation. Sometimes in the summer you could go to the fields and gather strawberries and berries because they were so cheap. The peasants could not make any money if they bothered to pick them. People started to hide things everywhere and things became unruly.

We were afraid of the war, but secretly I was excited that something was going to happen. I saw Poland from my Jewish eyes and my Polish eyes. I was abused by the Polish reality, but I figured a war would destroy Hitler and his awful fascism. I saw mighty Russia as a savior, but the Poles saw Russia as a danger. My father was afraid of the war, he would tell me what had happened in 1914, how the Germans could be such ruthless killers. They came into Kalisz, it was the first town, and they destroyed half of it. They killed so many Jews.

I was more integrated into the Polish sentiment because I

went to that school. I did not see the other reality, how Poland was before. I was born two years after Poland began again. I was brought up in that Polish school as a real patriot caught up in Polish literature, Polish pride, and Polish strength. I fought the negative parts of Poland, the anti-Semitism and the hoodlums, but I saw the progressive parts too. My father felt negative towards Poland because they abused him financially, taxing the Jews so heavily. They would come to the butcher shop and tell him that he had to pay for 'a brick for the school', and he had to give it. The gentile butchers gave much less. My father was a provider, these taxes, plus new laws that hurt his business by threatening the process of kosher killing, angered him. His attitude towards Poland was ambiguous; he had no Polish eyes.

We heard rumors and we heard news, indecipherable from each other and none good. We heard that the Polish government had barred Soviet troops from crossing through its borders to assist Czechoslovakia. We heard that Stalin had broken off ties with England and France and was now instructing Molotov to make a pact with Hitler. In local affairs, we heard of Poles in western Poland massacring *Volksdeutschen*, an extension of a centuries-old struggle. More importantly, we heard that war was imminent.

The Nazis dressed some prisoners in Polish clothing and made them blow up a German radio station. This deception was the justification for war.

*Note*

1.  Slavoi Sladkovski the former prime minister of Poland, ironically, became a butcher in Tel Aviv.

*Part II*
*Nazi Occupation*

# 5 Caught behind the lines

On 1 September 1939, Germany declared war on Poland. It was a Blitzkrieg, a lightning-quick attack across the entire Polish border, too mobile and too powerful for the Polish army, hampered as it was by its old-fashioned doctrine of fighting, to withstand. The Nazis came with tanks, trucks and motorcycles, mobile artillery and near flawless planning. The Polish army was a mass of soldiers and horses, armed with bayonets and unprepared for modern, industrial warfare. The defensive lines were not ready; the bluff had not worked. The Polish army saw what was happening but they were almost powerless in defense. The first terrible battles were in Danzig, and the city fell quickly. It was just a matter of time before Kalisz was overtaken.

The war started in the morning and immediately Kalisz underwent a total change. The radio barked coded signals, calling the different levels of organized defense to their duties. Before the war you never saw a Polish soldier carrying a rifle. Now they had a rifle, a bayonet, a gas mask, and a hat with a strap. When a soldier wore the strap of his hat around his chin it meant he was on duty. On our street we did what we perceived as necessary. We knew the locks in the river were to be exploded to slow the German advance, so I helped my master prepare for the flooding in his workshop. We put all the furniture on blocks to keep it dry. We were saving furniture, it was so naive, but what else was there to do?

In the afternoon Polish soldiers came to our house and told us that the bridge behind our home would be destroyed at night and that we were to open all our windows, otherwise the force from the blast would shatter the glass. The soldiers told us that if we were planning to escape we should do so now. Having been brought up to follow the government's orders – if they suggested something, we did it – we put our things together and prepared to join the massive exodus from Kalisz.

We had my father's butcher carriage, sturdy and lined with metal, which we filled up with food, clothing, an ax and a big jug of homemade wine. My grandmother would not go with us. She was in her eighties and the excitement was already causing her to vomit. She told us that she would look after the home and keep it for us until we returned. Can you imagine my mother and our feelings? The Liebeskinds also stayed, and we were relieved that the Szwiger would not be alone.[1] We took everything downstairs to the backyard where we saw our neighbours. They too were running.

My father closed the door and he broke down. 'My God, what is going on?', he cried. It broke my heart to see my father in this state, my mother's condition was not good either. She was sick at that time, with an ulcer on her leg that bled and suppurated continually. We laid her in the carriage and tried to make her comfortable. We headed across the bridge, past the prison and out to the road. Maybe 15 minutes later we heard the bridge explode.

The road itself was a river of people. There were complete villages walking with cows and chickens, but where were they going? We were swept into the current and taken away from Kalisz. On the side of the road I saw Yetka, the shoemaker's wife. She had her two children with her, but was lost without her husband. She yelled to me, 'Henrik! What shall I do?'

'What can you do?', I yelled back – I could not leave the road or I would have lost my family. Poor Yetka, alone with two children, but what could I have done?

I was like the carriage-horse, pulling our carriage from the front while the others pushed from the back. Moishe became tired, he too was sick, so we put him in the carriage with my mother. I was walking behind a couple of horses and I thought of hitching our carriage to them, but a peasant with a whip looked down at me as if to say, 'don't you dare'. We walked like this for hours through the night, and we were exhausted. My imagination was working as usual, in my head I pictured we were being expelled from Spain. Sometimes I slept as I walked.

We came to the little town of Kosziminka whose inhabitants had also fled; each town retreated into the next. The road took us straight through the marketplace and on to the synagogue, our destination. The town was overflowing with people and in chaos. We came to a marketplace where I stood in line to wash myself at a pump. I caught a glimpse of a group of Polish soldiers in a state of disarray that I could never have foreseen in my wildest dreams. A Polish soldier was such a symbol of power and strength, always at the ready whether he was Jewish or Polish. This group was already without hats, belts or bayonets. In their eyes you could already see defeat. My father and I looked at each other in disbelief. I would more readily have believed that the moon was going to fall from the sky, and this was only the second day!

I was exhausted because I had not really rested for days. With the approaching turmoil I had spent most of my free time getting in touch with my friends and planning our activities if a war should break out. Of course, everything fell apart. We were living too far away from each other to make contact when our families started to flee. All our planning was futile; it really was chaos.

We had to take my mother out of the carriage so she could rest a spell and change the dressing on her wound. My sister applied a strong smelling ointment to her leg and covered it with clean bandages. As she did this I looked to my right and saw a German plane. It was flying so low that I could see the swastikas on its wings and tail. It began spraying bullets: *drat-drat-drat-drat-drat*. This was our first tangible encounter with the Germans and it terrified us. We helped my mother and Moishe, who was crying, back into the carriage, and as I looked at my father my heart began to break. He had no control over the situation and he could not protect his family. He was close to collapsing again, so I suggested we find a place to settle down.

We took the carriage to the edge of town and came to an empty farmhouse. There was a set of stairs on the outside of a barn leading to a loft. In the middle of the yard there was a compost pile and on the other side was the house. We climbed the stairs to find other Jews resting from their travels. We laid my mother down on the floor, making her as comfortable as we could, then my sister took care of the food while we rested for a few moments.

We were all so tired, we had had to push that carriage over

the gravel road and my mother was very heavy. The carriage was not prepared for this, but we were lucky that my father was my father.[2] He was forever the perfectionist, making the carriage the best it could be – it even had shock absorbers! Why did a butcher need shock absorbers on a carriage? As we fled from Kalisz, we saw plenty of broken carriages on the side of the road and we were thankful for his excesses.

After a short break, my father and I went out to see what was happening. I was more excited than fearful, still caught up in the adventure of the situation. We walked through that unfamiliar town in the direction of the synagogue. Two soldiers on horses, *ulanis* with sabers, galloped into the center of the town and yelled instructions through a megaphone: all Polish citizens, all men above 18, were to go in the direction of Lodz to join the fighting Polish army. The two quickly rode off to repeat the message elsewhere. This was an order both my father and I would follow, although I was a month shy of my eighteenth birthday. We assumed that if we did not register we would be shot as deserters. Regardless, I was willing to fight because I was such a patriot. We went back to the farmhouse to tell the others. Upon hearing the news my mother cried.

Tearfully we left them in that loft, leaving all the supplies, and started down the road to Lodz. After a short while, we came across a little river. The bridge was already destroyed, and in the water and on the banks there were dead people. The Polish forces must have destroyed the bridge while people were still crossing. We waded through the water and continued walking until we came to the famous Liskuv village.

Liskuv was a model village designed by the government as an example of Polish rural life. We learned about Liskuv in my contemporary geography class at school and I was excited to see it for myself. There were fruit trees lining the main road, the streets were clean and beautiful and the roofs were made of metal, not straw. Like the rest of the towns in our region, it was already half-abandoned. We saw men hurrying towards the road, towards mobilization, just as we were.

We were having two different experiences, my father and

I. He was completely destroyed, while my sense of adventure continued to heighten. We walked along the side of the road until the evening when we suddenly heard to the side the sound of a machine gun. There was a group of civilians, *Volksdeutschen*, sitting on motorcycles and in sidecars firing in our direction. We dove quickly into the drainage ditch until the shooting stopped. We looked up and saw that the group had left, but not before they started setting fires. There was no real point to this other than to create chaos.

After this incident we decided to get off the road and get into the forest. The forest air was so new to me. We were not exposed to such smells in Kalisz. It was beautiful, there were lots of pine trees and it was cold and crisp. I was very tired and my feet hurt a great deal. I had on new shoes, a terrible mistake – you should never run with new shoes. By nightfall we could not continue any further because of the darkness. We were walking into trees, so we stopped to get some rest.

Unknown to us, there was an asylum nearby that had been unlocked at the time of the invasion. In the middle of the night my father and I were attacked by a group of escaped inmates. They were falling on us, still wearing their strait-jackets and talking nonsense. This made me afraid, but my father started to become more himself, he began to beat them up, pushing them off of me and taking us both out of the forest.

Finally we came to a village and found an empty barn. With the smell of that barn and the comfort of the straw, it was not long before I was asleep. When I woke up, I did not know where I was – a Jewish boy always sleeps in a bed and I was completely lost. When I saw my father I came back to reality and remembered what was happening.

We did not really know what to do, just that we were supposed to join the Polish army. There was only one road, so we started towards Lodz until we came to the outskirts of a town named Dobra, meaning 'good'.

There was the distinct smell of fresh bread in the air and when it hit my nose I became incredibly hungry. We found the source, a little Jewish bakery on the right-hand side of the road. In the small towns that were not *Judenrein*, Jews were more integrated, like part of the town, not in separate sections. We went in and said, *'Sholem Aleichem'*. He was a typical, elderly Jewish baker, working diligently in his long underwear and a white apron covered with flour. He asked us what was going on. We told him that we were running away from the Germans, that there was a war. He knew nothing! He probably slept during the day and worked through the night with little contact with the outside world. We took two loaves of bread for which he did not want money, but we insisted on paying.

My father had a leather pouch with money, mostly coins; paper money started at 20 zlotys and higher. We took the loaves and walked into the center of Dobra. My father began weeping heavily. He saw people in distress and said, 'Oh my God, where is my family?' I was so heartbroken and so full of love for him. I recognized the enormity of such a man crying. It was killing him that his family was in danger and he could do nothing to protect them. I just tried to calm him down, saying, 'Father it will be okay. The Germans will be destroyed and we will go back.' While I was talking he cried, 'Henrik, Henrik what will be? Where is your mother? Where is our family?'

We came to the market in Dobra where I saw David Gelbert, my master. I asked him what he was doing, and he asked me the same. We had similar stories and he too had no idea where his wife or children were. But what news he had: my Aunt Rifkah was in Dobra! He pointed out the house to us, which was abandoned, and told us to go downstairs to the barber's quarters.

There we found Aunt Rifkah, still piously wearing the *szeitle*, and two of her girls. When we saw each other, we cried. She did not know where her boys had gone, but her husband, Uncle Herschel, had taken the other two girls to Warta. The occupants of that house had fled to another town and other people from Kalisz now filled it. She gave us something nice to eat.

In the evening I went out to inspect the situation. I came to the road by the marketplace and the churches and saw two *ulanis* coming from the direction of the Wartar river. They galloped into the middle of the town and circled around the water pump before – like Cossacks – they dug in their spurs and galloped away. I figured they were on a reconnaissance mission. I went back to the house and slept in the barber's bed. It was such a nice bedroom with beautiful furniture.

In the morning Aunt Rifkah prepared a small breakfast for us. We started talking about the war, how we heard rumors that Great Britain and France had declared war on Germany just as they had promised to do if Poland was attacked. It was very uplifting for us. Some were saying the French and British would be sending their *descentes*, paratroopers, to join the Polish army. Everyone had their own rumor and our spirits were good. We knew that Poland still had an army because of the two *ulanis* I had seen the day before. We intended to gather our things and continue to Lodz to join the Polish forces.

At about noon we heard motorized vehicles coming into the center of Dobra. We were hoping it was the English, I do not know why we were not hoping for the French. I jumped to my feet and ran to the backyard fence, which was full of holes. I saw a procession come into the town center. First came something like a jeep but smaller, with a machine gun and four soldiers. Flanking it was a series of motorcycles with sidecars, also with machine guns. Then came a tank, something I had never seen before, not even in the movies. Then came two more motorcycles. They went around that market, circling the water pump as the *ulanis* had, and then opened fire. The shooting was chaotic. As they circled, I could see the mark of one of their helmets: it was the German eagle. We were under German occupation.

I ran back to the adults and told them it was not the British, saying simply, 'the Germans are here'. People began to panic and some ran out of the room. My father and I were left and we began to talk. What were we to do? Should we run? Hide under the beds? We decided just to sit and wait. After 15 minutes we heard a loud painful yell. The rabbi from Dobra was living nearby. How the Nazis knew where to go, I never knew, but they went to his home and they killed him. Immediately after that horrible scream, a soldier kicked down our door and came in with a pistol in one hand and a grenade in another, yelling, *'Juden, Raus!'* Jews get out! It was a good thing that we were not hidden under the bed, I felt they would have killed us for sure. I took my leather jacket and ran with my father down the steps.

On the entrance to the street there was a soldier with a bayonet raised, ready to strike. We ran out to the street and saw a horrible scene. The whole marketplace was filled with German cars and tanks, and the air was blue with exhaust fumes. The gasoline smelled different to me – it seemed somehow dirty. I saw soldiers with big axes destroying the windows and doors of houses and running into stores. There were a few elderly Jews running towards the church. I saw a German soldier with his bayonet stab one in his behind. The Jew fell down. The soldier extracted the blade from the victim and chased after another. You could see other people running towards the church, not only Jews but Poles too. The only ones assaulted were Jews in orthodox clothing, easily identifiable to the Nazis.

There was like a net, a cordon of soldiers pushing people in the direction of the church. They herded all the people up against a wall, which was like a gate outside the church. They forced us to stand with our backs to the wall, which stood in front of a beautiful, white church. The more people that came, the more pushing there was. I was already pressed against the wall next to my father, waiting for something. I was thinking, 'My dear God, why have we run the whole night with blisters on our feet only to come here to be killed?' The sun was shining, it was a beautiful day but it was slipping away.

Two trucks with machine guns and the mini-jeep faced us. A civilian priest, standing next to a German officer, stood up and addressed us. He spoke to us in German, which nobody understood, so he repeated himself in Polish, 'You will be hostages here. Not far is Euneuf on the Warta river, where there is a battle. If we do not succeed, you will be destroyed together with the church.' The soldiers on the trucks pointed their guns at the crowd and started a terrible panic. People were stomping and running, tearing up their shirts and yelling, '*Shema Ysrael!*' You could see the behavior of the Jews was more agitated, panic stricken, than that of the Poles who were more passive. People started to faint, my father too.

In the cordon of Germans there was a young soldier with a pistol, and I ran to him. '*Wasser, Wasser*', I pleaded. The soldier, who was overwhelmed with the yelling, shrugged and showed me the palms of his hands as if to say, 'What can I do?' I went back to my father and took off my shirt and fanned him. Eventually, he got up. They did not shoot at us, so the people calmed a little.

The priest spoke to us again. 'Every valuable, every weapon, all money, all knives are to be put in this hole. If you do not comply, you will be shot.' My father had that leather pouch of money and I told him to give it to me. I put it in my pocket and waited to see what would happen. The people were throwing in their knives and money and watches, there were many pocket watches.

They pushed us into the church. It was my first time in a church. There were four sections; you could not just go straight in. There was a place to wash your hands, decorated with a figure of Jesus. I saw what the Poles were doing. They went to this place, washed their hands and crossed themselves. We went into the church, which was long and lined with pews on both sides and separated by a nice carpet. The woodwork was very good, everything made from solid oak. At the back there was a beautiful altar, raised slightly higher than the pews. There was a priest wearing a black cloak and a white shawl standing by the altar.

We were crammed into that church and separated – Jews on one side and Poles on the other. The Jews were telling each other to watch the Poles, maybe one would pull a trick and convince the Nazis to shoot at us. In that swell of people I saw a friend, Richeck Pearlman, but we did not talk, we were so scared and overwhelmed with what was going on. The *misiganahs* from the forest were with us, walking around and relieving themselves in their pants. One was kicking a stone around and around, constantly mumbling something. It started to smell badly.

There was a proclamation: if a weapon is found, every tenth person will be killed. We looked around. Nobody wanted to be the tenth, so we started shifting to the left and to the right. If it were not such a tragic situation, it would have been comical. No weapons appeared, so we sat down, tired, not knowing what would happen next.

Night fell. The beautiful, long windows showed the fire of the distant artillery. Many of us needed to relieve ourselves, but the Germans would not let us outside. We ended up doing it by the entrance, next to a cross.

Later, two soldiers came in holding pistols in their sleeves. They went to the altar and took out the priest. We heard a shot. We did not know why they killed the priest, we did not know anything.

The next morning, while we sat around, exhausted, I spoke with Richeck Pearlman. He had run away with his girlfriend who was still outside, but he did not know where his family was. He desperately wanted to leave the church, as we all did, but it was not allowed. There were some clever people. A Jewish woman from the outside came up to a soldier and explained that a man in town was very sick and that his son, who was in the church, was needed at his side. The German soldier permitted this and released the son. Later, another complained about sickness. Maybe he was sick, maybe not – eventually he was released.

In the afternoon, a commandant came in and told us that the Germans had won the battle on the Warta and we would be released. We were not, however, allowed to leave the town under penalty of death. We walked out into a perfect day, typical of the golden Polish autumn. The Polish women cried when they saw the cross near the door; we had made a toilet out of their church.

We went back to Aunt Rifkah at the barber's house. Others from Kalisz joined us, including Master Gelbert and Richeck Pearlman, and we discussed what to do. My father said that we should go back to Kalisz. I loved what he said, he had regained his self-control after being so depressed. I agreed with him, but the others were too afraid. My father knew the land around Dobra from the cattle trade. He knew the fields and he knew the wetlands so we would not need to take the road. Still, nobody wanted to join us. I said to my father that it was better with just two, less suspicious, and we decided to go.

We said good-bye to everybody and, after receiving blessings from Aunt Rifkah, we left. We walked across a number of fields until it began to be too wet, just as my father had said. In some sections we were forced to take off our clothing, bundling it up with our belts and resting it on our heads, before wading through the waters.

After crossing a patch of wetlands, with our clothing still in bundles, we came to a village to find a bunch of Polish women coming out of their houses crying to us. There were no men in the area, they had all been mobilized. Even though we were undressed, the women began asking us questions about the situation and the Polish army. It was slightly embarrassing, but with the situation as it was, who cared about appearances? They did not know much, but neither did we. We told them that the Germans were already in Dobra. They cried, 'Jesus Maria, Jesus Maria!' We put on our clothing and thankfully they fed us.

We went through the village and headed towards the highway that we had taken out of Kalisz. On the road we saw a German checkpoint: three armed soldiers and a field cannon. They were controlling the road from the village to the highway. One yelled, '*Halt!*' I felt a pit in my stomach. He asked us all sorts of questions, especially about my father's boots. His butcher boots were big and sturdy, like a soldier's boots. I said in German, '*Fleischer! Fleischer!*' but they kept asking more questions. I was becoming increasingly frightened; if they could kill a rabbi and a priest so easily, what was to stop them from killing us? As we continued answering their questions I saw a column of tanks out of the corner of my eye, heading in the direction of Lodz. We continued talking, but at the right moment I yelled, 'Father, let's go!' and pushed him away from the soldiers. They had not expected this, so we were able to get away while the column of tanks separated us. In the end they did not follow us and we made our way safely back to the road. I believe that if we had not run, sooner or later the conversation would have come around to: *Jude* or not? I took a lesson from this: once a decision has been made, do not hesitate.

We were walking towards Kasziminka when we came face to face with the German army. The incredible might of the Nazis was on display; we had never seen such a picture. It was not just the masses of trucks, motorcycles, cannons and tanks, but also the organization. The spacing was perfect, the uniforms were made of such fine material, and the machinery was impressive. The motorcycle drivers, wearing rubberized jackets and silver goggles, zipped up and down the columns of trucks filled with infantrymen with their rifles by their sides. The tanks rolled past us, one after the other, while planes flew overhead. I could see that Poland did not stand a chance. The Polish army, which had been so invincible in my eyes, now looked like nothing. How outdated our army had become – against whom would we use our bayonets?

In the afternoon we passed once again through the model village of Liskuv, now partially destroyed, and came to the river with the broken bridge. The Germans had already repaired it, so we crossed and arrived at Kasziminka, going straight to the house where we had left my mother.

Our carriage was still in the backyard, which seemed like a good sign to us. But when I ran up the stairs, I found no one. The loft was in disarray and it looked like something had happened. We looked around the farmhouse and found a dead Polish man, head down in the compost pile, not far from a casing of bullets. He had been shot. Later my mother told us that he was a former soldier who tried to resist the Nazis, but to us it looked like a murder. My father was in a terrible state, as was I. Where was our family? We opened our carriage and found some wine and food. We took a little, washed ourselves and then fell asleep, it was already dark.

The next morning we decided that I should go out to see what was going on. As a boy I attracted less suspicion. I saw no civilians, only German soldiers. Not far from the market place and the synagogue there was a German army commandant standing in a store. I returned to my father and I told him what I had seen. We discussed the situation and we agreed that I should go to the commandant and ask for his permission to go back to Kalisz.

I approached the commandant, an elderly man, and told him we would like to return to Kalisz to continue our trades. I still had my certificate of apprenticeship, decorated with the Polish eagle, which I presented to him. I told him about my mother and my siblings, how we wanted to find them. He looked at me and said, 'I remember such a woman. I put them on a bus back to Kalisz.' This news hit me so hard that I began to cry. He said, 'Oh young man, young man, everything is all right, everything will be fine.' He gave me a *Schein,* a stamp with the swastika and the German eagle, on a piece of paper stating that my father and I had permission to return to Kalisz. I went back to my father and told him the story. He was so happy he almost cried like me (I was a crier).

After putting a few things into the carriage, we headed down the road back to Kalisz. Soon we were pushed to the side to make way for another huge section of the German army to pass. We came to a bridge that German engineers, looking happy, singing and talking loudly, were repairing. They were big, strong men, wearing light, linen clothing with workers' boots. They did not look like the rest of the army. As we passed our carriage got stuck in the sand and we could not move it. They came over, laughing at us good-naturedly, then two engineers lifted that carriage like a toy and put it back on the road. In my eyes they seemed stronger than my father, such good-looking, husky men.

There was a well by that bridge and I stopped to drink some water. I hoisted the pail and drank from it like a horse. The engineers were laughing like crazy, even taking pictures of us. We were disheveled, it was hot, and my father's boots were dirty from the wetlands. We had no difficulties with them, just that they laughed at us.

We continued on the side of the road, as endless army columns passed by. Cannons were transported on trucks, flanked by two soldiers. The infantry trucks held three or four lines of soldiers, sitting back to back like in a picture. No one walked. There were soldiers on bicycles with rifle mounts pedaling beside the trucks as the motorcycles moved quickly up and down the columns like sheep dogs. And the planes continued to come. It was such a show of force.

We passed the suburb of Vinjare, where the antiSemitic policemen had built their retirement homes. The people were frightened, subdued. I felt strange. The strength of the antiSemites had brought my friends and me here on Saturdays to fight and its absence seemed unnatural. I did not like it.

The Germans were repairing another dismantled bridge. There was only enough space for one party to cross at a time and we had to wait for German soldiers to cross. As we were waiting, one German soldier looked at us and said in Polish, '*kykes*?' He probably was from Poland originally because the Germans generally could not recognize who was Jewish. He looked me in the eye and, with his finger, made the movement of a knife across his neck. This let me know what they had in store for us.

We reached Kalisz. The bridge from the road to our house was still destroyed so approached our house from the other side. It did not look good. The house was partially demolished, the small stable out back was ruined. From the backyard we could see that all the windows had been knocked out and all the doors blown open. With trepidation we walked to our floor. We saw that the door was open to our apartment, so we went in. 'My God,' I said.

My mother, my brothers, my sister and my grandmother were all sleeping on the floor. The furniture was destroyed, the window glass was shattered, and one wall was cracked so badly you could see the outside, but there was our family! We woke everyone up. Can you imagine what happened, how wonderful it was? My father made a blessing for our safe return as we fell into each others' arms. We were the only family in the building.

*Notes*

1. Szwiger literally means mother-in-law and has a particular sentiment associated with it, in this case she was our maternal grandmother.
2. In the winter, Shloime Gerszin took four pieces of wood and gave them to his children as sleds. My father, instead, made a sled with a seat, handles, a curved bottom, iron runners and room for two – that was my father.

# 6 The Gestapo moves in

To see each other again and to be safe in our own home was like a miracle. We were overjoyed. My mother explained the ordeal in Kosziminka. From the farmhouse loft she saw the Nazis come in quickly, just like in Dobra, firing rounds of ammunition above people's heads as the commandant shouted his commands, 'Fritz Feuer! Fritz Feuer!' A Polish man, probably a former soldier, came out of the farmhouse and started shooting back, but he was gunned down quickly. This was the man we had found in the compost pile. That was all the resistance she saw, the Nazis had few troubles in Kosziminka. Soon they were led out of the loft and, later that day, sent back to Kalisz.

My grandmother remained in our apartment with the gentile maid and waited for our return. They were unharmed by the explosion, but my grandmother had been sick. The Liebeskinds had mysteriously left on the second day, fueling the rumors of their spying.

I began to fix whatever I could with my carpenter's tools, but the damage was massive. We did our best to put back our home as we waited for the other tenants to arrive. I went around to all the apartments in the building, checking for damage and closing the doors for protection, but from whom did we need protection?

People came into the building sporadically. The first to return was Ferdunos, the Polish policeman, arriving the next day. Sons and daughters arrived without their parents and husbands appeared without their wives – such was the confusion. Soon almost everyone had returned, including the Kawes, the Sziveks and the Zelvers. We were reunited with our families and it was joyous, even under German occupation.

The Germans destroyed many synagogues in the attack. Since the synagogue was where we convened in strange cities, many Jews were injured or killed, including a classmate of Nuchem's. Each person had a story to tell about the German army's brutality, each person had seen incomparable destruction. The older people were reminded of their experiences in 1914 and recounted the conduct of the Germans then. They explained how cruel, how dangerous a German soldier could be, yet they still had a sense of optimism, they were sure we would survive as we had for centuries. To them, it was just another ordeal the Jewish people would overcome.

The next day, my father and I walked down Babina Street towards the butcher shop. The city was desolate and littered with debris, the after-effects of the invasion. The Endeki, unbelievably, had bothered to hang an enormous banner reading: 'Kalisz without Jews!' Animal pens must have been destroyed during the fighting because there were more beasts on the streets than there were people. We came to the Jewish complex of buildings holding the *kehila*, the *mikvah*, the hospital and the kindergarten. Everything was closed, as was my father's butcher shop, but nothing was destroyed.

My father surveyed the situation and, after deliberating for a while, decided that he wanted to open the butcher shop, and why not? We took a few of the cows off the street and put them in the partially destroyed stable at our house. We were a little afraid, we knew we needed permission from the Germans and we knew there would be new rules. Even at this time the Germans were grabbing people to work, whether you were Polish or Jewish. If they discovered you were a Jew, then there would be more problems. We approached the Germans in the most humble way, sending my mother and sister with my father's official documents from before the war. They went to the German administration and asked for permission. Thankfully they were given a *Schein* and we were in business. We were already learning how to deal better with the regime.

My father and I brought one of the cows to the slaughterhouse, which was totally deserted. It was not a kosher killing, how could it be with no *szoscshet*? My father killed the cow himself, cut it into parts and loaded it into our famous cart. This meant we could sell every cut, just like the gentile butchers. I washed the shop, top to bottom, with water from the river, preparing the store for business. We opened the next day hoping to bring some normalcy back to our lives.

You should have seen the business we were doing; the Germans bought everything! The soldiers that came into the shop fascinated me. It was clear that they were not front-line soldiers, but second-tier soldiers – older, more relaxed, some even friendly. They wore hats without brims and smoked little cigars as they joked with each other. My father was doing a great business with them, in a very friendly fashion. They would pay for the meat in Deutschmarks (one Deutschmark equaled two zlotys) and give some of their cigarettes to my father. These were such beautiful cigarettes, perfectly rolled and wrapped in metal foil, which pleased my father. Soon we had peasants on the outskirts of town looking after our cows – business could not have been better. Later some of the gentile butchers returned and started to work again, but no Jewish butchers; my father was the only one. Still, he was very happy. In his opinion, if we were able to do business with them, we would survive. I was not so sure.

There were rules posted on placards around the city, which we assumed to be normal laws for such a situation. Polish citizens were to turn in all weapons, radios and items adorned with the Polish eagle or other Polish insignia. Also, no Polish citizen was allowed to pick up debris from destroyed buildings or bridges. Any citizen caught violating these rules would be immediately sentenced to death. These were not terrible hardships and we were experiencing prosperous trade, so it gave us a reason to believe that life would not be so bad under German rule. Other tradesmen had similar experiences and for two or three weeks the mood was generally good.

Things changed dramatically. The second-tier soldiers moved out of Kalisz and the Nazi civil administration moved in; we were suddenly under the jurisdiction of the Gestapo. Placards decorated with anti-Jewish propaganda and new regulations were immediately disseminated throughout the city. Jews were not allowed to walk on the sidewalks, only in the middle of the streets. We were forced to remove our hats in the presence of a German soldier. No Jew was allowed to keep his hands in his pockets; we were considered thieves. Later, we had to wear yellow armbands around our left biceps. Failure to comply with these rules resulted in death. These regulations were of a different, chilling nature, and we suffered.

The Gestapo set about destroying our Jewish life in Kalisz step by step. First they hit us economically, just as the Poles had done. All Jewish businesses had to post a sign: 'Jewish store'. These were the first to be vandalized by the German soldiers, who smashed down the door and broke the windows, taking out anything of value and loading it onto trucks. They humiliated and beat the proprietor, and made him carry his own merchandise to their vehicles. Polish businesses also suffered, but not to the extent of the Jewish shops. It was clear to us that our livelihood and safety were in danger. With a heavy heart, my father decided to close the shop. It was a terrible defeat for him. He felt helpless again, powerless as a provider for his family.

My father sent me to turn in the keys to our landlady. She was a typical Polish woman, very religious and old-fashioned. Before the war I went to her home to pay the rent and I treated her with great respect, removing my hat and kissing her hand. She was very sympathetic to the Jews and to me. She always asked about school and my family, and I enjoyed speaking with her.

She opened the door and that strange smell hit my nose, such a gentile smell, maybe from the dry grass she kept surrounding her holy pictures. I told her the situation, explaining that we would not be able to run the shop under the regulations of the Gestapo. I kissed her hand and gave back the keys. She was very moved. She cried to me, 'What will become of us? What will become of Poland? What will become of you, the Jewish people?'

'We are in God's hands,' I replied.

What was there to do? With the shop closed we had no way of making a living. At least, we thought, we could collect our animals and sell them to the gentile butchers. My father sent me to retrieve the three remaining cows from the peasant farmers. I came to the first peasant and asked him for our cow. He was immediately abusive, calling me a *kyke* and threatening to call the Germans if I ever returned. He was like many of the Poles at this time, seeing the German occupation as an excuse to mistreat the Jews without fear of retribution. The second peasant also kept the cow, but he gave me a barrel full of vegetables, which I happily accepted – how could I decline food? The third peasant offered a bushel of wheat, which I took to the mill and had ground into flour. It was not ideal, it was unjust, but I was learning that in our current situation we had to be thankful for whatever we could get.

Soon I found work with Master Gelbert in his carpentry shop, though we were not making furniture, only brushes and oddities ordered by the Germans. I do not know how he found this commission, but we were happy to have it. Inspectors from the Gestapo would come into the shop periodically to view our workmanship. They would say in a half-joking, half-threatening manner, 'Juden, are you working?' Sure we were working, working for those who were preparing our death.

Coming home from Gelbert's shop one day I heard a German soldier yell to me, '*Jude! Halt!*' I had no idea what he wanted but I was not going to find out. I ran down streets and alleys until I came to our neighborhood. I ducked into our house, but he followed me inside. I sprinted up the stairs, all the way to the top. I did not want to go inside our apartment or anyone's apartment because I would have involved others in my predicament. I reached the end of the staircase and waited, breathing heavily and terrified. For some reason, the soldier never came up the stairs. I was sure that if he did he would have killed me. This incident took away any sense of normality I had left.

Master Gelbert closed the shop a few days later and again I found myself with nothing to do. Just like my father, I began to feel helpless.

The first weeks of October was a time of terror in Kalisz, even in our homes we were in danger. The Gestapo started taking people out of their apartments at night in addition to catching people in the streets during the day. The fifth column, so interwoven with the Polish civil administrations, gave the Gestapo lists of prominent Jewish leaders and potentially dangerous Polish citizens – such as those with guns. We heard that these people were taken to the fire station in the middle of the night and forced to exercise for hours until they were utterly exhausted, then some would be killed. In the morning the Gestapo posted the names of those executed the night before, just as the Polish government had previously listed the names of German spies. The extent of the fifth column's penetration into Polish government was seen at the Shreier toy factory; the very men said to have been executed for espionage before the war were now running the factory.

Normal citizens were also in danger, not just the leaders. My brother Nuchem, just hanging around with some friends, was caught and taken to Gestapo headquarters. He and his friends had to do calisthenics for hours as they were beaten constantly. They put a pail on Nuchem's head and forced him to climb a ladder. When he fell they beat him and sent him home, swollen and humiliated. What kind of terror was this, such a senseless beating of boys? It was so illogical, so pointless.

Gestapo officers on motorcycles patrolled the streets looking for crazy people, killing them on the spot. All the synagogues were closed and prayer was forbidden. Our rabbis still prayed, but only when others stood guard. The Nazis attacked the Jews they could recognize, cutting off pieces of the Orthodox Jews' beards and forcing the Orthodox women to wash the toilets and the streets with their *szeitles*. To help them identify non-Orthodox Jews, the Nazis employed young Polish boys who would stand in front of a bread line and point people out, saying, '*Jude! Jude! Jude! Jude!*' Those indicated were beaten or taken away for work.

This terror forced us into submissive, sheep-like behavior. No one wanted to stand out and no one wanted to be the cause of a massacre. If one person fought back, many others would be killed. This preyed on the Jewish intellect as we were afraid of what would happen to our family and friends, not to ourselves. I was beside myself with anger, outraged by these offenses to our humanity. I felt I could strike back, I could kill anyone, but I did not want to be the reason for a pogrom.

Yet in my own way I did start to rebel. I would take chances, break the rules when I was alone and risked endangering only myself. There was a destroyed bridge over the Prosna river. A sign posted above the wreckage warned of execution for anyone caught stealing the debris. I took the handrails from the pile and cut it into smaller pieces in my backyard, distributing it as firewood to our relatives. Once, on a cold day, I walked through the streets with my hands in my pockets. A Nazi soldier caught me. He beat and kicked me so hard that it felt like my ribs were bending, but I was defiant. I pulled the hood of my jacket over my eyes and fell to the ground with my knees to my chest. As he beat me, he never saw my face or my tears – I never gave him that satisfaction.

My father was a broken man – he could do nothing to help his family. I took over the burden of supplying food not only for us, but for our relatives as well. I learned from the ordeal with the peasant farmers to take whatever I could get, and soon I had developed some trade connections. It started with the peasant who gave us vegetables for our cow. He was not a bad man. I exchanged clothing with him for potatoes, beets and butter, which we shared with our neighbors the Kopels. My mother saw that I could get food easily, so she suggested that I bring some to all our relatives, first of all the widower Uncle Josef and his children. I was soon bringing provisions to Uncle Shloime Gerszin, Shaya Kawe, Aunt Blima, Aunt Rifkah, Aunt Figa and anyone else known to be needy. I did as she told me, but I never let her know how dangerous it had become.

I needed to use the carriage to haul the food from the outskirts of town to the Jewish section. With the help of my sister and her friend Else, I developed a system to avoid capture. By this time we were required to wear the yellow armbands, which my sister and I removed. The girls would walk a little way in front of me and give me signals with their hands. If a Gestapo officer was coming, or if the Germans were rounding up Jews for work, I would pull the cart into a backyard and kneel down pretending to fix the wheel, never

71

looking up. I always kept a hammer, pliers and some lubricant with me for this reason. Normally the Jews would be running around, so I would pretend to be just a Polish boy with his cart, something of little concern to the officers. We learned that normal behavior usually kept the Germans away.

Else helped out in many ways during that time. She and her father were so dedicated to us; they saw how horrible things had become. She would often bring us bread or take my sister shopping for groceries. It was important to buy things quickly because merchandise was disappearing from the stores and people were hiding things. They also had armbands, white ones, distinguishing them as ethnic Germans, although as it was not law that they should wear them, they never did.

In this demoralizing time there could be seen good, decent Germans like Else and her father. Also some soldiers were sympathetic to us. Elias the glazier, a tenant living downstairs near the Linchinzkis, was a Jew who had fought in the German army in 1914. A German officer, an old friend from the war, came into our home from time to time and visited him. He was so friendly, as if everything that was happening outside stopped for the few minutes he was at our house. Individual Germans could be good, but the whole system was the purest evil.

The Polish people were divided in two: those who profited from our terrible situation and those who were too frightened to show their sympathy. We were constantly attacked and robbed by the Poles. In our building the shoemaker Staszik and his two boys, especially Emanuel whom my father had scared so badly, would enter our apartment and start taking whatever they wanted. There was nothing we could do, all it would take was one complaint to the Gestapo and then what? My father had two axes in the house from the butcher shop. I wanted nothing more than to swing the ax and take off their heads, but I was bound by that personal responsibility to my family.

I kept busy helping my relatives. I built a fake wall within a closet to conceal valuables for an aunt. I thought it was absurd, what good would saving valuables do if we would be fortunate just to survive? My friends, young and strong like me, provided for their families as well. It was an odd transfer of responsibility from our fathers' generation to ours, but we did not think of these things then. We would help each other with connections and information, creating our own network of supply lines. We worked together building stretchers and hauling large loads of wood to each others' homes from the lumberyard.

If the Gestapo tried to capture us or blockade our street, we would disperse like it was the end of a *masuwka*, darting between fences and threading our way through backyards and buildings. It was no problem for us – as long as we were alone we would never get caught to work. Then the Gestapo became more organized, they created the *Judenrat* and suddenly it was no longer possible to avoid work.

The *kehila* was now defunct, the leaders having either run away or been executed. In its place the Gestapo set up the *Judenrat* as administrators of the community, composed entirely of Jews. The *Judenrat* was required to ensure compliance to any demands the Nazis made on the Jewish people. They would come to our homes demanding kilos of gold, ostensibly to buy freedom for Jewish soldiers held in prisoner-of-war camps. I believe this money went straight into the Germans' pockets, and probably some never left the *Judenrat* members' pockets. They enlisted Jews to work for the Gestapo, coming to our homes the night before to tell us we were needed the next day. A lot of it was senseless labor, used only as a tool to further the insult of occupation. A market soon developed in which the wealthier people would pay others to do their work. When my cousins received their orders I went in their place. They had never done physical labor and I was not afraid.

I reported for the first time and found myself being marched to the end of town, near the railroad station. We were told by an officer to haul rocks from one side of the road to another. When we had finished, we were to haul the rocks back again. The commandant left us under the supervision of a young soldier. After a while the soldier came to us and told us to sit down and relax. He was an Austrian, not a German.

He thought the work was senseless, so he let us sit. He signaled to us to start working again when the officer returned.

There were such episodes of humanity from individuals. I was with Chaim Katz's brother, a deaf boy, when a soldier yelled something at him and he did not respond. The German became furiously angry and came after him, but another soldier got in between them and explained that he was deaf. At a time when killing Jews came as easily as killing flies, this was an astonishing act.

I was taken to work almost every day, and each day I witnessed some form of brutality from the Germans. We were inside the *gymnasium* once, and told to smash the benches with axes. I enjoyed the work – one, two, three, smash! – because I was used to physical labor and I was strong. Others were not coping so well. There was a Yeshiva boy who was totally confused, not accustomed to such work and unable even to lift the ax. I was destroying the benches for him, and I told him to get a pail of soap and water and to wash the Germans' bikes. I thought that if they saw him working, they would leave him alone. However, the Germans did not like this. They picked up the boy by his neck and dragged him in front of us, then with the butt of their rifles and with their fists and boots, they beat him to death. They beat me up too, telling me not to help anyone anymore. There was no reason for that murder, they only wanted our suffering.

The work crews were taken deeper into the countryside and outlying villages around Kalisz; sometimes those taken would not return. One day I was put onto a truck with other Jews and transported outside the city. We drove for some time and eventually entered a forest. This was my first time in a truck and so, although I was afraid, I was excited by the adventure. The people were getting nervous. 'They will kill us out here,' they shouted, and they threw all kinds of money out of the truck – I do not know why. I wanted to see if we could escape, but there was a jeep following us, armed with a machine gun and three soldiers.

We eventually stopped at a river where we saw a crew of elderly German soldiers fixing a bridge. Our job was to help them, hauling materials and cleaning up the debris. The work was tiring, but the soldiers were friendly and down-to-earth – real horse-and-wagon people. They were good-humored and kind, even offering wonderful loaves of bread and canned meat to us. We declined because it was pork, but we appreciated the gesture. They called it their 'Herman Goering food'. We witnessed their kindness during the day, as an elderly soldier spotted two Polish prisoners of war heading home through the forest. He called them over and begged them to sit down and rest, later bringing them home in his carriage.

Despite their good nature, these soldiers almost caused our deaths. They brought us back to Kalisz in the truck, but not until after our curfew. At the hour we arrived any patrol had license to shoot us on sight. We ran home as fast as we could with our hands straight up in the air. I was stopped by a patrol, facing the barrel of his gun, but he did not shoot. He only yelled, 'Get back to your house!' I did just that.

Every morning I went to the market to hear the most recent news and to find out where I could get some bread. Many times there would be dead Jews on display, mostly prominent Jews, lying on the ground, shot or beaten to death with the butt of a rifle. Rumors more than news circulated around the market, but these rumors kept us going. We waited for an imminent invasion by either the English or Soviet forces, but of course it never came.

We heard that Stalin had made a pact with Hitler, that the Russians would take over everything they had occupied in 1914, including Kalisz. We saw this as a miracle, sent to us by God. Later we found out that the Russians had occupied territory only as far as the Bug river, but this was still cause for hope and joy. A few Polish–Jewish communists had come over from the Russian side to tell us that it was just a matter of time before the Russians marched into Kalisz – they were to be the angels of our salvation.

My friends and I attempted to form escape plans as soon as we heard about the Russian agreement. We discussed how to run away with our families, not by ourselves. So many had made the mistake of fleeing without their parents during the

German invasion. It was our responsibility to save our families, so the planning was difficult. We wanted to get to the Russian side legally. One of our first plans was to change the word Kalisz to Kalusz on our documents because there was such a city on the Russian side. We would tell an officer in another town that we were here for school and wished to return home. He would give us a *Schein* and we would be allowed to take a train. Ultimately we never agreed on any plan, but the discussion helped, it gave us hope.

We did determine a rendezvous point on the other side of the Russian/German divide. We would meet in Baranavicy, a city near the former Russian border, at the street address Minska 57. This was the home of a family that had come to Kalisz before the invasion. The eldest son, Haszera, was working on a kibbutz near Kalisz in preparation for his emigration to Palestine – every Zionist organization maintained a kibbutz so émigrés would be well trained for work before arriving in Palestine. His mother and two sisters came to live with him in an apartment not far away from the home of my friend Mendle. One of the sisters, Milsza, went to school with my brother.

They came to my father's shop to buy meat, where I would occasionally be helping out. I loved the way Milsza spoke, she had such a strange accent. It was so beautiful to me, so exotic. It seemed they had come to Kalisz from so far away, from such a different culture. The people from that part of Poland were so close to nature. We did not see such people in our part, so I was very intrigued by them, especially by her.

I asked my brother how well she spoke Polish. He told me she spoke it poorly, so when I met her once on my way to see Mendle I asked her if she wanted a tutor. We began to meet periodically, and I was captivated by this tiny girl with beautiful eyes. Some people laughed at her accent, but I felt a need to protect her and I loved spending time with her. Her family went back to Baranavicy when the signs of war came to Kalisz.

There was a bookstore in Kalisz that displayed a huge map of Poland. After Milsza left, I loved to look at the map and chart the route I would take to go see her. In my mind I would go from Kalisz to Lodz, to Warsaw, to this, to that, until

Baranavicy. I told my friends this route and we agreed to meet there, or at least send word to Minska 57 if we ever made it to the other side.

Under German occupation the bookstore displayed a new map: Europe, highlighting the newly acquired German territory.

The city was rife with panic and the violence continued, often randomly. The Nazis shot a priest on the street and forced the rabbis to carry his body away; we did not know why. There was plenty of organized terror. Jewish streets were systematically being cleared by the regime, you were given 15 minutes to leave or be shot. The homeless Jews were taken to the railroad station and sent on trains to Lublin, to a concentration camp. *Volksdeutschen* and Poles moved into vacated apartments immediately, claiming the homes and all the possessions left behind. Babina Street, with its wealth of shops, was cleared quickly along with other richer streets. Ciasna and Pierackiego streets remained untouched, it was a benefit of being poor. Still, we were prepared. We had many packed suitcases sitting in the kitchen, ready for when they knocked on our door.

Occasionally I would take Moishe outside the apartment for short walks. It was dangerous, but it was so horrible for him to be stuck inside all the time. Once we heard the German soldiers singing in the streets, taking a break from their patrols. Moishe loved to listen, he was such a musical boy. Since the occupation he had not been able to sing very much with my father. Before the war, they gave small concerts in front of the family on Saturday afternoons. They both missed singing very much and hearing these songs raised his spirits. We removed our armbands and walked closer to the soldiers, listening. They sang such beautiful songs, some of which I remember:

> *Wenn die Soldaten*
> *auf die gasse marchieren*
> *Offenen die Mädchen*
> *die Fenster und die Türen*

77

After a while I said to Moishe, 'Let's go, or they will kill us.'
He looked up at me and said, 'Ehh … one more song.'
One more song!

Soon I stopped going out with Moishe or anyone else. We implemented a rule which stated that no two family members should be outside at the same time. We felt that the loss of one person would be a tragedy, but to lose two would be catastrophic. Strange things happened to people on the streets. Aunt Figa and Uncle Szama were riding in a carriage that was stopped by a patrol. They only took Szama away – perhaps Figa looked too much like a gentile. He was part of a group of people put on a train and carried across Poland. They were in a show, though I never knew what kind of show it was. In the end they released him, half dead. We were eager to hear what he had seen and learned. He told us he had seen the Russian border and there were soldiers there, waiting. This was good news, great news – any word of Russian soldiers was good news.

I had trouble keeping my friends' spirits up, and no wonder. Everyone in Kalisz was demoralized and depressed. Walking with Chaim Katz one day, I ran into the director of the Mikolai Reja school, Pan Browislaw Mjorkowski. He was barefoot, unshaven and dirty. This was shocking to me because he was always so clean and exact. I ran to him and asked him what was happening to us and to Poland. He started to cry, right there on the street, and gestured with his hands that he did not know. It was demoralizing for both of us.

Aunt Figa and Aunt Blima both lived on Ciasna Street with their husbands, not far away from Aunt Hayasura and Uncle Yidah. Aunt Figa came running to us one day, screaming that Aunt Hayasura had been forced out of her home and was now waiting at the new market with her husband and daughter for the next train to Lublin. What could we do? I ran over there as fast as I could. It was an indoor market, guarded from the outside. I climbed a gutter until I was on the roof, then I crawled carefully down to an opening and saw them, saw everyone just sitting there without food or water, completely defeated. I saw Aunt Hayasura and asked her what I should do. I wanted to take the child home with me, such a beautiful redheaded child, so smart (she always knew where the candies were hidden at our house, such a happy child). Aunt Hayasura said no. She said they would be fine in Lublin, they would find work over there. I begged her, but she would not change her mind. I came back to them later with some food and some sweets. They were taken to the camp and we never heard from them again.

There was no way we would survive the occupation, we could all see that now. Every family had someone taken away to Lublin, but none returned. Anxiety and gloom were taxing our strength. I could not sleep from worry. I would listen to my parents talking during the night; it was their only time alone. One night I heard my mother quietly crying to my father, 'Josef, how will we save the children?' My heart burst with pain and I prayed.

'My dear God, if you need a sacrifice, take me. Let me die for them. Let me save them.' I was not afraid to die; I was ready to die for them.

# 7 Moraviny

By mid-October my brothers rarely left the apartment. My sister Henya went out with Else on occasion and I had my usual routine, but Moishe and Nuchem lived like prisoners. I wanted to bring them with me on my errands, but we had our rule: only one of us should leave the apartment at a time. I especially wanted to bring Nuchem with me. I could see how he was affected by his inactivity, becoming very depressed. He was 13, and a boy of that age needs to keep busy. Plus, since the time he had been beaten up by the Gestapo, he had become so afraid. The fear had made him subdued, which, to me, was even more dangerous than his being outside.

I was also afraid, but I learned to control my fear by growing more confident in my actions. I was constantly outside, and that gave me countless opportunities to react to dangerous situations. For example, the first time I pretended to fix my carriage during a roundup of Jews it was a split-second decision, but it had worked. It proved to me that the Germans could be outwitted, and that gave me tremendous confidence. I became more streetwise every time I left the apartment. Nuchem, on the other hand, went in the opposite direction, becoming less assured and more apprehensive.

Fear was the Nazis' greatest weapon against the Jews. They implemented a campaign of absolute terror, knowing that we had to be destroyed psychologically before they could eliminate us as a people. We feared reprisals and mistreatment not only as individuals, but also as a group. We were afraid to break laws we did not even know existed, afraid to jeopardize the safety of our friends and relatives, and afraid to think about tomorrow. The Nazi's precision of action, their carefully crafted uniforms, and their military brutality led us to question our own self-worth. We became small in our own eyes. As most people in Kalisz sat in their homes, their foreboding increased.

One Sunday morning, a very cold morning as I remember, I went downstairs to the pump to get fresh water for the day. Mr Szivek, our neighbor the blacksmith, came to me and told me that the Katz bakery was selling bread. At the time it was rare for a bakery to be open and, as we had no bread, I decided to go. I went upstairs and told the others and Nuchem immediately started begging to come. The bakery was only a few blocks away and nothing would have made me happier than to see him get outside for some fresh air and exercise, but a rule was a rule; I told him to stay at home. My mother saw how Nuchem suffered and she felt his suffering. She asked me to make an exception this one time. That, of course, was really an order, so Nuchem and I went out into the cold street and headed towards the bakery.

The Katz bakery was located next to the Jewish *gymnasium* – where I had been taken to break the benches – in an open square called the Platz Kilnickiego. The *gymnasium* stretched along one whole side of the square, and, along with the bakery, marked the border between the Jewish section and the gentile neighbourhoods. Behind the square the open fields began. In this time of need, both Jews and gentiles went to any bakery that was open.

Even as times became so terrible, my friends and I used to meet outside bakeries to discuss our situation, catch up on gossip and exchange ideas. Most people who met for such things did so outside the *Judenrat*, but we were young men with the ability to outrun the Germans, we did not worry about capture. Still, at these times we would place lookouts to warn us if the Gestapo men appeared.

Nuchem and I arrived in the square at around 7 a.m. That was very early, too early for any lookouts to be in place, but, since we saw some people lined up outside the bakery, we took a few steps into the square. We soon spotted Mr Szivek from a distance, waiting in line. Built as solidly as an oak tree, his hands and fingers stained black from his years in the smithy, he was easily recognizable.

We had taken no more than a few steps before the confusion began. Without warning, two Gestapo trucks screeched into the square, cutting off both the Babina Street and Pierackego Street exits. I knew immediately what was happening: it was a *lapanka*, the Germans were rounding up Jews. People ran in every direction as panic set in. The Gestapo soldiers grabbed people, beat them and shoved them into the backs of the trucks.

I remained calm, or at least under control, because I had been in such situations before. My first priority was to get my brother out of danger. I wanted to run into the *gymnasium*, a building I knew had three entrances: one on our street, one on Turecka Street and one on Kilnickiego Street. If my brother and I could make it to Kilnickiego Street I knew a route to safety. If it came to it we could throw ourselves into the garbage dump nearby, something I had done in the past, or even into the toilets.

Instead, I did nothing. I took one look at Nuchem and I could tell he was paralyzed with fear. I could see it in his eyes; I knew he would not be able to run. What could I do? I considered pushing and pulling him along, hoping we would be able, by some miracle, to escape unnoticed, but if we were caught I could only imagine the consequences. So I did what I thought was best for Nuchem: I held him and waited for them to take us, hoping that our lack of resistance would spare us from mistreatment.

'So,' I thought, 'it is time.' We were netted like fish, and they took Mr Szivek too.

We quickly sped off on a ride filled with praying and crying, of panic turning into despair. In a few minutes we arrived at the city hall where a crowd of Jews, also captured that morning, stood huddled together. I recognized some people, such as Moishe Obol, my father's friend from the Butchers' Union. I also saw Arkusz, the choral director from the synagogue. It was a real mixture of folks: businessmen, Chasidim, laborers, everyone. In the Nazis' eyes there was no difference. They shoved the others into the truck with us.

The vehicle was enormous, bigger than the infantry transport trucks I had seen in the past. A lot of us were crammed inside, so I tried to make sure my brother was all right. When the space was filled, the Germans pulled a tarpaulin down over the back of the truck. It was a tight, dark canvas cover that blocked our view in every direction.

Most people felt very uneasy – I felt uneasy – but even in that horrible drama, I admired the Germans' craftsmanship. I could see the detailed engineering in the simple canvas cover. The tarpaulin was held down by a series of pulleys and I found the mechanism fascinating. I always found myself amazed by the Germans' horrible efficiency, even in my most desperate moments.

The truck pulled away and instinctively we tried to figure out where it was going. I lost track of our route once we left the city limits. I was not used to riding in a truck; this was only my second time. It was horrifying, yet I was swept up in the whole, terrible adventure of the situation. Everything was new to me: the feeling of speed, the sounds of the branches scraping the canvas, and the smell of the truck's exhaust. I observed it all and felt a rush of adrenaline, but I was very afraid.

Our anxiety increased as we rode for miles and miles. Thinking that maybe Nuchem and I should jump, I lifted the tarpaulin a little and looked out the back. And just like the last time, a small jeep, a *Kopelwagon*, with a mounted machine gun was following closely behind. Again I was impressed – you had to admire the German war machine. I saw how every-thing fit together perfectly, how it was engineered with such precision, never casually. The Germans considered every-thing, right down to their wardrobe. The soldiers wore special rubberized outfits and goggles to protect them against the dust. They found it very dusty in Poland, while for us the dust was a normal thing.

After an hour or so we took a left turn and the ride was finally over. I had a terrible feeling inside, and I am sure the others felt the same. I had no idea where we were, only that I was farther from home than I had ever been. What could they want from us way out here but to kill us? None of us knew what was going on, only that there was no escape.

Arkusz, the choral director, thought we were near the town of Cekov. He knew this part of the countryside well because he was in the feather business – he bought and sold down for jackets and pillows. He often dealt with the estate owners in western Poland. Somehow having even only a general idea of where we were was strangely comforting.

Two Gestapo handlers led us out of the truck. The driver looked like a boxer, squat and solidly built, like a tree stump. The other, an officer, was tall, with chiseled features and he was so impeccably dressed that I could not help admiring his outfit. Everything was so well made: the leather boots, his pistol tucked into a shiny belt, his well cut uniform. Immediately we felt small and helpless in the face of this authoritarian presence.

I looked around and I could not believe my eyes. I thought I was standing in front of a palace. The left turn had taken us onto a long driveway lined with ancient lime trees and leading to an impressive estate. Directly in front of us was a small pond flecked with lilies, and beyond it stood an enormous mansion. The mansion was palatial, made of stone and wood and adorned with a huge Nazi flag. To the left of the mansion stood a series of workshops, and to the right, set slightly back, was a barn. I could not see them at this point, but beyond these buildings were huge fields of sugar beets, potatoes, corn and other crops. I was amazed – what a beautiful property!

Arkusz was correct, we were just outside the village of Cekov, about 30 kilometers outside of Kalisz. He recognized the property as Moraviny, an estate owned by an old, ethnic German woman and her daughter. They had asked the Gestapo for workers because the war had kept the factories from collecting the season's sugar beet harvest; she needed us to cut and store the crop. During the initial invasion, some of the Poles had overtaken the estate, plundered it and killed her husband. The *Volksdeutschen* and the Gestapo retaliated, and, as a result, many Polish peasants now toiled in her fields – as slaves, most likely.

The officer, that devil, lined us up next to the pond. Nuchem stood next to me like a little child, but he was brave.

The officer told us that we were to work in the fields of this estate until the season's tasks were finished. If any one of us tried to escape, or if any one of us broke the rules (we were not told the rules), there would be a *Kurzgericht*, a short trial. The officer would be the judge and jury. He took out his pistol and said, 'The sentence is simple: ten will be killed.' He said all of this in such a way that any thoughts I had of escaping quickly ended. He would be looking for excuses to kill us.

The officer finished his barking and turned to the old woman. She had come out to inspect the line of workers and to greet the Gestapo men. He transformed instantly into a gentleman, clicking his heels together and standing with perfect posture. They spoke, I do not know what about, and he handed her a copy of the *Kaliszer Echo*, our city's newspaper which was now printed in German.

After a short talk, the two of them turned to us and asked us our professions. Mr Szivek said he was a blacksmith, and was put to the side. I said I was a carpenter, and was put to the side along with some others. When the woman saw Arkusz she greeted him as 'Herr Arkusz'; they had done business in the past. The others – the butchers, the barbers and so on – were taken out to the fields along with Nuchem. I did not like being separated from my brother, but I had no choice.

They took those of us with useful professions into the workshops beside the mansion. Mr Szivek was given a smithy to perform his trade, while I was put into a woodworking shop. I saw that the workspace was used to make and repair carriages, something I could not do – that was an entirely separate profession. Mr Szivek told me to do whatever I knew how to do, just to keep busy. I found some lacquer in the shop, so I set about lacquering anything I could find. That was my specialty under Master Gelbert.

Eventually the old woman came into the shop and asked me to fix a carriage wheel. I told her that I was not able to do so, that I had not been trained in that profession. She started yelling right away, screaming that I did not want to work, that I was a lazy bum and a filthy Jew. She marched me out to the fields, hollering the whole way, so much that she was hoarse by the time we reached the others in the sugar beet fields.

From that point on, I was a lazy bum in her eyes.

The work in the fields was horrible. My hands bled from the rough sugar beet stalks and the cold weather. We did not have the proper tools nor did we know the proper methods, but we were still expected to keep pace with the group of Polish peasants working beside us. A band of *Volksdeutschen* patrolled the fields wearing white armbands with the Swastika, and brandishing Polish bayonets and rubber clubs. They beat us as we worked. They especially beat a Jewish barber whom they named our supervisor, unfortunately for him. They made him responsible for our production, but, like the rest of us, he did not know what he was doing, so, inevitably, we were unproductive – we were working only with small knives and our hands alongside skilled farmers with machetes and pitchforks.

There were two types of Poles working in the fields: those who laughed at us and enjoyed our suffering, and those who sympathized with our struggle. There was a Polish foreman who took great pleasure in our hardship. He mocked us, saying 'No more chickens and no more ducks for you Jews!' We did not have much personal contact with the Poles, but some of them helped us to survive by leaving pieces of bread for us out in the fields – generally we subsisted on sugar beets, raw and covered with dirt, which made us vomit.

Our nights were spent in the barn, sleeping in the hay. Sometimes the *Volksdeutschen* put their German Shepherds in the barn with us. They were vicious, biting dogs, trained to attack. When they were inside the barn we had to spend the whole night up in the rafters to avoid their teeth. At times like these Nuchem and I would feel at our lowest. But Mr Szivek was our savior. He kept our spirits up by telling us stories about his time in the czar's army, how he used to fight with the Russians and beat them up so easily. He told us how he broke a Russian soldier's nose with his head once and how he could do the same to a German. When I heard him speak, I felt my heart growing. He gave us such strength in those horrible times.

We did this for days, for more than a month, and we were beaten constantly. We were losing hope and losing our mental strength as our bodies began to waste away. My eighteenth birthday came and went unnoticed. Something like a birthday meant nothing in these conditions.

My main concern never changed: I was always looking for ways to help my brother, who was by far the youngest of all the prisoners. I kept him by my side as much as possible and tried to help him with his work. Still he suffered, and as days went by I could see that he was losing strength. He was too young for this type of work and he needed protection.

As time passed, we all lost our strength and the *Volksdeutschen* became more violent. There was an old Chasidic man working with us in the fields who had lost the strength to lift the baskets of cut sugar beets. He was in his mid-sixties and probably had never done work like that in his life. I tried to take the load from him, but one of the supervisors saw what was happening. He called some other *Volksdeutschen* over and, with the butts of their rifles, they beat the old man to death. We carried him off to the side and went right back to work.

The old woman's daughter, who was probably around 18 years old, would come out to the fields on her horse and whip us for fun. She was a beautiful blonde, but we found her very strange. She used to wear riding pants, and we had never seen a girl wear pants before. The night the Chasid was murdered, she made us run after her horse with the body and put him in the ground.

When the leaves turned, we raked the long driveway after we were finished in the fields. On one of these evenings the old woman and a band of *Volksdeutschen* headed out to hunt Polish landowners – part of that centuries-old struggle which had claimed her husband's life. As they were leaving, they stopped for a moment and started to shoot at us as we raked. We could only assume they intended to kill us, so we threw ourselves to the ground. They were doing it just for fun, but if they had accidentally hit one of us it would have meant nothing to them. We were Jews, garbage, just something they could get rid of.

In these fields of misery, in the depths of our depression, we were surrounded by the contradiction of the beautiful

Polish autumn. We worked under perfect skies, amidst tall, golden trees on an unbelievable country estate. The surroundings represented everything, up to that point, which my life was not. I was fascinated by the corn, by how tall the stalks would grow, and by the fields of potatoes and sugar beets. I had never experienced such smells before, such country and forest air. It was as if the books I had read were coming to life in front of my eyes. I knew all of it existed, but my world had consisted only of my small, narrow life in Kalisz.

These things, so foreign to me, sparked my imagination. My head was filled with the stories of Polish history and its great literature. The estate, and especially the long driveway lined with lime trees, reminded me of the extravagant properties I had read about in Adam Mickewiicz's *Pan Tadusz*. Standing among those ancient giants made me consider the pieces of history they must have witnessed, and this made me feel like I, too, was touching history.

Whether from my schooling or from the books I had read, I had an ingrained predilection to observe the historical perspective, the bigger picture. I could not really separate myself from the suffering, but I did see our plight from two sides. On the one hand, I was one of an endangered species, at any moment likely to be struck down. On the other, I was simply a witness. Perhaps it was a mental defense, a way for me to get through the days without concentrating too much on our pain, but it is an ability that has never left me.

Mr Szivek was allowed to select one assistant per day for his blacksmith shop. He would take the wounded or the most weary of us inside for a day of rest. Once, when I was with him, a German officer came into the shop. Mr Szivek had a small, unlit cigar in his mouth – he always had such a cigar. When he saw the German he reached into the fire, picked up a burning coal with his bare fingers, and lit the tobacco – all the while facing the Gestapo man. The German said, 'Good morning, good health', but Mr Szivek just looked at him and grumbled. He was my hero: how could a man not be afraid of the Germans?

I soon arranged a deal with Mr Szivek that put my brother inside with him for both our turns. It was such an obvious thing to me, the need to protect the youngest in such a horrible situation, but not everyone agreed. Our terrible conditions had taken their toll on the psyche of the others. They complained bitterly over the special treatment my brother received. Even Moishe Obol, a friend of my father's, complained to me. I was ashamed for them, not angry with them, because I could recognize that it was our predicament, not their spirits, which was the cause of their bitterness. None of us had ever been exposed to such horrors, such mistreatment – we were fighting to survive. I witnessed this deterioration of personal character and I felt that it was just the beginning. What was going to happen if we stayed much longer with the Germans? Would we cease to be human?

I believe that there is a time, in these situations, when you have to make a decision. You have to decide how you are going to cope, because later you will not have the strength to change your mind. Will you walk over people to save yourself, or will you refuse to cross that line? We had already seen what people would do to survive. The Germans were killing us with gloves, using the stronger Jews who had joined the police to do the dirty work in the ghettoes. I knew that if I did not make a decision now, never to put myself above someone else's suffering, then I would eventually be lost. I could see it coming, it was like a fire in a cinema, with people getting trampled.

The way my fellow captives turned against my brother was my first baptism into that reality; it was like seeing into the future. To make up for the special treatment, I agreed to work on Sundays, the day all but a few of us had to rest.

Added to our troubles was the fact that the barn had become infested with lice. Soon we ourselves were infested. This problem was in a way a blessing for Nuchem because it kept him out of the fields. With his dexterous hands he started a new profession. He would take four or five sets of clothes into the shop with him every day and put them over the fire, working the smoke into the creases to expel the vermin. He was a marvel at it. By doing this he made himself invaluable to the others, and they stopped complaining about his special treatment. Sometimes he was even able to wash the clothes in water, but that was rare. Even so, I had to continue working on Sundays.

We did not have much contact with the Gestapo on the estate; the *Volksdeutschen* supervised us. There was one Gestapo truck that came to Moraviny and filled up with produce every morning. That was the job of a military policeman, a gendarme, from the town of Cekov. Like all Nazis, he had a very impressive uniform. He wore a metal chest plate, carried a rubber club and kept a large automatic pistol in his belt. I admired his gun, it was another technological marvel in my eyes. He was intimidating. He appeared so big and strong to us. But, as I have said, all the Germans looked this big in our eyes.

A Jewish boy came with the gendarme in the mornings. I was amazed that he worked for the Gestapo. I knew him from Kalisz – he was a member of the Betar youth group. Never in a thousand years would I have expected to see a young Jewish boy from my city working with these devils. He was a blond, good-looking boy, maybe they did not know he was a Jew. There was seldom a chance to talk, but I was able to speak with him once as we loaded potatoes. I appealed to him for help, explaining our situation as best I could. I told him that we would die on that estate unless he could contact the Jewish committee. I thought the *Judenrat* would buy us out if they knew about our horrible conditions. He listened to me and I knew he understood, but I do not know if he ever told anyone about us.

Every morning, after loading the truck, we lined up by the cornfields in front of the old woman and the gendarme. The two of them would choose someone to be beaten. Only Arkusz was spared, she always took him out of line. Because I was the 'lazy bum', I was beaten on two different occasions.

The gendarme acted so friendly with us sometimes, coming towards us saying, *'Halo Juden, Wie geht's?'* – 'Hey Jews, how's it going?' You could tell he was a nice man on some level, but I made the mistake of believing in him. I showed him my hands in the hope of appealing to his humanitarian side. They were cut up and bloody from the corn stalks. He took one look at my hands, pulled out his whip and cracked me directly on my wounds. It reminded me again that we were not humans in their eyes.

One morning, just for fun, the gendarme told us to beat up the person standing next to us. Of course my brother was always near me, so we were supposed to fight each other. I decided that I would go no further and I refused to fight. The gendarme took out his club and gave me a severe beating. Soon my leather jacket was shredded like noodles, but he continued to swing that club. He beat my legs, my back, my arms around my head, but he never reached for his pistol. That is what I thought about the whole time. 'As long as he doesn't reach for the pistol', I thought, 'it will be okay.' I was badly hurt, but by some miracle I could still walk. If I had been unable to work, who knows what would have happened?

The next day was a Sunday and I had to work in the fields. I could barely move, yet even though I was in such a terrible condition, no one volunteered to take my place. They had become so base. Even before that brutal beating I had been exhausted from working so hard and getting so little sleep. How could I continue?

On that Sunday the work was particularly difficult. As the weather worsened, the work on the farm changed. We had spent the last few days building *kopiets*, mounds of mud and straw used for storing the unused portions of the harvest during the winter. It was exhausting work, requiring more physical strength than I could muster in my condition.

I dragged myself from mound to mound in driving rain. The ground was saturated and uneven, and I had trouble lifting my feet and keeping my balance. I remember we were working with pitchforks, but I could hardly lift one off the ground. Big wagons lurched and swayed around me, their huge wheels turning up the cold, wet earth. I saw the wheels moving through the mud and I had a comforting thought: 'How about killing myself? How about throwing myself under the wheels?'

For a moment I was sure I would do it, but my concern for Nuchem stopped me. Instead I prayed to God to give me the strength to continue. I wanted to end my life that day, and it would have been so easy, but with the help of God I remembered that my responsibilities to my brother and to the Jewish people outweighed my suffering.

We were haggard. We struggled to get ourselves out to work after fitful nights of sleep. If something did not change, we were sure to die of hunger, or from lice, or maltreatment. I held onto the hope that the *Judenrat* would hear about us soon and surely, I believed, bring us home.

On the night of 9 November, the Gestapo truck pulled into Moraviny and we were told to load potatoes into the back as we normally would. It was strange that we did this in the evening, but with the change of weather, routines were no longer the same. After we finished the loading, the gendarme said to us, 'Everyone get in.'

We could not believe what we heard, but it did not take long for us to understand what it meant. We jumped into the back of the truck, happy, all of us so happy. I thought this was surely the result of the *Judenrat* buying us out, but when I looked to the Jewish boy for confirmation I noticed something queer in his behavior. He was reserved, refusing to make eye contact with me. Was he afraid of reprisals from the Gestapo for helping our cause, or was he hiding something terrible from us? It did not give me a good feeling, but when the truck started down that long driveway, I was optimistic.

As we drove the 30 kilometers back to Kalisz, I felt anxious. The behavior of the Jewish boy worked its way into my thoughts, and I was overwhelmed by its effect. I figured I would know soon enough whether or not we were saved. If they took us to the *Judenrat*, I believed we would be released. If they did not, surely we would be in trouble.

The truck entered Kalisz and turned onto Luminus Street, straight to the Gestapo offices. The joy felt during the ride was replaced by a wave of dread – why were they taking us there? A crew of young officers met us outside the headquarters and directed us off the truck and into a line. We were marched quickly into the building.

In the hallway I came face to face with an old classmate of

mine. It was Zelzer, an ethnic German who had come to my family's apartment to work on his homework. He was always such a stern boy, not very friendly, but I considered him a friend. After he finished school he went to work at the piano factory, but now he wore a Gestapo uniform and carried a pistol. Probably with the arrival of the Germans he had become a big-shot – a result, I figured, of his work with the fifth column. I looked at him and he looked at me, but he said nothing and walked past.

They led us down some stairs to a damp basement and left us alone in the dark. We spent the night there, cold and hungry, as we listened to the sounds above us. There was an interrogation room or a prison cell of some kind on the first floor. Through the night we heard the Gestapo abusing and thrashing people. It was terrifying for Nuchem. We held each other and waited for morning, trying not to visualize what we could hear. We were too heavy with fear to rest.

In the morning, Zelzer and a few other officers came down to the basement to collect us, and again he ignored me. We were hurriedly raised and directed up the stairs and out of the building. Many of us struggled to stay on our feet; they had not given us any food or water and we had not slept. It was very early in the morning, the light was still gray as the sun just started to rise. I tried to be optimistic. I wanted to believe that we were held overnight because we had arrived after curfew the night before, but deep down I knew our situation was still severe.

We walked away from the headquarters in an orderly fashion, flanked by Gestapo officers, and headed towards the Jewish complex of the *Judenrat*. The march took us across a long stretch of Kalisz, through a variety of neighborhoods, until we came to the Jewish section. The *Judenrat* had its headquarters in the central building of the complex, but we walked right past it.

They took us instead to a small building behind the Jewish hospital, a building used for preparing the dead for burial. It was a one-room structure with little decoration and a mass of shovels collected in the corner. On one side of the room there was a small door – almost like a window – used for passing the prepared corpses outside to be buried. It was a dismal space, and we were crammed inside it. There was a *Judenrat* man there to greet the officers, but we did not speak with him. One of the Gestapo officers told us each to grab a shovel.

I knew at that moment that we were never going to be set free, that we were truly sentenced to death. My thoughts, of course, turned to Nuchem. How could I save him now? Then a miracle happened: there were not enough shovels.

The Gestapo officers and *Judenrat* man took a few people, including Arkusz, and went to retrieve more, leaving the rest of us alone in the building. It was an opportunity given to us by God. As soon as we were alone I shoved Nuchem out the little door and told him to run. I shoved others out yelling, 'Run! Run!' I was so desperate to save others that I ran out of time to save myself. By the time I was prepared to flee, the officers had returned. Still, four or five people were saved, including my dear brother Nuchem.

I was shaking as they lined us up again outside that building. I did not know if Nuchem had the strength to run all the way home, or if he had the savvy to avoid capture. I had no doubt, however, that I had done the right thing. He was better off apart from this group.

We marched through the streets of Kalisz, each of us carrying a shovel. We came to some Jewish streets and some mixed streets outside the old city, but we saw no Jews. They had been taken away or sent to the ghetto. In their place were bands of Polish hoodlums, who watched our procession and clapped as we passed. They knew we were going to the cemetery. They applauded the fact that we were being led to death.

We walked down Widok Street, a Polish street that led to the Jewish cemetery. On the side of the road there were a few old, Catholic women kneeling and crossing themselves as we passed. I had seen this before. During a Jewish funeral procession, professional mourners and family members, all dressed in black, would pass down Widok Street as the Catholic women prayed for the dead. This time their prayers were meant for us.

We arrived at the Jewish cemetery. For weeks the Germans had forced the rabbis to bury the dead in Kalisz and you could see the fresh marks on the soil. We knew priests and prisoners were buried there and we knew we were next. A feeling of nothingness, beyond helplessness, weighed down upon us. The Gestapo officers wore black; I had never seen them in black. They measured a long trench and ordered us to dig.

These men did not even consider us enemies – we were nothing, garbage, and this somehow felt worse. At least with a Pole they had a reason to kill, there was a war. The murder of the Jews held no logic.

We dug in the morning and did not rest until the late afternoon. We had not been given food or even a drink of water since leaving the estate. The earth was sandy, and as we dug, the trench constantly collapsed into itself. The Germans beat us and told us to dig at an angle, and we did as we were told.

We finished digging the trench at three or four in the afternoon. We climbed out and laid down our shovels. Nobody spoke. Two trucks carrying more prisoners entered the cemetery. More officers clad in black directed them off the trucks. I believe there were over 100 of us now.

The Germans suddenly started firing their guns. I do not know whether they used blank bullets or fired above our heads, I just know that we all threw ourselves to the ground. They yelled at us and forced us back to our feet. They moved us near the wall of a mausoleum and lined us up facing the ditch.

'Look straight ahead!' the commandant yelled.

A young German officer stood in front of the first person in line, face to face, and pulled out a pistol. He held the gun to the side of the person's head and pulled the trigger. The body crumbled to the ground. He then shot the next one, and the next one, moving down the line. The bodies fell in succession. He smoked a cigarette as he did this.

I did not know what to do. I could not figure it out. Why were people just standing there letting themselves get killed? Could I hit the German when he came to me? Could I run? What would happen now? What would happen now?

I was not myself any longer. Something almost like a sickness overcame me. I could see myself standing on the other side of the ditch. As the falling bodies came closer I saw myself more clearly. I saw myself watching the whole thing and pointing into the grave. I leaned forward an inch, not much more, as if following the direction of my own ghost. As I leaned out an officer was in the process of choosing four prisoners to haul bodies. '*Eins, zwei, drei, vier,*' and I was the fourth. They needed two people to haul the dead to the pit and two people to lie the bodies down inside the grave. I was chosen, along with a boy named Herska, to go into the grave. That is what saved me.

Bodies were thrown into one end of the trench, where Herska and I picked them up and laid them down neatly, side by side. Some prisoners collapsed from fear before the Nazi pulled the trigger. They rolled into the trench still alive, still breathing. With every breath they exhaled a fountain of blood. I was soon completely covered with blood. It was on my chest, on my face and on my shoes.

I picked a girl up and she was so heavy, so heavy. I fell apart emotionally. You see them alive and then you see them dead. It was so horrible.

The Nazi shot an older, very well-dressed man. I do not think he was Jewish because he had a big, Polish mustache. I noticed he was wearing a pocket watch, and for some reason, maybe to give him back some dignity, I tried to put it back into his waist pocket. When I touched the watch, he grabbed my arm with a powerful grip. He was dead, but I was not able to free myself from his grasp until I pushed off his chest with my other hand.

Herska and I hauled the bodies as quickly as we were able, but we still could not keep up with the pace of the executions. Herska whimpered like a dog and I told him to be quiet. He was going crazy, and I also felt like I was losing my mind, but somehow I was able to keep myself together.

They were nearing the end of the line; so many had been killed. Surely they would kill me soon. I adjusted myself philosophically; I was no longer afraid. I believed that in a few minutes I would cease to exist, and no one would ever know I existed. I noticed again how the autumn in Poland was so beautiful. The sun had begun to set, and I considered it a beautiful day to die.

# 8 Escape

With only a handful of prisoners still standing in line, facing the pit, the Commandant looked at his watch and yelled, *'Feierabend für Heute!'* – 'Finished for Today!' It was as if a factory whistle had blown. My mind, so lost in preparation for my own death, quickly snapped back to reality. I sprang up like a cat and peered across the level ground. The young German executioner had sheathed his pistol and walked away from the line of prisoners, the executions were truly over. 'What will happen now?' I wondered.

A German doctor climbed into the pit wearing civilian clothes and carrying a Polish pistol. From the far end of the grave he began walking on the stomachs of the fallen prisoners. If one made a sound or twitched, he put a bullet in his belly. After a few shots his pistol jammed and he yelled out, *'Polnishe Sheisse!'* and threw the piece to the ground. A soldier gave him an automatic rifle in replacement. He used it to spray the sides of the pit, ensuring no survivors and ending the pain of the slowly dying.

Herska began howling, more like a dog than before. I pleaded with him to keep quiet, but he could not. He had lost his mental faculties completely. The doctor walked up to him and shot him. I kept my mouth shut because I did not want to be next.

Somebody called me out of the pit. I lined up with the other surviving prisoners. There were maybe 15 of us, including Mr Szivek. The Nazis marched us away from the grave.

They led us to a little house within the cemetery normally used by a rabbi in preparation for religious ceremonies. There were no windows, but the roof was old and coming away from the stone frame, letting in some air and a small amount of the day's fading sunlight. The Gestapo officers left us in there under the watch of just one guard. We could hear the rhythmic scraping of gravel underneath his hobnailed boots as he paced back and forth outside the cemetery walls.

For a time, I'm not sure how long, I was lost in thought and confusion. I took no notice of the wailing and mourning around me; I simply retreated within my own mind. Eventually I caught myself and realized we were making too much noise. People were going crazy, they did not know they were screaming.

I tried to keep everyone quiet. I told them to put sand in their mouths, anything, just to lower the volume. I said, 'That guard will kill us if we continue to make such noise.' But these people were already destroyed. They had not eaten or had a sip of water for a night a day, and now another night. They had just witnessed the execution of about 100 innocent people and they knew they would be killed too. The insanity of the situation, the cruelty of staying their execution for one more night, was just too much.

I saw only one option: to try to escape. There was only one guard, and even if he killed half of us we would be better off than if we did not try. I told the others that I was going, but no one wanted to go. They said, 'They will kill us.'

'They will kill us anyway,' I said. I asked Mr Szivek to come, but he was at that point a walking ghost. Nobody had the strength to join me. Although their hearts still beat, the Nazis had already killed them.

I went alone. I listened to the rhythm of the hobnailed boots and crawled through the opening under the roof when the guard was at his furthest point. I hit the ground and immediately turned on my back to better hear his steps. The cold air hit me like a fist, and the smell of the blood on my chest became more pungent. I started to vomit uncontrollably.

Miraculously, the guard never heard me. I lay there, on my back, for minutes, not knowing what to do next. I rubbed sand into the blood on my clothing to lessen the smell and I started to breathe deeply again. The cold air refreshed me, but I needed a plan.

In the distance I heard a whistle blow, a train whistle. A motor started working in my mind. I envisioned the train coming into the station, which was in the opposite direction from the guard in a straight line through farmers' fields. It was my only option.

Once I had a plan, once there was a purpose in my life, the energy became available. I was paralyzed without an objective, lying in the cold, but when I decided to go to the train station, I was on my feet and running in seconds. I climbed the cemetery walls, cutting my hands on some glass mounted on the top, and landed on the other side. I heard the cadence of the hobnailed boots for the last time and I ran across the fields.

The Jewish cemetery ran parallel to the stretch of land I traversed, giving me some cover as I made my way towards the trains. Nearer the station I was able to utilize the cows in the fields to help hide my suspicious approach to the platform. I saw plenty of people milling about, mostly, I supposed, Polish prisoners of war. There was a general state of turmoil in all the stations in Poland; so many families were running. I did not see any Jews, but with everyone looking so shabby, how could I recognize them anyway? People were in such a state that I was able to blend right in, even covered with blood and sleepless for so many hours.

Eventually a train came to the station. The Germans started loading people onto the cars so I got on board; it was my first time on a train. After only a few minutes the train began to roll, but I had no idea what direction we were heading. In one direction I would soon be in the belly of the enemy, in the other, who knows, perhaps in the arms of my Russian saviors?

By chance the train headed east. I recognized the station names – Siersadz, Lusk, Loskavora – until we came to Lodz, which had already been re-named Litzmannstadt. I alighted from the train into a big railroad station filled with people. There must have been hundreds, if not thousands, in there, but I could not tell who was Jewish and who was Polish. I had never been to Lodz, but I knew there was a big concentration of Jews there because our neighbors, the Kopels, moved there to avoid maltreatment in Kalisz. I remember Mr Kopel saying to me, 'There are 300,000 Jews in Lodz, what could the Nazis do to 300,000 Jews?'

I made my way through the people with my eyes averted and went into the restroom to get a drink of water and to wash up. I took a look in the mirror and I was shocked. I looked like a wild animal, completely unrecognizable to myself. I did my best to clean the blood and filth off of my skin and clothing, and the water helped refresh me. I began thinking clearly. I knew, undeniably, that there was no future in German-occupied Poland for the Jews; I would have to make it to the Russian part if I were to survive. Perhaps I could make it to Baranavicy, to Minska 57 and meet my friends from the youth group – if they had managed to escape.

I came out of the restroom and observed the movements in the station. I did not want to seem out of place because there were Germans walking around, checking papers, and taking some people away. I saw a very decent-looking woman sitting alone. I walked over and sat next to her. I could not tell if she was Jewish or not, but I could sense that she was a good person.

Shortly after I sat down there was an explosion outside the station. People ran into the station shouting that the Germans had destroyed the monument of Tadeusz Kaszucka – a Polish war hero who had also fought for America in her war for independence. The Germans had also destroyed the main synagogue of Lodz. It was after midnight, making the date 11 November, Independence Day in Poland. The explosions were symbolic messages to the city of Lodz.

I started speaking with the woman, asking her where she was going. She said she was going to Kutno to bring some people back to Lodz. Kutno was the site of a horrible massacre of Polish soldiers, completely outclassed by the German war machine – another example of sabers versus tanks. I told her I had come from Kalisz, and she said she had heard terrible things were happening there.

I still could not tell if she was Jewish, but I took a chance. I asked her in Hebrew, 'Are you Jewish?' She replied, 'Yes, I am a Jewish daughter.' I showed her the blood on my shirt and I told her my story – what I had been through at the cemetery and what the Germans were doing to the Jews in Kalisz. She helped me. She gave me food and real coffee from a thermos. I had never had real coffee before, only a chicory substitute. She asked me where I wanted to go, and I told her, 'To the Russians.'

She explained that I would have to stay the night in the station because it was already past curfew, but in the morning I would have to take a tram to another station. There I would be able to catch the train to Warsaw, and from Warsaw I could find another train to a border town.

The Germans patrolled the station periodically through the night, sometimes taking people away to work and sometimes beating people up and robbing them. I spent much of the night hidden underneath the skirt of that woman, who sat on me whenever the Germans passed. In the morning I thanked her and we said goodbye, and she gave me a little money.

I waited until I saw a tram with the sign: Lodz Fabryczna, the name of the other station. There were plenty of people on board, but I did not see any Jews. Jews were no longer working normal jobs in Lodz and rarely used public transportation. The tram was mostly filled with *Volksdeutschen*, and I overheard one of them say, 'If I catch a Jew on this trolley, I will throw him to the street!' to the approval of his friends. The industry in Lodz was divided between the *Volksdeutschen* and the Jews. In terms of business, the occupation of Poland was the greatest thing that could have happened to them. I kept my mouth shut and my head down, though I was boiling with rage every second of the ride.

At Lodz Fabryczna I bought a ticket for Warsaw and we soon departed. The train stopped a short while later on the border between the German-controlled section and the self-governed section of Poland, at a station called Koluszki. We waited there for hours. I spent the day listening to other people speak, trying to piece together what was going on in the war and with the Jews. Finally, at night, we boarded the train and departed again. I chose a seat by the window.

The train was filled with people, so many people on the run, and so many gentiles. There was no interior lighting, which gave me an unhindered view out the window. As we rolled along I kept my eyes away from the other passengers; I was afraid to be recognized as a Jew. Staring out that window, I lost myself in the dance of smoke and spark that kicked up from the locomotive, and then in the patterns formed by the distant lights of villages I had never seen. My ears, however, were trained on the passengers seated around me.

They were talking about the war, specifically a hopeless battle in Klupyo where the bodies of the slaughtered *ulanis* had been stacked two stories high. The war was a terrible tragedy for Poland, but these passengers saw a silver lining. 'At least Hitler is ridding us of the Jews', said someone. And others concurred. How these *chams*, the worst type of person, could see a victory in the Jewish tragedy while our country was violently torn apart was inconceivable to me. My disappointment in them, and in humanity in general, made me sick to my stomach. I tried not to listen any more and I stared out the window, wishing I could be a dog or a fly, anything but a human being. When morning broke and light filtered into the cabin, I made sure to look at all their faces – I wanted to recognize these human vultures.

We arrived in Warsaw in the morning. The train station was almost completely destroyed and the outlying streets were torn up and barricaded. The citizens of Warsaw held out the longest against the German forces, even tearing up the Belgian stone of their streets to create trenches to slow the advances. Their struggle, although a losing cause, exemplified the proud nature of the Poles – it was fought without the Polish army.

To me, and to anyone from Poland, Warsaw meant much more than its position as the nation's capital. Its historic and romantic significance in some ways surpassed its political importance, a trip to Warsaw was like a pilgrimage.

I was simultaneously saddened by the city's destruction and awed by its character. There were so many people walking around the station, hundreds and hundreds of people. I recognized many Jews, I could see and I could smell that they were Jewish. I was fascinated by the activity around me, but I was more concerned with finding a route to Russia.

I noticed two gentile boys walking by in uniforms from a *gymnasium*. As they approached, I overheard them talking about Bialystok and Malkinia, cities to the east. I trailed them and listened to their conversation. They both studied in Warsaw, but their homes were in the Russian-occupied territory – they intended to cross the border. I followed them through the city, listening to their instructions.

I saw the extent of the destruction of Warsaw as we passed through main roads and side streets, not one untouched by an explosion. The damage was massive: bridges lay crumbled, dead horses rotted on the streets, buildings were obliterated – it was a frightening scene. Finally we came to Vilna railroad station, the station for trains heading east. I followed the boys right onto the train, not bothering to buy a ticket.

I sat within earshot of the boys as the train rumbled out of the station. As we traveled I watched the countryside transform outside the window, becoming more eastern. It was like pictures I had seen, so poor and old-fashioned. The farmers wore homemade clothing and shoes made of bark called *lapcias*. The horses wore the Russian *duga*, an ornamental yoke. I was fascinated; it was like a history lesson to me.

The train was very nice, extremely smooth and fast. As we rode, I noticed subtle differences in people's demeanors. The Polish passengers were recognizable by the defeat in their eyes, the Jews by their fear and the Germans by their confidence. I was already taking precautions to remain unnoticed – keeping my head down, not reacting to Yiddish words, not making eye contact with Germans – but I saw that there was more I could do. I was gaining confidence, much as I had when I collected food for our friends and relatives in Kalisz, and this confidence showed in my eyes.

The train pulled into Malkinia, a station on the border of the Russian-occupied territory. The tracks had been dismantled, so we disembarked. I followed the Polish boys again, taking no notice of the Gestapo men asking all the passengers, '*Jude? Jude? Jude?*' as we walked along the platform. They took a few people away; I am sure they were betrayed by the fear in their eyes.

I followed the boys outside the station, down a street to the right and straight ahead. Eventually we came to a big field filled with people, to the left and to the right, as far as my eyes could see. There were thousands of people, maybe tens of thousands, sitting in groups, walking around. I walked through the crowd until I came to a fence. There was an enormous gate adorned with a red star and the hammer and sickle – this was the Russian border. 'Oh my God, I made it,' I thought.

Why were the people waiting in this field? I asked a group of young people sitting near the fence and they told me that the Russians were not letting people in. 'What? Our saviors, the Russians, are not letting us in? It can't be!' But of course it was. Refugees were kept starving and filthy within the confines of no man's land.

I walked right up to the fence and caught my first glimpse of the Russian reality, shattering the mythic image I held in my mind. A short, shabbily dressed Mongol holding an unimpressive rifle guarded the fence. His beard was unkempt and his greatcoat was frayed; the complete opposite of the six-foot, impeccably dressed German. I thought to myself, 'So this is our protector?'

I was going to the Russian side, there was no doubt about that. I waited until nightfall and simply lifted up the barbed wire and started walking along the path of the torn-up train tracks. I assumed this would eventually lead me to Bialystok, the first big station in the Russian territory, where I could wait until I met someone I recognized. I had not walked 100 meters before a Russian soldier dropped out of the trees and pointed his bayonet at me.

'Stop! Go back!' He yelled in Russian.

'No. Germans.' I said in Polish, gesturing behind me. We haggled like this for a while, neither of us willing to budge. He stepped forward and pressed the tip of the blade into my chest, still I held my ground. Finally he said, 'Go!' and let me pass. I saw him climb back into the tree to await the next refugee.

A little further on, the train tracks began again. I continued for an hour or so when I heard singing in the distance – in German. I thought, 'My God, that soldier has sent me to my death.' I got down on my knees and approached a group of young people sitting at a train station. With a touch of shock, I realized they were singing in Yiddish; they were Jewish. It never occurred to me that any Jew could sing in these horrible times, but these people had no idea what atrocities were committed back in western Poland. I stood up and walked towards the group.

They were very friendly and welcomed me to their circle. I was given some food and water as I told them my story. They did not believe me. I heard someone call me a *misiginah*, so I opened my jacket and showed the blood on my shirt. After that, they were more sympathetic but not necessarily convinced. Soon, from my exhaustion and from the frustration of their disbelief, I fell asleep.

In the morning they woke me up and told me the train had arrived. They gave me coffee and some food before we boarded. I sat apart from the group as I did not think they trusted me.

It was still a Polish train with Polish conductors, but the atmosphere was completely different from the trains on the German side of no man's land. The Jewish people were not afflicted by that deep fear; they were more pained than frightened. The Poles were no longer subdued, but angry. They wore their hearts on their sleeves, unlike the Jews, and made no secret of their hatred for the Russian occupiers. The conductors were very arrogant, outwardly showing contempt for Russians and hostility towards Jews. This behavior was possible on this side of the border because of the different roles the soldiers played: a German soldier was a known killer, you could sense the animal in him; a Polish soldier was tough, but not a killer; and a Russian soldier was a joke.

We traveled throughout the morning and into the early afternoon. Shortly after crossing the River Bug, we entered Bialystok train station. This was the first big station after the border, so the platforms were lined with people waiting for relatives and friends, or anyone they might recognize from their hometowns. I walked off the train and made my way towards the exit, not knowing where I would go or what I would do. The station was filled with Russian soldiers and officers, some sleeping on the floor. 'An officer should sleep on the floor?' I thought. You would never see a Polish officer do such a thing, but somehow it fit the atmosphere.

Surprisingly an old friend, Wroclawski, approached me. His father was an electrician who had worked on Ciasna Street near our old home. I had not seen him in years, but I recognized him immediately. He had run away during the initial invasion and was so far away when the Germans occupied that he was stuck on the Russian side. Every day he came to the station and waited for somebody he knew, hoping that his family would arrive.

He asked me what was going on back home and I told him my story. I could sense, just like the group of singers, that he did not believe me. It was as if they could not put it together, perhaps as a self-protection devices. In their defense, I do not think I was normal at that time. It may have been hard to believe anything I said at all.

We came out of the station into a beautiful, sunny day. I could not believe the scene: music was playing; people were dancing; banners heralding a politician were draped across the streets – written in Yiddish! It was a paradise, it was more than I could have hoped for. As I experienced the joy of seeing such a sight, my thoughts immediately turned to my family. 'What am I doing here? How can I enjoy this without them?' I asked myself. I turned to Wroclawski and told him that I was returning to Kalisz the next day, that he was coming with me, and we were going to save our families. He agreed.

We went to his rented room and ate Russian *kasha* (a porridge-like dish made from crushed cereal) with fried onions. It was my first experience of *kasha*, and I found it very tasty. I washed up a little and together we went to the synagogue. I was amazed at how many Jews I saw and how they lacked fear, it seemed to me a paradise. Of course there were probably countless problems with their situation, but coming from Moraviny I could see only the positive.

In the morning I prepared to go back, but Wroclawski decided he would stay. He was too afraid. I tried to convince him that it was his duty to go back, to save what we could of the Jewish people and our families, but eventually he stayed. He gave me some chocolate, some things for his parents, and a sweater to replace mine, which was still covered with blood. We said goodbye and good luck and I went back to the station.

I caught the first train back to Malkinia, following the same route in reverse. At the border I discovered the Russians were not letting people out. It was another lesson in the ways of the Soviet system: first they will not let you in, then they will not let you out. I needed to find a way into no man's land, so I listened to the conversations people had with the Russian soldiers. If somebody said they wanted to go to Bialystok, the Russians pushed them in. If they said they wanted to go to no man's land, the Russians pushed them towards Bialystok. It was so ludicrous, but it worked. I told a soldier I needed to get to Bialystok – one minute later I was in no man's land.

I was afraid to go back to the Germans, but I had a mission, I no longer felt like a vulnerable, little Jewish boy. I found a spot to observe the crowds, hoping to determine the best way through and onto a train for Warsaw.

I was amazed to see such an increase in the number of people. It seemed like the population had doubled in just these two days. The crowd was like a river with many currents. In the middle I saw whole families, stuck in limbo with no idea what to do or where to go. By the Russian gate the crowd was more desperate, but by the Germans there were bands of people with a different look in their eyes, a business-like look. I went near these people and watched them for a while. They were assessing the situation, making up their minds about something or other. Probably they were extortionists or smugglers, but above I could tell they were survivors.

I saw a group of boys over there, strong-armed boys hanging around like hoodlums. I could tell they were Jewish – they were a lot like the Black Hands. I talked to them in Yiddish with my funny Kalisz accent, telling them my plans to go back to the Germans. They laughed at me and said, 'Hey, *Yoldel* [a naive or innocent person] you're an amateur!' I told them what had happened to me and they became serious.

The leader of that group was a man they called the Schwartzer Yankel, a real hardman, with a knife in his boot and a cynical way of talking. They were professional smugglers selling Jewish merchandize, such as jewelry, in Russia. He said he would help me and he told me what to do. They bought my ticket for me, told me a few tricks to help avoid the Gestapo, gave me a salami, some Polish money, some German money and a final piece of information: 'If you need help in Warsaw, just ask for the Schwartzer Yankel. And God help you.'

I was afraid to proceed. I was on a mission, feeling almost immortal at times, but without their help and encouragement I would have had a great deal of trouble getting back on a train to Warsaw. In my imagination they were angels sent down to protect me, for which I am eternally grateful.

I arrived in Warsaw at Vilna station and made my way through the city again. I remembered the path I took and found the other station in no time. I took a train to Lodz without incident. There probably were faster or better ways of getting home, but I knew this one would work.

Since my meeting with the strong-armed boys in Malkinia, I was a different person. I was not afraid to die, herefore believed I could carry out any plan. I made up my mind to save as many people as I could by simply telling them the route to take to Russia. I would start with the Kopels.

At Lodz I made my way from the train station to the Kopels' house as fast as I could. They lived in a northern neighborhood, which gave me a chance to observe the character of the city. The Jews were already in hiding, not one walked along the streets that I saw. The *Volksdeutschen* wore Nazi pins, swastikas, proudly on their lapels and strode along with an aggressive air. It was not a safe place for a Jew, that much was clear.

I found the Kopels' building and made my way down a long corridor to their apartment. Mr Kopel opened the door and shouted, 'Oh my God, Henry is here!' The entire family greeted me with hugs and kisses, and soon we were seated at the table enjoying some food and drink.

I told them my story, what had happened to me and how

I had found a way to escape the Germans. I told Mr Kopel I would first go to Kalisz and then return through Lodz to pick them up. He said to me, 'What? We are going to Russia? People are coming back from Russia; they are living there on the streets, no one helps them and they are getting arrested. It is a terrible life. Here I am selling merchandise and soon they will make a ghetto. It will be like a small Jewish country. I'm sorry Henry, but we are staying in Lodz.'

I asked if I could at least take the children, but this was not a possibility for him. I told him to think it over, that I would return soon and try to convince him again. I had to get back to the train station so I started to leave. Mr Kopel gave me ten packs of stockings, silk stockings that could be used as currency at that time. I thanked him and offered him money, but he refused. Mrs Kopel was crying when I left, I believe she wanted to leave but was under the influence of her husband.

Before I departed I took Lola, the oldest daughter, into the corridor for a word. She was maybe a year older than I and could understand the gravity of the family's situation. I begged her to take her siblings and come with me when I returned from Kalisz. 'Horrible things will happen here, Lola, you will not survive,' I said. But she believed in her father's words more than mine and declined my offer.

I slipped out into the streets and made my way to the station, saddened that someone so close to me, having heard my own story, could still believe they could have a good life under the Germans. It was so clear to me that they only wanted our destruction, why was it so hard to convince others?

I felt fairly civilized when I entered the Lodz train station, so I bought a ticket at the window. I looked more like a Polish hoodlum than a Jew at that point, plus it was not yet illegal for Jews to travel – that came with the ghettoes. Soon the train departed and I was on my way back to Kalisz.

We arrived in Kalisz station late in the evening, well past the police curfew. Although I had gained confidence in my ability to appear Polish in the other stations, Kalisz was a different story. I could easily be spotted by a classmate or a neighbor, and then what would happen? I spent the night in the station alternately looking at the timetables and hiding out in the restroom.

Very early in the morning I left the station and made my way through the old gentile neighborhoods towards the park. I chose a route where I was least likely to be recognized because I did not know how people would react. From the park I made my way to the back of our house. I came up the stairs and pushed open our door.

The whole family exploded with joy. Nuchem (he had made it home!) ran to me, crying as he kissed and hugged me. I embraced Henya and Moishe before my father gave me such an enormous bear hug that I felt that my bones would break, but it was perfect. My mother fainted when she saw me and my poor grandmother started to vomit. I was so overwhelmed with happiness, so proud of our love for each other and so sure we could get to Russia together.

Things were hard for them at home, much worse than when Nuchem and I were captured. The kitchen was filled with packages and luggage, ready to be carried out at a moment's notice. The Gestapo continued to clear out the Jewish apartments systematically, street by street, and the rumor had it that our building was coming up soon. My family had gone through the trauma of believing two sons were dead, then of only me – such things take their toll. Henya and Else had been supplying the family with food, but everything was harder to get. They were ready to leave and I was to show them the way.

I told them my story, how I had been to Russia and found it a paradise. It was so easy, I said, to take the trains to the border. If you removed the yellow sash, kept your eyes straight ahead, and walked with a purpose, no one would think you are Jewish. In truth, it was extremely dangerous and far from easy, but I believed it was my duty to instill confidence in anyone willing to take the trip. I explained that if something happened, if the Gestapo took one of us away, the rest of us could not react – this would be the hardest part.

The family agreed to go, we would leave the next day. My sister and I left the apartment – I would not let Nuchem go outside – to tell our friends and relatives what we had planned. It was our intention to tell as many people as possible that there was a way out. Even if they could not go tomorrow, perhaps they would go soon.

I stayed on the gentile streets and away from the *Judenrat* because I was afraid of what might happen. On Fabryczna Street I encountered my old friend Buresh Weinstein. He was a little boy in glasses, the consummate philosopher who was very active in the Poalei Zion youth group. I told him the situation and asked if he could spread the word instead of me – I was very paranoid walking through those streets. He said he would, so I returned home.

As I entered the apartment I saw our anti-Semitic neighbor Staszik and his boy Yanik harassing my father. Staszik was telling his son to take things out of the apartment, like tables and chairs. My father was livid, but I convinced him to calm down. It did not matter what they took from us, nothing in that apartment was important any longer. I was very polite to them, it was almost like setting an example for my father to see show how we would need to act on our trip.

When Staszik and Yanik left, I made my way through our building explaining our intentions to the tenants. I spoke with the Lenczeckis, the Zelvers, to Bilbaum and to Elias. They told their relatives and the word continued to spread. Henya came back and said she had spoken with Shloime Gerszon, the Fleks, the Stockmans and Mr Kawe, among others. Nuchem had slipped out when I was away, but he returned safely after speaking with Mendle Bergman and Chaim Katz. Aunt Blima and Aunt Figa had disappeared from Kalisz, no one knew of their whereabouts.

We created an avalanche of talking, which was my intention. Our community had been stripped of its leaders at the outset of the war and subsequently had no voice. This was something, a way for us to take control of our destiny. It was dangerous, most likely many would not make it, but I prayed that our friends would have the courage to leave.

1  Military Identity Card in the Red Army, 1942

*This identity card was issued to me when I was mobilized to the Red Army in 1942. I was 21 years old. Every male from the age of 18 and older was forced to serve in the Red Army, which was the official armed forces of the Soviet Union. Its accurate name was (in translation): 'The Workers and the Peasants Red Army'.*

The card reads as follows:

*SSR = Soviet Socialist Republics [Red Star with Soviet hammer and sickle, to symbolize the workman (hammer) and the peasants (sickle)].*

*Scorupa Genoch son of Joseph [such was my official name under the Soviets]. This document is given out by the Czerepowicz Military Command on 30 May 1942.*

*[Signature of Commanding Officers at bottom].*

Note: Czerepowicz was located in the Soviet Union between Vologda and Leningrad.

2a Fire Department Identity Card, 14 January 1945

Translation from the Russian:

*This document is given out to Comrade Scorupa G.I. [abbreviation for Genoch, son of Joseph] that he works in the Czerepowicz Fire Department as the Assistant Fire Chief and he has the right to inspect all factories and military objects on the territory of Czerepowicz. Signed by Chief Susin (head of the Fire Department).*

On the left side the stamped information reads: *SSSR [Soyus=Union meaning Union of Soviet Socialist Republics] NKVD [the precursor to the KGB, the Soviet Secret Police] in the Volagodska Province, Czerepowicz City Fire Department.*

2b City Pass in Czerepowicz, Soviet Union, in 1944

*When the curfew required people to be in their homes from midnight until 4 a.m., this document permitted me to be on the streets.*

Translation:

*This document is given to Citizen Scorupa Genoch Josephivich [son of Joseph] to have the right to walk on the street between 12 a.m. and 4 a.m. by the Military Commander of the City of Czerepowicz, Colonel Dubrovitsky.*

3a/b Joseph Scorupa's City Work Pass, Soviet Union, valid until 31 December 1941, with his identification photograph

*My father, Joseph Scorupa Genochovich (son of Genoch, my paternal grandfather after whom I was named) was given this permit to enter and walk around the meat factory where he worked. Without this pass, he would not have been able to enter the factory, and thus, he could not have worked. The pass was issued on 16 May 1941 and was valid through the end of the year.*

Translation: Document Number 255

*Scorupa Joseph son of Genoch working in the Meat Factory, who lives on Nekrasova 10, has permission to enter the factory.*

*Signature of Director Zacharov (head of the Meat Factory).*

[Front]

[Back]

4 a/b Letter from Uncle Herschel Boms (front and back) written in the Warta Ghetto, Poland, 16 November 1940

*My mother's brother, Herschel Boms, with his whole family, was imprisoned in the Warta Ghetto, located near my hometown of Kalisch. They escaped to Warta after the Nazis made Kalisch Judenrein ('free of Jews') in 1940. However, they were soon imprisoned in the ghetto formed in Warta, and after this letter, we never heard from them again.*

*When we (my mother, my father, my two brothers and one sister) were in Czerepowicz, we learned about Herschel and his family's plight in the Warta Ghetto, and we began to send them packages of food. At this time, it was still permissible to do so.*

Translation of my uncle's letter from the German:

[Front]
*Beloved Sister, Brother-in-law and Children,*

*We are very happy to receive your letter and [news] that you are healthy. We thank you for the packages that you are sending to us. We miss you very much. Please continue to send us packages and letters.*

[Back]
*I end my writing with the best regards of my wife Rijka and her brother.*

*Avrum Hirsch Boms*

*Did you receive some letters from my brother Shlomo din Brazil?*

Henry explains:

*This family, like many families, did not run away from the ghetto because they thought it would be safer if they followed the rules. Avrum Hirsch and Rifka refused to run away with us when we came back to take them out. It is a terrible tragedy that they all died, especially their beautiful daughters, Miriam (aged 22), Shfta (aged 21), Ratza (aged 20) and little Dvora (aged 6). These girls were like beautiful blossoms coming into bloom.*

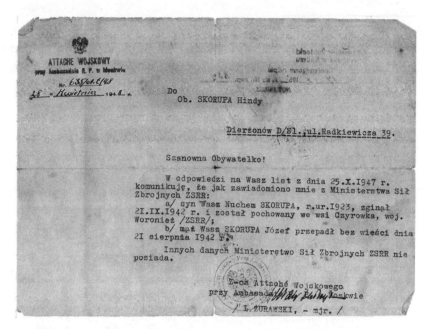

5 Letter from the Polish Military Attaché in Moscow, 28 April 1948

*This was the saddest letter we ever received, telling my mother about her husband and son.*

Translation reads:

*To Citizen Skorupa Hinda*
*Dzerzonuw n. Sl. ['n. Sl'means 'Lower Silesia']*
*Radkiewicza Street 39*

*Honorable Citizen!*

*In answer to your letter from 25 October, 1947, I am communicating to you what I was told from the Minister of Defense of the Soviet Union.*

*A – Your son, Nuchem Skorupa, born in 1923 was killed 21 September 1942 and is buried in the village of Szyrowka.*

*B – Your husband, Skorupa Josef, was lost without information on 21 September 1942.*

*No other information is available from the Russian Minister of Defense.*
*Military Attache from the Polish Embassy in Moscow L. Zurawski, Major*

*[The official seal signifies the Polish Embassy in Moscow].*

Although the official cause of death is listed as unknown, Henry later learned that his father was killed when the Germans bombed a military train he was riding near Moscow. Everyone on the train was killed.

Henry's younger brother Nuchem was charged with the task of reporting on the accuracy of artillery fire for the Red Army. He was killed in performing this duty, a duty he was forced to do. He was buried in a mass grave numbered 26, in the village of Szyrowka. Nuchem was only 19 years old when he died.

6 Medal Awarded to Sheva (Shelly) Welcher, who later became my wife, for her participation in the 'Great Fatherland War', 8 March 1946

Translation:

*Official notification for being a part of the Great Fatherland War, Welcher Sheva daughter of Israel [her father's name was Israel] by order of the Presidium of the Supreme Soviet SSR [Soviet Socialist Republic]. On 9 May 1945, a medal was approved for the victory over Germany in the Great Fatherland War 1941–1945.*

*In the name of the Presidium of the Supreme Soviet, this medal was presented on 8 March 1946*

*Signed by a representative of the Wologda Military Committee*

Sheva was a military nurse in the Red Army. She got her medical training in a nursing school in Czerepowicz, Wologda Province, in the Soviet Union in 1941. At the start of the German aggression against the Soviet Union in July 1941, Sheva was mobilized as a nurse for the Red Army, first working in the field, and later in the hospital.

The Russians referred to their war with Germany as the 'Great Fatherland War' in an effort to mobilize the entire Russian population against the Germans.

Henry explains:

*The Russians had slogans to extol their war preparedness. One song said it most succinctly: 'If tomorrow will be a war, we are ready, already, today.' But the reality was quite different from the slogans.*

*The Russians were prepared, not in their army and not in their minds. In fact, on the first day of war, there was already utter chaos in our town. There was no bread delivery. There was no transportation, and we were already experiencing electrical blackouts. Stalin disappeared from view, and the only sign of a leader was when Molotov made a speech on the radio. He said that we were attacked by the Germans, and we will start to fight, and in the end, victory will be ours.*

Note: Vyacheslav Molotov was the Russian Foreign Minister who, in 1939, negotiated a Non-Aggression Pact with Hitler's Foreign Minister von Ribbentrop, pledging that neither side would attack the other. Furthermore, they divided Poland into two, one part up to the Bug river would belong to Germans (the western side) and one part (the eastern side) would belong to the Russians.

IZBA RZEMIEŚLNICZA
WE WROCŁAWIU

Wrocław, dnia 12 grudnia 194 9 r.
Plac Muzealny 16. Telefon 3138

Znak 31 | AF/4/9/49.-

W odpowiedzi należy powołać się na nasz znak

Z a ś w i a d c z e n i e

ob. Skorupa Henryk,

Kierownik Biura Cechu, Stw. Chołek, Rewicz Pod. w Dziwiomowie.

brał udział w 5-cio dniowym kursie administracyjno-finansowym, odbytym

we Wrocławiu w okresie od 8.do 12.grudnia 1949r. i wysłuchał następują-

cych wykładów:

1) O Polsce współczesnej. . . . . . . . . . . . . . . . . . . . 4 godz.
   Dr.WIŚNIACKI

2) Struktura organizacyjna rzemieślniczego samorządu . . . . . . 2 godz.
   gospodarczego.
   Czesław DRZEWICKI - Dyrektor Izby Rzemieślniczej

3) Organizacja biura cechowego. . . . . . . . . . . . . . . . . 2 godz.
   Kazimierz KUŹNICKI - Inspektor Izby Rzemieślniczej

4) Gospodarka budżetowa. . . . . . . . . . . . . . . . . . . . . 4 godz.
   Stanisław ZRANOWSKI - Naczelnik Wydz.Administr.-Finans.

5) Rachunkowość. . . . . . . . . . . . . . . . . . . . . . . . . 13 godz.
   Mgr.Bolesław SITKO

6) Spółdzielczość rzemieślnicza. . . . . . . . . . . . . . . . . 2 godz.
   inż. Franciszek CHUDZYŃSKI - Kierownik Sam.Ref.Spółdz.

7) Rozgraniczenie rzemiosła od przemysłu-rejestracja-przeróbki . 4 godz.
   Jerzy ROSZKOWSKI - Naczelnik Wydziału Planowania

8) Świetlice i biblioteki. . . . . . . . . . . . . . . . . . . . 1 godz.
   Zofia BIRKENWALDA - Kier.biblioteki i świetlicy

9) Komisja egzaminacyjna. . . . . . . . . . . . . . . . . . . . . 1 godz.
   inż. Alfred BARTEL - Naczelnik Wydziału Szkolenia

10) Organizacja obrad i dyscyplina pracy. . . . . . . . . . . . . 1 godz.
    Mieczysław SZCZEPEŁ - Kier. Sam.Ref.Personalnego

11) Zagadnienia prawne i formy pomocy prawnej. . . . . . . . . . . 4 godz.
    adwokat Wacław CYWIŃSKI

Delegat P.C.Z.Z.                                    Prezes Izby:
                                                    (Stanisław Tarnowski)

(Stanisław Kaczmarek-Płucek)                        Dyrektor Izby:
(Stanisław Zdanowski)                               (Czesław Drzewicki)

7 Henry Skorupa's Education Certificate, 12 December 1949

This document attests to the completion of Henry's course of study in the Artisan's Guild. When Henry returned to Poland from the Soviet Union in 1946, he began to study Industrial Law for Artisans in Breslau (Wroclaw), Poland.

*cont.*

*cont.*

Translation:

*Wroclaw*
*12 December 1949 Museum Place (Plac)*

*Chamber* of *Artisan Industry Phone in Wroclaw: 31-AF-II-949*

Citizen Scorupa Henry, the head of the office of the Guilds of Shoemakers, Tailors, Bakers, Makers of the Leather Shoe Zippers in Dzierzoniowie, participated in the five-day course in Administration and Finance in Wroclaw, 8–12 December, 1949.
*Lectures:*

*1 – Temporary Poland — 4 hours – Dr Serwatski.*
*2 – The Organization of the Inner Structure of the Guild – 2 hours – Czeslaw Drynkowski, Director of the Chamber of Industry.*
*3 – Organization of the Guild Office – 2 hours – Kazimierz Kusznitski, Inspector of the Chamber of Artisan Industry.*
*4 – Budget Planning – 4 hours – Stanislaw Zarnowski, Director, Department of Administration Financing.*
*5 – Accounting – 15 hours – Magister Boleslaw Siwon.*
*6 – Guild Cooperative – 2 hours – Engineer Francicek Brudnotski, Leader of Guild Cooperative.*
*7 – Dividing the Guilds from Industry Registration and Changes – 4 hours – Jersey Roszkowski, Leader of the Planning Department.*
*8 – Sitting Library – 1 hour – Sofia Nigelowska, Head of Library Department.*
*9 – Examination Commission – 1 hour – Engineer Alfred Bartel, Head of the Education Department.*
*10 – Organization of Meetings and Discipline of Labor – 1 hour – Miszyslaw Szefel, Personnel Director.*
*11 – Jurisdiction of Law – 4 hours – Lawyer Waclaw Czyrzwski.*

*Signature*
*Delagate PSSZ Krzyrzewski Stanislaw Zdonski*
*[Official Stamp with Polish Eagle]*
*Chamber of Industry in Wroclaw*
*Presis Tarnowski, Director of Chamber Czeslaw Drynkowski*

**BIURO CECHÓW**
w DZIERŻONIOWIE                        Dzierżoniów, dn.10.5.1950 r.

Z a ś w i a d c z e n i e.

    Biuro Cechów w Dzierżoniowie zaświadcza niniejszym, iz ob.Skorupa
Henryk, ur.dn.8.X.1921 r.w Kaliszu zam.w Dzierżoniowie przy ul.Nowogródz-
kiej Nr.4 był zatrudniony w biurze Cechów w Dzierżoniowie od 1 grudnia
1947 r.do 25 maja 1950 r.w charaktrze sekretarza biura a następnie w cha-
rakterse kierownika biura.
    Za okres swej pracy ob.Skorupa Henryk wykazywał się jako sumien-
ny i oddany pracownik poświęcając maksimum wysiłku dla prawidłowej organizacji biurowości.
    Pracując na odcinku rzemieślniczym walnie się przyczynił do us-
półdzielczenia rzemiosła na terenie powiatu dzierzoniowskiego współdzia-
łając przy organizacji Pomocniczych Spółdzieln Rzemieslniczych i następnie przekształcając je w Spółdzielnie Pracy.
    Ob.Skorupa Henryk został zwolniony na własną żądanie w związku
ze skierowaniem go na inną pracę.-


Sekretarz:                                    St.Cechu:

/Gryz Antoni/                                 /Gandelm

*Gyz Antoni*

---

8 Testimony about Henry's work in the Guilds, 10 May 1950

Translation:

*Guild Office in Dzerzoniowie [Seal]*

*This is to testify that Citizen Henry Scorupa, born on 8 October 1921 in Kalisz, living in Dzerzoniow, on the Nowogrudza #4, was employed in the office of the Guild in Dzerzoniow from 1 December 1947 until 25 May 1950, first as the Secretary of the Office, and later as the Director of the Office of (all) the Guilds. During the duration of his work, Citizen Henry Scorupa showed himself to be excellent in the organization of the Guild. Working in the sector of the Guild, he was very active in organizing the Cooperative Guilds in the outlying areas of the District of Dzerzoniow. Citizen Scorupa was discharged from his duties on his personal request in order to begin other work.*
*Secretary Griz Antoni Elder of the Guild Gandelman Froim*

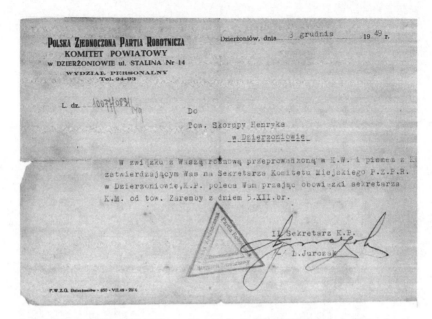

POLSKA ZJEDNOCZONA PARTIA ROBOTNICZA
KOMITET POWIATOWY
w DZIERŻONIOWIE ul. STALINA Nr 14
WYDZIAŁ PERSONALNY
Tel. 24-93

Dzierżoniów, dnia 3 grudnia 19 49 r.

L. dz. 10077/0891/49

Do
Tow. Skorupy Henryka
w Dzierżoniowie

W związku z Waszą rozmową przeprowadzoną w K.W. i pismem z KW zatwierdzającym Was na Sekretarza Komitetu Miejskiego P.Z.P.R. w Dzierżoniowie,K.P. poleca Wam przejąć obowiązki sekretarza K.M. od tow. Zaremby z dniem 5.XII.br.

II Sekretarz K.P.
L. Jurczak

P.W.Z.G. Dzierżoniów - 850 - VII.49 - 20/0

9a/b  Letter from the District Committee of the Polish United Workers Party of Dzerzoniow, Poland, 3 December 1949

Henry Skorr:

*They sent me a letter telling me that I am nominated as the Secretary of the Party's City Committee of Dzerzoniow. This was a big honor because the secretary's function was to be the de facto leader of the city. I was responsible for the political and financial well-being of all the people, all the factories, all the cooperatives and all the guilds of the city of Dzerzoniow, including the government and everything.*

Translation:

*Polish United Workers Party District Committee of Dzerzoniow
Stalin Street #14*

*Personnel Department Telephone: 24-93 Number 10077-0891 Dzerzoniow 3 December 1949*

*To Comrade Scorupa Henryk in Dzerzoniow*

*In reference to your discussion with the Province Committee [the highest committee of the Province of Bratslaw, or Breslau in German] in a letter from them the District Committee appoints you as the Secretary of the City Committee of Dzerzoniow. The District Committee informs you that you should take over responsibility as Secretary of the City Committee from Comrade Zaremba beginning on 5 December of this year.*

*Signed,*

*Second Secretary of the Committee L. Jurczak
['Jurczak' is pronounced 'Your chuck']*

*[The red triangular seal represents the Polish United Workers Party in Dzerzoniow District Committee]*

*cont.*

*cont.*

Henry Skorr explains:

*This was a shocking development for me. Becoming the Secretary of the City Committee meant that I would be forced to make decisions that would hurt people, and that I would be a part of the criminal activity of the party. Until now, whatever jobs I held, I was able to find ways to help people, and not only help them, but to protect them against the criminal brutality of the Communist Party. For example, when the Security Department wanted me to release inside information about the 'wrongdoings' of other people, I found ways to warn these people and help them escape. I also worked very hard to protect people against the unjust taxation of the government. The government was the Communist Party and the Communist Party was the government. In this regime, especially against the Jews, these unjust taxes were levied. Now I was being forced to accept this position, and by accepting the position of Secretary, I would be forced to become the oppressor of the people, instead of their protector. I could not do this, and therefore I decided not to accept the position of Secretary because it would force me to violate my moral code.*

*What then were the repercussions? My refusal to accept created a situation that was unheard of in the channels of the Party! I was invited to a meeting of the District Committee where I declared my decision to resign, and the discussion, very early on, started to take on an anti-Semitic turn. The Secretary of the District Committee accused me, on behalf of all Jews, 'You all want to go only to Warsaw!' He spoke in such a tone of hate to me.*

*I continued to protest this kind of anti-Semitic statement. When I had had enough, I picked up my hat and I walked out of the room.*

*I didn't know what danger this action might bring, or what kind of severe punishment I would suffer. I knew nothing about my future anymore, and one of the worst parts of the experience was that I could not even share any of these details with my family, especially my mother and Shelly, because I knew I had to spare them any worry.*

*This episode reminds me of the time when I testified before the Russian–Polish Committee of Diwowo [pronounced Dee'voh voh] in the Province of Riyazani [a large province not far from Moscow which was the political seat of the Polish Army]. At that time, I testified that I did not want to go to the Polish Army because of their anti-Semitism. The Polish officials were shocked, and the Russian officers understood. I made a speech in front of the Polish and Russian officers and here is what I said:*

> *If I join the Polish Army, I am afraid that I will be killed, not by the Germans, but by my Polish Comrades. If I am to die, I want to die in the Red Army, like my father and my brother!*

*When I finished this speech, I was sure that if I was sent to the Polish Army, I would be killed by the Polish gendarmes [military police]. In the same way, when I refused to accept the big honor of becoming Secretary of the District, I likewise thought I might be killed.*

*The fact that I am writing these words proves that I'm here. In this experience, I again saw where my red line was – that is, the line beyond which I was not willing to go, even if it meant my death.*

*I think the reason they didn't punish me is that they were simply too shocked to do anything. No one had ever refused such an honor! In the end, to save themselves any embarrassment, they kept the whole episode a secret and I also kept it a secret.*

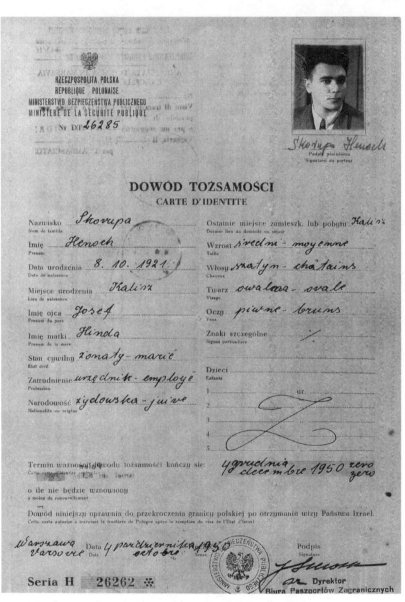

10 Polish Passport of Henry Skorr going to Israel, 4 October 1950

*cont.*

*cont.*

This passport gave Henry permission to leave Poland and to go, legally, to Israel.

Henry Skorr:

*It is interesting to note that my address is listed as Kalisz, the city of my birth, and not Dzerzoniow, the city in which I was actually living, because if I listed Dzerzoniow, I would be arrested – ironically, especially by the Jewish Party activists. They would find a million reasons to keep me in Poland or in prison, because they were very vigorously opposing Jewish emigration out of Poland to Israel. They wanted to keep the jobs and to keep Jewish people in Poland.*

*There is a paradox in this whole situation: The paradox is that, while the Jewish Party leaders were trying to keep the Jews in Poland, the Polish government and the Polish Communist Party leaders wanted to send all the Jews out of Poland to Israel, in order to rid Poland of its Jews. In a sense, they were trying to make it 'Judenrein', not by murder as the Nazis had done, but by immigration. As a result, there were no difficulties in the old Poland, which was the part of the country that existed prior to the First World War.*

Translation:

*Polish Republic [photo of Polish eagle]*
*Minister of Public Security*
*Number 26285 Identification Document*

> *[Photo of Scorupa*
> *Henoch (Henry Scorupa)]*

*Name: Scorupa, Hanoch*

*Date of Birth: 8 October 1921*
*Born in Kalisz (Poland)*
*Father's Name: Yosef (Joseph)*
*Mother's Name: Hinda*
*Civil State: Married*
*Profession: Office Worker*
*Nationality: Jewish*
*Last Address: Kalisz*
*Height: Average*
*Hair: Black*
*Face: Oval*
*Eyes: Brown*
*Time of the Document: 4 December 1950*
*This document permits you to cross the Polish border by getting a visa from Israel. Date is 4 October 1950.*
*Signature [illegible] Director of Office Out of Border Passport Division*
*Official Stamp: Ministry of Public Security Serial Number: H26262*
*Sheet # C*

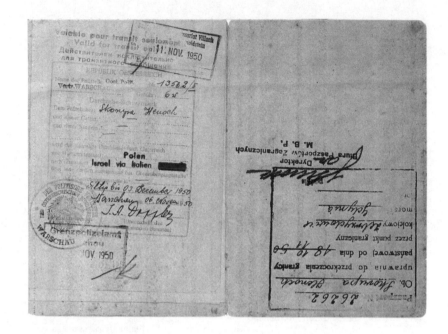

11  Passport of Henry Skorr

Translation:

*Passport Number 26262*

*Citizen Scorupa Henoch has the right to cross the border as of October 1950 through the border point by train at Zebrzyedowice [pronounced Zeb' zhe dobee'zeh] and by sea from Gdynea [pronounced Geh Been' ya, a new Polish port built by the Polish government very close to Gdansk/Danzig, which was used as an alternative port to Gdansk (Polish name)/Danzig (German name)].*

Henry Skorr recounts:

*Gdansk was supposed to be a free port but the reality was that it was really a German outpost, with a very high percentage of its people supporting Germany and acting in a very hostile way to Poland. As a result, Poland was forced to build an alternative port for its own use located on the delta of the Vistula river. I remember my father complaining that we had to pay so much in taxes to build this Gdynea port.*

12  Government War Loan Treasury Certificate, 200 rubles

13  Government War Loan Treasury Certificate, 100 rubles

Henry Skorr explains:

*These bonds were supposed to be voluntary but in reality they were forced upon us. The government organized meetings and the political leader announced how much each person must pay. It was not voluntary at all. But, though it was forced upon all the rest of us, the head of the Fire Station, Susin, and the political leader of the Party did not contribute at all. In addition to these 'voluntary' mandatory certificates, we were also forced to buy a tank for the army, a T-34 tank in the name of the Fire Department.*

*Unlike our treasury notes today, we could not redeem these certificates to get our money back. No, we would not even dare to ask for the money. In reality, these notes were more like forced taxation.*

*In fact, if you were childless, the government also forced you to pay an additional tax. It's not bad enough that you couldn't have a child. You were also penalized by the government to pay more taxes!*

*cont.*

*cont.*

To make matters even worse, we were forced not only to pay what we did not want to pay, but also to pretend to be wildly enthusiastic. In fact, every time there was a 'vote' about these matters, we always had to have unanimous consensus.

The leaders were so corrupt that they forced us to pay, but they didn't pay even one koperick [5 cents]. How do I know that they didn't pay? The bookkeeper, Maria Georgewna, the mother of my friend Vera, told me this information in strictest confidence. I remember her words as if they were spoken yesterday. She came to my table and said to me 'Henry, they didn't pay again.'

Every paycheck, they took out these rubles that we 'volunteered' to give the government. Let me give you a comparative value of what 100 rubles meant: The cleaning woman whose husband died in the Red Army, Dmytrova, the mother of two little orphaned children, for her whole month's work, she made only 100 rubles. And with this 100 rubles, she could only buy, even on the Black Market where values were better, a mere 2 kilos (2 Yz pounds) of bread! That tells you how much 100 rubles meant to us!

13 Government War Loan Treasury Certificate, 100 rubles

*Part III*
*Life in Russia*

# 9 Refugees

Our city had changed irreversibly since the invasion, but it was still our home and the cradle of our history. My mind was focused on our mission, yet a feeling of nostalgia swept over me as we passed familiar street corners and shop windows for the last time. I wondered if we would ever return.

My grandmother remained in Kalisz. She knew she would not survive the journey and she did not want to jeopardize our chances. It was an awful parting, so many tears were shed. Although we promised to return, we understood that these were probably our final moments together. Moishe was particularly upset, he worshipped our grandmother.

Buresh Weinstein arrived at our apartment shortly before we departed. He wanted to join us, but I told him he could not leave his parents behind. He tried to convince them to leave, he said, but they refused. I could not stop him from coming, so I handed him a valise holding some of our valuables – he said he wanted to help – and we headed to the train station.

I saw the Blitzblaus, the Zelvers, the Fleks and some others spread out along the platform. They watched us but kept their distance. This was the way we intended to travel, knowing we had a better chance of success in smaller numbers. The train arrived and we entered the cars without incident; it was already a victory in my eyes.

The city of Lodz had become a city of hatred and anti-Semitism, as if a fire burned constantly around the Jews alone. Perhaps it was particularly violent because of the long-standing economic rivalry between the Jews and *Volksdeutschen* in the textile business. Probably it was because there were so many Jews in Lodz, and therefore so many vermin to erase in the eyes of the anti-Semites.

We exited the train and walked into the station. We sensed a general panic, but not a frenzied one. Germans were rounding up Jews for work. This was the first of many dangerous situations for us. My mother sat on Nuchem and my sister sat on me while Moishe bumbled around, leaving my father in the open. Looking so strong and so Jewish, of course they took him away. 'I will catch up', he said, and he was gone.

We were shocked. I was beside myself with grief and guilt. My family had left Kalisz because of me and already we were falling apart. What about our friends and relatives, would they be torn apart as well? It was inconceivable to lose someone so early, but we had made a pact to keep going no matter what happened, so we pulled ourselves together and headed towards Lodz Fabryczna station.

Our initial plan was to go to the Kopels and convince them, if we could, to join us. But with the city being such a cauldron of hatred and our father already pulled away from us, we thought it best to leave Lodz as soon as possible. We boarded a train at Lodz Fabryczna, stopped at Koluszki again (the border between the German-occupied and the self-governed sections) and ultimately arrived in Warsaw.

Here my mother revolted. She refused to continue without our father. 'How do you know he will come back, Mother?' I asked.

'He will come back, Henrik. This I know.'

We waited in the station for the remainder of the day. I was anxious and preoccupied. Of course I wanted to wait for my father, but I did not have faith that he would return. I tried to accept that he was gone and the right thing for the family was to continue our journey. My mother would not budge, however, so we stayed not only that day, but through the night and into the next day.

My father walked off a train in the early afternoon, tired but healthy. They had taken him to load bags of flour onto freight trains, and had only released him that morning. My mother said to me, 'You see, Henrik? I told you he would return.' I told her I was thankful she made us wait.

My mother's leg troubled her; it was, as far as any health

professional in Kalisz could surmise, an incurable ulcer. The traveling had thus far only served to aggravate the wound. We had made a makeshift bed for her out of our luggage, so she was able to rest in Warsaw while we waited for my father. The walk to Vilna station, however, was too much for her to handle. We had to spend the money on a horse-drawn taxi, a *rysarka*.

The driver loaded our luggage into the back as we climbed into the carriage. He could tell we were Jewish, but he did not say as much. He simply said, as we clattered down the half-destroyed streets, 'Oh, today the Jewish bones will crack.' We remained silent. What could we have said?

The carriage ride took us through different parts of Warsaw, including a few Jewish sections. We pretended to pay no attention to the Jews being forced out of their homes and the anti-Semitic signs hanging in the streets. We just sat and prayed the driver would take us to the station with no interruptions.

We could only get as close as the square in front of the station, which was in a state of turmoil. German soldiers were shooting in the air and people were panicked, running back and forth. At first glance it seemed we would never get through to the station, how could a family pass through a corridor of bullets and screaming peasants?

I had the burden of my entire family's survival on my shoulders; I needed to find a way onto the train. I calmed my nerves and watched the chaos for a short while. Behind the Germans, on the side of the station, there was an alley we could get through. In effect, the Germans had created their own diversion. I saw this and immediately reacted, crying out, 'Come on, let's go!' We scrambled behind the Germans' backs and straight onto the train. Buresh was still with us, but I did not see anyone else from Kalisz.

As we waited for the train to leave, I watched the madness the Germans had created. It was pointless, apart from reminding the citizens of Warsaw that they were under the undeniable authority of the Third Reich. The most disturbing sight, however, was the collaboration provided by the Polish police, already wearing uniforms stripped of the Polish eagle. We were on a train to Russia, but those who remained also said goodbye to Poland.

The troubles in Warsaw and Lodz made me extremely nervous. What would we see in Malkinia? Surely the Nazis would be scouring the last stop for Jews, hoping to rid the world of every bit of garbage they could. I was particularly concerned for Nuchem. His eyes showed the dread I had seen in the Platz Kilnikiego, that paralyzing fear. Before we arrived in the station I told him to pull his ski hat down over his eyes. It was an alpine hat, a model the Germans also wore at the time, so it would not look out of place, I thought.

We arrived at Malkinia station. We walked down the platform with the train on our right side and a line of Gestapo on the left. They stood with dogs and flashlights, peering into people's faces asking, '*Jude*? *Jude*? *Jude*?' We had to walk straight through. If we were not *Juden*, why should we answer?

I walked with my mother, and my sister walked with Moishe. Nuchem and my father stayed close behind, with Buresh following them. There were hundreds of people coming off the train, making the odds for our safe passage fairly high. My family passed the Gestapo men without incident, but poor Buresh, looking so frightened and so Jewish, was taken away. We had to continue without him.

We left the station and made the short walk to no man's land. There we discovered that Shloime Gerszon and his family, plus my friend Shaya Kawe, had been on the same train. They had also waited for my father in Warsaw, unsure of where to go without my lead. It was wonderful to see them, especially after losing Buresh at the station.

In no man's land I told my mother and father that we were free, but the situation had changed completely. Thousands and thousands of people crowded into the space, which was now lined with impenetrably strung barbed wire and additional blockades behind. The gate adorned with the red star and hammer and sickle was not going to open for any refugees. In short, I did not know how to make it through, not even on my own.

We found a spot to lay down and have a little food. My mother was extremely tired and sore, so we made a bed again from the luggage. Looking around I saw families with sick children, desperate looks on people's faces and the beginnings of starvation. Where had I brought my family?

Buresh found us in the middle of that sea of people. The Nazis had taken him to a room and beaten him up. They stole the valise he carried, which held our most valuable things. We were happy he survived, but we knew we would be in need of currency in the coming days.

The next day we began to run out of food. My father and I set out to negotiate for some food from the peasants who had lived near Malkinia. We had my father's ring, a large, heavy black stone with a gold band, which we intended to trade for bread. I did the talking, but we were only met with hostility. 'That ring', one said, 'I will get when you die.'

Could you blame them? Imagine thousands of refugees, almost all Jewish, asking you for food every day. If you were predisposed to anti-Semitic feelings, plus barely finding enough food for your own family, perhaps you too would become callous. In addition, it was not wise to be helpful to Jews under the watchful Nazi regime. Who knows what repercussions could follow?

Uncle Shloime Gerszon, such an admirer of the Russians, such a good communist, came with me to the gate to speak with a soldier. By now it was not just the shabby Mongol guarding the gate, but many soldiers with better rifles. Uncle Shloime had fought in the Russian army when he was younger and still felt a sense of camaraderie with these men. 'Comrade!' He yelled in Russian, 'How can we get to the other side of this mess?'

The soldier turned to him and said, 'Go back, *Judofsky Spekulant*' – 'you Jewish Speculator!'. Uncle Shloime deflated like a balloon. He had been certain, as I had been, that the Russians would welcome us with open arms.

We stayed in no man's land for a week. Winter was approaching fast now and snow and ice were no longer strangers to us in the fields. We made a tent out of our bedding, but everything we had was wet. I spent the days searching for food for my family, but I was not eating. Moishe's feet and knees began to swell, he was getting sick in the cold climate. My mother gave him more food, but he did not improve. At night the Germans and the Polish peasants came into the pass and robbed the refugees. There was nothing we could do to stop them, who had the strength?

Then a miracle happened in the night – the Russians began to dismantle their border. Apparently they had to realign no man's land to maintain their pact with the Germans, but that meant little to us at the time. It was just a small opening, but thousands of us rushed through after the barbed wire was lifted. We were part of a tidal wave of refugees, pushing and pulling in a frenzy, trailing a group of soldiers.

'Yankel? Moishe? Chaim?' People were calling out their relatives' names; they were getting pulled apart. I knew we had to stay together. Within minutes we had lost Uncle Shloime, Buresh and Shaya Kawe, but we did not lose each other. My sister and I were partially carrying my mother, my father carried Moishe and Nuchem stayed next to me. We were running, actually running through the night. Can you imagine the strength and courage it took for my mother to run such a way? We probably covered a distance of 10 kilometers over soggy and beaten fields before we stopped.

The Russians would let us go no further. Cossacks yielding sabers and yelling 'Go back! Go back!' circled in front of our path on horses that reared up in terror. Everybody, thousands of refugees, began yelling at the Cossacks to let us through. Can you imagine the noise thousands of refugees can make at night in such a situation? It was deafening to the Russian officers, who blew their whistles and tried to calm the crowd. There were plenty of armed Russian soldiers looking down at us, so we all laid down and continued our wailing. It was clear they would have to kill us or let us through – we were not going back.

A high-ranking officer approached the crowd on horseback and gave a speech in Russian. We did not understand completely, but we got the gist of it. This was to be the new border, but we were all to go back to the other fields for now. Stalin was aware of the situation and would be letting in all the refugees in an orderly and legal fashion very soon. For now, we were all to go back.

We were not going back. The horror of getting to the new border was price enough to pay for our passage. The rush had trampled children and separated families. The mud in the fields covered our bodies and clothing and our few remaining possessions. It was hell. None of us cared if our immigration was legal or not, we just wanted to get out of no man's land. The soldiers left us and we waited in the damp of that night.

A Russian officer on horseback rode out to us. He began to speak and we could hardly believe our ears: his words were Yiddish! This Russian, Jewish officer told us not to believe what the officer had said. 'Don't go back, Jews, there was never a conversation with Stalin. Wait here and I will help you.'

After two hours or so, he returned with a string of Russian soldiers. He took a group of us, around 200 I would guess, through the woods and onto the path of the railroad tracks. Nuchem, my sister and I were again helping my mother and anyone else we saw needing assistance, as were others still left with strength. Up ahead was a station, Czirzow, the second one from Malkinia – we had overshot the first (Zarembe Koscielne). The officer pointed in the right direction and disappeared through the woods. Who was he? Who was this miracle worker? We never found out.

We rested for a while before making our way to the station. My mother needed to lie down and my father was nearly destroyed. Moishe could not talk, but I could see he was in tremendous pain. I offered to carry him on my back *koppichella* – piggyback – which cheered him up. Eventually we made our way to the station, Nuchem carrying most of the packages and my sister and I helping the others along.

There was a mass of people at the station. We joined them at the platform and waited for the first train. When it arrived so many of us crammed inside that any comfort for my mother and Moishe was simply out of the question. This was all night, it was enough to be away from the Germans.

The conductors were still Polish, but their hostility seemed to have increased. About halfway towards the next station, the train stopped and we were all forced out. Those with tickets were let back on, but those without had to buy one from the conductors with Polish money or be left behind. We had enough to buy tickets to Bialystok, but many, many others were left on the side of the tracks.

From what I could tell, the only passengers on that train were Jewish. We sat in silence as the train rolled through the countryside en route to Bialystok, reeling from our crossing and fearful of what awaited us. It would be a relief to reach the city I saw as a paradise. Then, perhaps, I could relax.

The station at Bialystok overflowed with people, most waiting to see if friends or relatives had made it to Russia. I brought my family to the only familiar address in the city, the house with the room Wroclawski had rented.

The landlady answered the door and recognized me immediately. 'Your friend is not here', she said, 'and I do not know where he went.' I explained our situation, how I had returned with my family through such hardships. I asked if we could stay the night, just one night, but she refused. She was afraid we would take over her house.

The refugees, the *bergenses* – runners, as we were called, were taking over the city of Bialystok, entering apartments as guests and not leaving. It was not easy getting a policeman's assistance to kick out unwanted guests, there were so many in the city. As a result, even the good people, those who wanted to help us like this woman, were afraid to offer their homes.

Bialystok's history as a proletarian city, a place of rebellion against the czar and the center of many Jewish movements, made it an ideal place for refugees to begin life in Russia. The sheer numbers, however, were too much for the city to handle and it failed as a conduit for refugees hoping to find a better life under the Soviet umbrella. Instead it became a seat of chaos, indicative of the Soviet knack for disorganization.

The landlady felt that she had to do something for us, so she boiled water to wash my mother's bandages, by now soiled with mud, dirt and pus. She then boiled enough water for all of us to wash, starting with Moishe. She would not let us in for the evening, but we left our bedding, so filthy from our stay in no man's land for her to wash. She gave us a little bit to eat and even spared a pot and a metal cup for the rest of our journey. We spent the night at the railroad station in uncomfortable conditions, but clean.

In the morning my father and I went to the synagogue,

where else would we go? It was a horrible sight. The people were filthy, the smell was putrid and the building and the grounds were littered with people and their possessions. 'What has happened to us? Are we no longer people?' my father asked. 'A few months ago we had houses, we had jobs, I had a business ... ', he was terribly upset.

'Papa,' I said, 'no one is killing us here. No one is killing us, and so we will straighten ourselves out. Jews have lived here for as long as they've lived in Poland. We will straighten ourselves out.' I just wanted to calm him down. He did not blame me for our predicament, but he was lost in turmoil and confusion.

We went back to the station because we saw the situation at the synagogue as hopeless. I had developed a number of half-baked plans in my head at this time. I did not want my family to be tossed around like leaves, we had to have a directive to give ourselves the feeling of control, even if it left us in no better standing. I thought we should go either to Kovel or Baranavicy and I discussed this with my father.

In Kovel there was thought to be a big-shot communist from Kalisz named Yanik Stulman, so much a party man they had already named him a commissar. He was active in the party on the same level as Uncle Shloime Gerszon, and had recently been released by the Russians from Kartuz Bereza, the Polish concentration camp for communists. His girlfriend, whom he called his wife, was Saba Linchinsky, one of our downstairs neighbors. My plan was, naturally, to go see our old friend the commissar who would surely help us find a place to live and a job or two.

The other option was to go to Minska 57, the address in Baranavicy, to the family Bilfiks. This was less appealing because we did not really know that family. Yes, they bought meat from my father, and I knew their daughter, but we were not really in a position to burden them with our whole clan. The biggest attraction was the thought of meeting my friends from the Poalei Zion who might have escaped from Kalisz by then.

I told my father I thought we should probably go to Kovel and he agreed. We walked into the railroad station with a plan, and my father's confidence was restored.

While we were gone Henya began speaking with a young woman, maybe a year older than her. She was from Lodz but was now living in Kovel. She had come to Bialystok to meet someone, but he or she had not shown up. Her name was Marisza Kohen, a name we knew. Her family was prominent in the Lodz textile business, and her mannerisms reflected an upper-class upbringing. Her Polish, for instance, was much better than her Yiddish, and her clothing, although slightly shabby, was much nicer than our own. She was taking care of my mother with Henya when we arrived.

Her appearance worked wonders for my mother's psyche. The people from Lodz are known for their friendly nature, their humor and their energy. Marisza was a classic example. For a moment she slipped away in search of clean bandages, hoping to find a representative from the Red Cross. My mother, despite her pain, smiled at me and said, 'She talks like a dog barks', making fun of her talkative nature.

Marisza returned with bandages and ointment she was able to obtain from a group of soldiers. While she and Henya looked after my mother, I took Moishe and Nuchem around the station for a walk. 'Come on,' I said, 'let's investigate.'

Music was playing loudly throughout the station, modern songs of propaganda: 'If tomorrow we wake to war, today we are ready ... ' At that point I could not understand the words, but in time I knew all of them by heart. There were posters plastered on every wall, pictures of the entire Politburo. I noticed the difference between the Soviet and German propaganda immediately. The German intent was to frighten you with the awesome power of the Reich; the Soviets wanted to be seen as protectors and comforters.

Moishe began to cry, 'Where is Baba? Where have we left Baba?'

He had cried like this before in front of our mother, which inevitably reduced her to tears. I looked him in the eye and told him to stop. 'Moishe,' I said, 'we are in a terrible situation, our parents can no longer protect us. We have to protect them. Making mother cry does not help us. I will go back for Baba when we find a place to settle, just as I came back for you.'

'And if the Germans should kill you?', he asked. I did not

have an answer.

We walked around the station as I pointed out various tricks they could use on our journey. I instructed them to grab any piece of paper, any wire they might see on the ground because all things come in handy at some point. I stressed to them the importance of washing our faces and bodies at all opportunities because it could be many days before another chance arrived. By educating them in this way, I thought they could become decision makers and problem solvers if something should happen to me.

We walked near the platform and Nuchem yelled out, 'I see the family Zelver!' Sure enough, our neighbors were in the window of a train beginning to roll out of the station.

'Nuchem! Henrik ... ' they wanted to tell us something, but the train disappeared before we heard. We rushed back to tell our mother.

'You did it, Henrik, the people will be saved. Everything will be okay.' She was very happy.

We purchased tickets to Brest-Litovsk – for some reason we were unable to get tickets all the way to Kovel. Marisza decided to come with us and bought the tickets with some Russian money she had. I had never seen Russian money; the sight of 3-kopek coins, half-kopeck coins and rubles intrigued me. We boarded the train and rode to Brest-Litovsk, Marisza talking the entire way.

Brest-Litovsk was a big place, a border town on the Bug river with great historical importance. Lenin signed an armistice with the Germans here in 1918 – a precursor to Stalin and Hitler's pact in 1939. There was also a tremendous complex built by the czar in this city, a classic remnant of the awesome wealth of the former ruling class.

The station itself was a fortress. Platforms were connected by a series of bridges arching over the tracks and above the earth. Queues of people formed on every corner, the famous Russian queues, waiting for something or other. The buildings were decidedly Russian, so gray and drab. This was Russia and the sight of it sent me into a downward spiral of depression.

I climbed one of the footbridges and stared down at the

earth below. I was all alone and feeling miserable. My hands, infected from the work in the fields and the officer's beating, throbbed with pain. I had not slept decently for many days, and I was terribly hungry. I had brought my family to Russia, this dark and disorganized place, and forever I would be the reason for this existence. My head was hurting, giving me no break from the depression. I wanted just one thing: to throw myself off the bridge and end the pain.

I could not do it. I was no longer a free agent. I was responsible for the safety of my family, of the Jewish nation. Just as in the fields of Moraviny, I had to overcome my selfishness to avoid ending my life. I cried alone on that bridge for some time. It helped me enough that I was able to collect myself before I went in front of my family.

My father wanted to go to the synagogue; it was a litmus test for the state of Jewish affairs in the city. It was a minor horror compared to Bialystok, but better than the train station. We set my mother down in a bed of our possessions and my father began drying our linen. I went out of the synagogue to explore the city a little.

I found a soup kitchen for refugees not too far away. With the pot the woman in Bialystok gave us, I brought back soup for the whole family. Some women in the synagogue told me to get hot water from the train station and bring it back. 'Huh? Where?' I asked. I soon discovered the famous Russian tradition of *kipjatok*. At every station in Russia there is a public spout of boiling hot water. At the station, people would come out from the train, fill their teapots, and return to make tea. *Kipjatok* is also a tradition in the home. A samovar is always at the ready for a visitor or a break in the day. I filled the pot a few times and brought it back to the synagogue. We were able to wash my mother's bandages and ourselves before we went to sleep.

Everything was good for us at the synagogue, apart from my father burning our linen. He was such a perfectionist; he overdid it drying the bedding in front of the fire. We woke in the morning, headed to the station and boarded a train to Kovel.

Kovel station was also enormous. Instead of bridges connect-
ing the platforms and track, there was a series of tunnels each
decorated with attractive mosaic tiles. This, I was told, was to
hide the movement of troops in times of war. Without
Marisza, we would have been lost in that labyrinth. She led us
through with my father as a shield – his strength made it
possible for all of us to scythe our way through the throngs of
people. I have said that the stations were filled with people,
but that does not properly explain the situation. In wartime,
people are hanging, standing, packed in, crushed, wailing,
everything. We were very fortunate my father was so strong.

The tunnels, as I said, were beautifully decorated. In
contrast, as we stepped into the open air, the city of Kovel was
a dump. I could not believe my eyes, everything looked so
shabby! All the houses were made of wood and looked dilapidated. Even the sidewalks were made of wood. I had never
seen this, nor had I read about it, but there they were, wooden
sidewalks. I was mesmerized by the state of the city and took
in what I could as Marisza led us to Lenin Street (by now,
almost every city in the Soviet Union had Lenin Street as its
main thoroughfare).

She led us to a little house and let us in through a back door
to a room she rented. Inside, an elderly woman, an old maid,
made it clear to Marisza that she was not pleased with the
arrival of these new visitors. She was a Litvak, a Jew from
Lithuania, and she spoke Yiddish with many Russian words
mixed in. She was not hostile towards us but she was, like the
woman in Bialystok, afraid of us. Small Jewish communities,
like this one in Kovel, were not unlike a small beehive. The
arrival of so many refugees was like someone took a big stick
and whacked the hive. People panicked, 'You can't sleep
here,' she yelled.

'Are you not ashamed of yourself', asked Marisza, 'that you
will not take care of a sick, Jewish woman who had fled from
the Germans?' She was arguing on our behalf, but it was a
hopeless discussion. The old woman was too frightened we
would take her house. She would not, under any circumstances, let us stay the night.

Despite her sour demeanor, she was extremely helpful. She

told us to go to the Russian committee for refugees, near the post office on Mickiewicza Street. I was shocked to hear that there was such a committee, so far the Soviet efforts to organize the arrival of the refugees had been nonexistent. So, we went to Mickiewicza Street.

A few Jewish boys wearing red armbands were seated behind a table. I explained to them where we had come from, and from what maltreatment we had escaped. They were shocked, but they did not want to believe what I was saying; they were under the influence of the official propaganda, that the Germans and Soviets were friends. I begged them for a place to sleep and some medical attention, showing them my mother's leg and explaining my sister's seven-year sentence for communist activity. Despite my pleading, there was no lodging for us in Kovel. They gave us tickets to a kitchen, but nothing else.

Before we left, one of the Jewish boys whispered something to another then called me back to the table. He said there was no lodging for us, but we could live in the jailhouse, a city detention center. I accepted.

The jailhouse stood not far from the office of the committee, on Komeroba Street. The road was made of mud and gravel, not even flanked by the odd, wooden sidewalks. Inside the jail we were given one bunk, not even a cell, for the whole family. There were three other bunks in the cell; each occupied by one or more persons. Ours was the bottom, left-hand bunk.

Above us was an old, Russian woman, an aristocrat who had fled with the czar at the time of the revolution. To the right, a pair of brothers shared the top bunk. They were former prisoners in Kartuz Bereza and they were both carpenters. Two girls occupied the bottom right bunk. Everything was like this at the time, mixed company crammed into tight spaces.

My father did not like the situation, but I convinced him it was the best we could do. After all, we had a bed in which our mother could rest and a roof over our heads. This was assistance, albeit small, from the country that had taken us in.

When things settled down with my father and when I accepted that things were all right, I tried to relax. One moment I was awake and the next I had fainted. My family thought I had dropped dead, such was the power of my collapse. The two brothers listened to my breathing and told them I was fine, but they should let me rest. I did rest, not moving for 24 hours.

My body had crashed from nervous and physical exhaustion; it was a breakdown triggered by my relief that something had been accomplished. When I awoke the next day I felt better. I headed out of the prison to explore Kovel.

There were many curious things about the city apart from its wooden appearance. The stores, for instance, did not give change after a purchase. Instead they gave a piece of paper with the amount written down. You could bring that note back later, only to that store, and use it as money. The stores had very little to offer, most anything of value was hidden in preparation for shortages that were sure to come – then the shopkeepers could get a real price. Again, every moment on the Russian side of the border provided a new lesson for me; I would have to learn to survive in this bizarre Soviet system.

I came to the corner of Lenin Street and Mickiewicza Street, to a huge silo. Behind the machinery was the refugee soup kitchen. I had the tickets in my pocket and thought I could bring some food back to my family.

I walked into the kitchen and whom should I see? It was the commissar, Yanik Stulman! Of course he was not a commissar, he worked in the soup kitchen. Saba Lenczecki, he said, was a waitress in a Russian restaurant for officers, but that was as close as he was to being a commissar. We laughed about the Kalisz rumor mill, how they had made a commissar out of a dishwasher, and then he gave me a load of heavy soup to bring back to my family.

Walking back I was passed by some local Jews who scoffed at my appearance and load of soup. They said in such a snide tone, 'I wonder what the refugees are eating today?' I wanted to throw the soup in their faces, but of course I did not. It was a strange hostility to comprehend, would not the Germans kill them too? Were we not the same? Later on I understood how the Soviet system turned a person's mind around, how resentment lurked in every corner, but at the time I was simply angry.

I came back to our cell to discover that the one light bulb had burned out. This was a terrible thing, especially for the women, because we could not see to go to the toilet. I went out to find a bulb. I went to the stores first, but I was greeted only with laughter, 'Can you believe it, he wants a light bulb?' Maybe they had one, maybe they did not. It did not matter, because they were not going to sell it to me. I went to look elsewhere.

I entered one of the big silos that lined Lenin Street. It had hundreds of lights, surely one could be spared. I asked a worker if I could buy one from him, but he refused. I started to tell him my whole spiel; I had developed a spiel by then, not forgetting my sick mother, poor brother and so on. He said, 'I will not sell you a bulb, but I will turn my back. I did not see a thing.' And so I took a light bulb when his back was turned and returned to the prison.

I was adjusting to our situation faster than the rest of my family. I was always outside, exploring and observing the city of Kovel and discovering the way things were accomplished in the Soviet system. For about a week I spent my days wandering around the city, providing food for my family from Yanik Stulman's soup kitchen, and trying to find a way for us to enter the city's life as citizens, not refugees. I would pass by the windows of houses and apartments and watch the inhabitants eat simple meals at a dinner table or drink tea and converse. 'Look how far away we are from normal', I would say to myself.

The streets of Kovel were no treat for the senses. The houses were generally dilapidated with paint peeling off the wooden frames, and the wooden sidewalks emitted a strange smell, which reminded me of poor people. The exception was the central section of Lenin Street, which was lined with concrete sidewalks and decent storefronts, countless propaganda posters and restaurants frequented by often drunk, Soviet officers.

I used to watch these officers as they made their way down the street. They bought everything they could get their hands on: clothing, shoes, trinkets, food, anything. They approached people on the street and offered to buy their jackets or boots. Why were they buying so much? Soldiers would come into our prison cell, sing songs on the accordion, and tell us how plentiful the great Soviet Union was, how it provides for all its citizens, yet here they were greedily collecting mostly useless material goods. I noticed, too, the Jewish storeowners were negotiating with the Russian officers without money. They did not want cash, but merchandise. I saw one storeowner give 200 kilograms of sugar for a beautiful English cape.

The Russians seemed odd to me, but I was learning to appreciate their spirit. One night my father and I took our laundry and went to the public bathhouse, the *banja*. I saw a line of Russian soldiers walk into the bath, led by a soldier wearing only a greatcoat and boots, rocking clumsily from one foot to the other. He was leading the group in a song as the whole line, for the most part naked, marched past the female attendants (female attendants!) and into the bath. The girls were laughing and singing along as well, as my father and I stood dumbfounded. They continued singing the whole time, sometimes boisterous calls to arms, sometimes beautiful, melancholy ballads.

Later I discovered the leader of the group walked with such a gait because he was still wearing his felt boots, a miracle boot lined with sheep's wool that can make your feet an oven in forty-below-zero temperatures. To wear the boots, the soldiers had to wrap their feet with a bandage because any other method, socks or barefoot, resulted in burned feet. Eventually, I too had to learn this method.

Every day I went to the railroad station to watch the flow of refugees, perhaps somebody from Kalisz would walk off one of the trains. It was also a good spot from which to observe the changes taking place in the city. I saw for the first time a band of civilian police patrolling the station. These were Ukrainian boys, young men really, wearing red armbands reading: *Polizia*. They moved about the station like the *Volksdeutschen* in Moraviny, with that hostile, murder-lust in their eyes. They intimidated most others, and me with their Polish weapons, bayonets and red faces. I avoided them whenever possible.

In the station I could see the Soviet officers dine, eating hearty meals on white tablecloths with fine cutlery. Through the windows to that restaurant my eyes saw the most amazing collection of people: Mongols, Uzbeks, Siberians. In Poland we had Slavs, here they had dark-skinned men drinking their tea with butter! They had a vastly different military dress from what I had seen. The regalia were not on the shoulders or on the collar, but on the sleeve. They wore tunics, not jackets, hanging over their trousers and buttoned all the way up. A belt lay across the chest, adorned with a star if he was an officer. They would sit and drink tea out of little glasses for hours, waiting for their trains to arrive.

In this week of exploration I came to one conclusion: our circumstances as they stood would not do. We needed to decide whether to move on to another city or begin putting down roots. I had many discussions with my parents and with my sister, but something was blocking our ability to decide. We all kept returning to the same question: when would we go back for our grandmother?

Henya would not let me return to Poland. I had been extremely lucky to make the journey twice, that was true, but even I did not think I could make it again. I was also very depressed; Kovel did not turn out to be the paradise I had promised, but a dump in which my family lived in a prison cell and it had drained all the strength from me.

Henya told me that she would go back to Kalisz to save our grandmother. She planned to go with Marisza, who had business to take care of in Lodz (she was definitely doing some business, with what and whom I did not know), and return with our grandmother, the Kopels and anyone else able to make the journey. It was much safer for a woman to travel in these times, but this was still an extremely dangerous proposition. We had to approach our mother delicately with this proposal. In the end she accepted it, after much protesting, and Henya and Marisza headed back to Bialystok. We figured Else would help Henya when she arrived in Kalisz, that it would be a quick operation. We estimated their return time to be 10 or 12 days.

We started counting the days. Meanwhile the two carpenters in our cell had taken jobs building stables and barns for the Soviet army at the new base in Kovel called the Red Hill. They got the job from a Jewish contractor, a Mr Szulek, who was subcontracted by the Soviets. Mr Szulek was such a pleasant man, very polite and respectful. He would chat with my father when he picked up the two brothers, and they became friends. It was exactly what my father needed, a man on the same level, to discuss things like a normal person. They were independent businessmen, Jewish, both weary of the world around them and he gave my father advice.

Szulek told my father to join a butcher's cooperative, if he could, to become a settled man. In the cooperative there would be money, a place to live and a job to do. Outside the cooperative things were not so easy. You had to have money, however, to join the cooperative. We considered selling a beautiful white coat, paying into the cooperative, then negotiating a salary and a place to live. It seemed the best plan.

Szulek took me along with the brothers and his son to the Red Hill. Again, as at Moraviny, my apprenticeship had not prepared me for this type of carpentry. Making barns and stables is a rough profession, lots of banging and little tapping. I was being so precise, as I had been trained, until one of the brothers came over to me and said, 'No good.' I asked him to show me how to do it and he replied, 'Take a hammer, take a nail, and bang it. Easy.' After that I was better, having fun even, knocking the boards together and banging in nails.

There was a Russian truck by the work site, which we used from time to time. I was not impressed with its appearance, its comfort or its odor. Of course I was comparing it to the German trucks I had seen in Poland, but still it was a ragged thing. Also nearby was a holding ground for various Soviet armaments, allowing me a glimpse at various tanks and vehicles with which I was very impressed. The treads of a Russian tank alone would cause me to surrender my army.

In the days that followed, my father and I both worked for Szulek as negotiations with the cooperative were in the nascent stages. The family Szulek helped us out in many ways, including bringing medicine to my mother for her leg and giving us advice we needed for survival in the Soviet system. They told us not to expect help from the Jews, not in the open anyway. The Jews lived in fear of the Soviets and they depended on the Soviets for their survival. Privately Jews will help, but under the regime as it stood, we were basically on our own. Arrests were made at the slightest infraction of the law. The only way to save the Jewish community was to keep it together, and that meant not getting arrested.

I continued going to Yanik Stulman's soup kitchen for our meals. One day I met the son of a tailor from Ciasna Street in Kalisz, his last name was Gross. He was a soldier in the Polish army and had retreated to the Soviets when things fell apart. He told me what happened to him, what horrible things the Soviets did to the Polish army. They shot the officers and they beat the soldiers while robbing them of their possessions, he said. They were worse than the Germans, he said, because at least the Germans were at war with the Poles. I did not want to believe him, just as others did not want to believe my story. He told me he was going back to Poland. I took him to see my mother, who tried to convince him to stay, but in the end he disappeared.

A week had gone by, then ten days, then two weeks and still Henya had not returned. To make matters worse, the Soviets started arresting refugees and sending them off to prisons in far corners of the Soviet Union. We had already met a few refugees who had been sent to prison, escaped and were making their way back to Poland. We heard how horrible it was in Russia from them. The Soviets put up placards on Lenin Street demanding that all refugees register with the Soviet government or face prison terms. The placards from the Nazis were bad enough, why now must we see the same thing from the Soviets? Our negotiations with the cooperative ceased and we decided to register with the government.

We heard the Soviets were coming into apartments at night, just like the Nazis, and taking out refugees. Of course there was a list with our name on, so what could we have done? My father and I went down to the office to register the family, not waiting to be discovered.

On our way to the office we came across a delegation from the German army. Since the treaty was still intact, I suppose this was not such an unexpected sight, but it was the last thing any of the refugees wanted to see. I could not believe my eyes, once again I was staring at the devils. Around me other Jews began shouting curses at the Germans, and my father and I joined them. I wanted to throw stones, but the military police came over and dispersed the crowd. Even in that small procession of soldiers and armored cars, I was reminded of how powerful the German army was in comparison to the ragtag Soviet forces.

We went into the office and were greeted by a Russian in an ill-fitting, broad-brimmed hat and an unimpressive tunic. I never considered the style of the Poles to be anything special until I saw how aesthetics were abused by the Soviets. The man was smoking an enormous cigarette wrapped in cheap rolling paper and the smoke filled the room. He gave us a summary of our situation.

We had to register to live somewhere else, where we would be provided with a job, a place to stay and a stipend. We had three choices: the timbers trade in Vologda province, a coal mine in the Ukraine, or an iron factory in the Urals. There was a young Jewish boy translating for us, though he spoke only a smattering of Yiddish words. I told him about our family, how my mother was sick, my brother Moishe was a little slow and Henya had not yet returned from Poland. I asked him where we should register with problems like these.

He translated this to the recruiter and together they decided we would be best suited for the forest in Vologda province. He told us the fresh air would be very good for us, especially my mother. We would live in a village and take a Pullman train to the forest back and forth daily. And, he said, there is no better butter in all of Europe. Everything would be provided for us by the timber business, including schools and clothing – we would have it all.

Had we known that everyone in the Soviet system is a liar, we might have hesitated. But, knowing only what we heard, we registered the family. Later we discovered the butter he spoke of was from a defunct Jewish factory and the mention of Pullman wagons, the luxurious American trains, was an outright lie. Still, they were sympathetic enough to let us wait until Henya returned before giving us a date of departure.

We ceased all our activities and waited for my sister to arrive. Every day I went to the station, and every day I had to tell my mother that Henya had not returned. She was beside herself with distress, and the rumors we heard about refugees getting slaughtered at the border did not help the situation. I was also tormented by her absence. I should have gone myself, I thought, and it was my fault she was in trouble, I felt like I had killed my sister.

I kept busy by making two trunks to carry luggage. The first was for us, the second for Yanik Stulman. He was going to Gorky in a special echelon made up of Communist Party members. Maybe if my sister had been here during registration, we, too, could have gone to Gorky. I got the wood from Mr Szulek and used the Polish method of interlocking pieces to construct the trunks. They were solid pieces, and the time to make them helped me keep my mind off our tragedy.

It had been about three weeks since Henya had left Kovel and still no sign. We received a notice from the Soviets that we had to leave by train to Vologda province in a matter of days. I went to the office to beg for an extension, but he said when the date came, with or without Henya, we had to go. He was a nice man, like most Russians when you could catch them outside the system, and promised me he would register Henya for the same village when she arrived.

It was nice to hear his promise, but I did not want to leave without Henya. As a family we discussed our options. No one wanted to leave, but if they sent us away to prisons there would be no chance of Henya ever finding us, so we decided we would go. We received the last notification two days before our date of departure and we sullenly resigned ourselves to leaving.

The day before our departure I went down to the station again. The train from Brest-Litovsk had stopped and there was a small commotion. They were carrying a sick girl out of the train on a stretcher. I went for a closer look, trying to see who was on the stretcher, and there she was, our Henya! She was suffering from frostbite, but she was okay. Marisza was also there, and together they explained to me what had happened.

They had gone back to Lodz without incident. Marisza

stayed there to do business while Henya continued on to Kalisz, which was officially *Judenrein*. Only a few Jewish men working for the Germans remained, like Butchinski the shoemaker (we found out that he was ultimately slaughtered like a pig, with a blade through the stomach). There were some women who had stayed to watch their homes while the men were away, but generally Kalisz had no Jews.

Else was still in Kalisz, but she was in terrible spirits. 'My dear Henya, run away. You don't know what kind of hell we are living in here.' She told Henya that our grandmother was taken to the 'old-people's home', Chelmoo, the first concentration camp in Wartegau. It is now known that the Nazis gassed the people in the trucks before they arrived, but this was only discovered later. There was nothing Henya could do in Kalisz but plead with the remaining Jewish women to leave. Some came with her, but most did not want to go.

She returned to Lodz and visited the Kopels. Again, Mr Kopel refused to leave and refused to give up his children, but he gave her another batch of silk stockings. She and Marisza tried, with some success, to convince more women to leave, but the majority stayed. A small group took a train to Warsaw.

In Warsaw Henya tried unsuccessfully to contact the Schwartzer Yankel. They met two women with children who had husbands in Bialystok and Kovel. They went together into no man's land. The Germans let them through – women and children were not taken at that point – and they came to the Russian border.

It was impossible to pass – the border was as if hermetically sealed. As they approached the border, the Soviet guards began to shoot. They were forced to lie in the snow, wearing only dresses and thin stockings. They stayed in the snow through the night, certain they would be dead by morning. Henya suffered worse than Marisza, whose clothing was better suited for the cold and of higher quality.

In the morning they approached the border again, yelling at the soldiers through the firing. 'Hello! Don't shoot! We have husbands in Bialystok and Kovel! Please let us through!' Miraculously, an officer let them through. He even brought Henya to a field hospital to treat her frozen knees and blisters that had formed from the cold. By the field hospital, Henya told me, there were many dead refugees, shot by the Russians and lying in the snow.

For some reason, the officer took pity on my sister and Marisza and put them on a train to Bialystok. He even gave my sister a package of ointment and bandages. They continued from Bialystok to Kovel and arrived the day before our departure, but without our dear grandmother.

We did not want to put our mother into shock, so we decided to soften the impact of Henya's arrival with a little talk. I went ahead to the prison cell while Marisza brought Henya home in a sled some distance behind. I said to my mother, 'I have some good news, Mother, somebody told me they had seen Henya in Brest-Litovsk. This is the Russian part, she will be here shortly!' My mother was so happy, but still worried we would have to leave before she arrived. When the news settled in, I opened the door and in walked Marisza and Henya. Can you imagine the joy? My mother and father were so happy.

Now that the family was together, we were prepared to make our way to the forest, even excited to do so. That night Henya went down to the refugee committee and registered for the same trip. My father and I also went down to some offices to pick up our new Soviet documents and our government-issued travel allowance. Throngs of people surrounded these offices; many refugees came to get their papers and money, plus we were near the railroad station. My father and I fought our way through the crowd and made our way back to the prison.

'Oh my God!' my father said, 'someone has stolen our money.' He had put the money in a pocket, but a looter in the crowd had cut away the bottom with a blade. We were stunned, how could we make it to the forest without money? I started to cry and my father started to lose control. I was in the habit of pulling myself together whenever I saw my father beginning to collapse. 'Father,' I said, 'maybe this is the price we pay to have our dear Henya back.' He calmed down a little, but things were not good.

Henya was given around 200 rubles because she had registered separately. This, plus the silk stockings, was all we had for our journey. We went to bed a little more anxious, but still ready to leave Kovel.

In the morning we put our things in the trunk I had made, stashed our papers in safe places, and made our way to the train leaving Kovel. We met Marisza outside, fully expecting her to come with us. She was, after all, a refugee as well. She told us that she was staying, but that she would keep in touch. She brought my mother and Henya more ointment and she brought me a set of tools. How she was able to get these things – a handsaw, a screwdriver, pliers – we never knew. She was always into something and she was a survivor. We said our goodbyes and left for the station, but we never heard from Marisza again.

# 10 The forest

Our echelon was put on a Pullman train, just as the recruiter had promised. Although lacking heating and lights, it was a commodious car and we settled in nicely. With the trunk we made a comfortable seat for my mother and we managed to find a good place to put my sister as well. Both needed to be looked after while their health remained poor.

Various people throughout the day joined us. The first was a family from Warsaw: the salesman Israel Perler, his wife Alla and their two children, Moishe and Regina. They spoke with a distinctive accent and were very friendly – apart from Mr Perler's lethal wit, which was so typical of people from Warsaw. Regina, about my age, was a very good-looking girl. Later on we discovered Alla was not Mr Perler's wife, but his mistress. She was such a fat, blonde woman.

The next family that joined us was from Chelmo, the city in Jewish folklore famous for its stupid people. This was the family Bubis, and they were far from stupid. Mr Bubis was a tailor, a very good tailor, who had arranged a pretty good life for his family in Kovel. They had voluntarily joined the retreating Soviet army when they pulled their troops out of Chelmo. Their transport, a large truck in which Mr Bubis was able to bring his sewing machine, was provided by the Soviets. Still, whether invited or not, if you were originally from Poland, you had to register as a refugee. He had established himself in Kovel even in that short time, but now he was moving his wife, two boys and daughter Blima to the forest. We were pleased to make their acquaintance.

Through the day the train filled up slowly. Finally we rolled out of the station sometime during the night. It was a comfortable ride, though a bit chilly. Temperatures were very cold at that point; it was the beginning of January. Tradesmen sold 'Grandfather Frost' trees at the station, the Russian version of a Christmas tree.

The train stopped in Sarny, the old border town of Poland and Russia before the war. The tracks were of a different width here, so we collected our things and gathered outside because we had to change trains. A few officials greeted us, including a politruk, a member of the Communist Party whose job, as far as I could tell, was to be a living mouthpiece of Soviet propaganda. They looked at our documents and told us some grand stories, but who could understand them anyway? They sang the national anthem and led us onto a Russian freight train.

It was a cattle train, set up much like our prison cell with four bunks on the side walls. In the middle of the car there was a *burzujka*, a wood-burning stove. The temperature was certainly below zero already and this was our only source of heat. People started asking about the *Pullmanovsky wagonin*, the Pullman trains that were supposed to bring us to the forest. Apparently the recruiter had given the same spiel to everyone. There would be no Pullman trains.

It was very cold and we had no wood to make a fire. There were no toilets on the train, and there were too many people in each car. We asked questions, but once a Soviet had done his job, he answered no questions. What choice was there but to settle in as best we could and prepare for a very cold trip? We were different people from different parts of Poland, speaking different dialects and coming from different social circles, but we were involved in this adventure together.

Everyone in our car claimed to be a communist: the Bubis family, the Perler family, a young couple from Lodz, a couple from Danzig; but what else would they say? One fellow from Danzig, Bronich Shanker, started barking orders. He tried to organize us, telling everyone where to sleep and put his or her things, but he was not getting much respect. We needed one of the lower bunks for my mother and, in truth, he was annoying everyone, so my father walked up to him and grabbed him by the collar. He said to him, 'If you don't quiet down I'll teach you a little lesson.' Then he grabbed Bronich's hand with his fist and gave it just a little squeeze. This quieted him down. My father said to everyone, 'Young people take the top bunks and children and the elderly take the bottom bunks.' Things were quieter then and we all went to sleep.

My mother was not well. When she woke in the morning, her hair was frozen to the wall. She could not continue in these conditions and I knew I had to get wood for the stove or surely she would suffer terribly. The heat was not the only issue – how were the women going to go to the toilet?

When day broke we stopped at a train station. Before I could search the area for wood, I helped the women off the train so they could use the toilet. I say 'use the toilet', but there was only the bare ground beside the train. With my mother and her bad leg, I had to help her balance as I turned away. How could a woman relieve herself in such conditions? Something had to be done, but there was no cooperation among us or from the Soviets.

We continued traveling, stopping infrequently at other stations and sometimes in the woods for no perceivable reason. Sometimes they would give us soup and bread, and sometimes we would go long stretches with little food. In our car we were disorganized, much like Moraviny, with all parties fighting only for themselves. If someone had wood, they used it to heat only their water. If someone had water, they used it only for their cooking. I could not understand how we could turn against each other so easily and I made it my main objective to bring the group together. Russia is an enormous country, who knew how long we would ride in these trains?

I decided to do a few things, hoping to show by example how we could get along and help each other through the journey. I took an assistant, Peretz Bubis, son of the tailor from Chelm. He was a scrappy, ten-year-old boy and a real thief! He smoked cigarettes and cursed like a bandit, but he was instrumental in helping me correct our situation. If we pulled into a station and saw a train across the tracks with something useful, like wood, coal or grain, he was already on top of the pile with his cigarette hanging from his lips, throwing down the plunder. Our stove soon burned through the nights and, with his help and the tools Marisza gave us, I made a stepladder for the women to exit the train. These little things changed people's attitudes for the better.

The other passengers saw the way I helped them and how I revered my father, and they started to respect us – or maybe they feared my father. In any case, we became the decision makers of that car and were consulted when problems arose. Most of them had not been exposed to such conditions before and could not see through their confusion to figure out solutions. I had been in Moraviny and in the grave, what more could I see that would hinder my thought process?

I was calculating, not cavalier or fearless, yet I appeared to be this way, a real big-shot to the two girls of my age in the car. Regina and Blima were both nice, pretty girls, but I had neither the time nor the energy to look their way. I had a responsibility to my family and everyone in the car. I spent my time figuring out what problems Peretz and I could solve.

Nobody wanted to stray too far away from the train at a station because they feared it would leave before they returned. As a result, I was the one to fetch water every time we stopped. Sometimes I had to run to catch up with the train as a result of which I would spill quite a bit. To solve this problem, I made a wooden cross to lie on the surface of the water, this prevented sloshing and saved a good amount.

One morning we entered the beautiful city of Korosten in the Ukraine, which seemed to me to be a completely Jewish city. We were told the train would not move for the entire day, so I went out with my brothers to explore. My sister was too crippled to leave the train, so she stayed with my parents. We came to a Soviet-style supermarket, stocked with just a select group of products and who knows what hidden behind the counter. The proprietor was Jewish, and he spoke with us in Polish Yiddish. He took a liking to us and made a special queue so we could buy separately from his regular customers. With the little money we had we were able to buy a pail of fruit preserves.

We started talking and I told him about the abuse of the Jews by the Nazis and our own troubles. He did not believe me, having heard no stories about the Germans' activities. 'So why are we here?' I asked him. In response he started praising Stalin, for what reason I do not know, I never mentioned Stalin.

I asked him if he could help us with something, if he had anything extra we could use on our journey, like a bucket or a pail. He told me all the metal was given to the government to make weapons, but he did have some empty wooden buckets from the fruit preserves. He gave us four wooden pails and some toilet paper. I wanted to kiss him, he was such a nice man.

Later the Germans overtook Korosten and slaughtered all the Jews, surely they killed him too.

One of the wooden pails was designated for water, which, in combination with the one we already had, gave us one for cooking and one for washing. This helped so much because there were children in our car who had not been able to control their bladders until the next stop – they were wetting their beds and the linen was filthy. When the stove was burning hot and the sheets were washed and finally hung up to dry, people's spirits were good.

With the other buckets we solved our toilet problem for the women and children. In one of the corners I made a triangular seat from wood stolen by Peretz, below which was placed a bucket. I also made a curtain from some of our bedding. Women could relieve themselves in privacy as the train rolled, and we would dump the waste when we stopped. For Russians this type of concern was frivolous. When a train stopped in Russia, hundreds of people, men and women, stepped out of the train and relieved themselves in all forms right next to the tracks. We were not ready to make this type of change.

In contrast to the rugged Russian nature we saw in their hygienic practices, we caught glimpses of the beauty of the Russian soul at every stop. No matter the temperature, no matter how hungry people were, somebody played an accordion and the people danced and sang.

If I was away getting water and the train began to move, I would simply run to the nearest car and wait until we stopped to rejoin my family. We were in car number 14, the same number as our house in Kalisz and the same number as my father's butcher shop. One day this happened and I jumped into the nearest car. To my surprise I saw the family Zelver, our old friends my brothers and I had seen in the Bialystok train station. Mrs Zelver was there with her two children and some other relatives, cousins I think. Mrs Zelver was in a bad way. Her cousins were mistreating her, getting back at her out of their jealousy for her wealth back in Kalisz. I felt like fighting every one of them. She and her children were relieving themselves, washing and drinking out of the same pot, so I gave them one of our buckets. She was so happy to see me and to hear my mother was just a few cars away.

In that same car was my future wife. I saw her in the corner, just a scared, skinny girl with beautiful eyes. I took pity on her at first glance, but I turned my attention to the Zelvers. We arranged that I would take my mother over to her car from time to time. It was a way to get my mother to take some exercise and a way to encourage some happiness.

Our car became the center for conversation after a few days. Young people, educated people, couples, families, they all came to talk together about the life they would lead in Russia. Alla, Mr Perler's mistress with the big behind, went on and on about how she went going to be a tractor driver and other women said the same. They all had ideas about their future lives in Russia, but their bombastic language did not convince me of its validity. I occupied myself carrying water, collecting wood and coal and seeing that my mother and sister were well taken care of.

There was also a Polish gentile in our car, an elderly man we nicknamed 'the Professor'. Why he was on a train to the forest, we did not know. Later we assumed that he was a German spy, but of course we never found out. He was quiet and kept to himself, he was certainly not one to join us in our singing, which became more frequent as the days went by.

In these long stops at stations there was a lot of flirting between the young men and women. It occurred to me that many of the young couples were not married, but conveniently posing as such to facilitate their transfer to the forest.

Blima was flirting with everyone, right under the noses of her parents. I hated the flirting and I hated the brash talk, but we were all in this together and if this was what kept people optimistic, then who was I to judge?

We became very close to the Bubis family on that ride. Mr Bubis was such a warm, energetic and entertaining man, but his wife was such a *kvetch* (a moaner). Regarding Peretz, I asked him how he could have raised such a devil, and he replied, 'you don't know the half of it!' I told him the Russians were going to slap the bad language right out of Peretz's foul mouth, not knowing that the Russians had even filthier tongues. Meanwhile, Blima flirted with any and all comers, including me.

I liked to be the one to stay up at night and watch the fire. Sometimes Blima would stay awake with me. Although a lot of men had their eyes on her, she seemed to take a special interest in me. I think I impressed her with the way I helped everyone and not just my family. I talked to her about literature, specifically about the famous Polish writers from before the war, such as Dolenga, Mickewicz and Jaszinski. I remember reciting *Pan Tadeusz* from memory as she rested her head on my shoulder. She enjoyed listening to me talk about such things because she had no knowledge of them. I liked talking with her, it took a load off my over-burdened shoulders. These late nights, however, led to many jokes from our mothers under their breaths.

Peretz, the thief that he was, stole for us miracle after miracle. When the car became unbearably odorous, Peretz showed up with a bail of hay. When my father neared a breakdown, Peretz handed him a few cigarettes. When we ran out of food, Peretz stole oats from the horses. I could do nothing but marvel at the feats of this little boy. Oftentimes he would only need to ask a group of Russian soldiers for tobacco or other goods and they would gladly comply. The Russians were so used to orphans from their revolutionary days that it was common practice to give to children of Peretz's age.

Conversely, we had two brothers in our car, the Viernik brothers, who were not much help at all. We called them *glodomori*, the hungry angels. According to them, they were near starvation at every moment. Much of what extra food

Peretz could find went to the brothers. Still, they were good-natured boys and we laughed at them more than begrudged them.

We were on the train for weeks, sometimes stuck in a station for days while the engineers tried to start the engine again in the bitter cold. The temperatures were consistently at minus 20–30 degrees and the snow piled high all around us. It was difficult to collect wood in such snow, so if a car had a fire in its stove, many other carloads would join them to keep warm.

Another problem arose: we were infested with lice. With the ashes from the wood and hot water, we washed our clothing. With Nuchem performing his magic with the smoke we were able to combat the problem as well as anyone. Still, as days went by the sanitation conditions could only worsen.

Although we were supposed to be nearing Moscow, it was impossible to tell the difference from the landscape. We passed through Mazyr, Homel and Briansk, each one indistinguishable from the others. We saw fences made of intertwined branches lining the sides of the tracks, keeping heaps of snow out of our path. There were hundreds of people, mostly women, sweeping the tracks with brooms, and just outside Moscow we stopped and spoke with one of them.

The Professor spoke Russian perfectly and asked her how things were going near the capital. She turned to us and lifted her *yubka*, a heavy coat/dress, and showed us her bare legs, she had no stockings in this terrible cold. 'Well Comrade, how do you think it is going?' she replied. She asked us where we were headed, and the Professor told her we were going to the forest. When she heard this she made the sign of the cross over her chest. 'No one goes voluntarily to the forest', she said. 'In Russia it is a way of life from which you do not return.'

I did not want to believe her, so I convinced myself that she was *misiganah*. Of course, her speech was not the only sign telling me that Russia was not the great land I thought it was. Everything was gray and drab in the cities we passed through, the streets no longer held together with a sense of civic pride. It was such a hardship to run and get water, hot or cold, at the stations, never mind trying to buy fruit or eggs.

Poland, in our eyes, was a backward country, but compared to what we had seen of Russia it was like a flower. Still, I only wanted to see the positive side of things. I had, after all, brought my family here.

An officer told us we were to remain in this station for two days and anyone wanting to travel to Moscow could take an electric train into the center of the city. An electric train? This was the developed Russia I was hoping to see. Nuchem put on his ski cap and I put on my dusty Polish hat, onto which my mother sewed earflaps, and we took that electric train to Moscow.

We were dropped in a downtown metro station, and to me it was like a museum. There were hundreds of people, each with something purposeful on their mind, striding around the platforms in *voilikis*, the warm, felt boots we saw the soldiers wear in Kovel. There was art hanging on the walls, not just propaganda placards. There were escalators going up and down (electric staircases!) and the people were dressed so well. My impression of Russia improved ten-fold that day, almost reaching the point it had been at before the war started.

Nuchem and I stood out like sore thumbs. First of all, no one wore normal shoes, certainly not like ours. Second, people were very well dressed and clean – we were neither. Because of our obvious refugee status we were approached by a very nice, middle-aged couple walking down the stairs.

They were teachers, Jewish I think, but they did not speak Yiddish. In Russian they asked us what we were doing. In Polish I answered that we were going to the forest. They seemed frightened by this and wrote down their address, or an address of a school. They asked if I had a pencil or a calendar, but we were not really getting things straight. In the end, my brother and I walked away with a curious shrug of the shoulders. Who knows what they were really trying to tell us?

Outside the station was Red Square. I had never seen anything like it in my life; it blew me away. The buildings and the people were so beautiful. The women wore white fur coats and matching *voilikis* as they moved in and out of the myriad stores lining the square. Every product imaginable was for sale in the square, not like the stores we had seen thus far. Soldiers dressed impeccably, wearing high-cut leather boots, marched with the Russian high-step outside Lenin's tomb. This was the Russia I had dreamed about.

Nuchem and I fell into the line outside Lenin's tomb and made our way quietly to the room where he lay. He was underneath glass, looking alive, though yellow, still sporting that inimitable beard. Nobody spoke when they passed him; it was a solemn moment.

We did not stray too far outside Red Square as there was so much to see right there. In time we returned to the train and recounted what we had seen to our parents and friends. Our optimism improved as we pushed out of Moscow and headed north, still north, for many more days.

My family was running out of money and we had not yet discovered a way to sell the silk stockings. Others in the car had prepared so well for the journey, but we simply lacked the means. The Bubis family, for instance, had lots of dried meat and chocolate, which Mrs Bubis tried to share with my mother. Mr Bubis knew the Russian mentality and had known he knew how to prepare for this trip. We had had our money stolen and had spent our last days worrying about Henya instead of preparing.

There was a young, incredibly handsome boy on our train we called Sinik. He was so rich and accustomed to nice things that he even wore pyjamas to bed. When we came to a station, he would put on his expensive fur coat and buy hard-boiled eggs, pirogues, dried vegetables and fruit for himself. He had such a childish arrogance, which made us laugh, always wanting this or that and pouting when he did not get it. How such a boy could end up in Russia, we never knew.

I, on the other hand, would buy one egg for Moishe and one for my mother. When I could I would try to get some dried cranberries. A woman wearing a shawl or a man with dirt-stained fingers would measure the cranberries in a glass and pour them into my hands. I did not have an extra bag, nor was there any paper just lying around in Russia, so this was how I transported the fruit.

The optimism I felt after our quick visit to Moscow

subsided as our journey continued. At night, sometimes with Blima, sometimes alone, I would go over and over again in my mind the betrayal I had felt at the Soviet border. How could socialists not accept with open arms the victims of fascism? How could the Soviet Union, defenders of socialism in Spain, a war in which our brothers' blood was also spilled, keep us out? If we had not overrun the border, they would have left us to die. Where was the socialist angle in that?

I stewed over their treatment of us, how we became untouchables, like criminals, in their system. I could forgive their poverty and their backward system, but I could not forgive them for breaking the cardinal rules of socialism. They had to accept us, the innocent victims of fascism, they had to provide safety and protection, but they did not. Instead we were stuffed into cattle cars and suffered from lice and hunger. For the first time I began to believe the son of the tailor Gross. I could picture the Soviets slicing the throats of the innocent Polish officers.

Mr Bubis heard my concerns and said, 'What do you expect from these Russian thieves?' He helped me to relax and see the positive side of things. He reminded me that I was still together with my family and we were heading to the forest to start a new life. This was not such a bad thing to happen in the middle of a war. I resigned myself to our fate and waited to see what would come.

The look of the towns changed as we continued. The stations seemed old-fashioned, the men wore thick beards and the churches were adorned with the classic, Russian onion domes. In my imagination we were on a journey back in time to the era of Ivan the Terrible.

A curious sight began to appear at many stations. Soldiers with rifles and dogs, German Shepherds, led lines of prisoners through the stations and onto trains. The prisoners kept their heads down and dragged their legs. They did not wear boots, just simple shoes made out of tire rubber. The strange part was the indifference of everyone else in the station, nobody seemed to notice. You would not have seen that in fascist Poland.

We passed through Jaroslavl, Vologda and then smaller villages before we came to a city called Cerepovec. This was our last stop.

A thick-bearded man came to our car and told us to unload. I stepped off the train and was convinced they had taken us to the North Pole; it was a sea of snow. On the horizon I could see only the tops of houses with smoke billowing out the chimneys, and few people. Those who were outside rode by on sleds pulled by horses over roads of packed snow. From time to time a truck rolled past with metal chains around its wheels. Boys with hooks, like the meat-hooks my father used in the slaughterhouse, would grapple the sides of the truck as it passed and be dragged to their destination. It was a strange sight.

Our entire echelon lined up outside the train and I saw how many we were for the first time. There must have been 1,000 of us, standing in regular shoes, cold and worried as we caught our first glimpse of our futures. Again I saw my future wife, shivering with a red nose and wearing a nice coat with a white fur collar. My heart went out to her because I could tell she was alone and she looked so lost.

I helped unload everything from the train and I put my mother on the trunk. Before we arrived I had managed to create a sled out of it, with two skis on the bottom and canvas straps with wooded handles on the sides. We were told to go to the town (where was the town?), so we started to walk. My sister was waddling like a duck, but, despite her injured knees, she was not the only one. So many of us had trouble walking after spending weeks on that rickety, rumbling freight train. Also, most of us had regular shoes on our feet, hardly suitable for the snow and cold.

Our caravan of people walked to the Peasant Inn, Dom Krestianina. We were given beds, not rooms, and told we were allowed to stay for just three days. There was not room for everyone, so a group was taken to a school near the river. We were so happy to be off that train and my mother was happiest of all. She was getting sick and needed a bed and a hot meal.

In time there were large tables set up with food, and we ate all we could. It was supposed to be chicken, but Mr Perler did not believe it. 'Is this chicken? I believe this is sparrow,' he quipped. His sharp Warsaw sarcasm prevailed at times like these. You had to be careful when speaking with him because he could insult you so easily. He was a little afraid of my father and had some respect for me, so we never felt the sting of his remarks.

After we ate we went to bed. It was difficult at first, trying to sleep in a bed without the floor moving, but once I fell asleep I was out cold. I got up the next day and followed my customary practice – I went out to explore.

It was a little city from olden times, one of the old northern settlements from the czars' time. The center of town was encircled by a large field, beyond which new, wooden houses had been built. It seemed there was another push to build settlements in the north, hence our presence. I stayed generally in the center of town, walking up and down Lenin Street. Not far from Dom Krestianina was a *sczaina*, a teahouse, so I went in to take a look.

As I stepped inside I immediately felt a lump rise in my throat. It was a dark room filled with the wildest looking people I had ever seen. The farmers, the peasants from the north, grow their hair and beards long and when they enter a teahouse they do not remove their jackets. They sit around like bears speaking in rough, growling tones, with steely looks in their eyes. They bought tea in a pot, not real tea but dried fruit soaked in boiling water, and sipped it out of bowls. The smell of the people mixing with the sweet tea combined to put me in a state of semi-shock. Was I in the den of criminals, I wondered? I did not stay for tea.

I headed further down Lenin Street towards the center of the city. To my left I saw a bazaar, an outdoor market. People were milling about, buying and selling like any market in the world. Near the market stood a water tower and across the street there was the butter factory. I did not want to get lost, so I stayed on Lenin Street and continued on my way.

Everywhere I looked I saw people standing in queues. I do not know what they were waiting for because the signs were written in Russian – I was unable to read their alphabet. I passed the city theater, a huge building, and came across the Sovietski Prospekt, the Soviet complex. This was a section of buildings made of brick, unlike every other building in

Cerepovec. The complex housed the city library, the Communist Party headquarters the communist newspaper and the offices of both factions of the secret police – the KGB and the police force of the NKVD. The NKVD was the general administrator of public safety, in essence responsible for the fire department, hospitals, community police and other civic departments. I did not see too many people walking in front of the complex.

After venturing only a little way further, seeing a tall school, a cemetery and fields, I made my way back to Dom Krestianina. I took Moishe and Nuchem to the bazaar, knowing well that I would have to buy Moishe something to eat – he was always so hungry. There were farm stands with dried vegetables – carrots, beets, potatoes, cranberries – which was the only produce available during the long, winter months. I bought a few glasses full for both of them, plus a glass of *mahorka*, Russian tobacco, for my father. I knew that would make everyone happy.

We went down to the end of Maxim Gorky Street and on one side we saw an enormous factory with the Red Star hanging on its wall. It was near the Sheksna river, which flowed through Cerepovec and was the center of its commerce. You could not see the end of the river or the start of the land because of the snow, but it was clear the river was gigantic, stretching as far as the eye could see. I saw wooden barges, frozen in the ice yet occupied by whole families. Smoke rose out of the chimneys and hay was strewn on the decks for cows and goats. Trucks and horse-drawn sleds made their way up and down the ice faster than they could in the city. Clearly the river was the highway during the winter. It was breathtaking.

In the evening I went to the school where the other refugees were staying to see what was going on. They told me they were giving out sweets around the corner. *Dajut* is the Russian word for giving and the Soviets enjoyed fooling you with language. They were 'giving' out sweets around the corner, but of course you had to pay for them. They were 'giving' things out every day, all for a price!

The children of Cerepovec started begging us for our

sweets as soon as we had hold of them. We could not understand why they were so desperate at that time. Later we understood the shortages that occurred here and the fact that we were being duped into thinking this was the land of plenty, but at the time we just thought it was strange. I gave most of my sweets to the children and the rest to Moishe.

Back at the inn, we discovered we were to be shipped out the next day to the forest. We were part of the Cerepovec Forest Trust Company, owners of basically the entire forest. Their offices were down the road from the inn, and there we would be given proper winter clothing.

Standing in line I saw our friends come back with *fufikai*, quilted Chinese jackets and pants and *voilikis*. As luck would have it, the Bubis family got the last sets of clothing. We were told we would get ours once we reached the forest. I did not like the sound of that. I asked my father, 'How can we expect to get clothing in the middle of the forest if they do not have any here at their headquarters?' Needless to say, we got no clothing.

We met Yastrobov in the morning. He was a politruk sent to organize our transfer to the forest. Unlike the one we encountered in Sarny, he did not fill our heads with party jargon (not exclusively anyway), but systematically explained what our situation would be. He told us we were going to the forest where we would have to work hard, but there would be money in our pockets. He said that with money in our pockets we would be given (*dajut*) boots, chocolate, whatever we wanted. I turned to my father and asked him, 'They give when you have money in the pocket, what's the big deal?' We still did not understand that there was nothing in this province. We saw trouble on the line, but we attributed it to the waves of refugees. The Soviet Union had recently incorporated parts of the Ukraine, White Russia, Latvia, Poland and Lithuania – where was the wealth?

Yastrobov divided us into groups of 20 and we loaded ourselves into the backs of trucks. The Perlers and the Bubis family joined us in our truck. Blima sat on my knees as the truck slid and skidded towards the river, the winter highway.

We had not gone far when we heard the engine give out. We had broken down.

Yastrobov's reaction to the situation was swift and somewhat frightening. He organized a dozen or so sleds with horses simply by telling the head of the local village he needed them. If he said he needed something in 20 minutes, he had it in 20 minutes, such was the power of a politruk.

We loaded everything into the sleds and we made our way north. The cold took its toll on many of us, especially when the sun began to set, as half of us did not have proper winter clothing. Yastrobov led us to a nearby village. We walked with him to random houses where he would knock on the door and say to the tenant, 'You will take four people in your home tonight. Put on the samovar and make some tea.' He would hand the tenant a bag of sweets and spice cookies and take the remaining refugees down the street to other homes.

This was my first look at a typical northern Russian home. It was very dark, with little lamps burning in the corners. The wooden walls were stained dark from constant use of the stove, an apparatus that occupied an entire wall. There were placards of Stalin and Lenin and pictures of tractors on the walls, plus a little icon with a small lamp in the corner. Our hostess put on the samovar and invited us to sit down.

We could not communicate well, so we drank our tea in relative silence. We learned to drink tea the Russian way. We placed the sweets Yastrobov left for us between our teeth and sipped the hot water. There were no leaves or dried fruit giving the water flavor, just the flavour of the sweets.

We turned in for the night. After securing my mother in a comfortable spot, I climbed the large stove and prepared to sleep. This was customary in the cold, to sleep on top of the hearth, which was an enormous unit.

In the middle of the night I heard a buzzing noise. I did not know what kind of noise it was, so I climbed down from the stove and investigated. In the dark I approached the icon, still lit up by the tiny lamp. I held the light next to the wall and I saw an ocean of cockroaches, climbing all over each other and buzzing loudly. I crawled back into my bed, but it was some time before I fell back to sleep.

In the morning my mother needed to use the bathroom, but there was no toilet in that home. My sister had to take her out back to the stables, where the cows, pigs and chickens lived, to relieve herself. It smelled horribly and was demeaning to my mother, but it was what we had to get used to if we were to survive in the forest.

After tea and biscuits, we loaded the sleds again and headed down the river. We traveled for hours on the icy river surrounded by the bright white of all the snow. Finally we came to the town of Beloz Orsk, meaning white lake. The flow of the river near there was controlled by a series of man-made locks. Yastrobov proudly detailed how prisoners, mostly Polish prisoners, had constructed the system. The town rested next to a gigantic lake with a similar name, Ozero Beloje.

Beloz Orsk appeared to be frozen in time. There was a *kreml* in the center of the city, a defense settlement on a hill holding a stone church and protected by a huge wooden fence. The keys for the gate were enormous, like theater props, yet they were still functional. The skyline was dotted with onion domes and the houses and stores were old-fashioned and made of wood.

We were taken to an inn, named Dom Kasia, in a very old house. I went out to explore with my brothers and sister, along with Regina and Blima. I was explaining things to the girls as we passed by the *kreml*, acting like an educated big-shot. We saw Russian children sledding down the *kreml*'s hill, which reminded us of what fun it should be to be a child. That night they fed us and brought us to a *banja*. My mother could not go because of her feet, but we were able to wash our clothes, which desperately needed it.

In the morning we loaded up again and headed down a canal to a port called Chaika, meaning seagull. From Chaika we continued on to Koniewo, the local center of the Cerepovec Forest Trust Company. In the spring, logs would float behind small boats from Koniewo to Chaika, then behind larger boats from Chaika to Cerepovec, where they would be distributed to different parts of Russia. Vologda was the province, Koniewo was the district, Cerepovec was the headquarters.

In Koniewo, Yastrobov began to organize us again. The

Jewish people were smart, they were yelling out, 'I am an accountant! A lawyer! A teacher!' and 'I am a professor of German!' and they were kept in Koniewo. We had no skills of this nature, so we were loaded up once again and sent still further north. A day and a night passed until we finally arrived in a small village called Semjenczewo.

We arrived in Semjenczewo in the daylight. There was a main road with houses on both sides, leading to a little grocery store and a building where political meetings were held. Yastrobov led us down the road, dropping off families and groups of people at houses along the way. We were placed in a house directly across the street from the Bubis family. When Yastrobov told the woman we were to be staying with her, she growled back at him, venomously, yet let us in just the same.

It was such a nice house, very clean with floors as white as snow. We had to remove our shoes before we entered after knocking off the dirt with a brush hanging by the door. There was a big chandelier and a bed with fluffy pillows, a quaint kitchen and no toilet – we already knew about that – the bathroom was next to the cow out back. She had placards of Stalin and Lenin, as well as a picture of a battleship on her walls. In the corner burned a lamp in front of a small icon. The windows were double-paned and the stove filled the house with warmth despite the feet of snow piled up outside. Some things in a Russian household had already become familiar to us.

We sat down and had tea with the sweets, as we had before, but the woman kept grumbling. She was hospitable, but she made no attempt to cover her contempt for our intrusion. At bedtime, when I went out back to the toilet, I saw a dead pig hanging from the rafters, frozen and vile. It reminded me of the Polish butchers in Kalisz, not an image I wanted in my mind before I slipped off to sleep. Amazingly, no one slept on the bed, not even the woman of the house. The bed was for decoration – the Russians slept in their clothing on the floor!

Yastrobov returned in the morning to collect my father and me for work in the forest. He told the landlady that the women and children would remain with her. Again, she made no attempt to conceal her hatred for Yastrobov. Later we discovered why he was so reviled. During the Finnish war, in which Russia lost tens of thousands of men to Finland's thousands, Yastrobov was responsible for recruiting soldiers in this area. So many husbands, sons, and brothers had died or returned crippled from a war that gained Russia only a few kilometers of land. Most of the women in Semjenczewo hated Yastrobov, but they also feared him. He had the power of the party behind him and with it the intimidation, not unlike a German officer during the occupation.

Our landlady told me to refuse to work if I was still without the proper clothing. Our shabby clothes, she said, were priceless in Russia; we would never have such nice things again. I felt sorry for her. Her husband was a brigadier, who fished the Ozero Beloje for long periods of time, and her son was in the army, leaving her alone and forced to take in a refugee family. I believe she felt sorry for us as well.

Before we left for the forest, we were taken to a real Russian *banja* by a few of the village girls. I would not say we were accustomed to men and women bathing together yet, but we were less surprised when a woman came into our steam room and poured the water on the rocks. It sounded like an explosion when the water hit, and my father and I started to run when the room filled up with steam. The Russians laughed uproariously, then they showed us how to wash ourselves as they did. After the steam cleared we scrubbed ourselves with brushes. The Russians were knocking them against their skin very hard, so I did too. More water was poured on the rocks and we watched the sweat and steam take the dirt off our bodies. Some of the Russians, including some girls, ran out of the *banja* and into the snow for a few moments. We did not have the courage to do this, which provoked more merriment. We returned to the village cursing and laughing, then we went into the forest.

We had plenty of room to move around on the sleds because only a few women came with us to the forest. One was Alla, the most boisterous of the women on the freight train. This was her chance to be a tractor driver. We left the village, passing through a wooden fence made in the Russian style with small, intricately cut pieces of wood, and sledded across a large field. We entered the forest and I felt a marked difference in the atmosphere, the whole world around me changed. There was a dampened noise surrounding us, yet I could distinguish the sounds of the sled much better than in the field. The sun shone through the trees and hit the gleaming snow, producing a sea of diamonds over which our sled continued. This was a virgin forest, so the trees were spaced far apart and rose as if to brush the clouds. It was an amazing, stunning sight.

We came to a road of packed snow and we began to walk. Yastrobov told us to stick to the road. If we meandered into the forest, it was likely that we would sink into the snow and be devoured by wolves – I considered this good advice. We walked for maybe eight miles, a decent walk, until we came to a large clearing.

The ground was rough and torn up, no longer covered with just snow but frozen mud and branches. Huge tractors with tank-like treads were pulling sleds the size of train cars loaded with timber stacked three stories high. There appeared to be some 20 loading stations and there was a lot of activity. We stood for a moment and took it all in as Yastrobov went off to find his contact.

We saw some familiar faces in the crowd of workers, people who had been in Kovel but had left with an earlier echelon. We asked them how things were going, and they complained bitterly. Mr Perler looked at me and said, 'Look at them, with their red faces and good physiques, how can they complain?' We assumed they were just not used to physical labor, that they would adapt and flourish, as we planned to do, in this industry.

Yastrobov came back with Master Osipow and then he disappeared; his job was finished. Osipow took us to our barracks, a long building called the Green Forest. The barracks were split between women and men; there was a store, a canteen and an outdoor latrine. Everyone was given a bed. There was one woman who cleaned our quarters and kept the fire burning, but the other women spent their days in a separate section.

We were expected to work immediately, but we refused to go out in the forest in our normal shoes, demanding at least *voilikis* if not the entire winter apparel. Osipow promised everything would come in time, but we held our ground. Eventually he reappeared with *voilikis*, not telling us that he had taken them off the feet of the women working behind the walls. So, wearing our long Polish shirts and ill-fitting *voilikis*, we began our work in the forest.

We were told to collect the fallen trees from the forest and bring them to the clearing. The trees were felled in such a way that they would lie on each other, which made the process of pulling them with horses easier. Also, tree stumps could only be two feet high, so there were holes in the deep, deep snow, making our work fairly dangerous. Unfortunately we did not know how to direct the horses, we could not get them to move. Out of necessity, we were moved to the clearing to load the trees onto the sleds.

Our supervisor was a young man named Mitja. We could see how he played favorites from the beginning. The Russian workers loaded sleds very close to the fallen timber, while we had to drag the logs great distances, yet we received the same pay. Still, the work was good for some of us, like my father and me, because it was physical labor that kept us warm through the coldest days. Not everyone, however, fared so well.

The women started leaving the forest immediately. The tractors, such prehistoric things, were fueled by wood; this was a time of experimental engineering. Those women who wished to be tractor drivers found themselves stuck beside a billowing engine, feeding it with pieces of birch continuously for hours on end. Many walked back to the village after only a few hours. Where was their bravado now, I wondered.

Mr Bubis, a tailor by trade, fell into one of the holes left by a fallen tree. We did not know he had disappeared until someone heard his yelling. He was in the snow for half a day and when he was fished out he simply told us that he was no longer working in the forest, so he took his things and walked back to Semjenczewo.

One person's misfortune turned into a mini-adventure for me. A young woman named Hella worked with us in the forest. She was from Warsaw and wore her rugged nature like a badge. She was a heavy smoker, by this time using the Russian *mahorka*, and her teeth were stained brown. One night she had an asthma attack and needed to be rushed to Koniewo hospital. Somebody had to take her, and, of course, it ended up being me. I had never handled a horse and sled before, but Osipow told me I just had to use the whip, the horse knew where to go.

We set out under the dark sky and I was a little bit frightened, but more excited by the prospects of a night-time sleigh ride through the Russian forest. I whipped the horse and away we went. It was fantastic, the feeling of speed while seeing very little was an adventure for me. Then, out of the woods, came a band of dogs. Six or seven big dogs – I thought they were wolves – ran alongside the sled, escorting us all the way to Koniewo. When I slowed down, they slowed down. At first I was afraid, but soon I enjoyed their company. I dropped Hella at the hospital and headed back the same way and the dogs joined me again. I never knew what happened to Hella and I never saw the dogs again.

For the first week or so my father and I worked very hard. I admired the way he did things effortlessly, never seeming to sweat or become exhausted, yet getting things done faster than anyone else. He developed a technique of rolling the logs using pieces of wood, while others strained to carry and lift their loads. I, on the other hand, sweated constantly, which froze my sleeves and caused them to tear. Our Polish shirts were not made for this type of movement as they were cut long with a belt-loop at the front.[1] The Russians wore short jerseys that reached to the waist and no lower, which allowed for greater mobility and less sweat.

As the days passed, Mitja became more snooty and arrogant. He did not try to conceal his contempt for us, calling us filthy Jews as he kept assigning us the most difficult assignments. My father and I watched him work one day, measuring the stacks of the Russian workers. 'Take a look', my father said, 'he puts a log on each end of the sled, but leaves the middle empty. This is how he measures their work.' In Russia wealth is measured in clothing and food, not diamonds and money. Mitja was fat, young and covered in fur. I felt like cutting off his head with the flick of an ax.

Still my father and I worked hard, and this work ethic caused a little friction in the barracks. We believed we were in the forest to work, so why not work? There was a Belgian Jew with us in the barracks named Naftali, a real hard man like our cousin Lazar Kaminsky. He was an older person, probably in his fifties and he had a knife wound. People respected him in the barracks, so when he laughed at us for working so hard, the others joined in. 'We all get eight rubles, my friends, so why work so hard?' he asked us.

In the end we saw that Naftali was right. What could we do with 16 rubles having to support a family and ourselves? With such little pay, it was like we were in prison. We had to buy our food at the canteen, a bowl of cereal, a piece of bread and coffee for breakfast, more cereal in the afternoon. This used up most of our money, yet the food was practically inedible. The bread was frozen solid. We had to take it to the fields with us and place it in the fire before we could eat it. I believe it was made of straw or something equally rough, because after eating it I could not bend over without my stomach burning.

We complained to Osipow. He told us that things would be straightened out, that we would be paid according to our work and the food would improve. He also said the winter clothing would arrive soon. He was a fountain of empty promises, but we soon learned to discount anything he said.

When we complained more ardently, Osipow let us know what kind of leverage we had. He explained that our papers allowed us to work in the forest and nowhere else; we had no choice but to continue working for him. He laughed and said, 'You will drop dead here.'

We were stunned. How had we been transformed from refugees seeking a better life under socialism to prisoners serving a death sentence? Something was not right.

Life in the barracks became tedious. Although personal relations were rough initially – like the first days on the freight train – we settled in for the long winter and grew accustomed to each others' behavior. The temperature continued to drop yet our clothing never showed up. If the thermometer read minus 40 degrees we would not have to work, otherwise we trudged outside into the bitter cold wearing tattered outfits. The latrine was outside, prompting Vasili to comment: 'We eat and pee like horses. We have become horses.'

We fell into a series of routines, such as laundry on Sunday and the *banja* on another day. Every morning there would be a prayer session led by a prisoner from the Polish army, Gostinsky. The sound of Hebrew echoing through the virgin forest was so wonderful to me. Also on Sunday Moishele Botner, a tailor from Lublin, would cut everyone's hair. He did not know what he was doing, but we called him 'the barber from Warsaw' just the same.

The girls from the village would visit us sometimes and stay in the women's section overnight. The shopkeeper, Viktor, was always fooling around with the girls, giving them sweets and joking with them after hours. When Blima visited me she would take sweets from him and I could hear her laugh through the walls of our barracks. I asked her if she was not ashamed of her behavior, but she did not seem to care.

Regina had fallen into a relationship with a man they called *stachonowietz*, a Soviet term for the best worker. This term, like most in the Soviet system, was mostly misused to perpetuate some sort of fraud. He was a Mongol, a huge man with great tree-cutting skill, and he deserved the term. Regina's involvement with him brought her a lot of criticism from the rest of us. In my eyes, she was not a nice girl.

Viktor's shop was open only about two hours every day, and he had very little to sell. You had to buy what he had, and this, combined with his behavior, was the source of many jokes in our barracks. Still, it was refreshing to see people enjoying themselves, not everyone felt despondent, some were single and full of life.

My family had its own problems, starting with my father's penchant for perfection. Just as with the linen in Brest, he burned his *voilikis* drying them by the fire. I had to take them into the village to my mother, who sold some things to have them fixed by a shoemaker. She also gave me some *mahorka* (Russian tobacco) to bring to my father. He would smoke it at night, giving everyone who wanted it a single puff.

My *voilikis*, on the other hand, were too small. I could put them on in the morning, but after sweating all day I could not remove them in the evening. Even with two people tugging with all their might, I had to spend some nights with the boots still on my feet. My clothing, like many others in the barracks, was in terrible shape. Sometimes I went outside to work draping my blanket around me to cover the holes in my shirt. Others did this too, making us look like prisoners of war.

My mother was not faring well at the house. The landlady forced her to do difficult chores like washing the floor, even though my mother could not bend down. She could not wear the *voilikis* because of her leg and therefore could not walk on the snow very much, making any outdoor chores at best a brutal hardship, at worst completely impossible. I would visit on Sundays and help the landlady with her chores, chopping wood and the like, but still things were not good.

I was concerned so I made a deal with Mr Bubis across the street. He had returned from the forest and set up a tailor shop. With his charm and good nature, he already had his landlady working for him! I arranged that my mother and siblings would spend the day over there, helping out with whatever they could. Only in the evening would they have to face our landlady. To get out of the chores, I had my mother give the landlady a Polish shirt. This was done and it saved my father and me a lot of worry, and it meant that Mrs Bubis and my mother could joke about Blima and me all day.

Back at the barracks, the clothing situation ultimately forced us into action. Naftali, no stranger to confrontation, organized a strike. In the morning we ate our cereal, then headed back to our barracks, not one of us broke ranks. Osipow and Mitja stormed in and demanded an explanation. Naftali simply told him that we would not work without the proper clothing, delivery of which had been promised long ago. Osipow was apoplectic, screaming at us: 'You are all counter-revolutionaries! Enemies of the people! You will all be locked up!' We refused to speak and he left in a cloud of fury.

Half a day later, three sleds of NKVD policemen came to our barracks. A band of rifle-toting Soviets barged into our barracks. 'What's going on here, you Polish fascists!' I was extremely frightened, but Naftali stood up calmly and addressed the policemen. 'We are not enemies of the people, we want to work. How can we work without clothing?' Apparently Osipow had told the NKVD something else, because they immediately dropped their weapons and turned to him and Mitja. The next day we were given second-hand clothing, short-waisted Chinese jackets perfect for working in the forest.

Two weeks later a special commission from Moscow came to our barracks; news of our strike had reached the capital. Then men from Moscow walked in and immediately I could tell that these were different people. Their speech was sophisticated, their clothing was refined and their manner was proper. I was very impressed. They took us down to the canteen and spoke with us for hours, trying to determine if we were potential counter-revolutionaries or the victims of someone else's corruption. We talked and talked.

I thought I recognized one of them as a Jew. When the talking stopped, I asked him privately if he was Jewish. He was, so I told him my story. I asked him how we could have run away from such horror only to be turned into prisoners through treachery? He was very concerned. First of all he did not know that the Germans mistreated the Jews, it was not part of the official party line. If the Soviet government did not want you to know about something, you did not know. Second, he could not believe we were given papers that locked us into one job and asked to see my documents.

Since they were written in Russian we were unable to read what they said – we had no choice but to believe what Osipow told us. This Jew from Moscow explained our situation to me. In our papers we, the Jewish refugees from Poland, were tagged with Article 53. This denoted a socially unreliable person, given only limited mobility within the Soviet Union. In our case it meant we could live and work only in Vologda province, but we did not have to stay in the forest. We were not prisoners after all.

Initially I was happy, but I angered quickly. Since this was the first person from the Soviet system willing to give me answers, I berated him with questions. 'If we are free to leave the forest, why have we been so mistreated? Why do we have no lights in our barracks? Why do we have nothing to read – no books or newspapers? Why do we earn only eight rubles despite having an entire family to feed?' He listened to me intently, but he had no answers.

A few days after the commission's visit, a politruk, like Yastrobov, came to our barracks carrying reading lights, newspapers and books. Viktor's store suddenly became filled with products and Osipow and Mitja were replaced. Apparently our clothing had been shipped to the forest, but Osipow had sold it to someone else. Our days improved considerably; just knowing we could leave when the ice melted was enough to get us through the coldest days. Not having the tyrants Osipow and Mitja hovering over us was another blessing.

I started reading the Russian books and newspapers, trying to decipher the Cyrillic alphabet so I could match the sounds with the letters. Russian was similar to Polish, so I studied a book I knew well, Tolstoy's *Peter the Great*, and compared the words. I could get through about a page a day, and in this way I eventually learned to read the Russian language.

I wrote a letter to Mircha, the girl from Baranavicy, hoping to discover some news about my friends. It was at her home, Minska 57, that we had planned to meet. The return address for the barracks read five lines long – this was the Soviet system. In two or three weeks I received a letter written half in Polish and half in Russian. She said she was glad to hear we were alive and that my friends Mendle and Mortich had been at her home. They had since disappeared, but the news had me kissing the letter and jumping around the barracks. I was so amazed that we could keep in touch even in the insanity of the war.

Life was tolerable because we now had respect from the Russians and we no longer felt helpless. Even the Russian girls, who had laughed at us for so long, started to respect us. As spring neared I began to think of the future. I was learning Russian rapidly, which gave me great confidence. I felt that if

I could read anything and I could learn anything, I would not be fooled into work like this again.

When the weather permitted, a group of us would head into town on Sundays and watch the activity in the village. I would go with my brothers to the main street and watch the Russian youth socializing with each other. The boys would begin playing music with a guitar and an accordion, singing together and separately. Then the girls would join in the singing, one at a time, improvising the words. This would go back and forth, each person making up the words to songs about the army, the politruk, sexual innuendoes, anything the youth sing about anywhere. This kind of musical session was called a *czastushki*; it was magic for my brother Moishe to hear.

When the street sessions were over, everyone would go into a club and dance. It was such a strange thing for me to be in that club. First of all, the Russian boys looked at us with hostility, but not the girls. They were checking us out, wondering about the strange boys with the funny clothes. Conversely, the Russian boys did not hesitate to speak to Blima or Regina. In these dance sessions one girl would dance alone for a while and then come to a boy on the side. If she danced in front of you, you had to join her on the floor. When I was approached for the first time, I did not know I was supposed to join her, so I did nothing. I was no dancer, but Nuchem was. However bashful he was in speech, he was confident in dancing.

At one point I had a problem with Blima. She showed up one night and told me I had to marry her and she would live with me at the barracks. What? She had had a fight with her mother and did not want to live with her any longer. 'Is this a reason to get married?' I asked her. In time I convinced her to go back and take care of her mother, but it was a tense situation for a while. I figured our relationship, which was really just her relationship with me, would bring me trouble someday and I needed a way out.

We continued working. Eventually the wind grew less harsh. It was not yet warm, but it no longer bit your nose when it whipped. The snow softened and the trees shook loose the snow and ice from their branches. It was time for the tree-cutting operation to come to a close. To continue the process of shipping the logs all over Russia, our supervisors wanted us to go to Krasniesello. This was a village on a tributary to the Cheksna river where the great summer log traffic began. Again, the families would live in one place, while the workers would live somewhere else. Because I wanted to put some distance between Blima and myself, I agreed to this arrangement. The ice on the river was not yet thawed, we had a couple of weeks to relocate and prepare for the new work.

My father decided to stay with my mother and siblings, and they were taken by sled to another village. Some of the young men, including the 'hungry angels', Sinek and myself, made our way on foot to Krasniesello. It was a few days' hike, and every day you could feel the forest come to life just a little bit more. By the time we reached the village, my *voilikis* were soaked with sweat. It was actually comfortable outside.

The village consisted of red houses, each filled with people who only worked on the river. We were supposed to live among these people in different houses during the warmer months, though this had not yet been arranged. We had been given some supplies for the trip, mostly bread and oil, which we ate once we arrived. Looking around, I knew I had made a mistake. Why should I work apart from my parents and not take advantage of our ability to move about the province? We were not prisoners, after all. Eventually the ice would melt and we could take a boat further south to a major city. The other boys agreed. We told our supervisors we wanted to go to our families. They gave us directions and we set out on foot, dragging our heavy *voilikis* but pleased with our decision to take control of our destiny.

After two days' travel, we reached the village where my family had been taken. Along with some other families, they were put in a beautiful country home situated on a peninsula jutting into the River Kowza. The property was a *chutor*, a rich peasant's homestead, or *kulak*, that had been requisitioned during the revolution. The former owner suffered the fate of many Russians at that time. He was an ambitious peasant, hard working and intelligent, and in time he had built himself a beautiful piece of property and made himself more comfortable. When the revolution came he was considered too rich, so his property was collectivized and he was either killed or shipped off to Siberia. In this way, the Soviets destroyed the best of the working class.

It was such a beautiful property. There was a mill to grind flour, a churn to make butter, and a smithery. The house itself was well crafted, put together meticulously and solidly, yet intricately decorated; each shutter displayed a hand-carved rooster. There was plenty of space inside the house, and we were given a whole room to ourselves. There was a family in the room beside us, the Zielberbergs, and a number of wartime couples with no children in the other quarters.

The river flowed around the peninsula and the fourth side was a virgin forest. It was such a peaceful property, only our neighbors, the Zielberbergs, had no appreciation for the beauty of the silence. They argued constantly, cursing at the tops of their voices. At first we laughed at them, thinking we had caught them at a bad time, but it soon ceased to be funny. Yitele and Reb Ysrael Zielberberg were an elderly couple with grown children, three husky daughters – ugly girls – and a son Yakov. They took care of their cousin Yankele also, a nice boy whom they mistreated. I had never heard such hostility in all my life, it was horrible.

The wartime couples were a strange bunch. Normally they would not have been married, and some even had families back in Poland, but the war caused people to do strange things. There was something temporary about their situation, something unnatural. Yet these people were quiet and friendly, unlike the horrible Zielberbergs.

We had to work to feed ourselves, so we began shaving wood in the forest for paper production. We did this directly behind the homestead, all of us working together. It was so wonderful to see my father teaching Moishe, while the two of them sang their famous songs together to our delight. This was the most beautiful time for my family because we were all together and in such a wonderful location. The only problem was food; there was a shortage of everything.

We were told a shipment of flour would reach us when the river thawed, but until then we would have to wait. In the local canteen we were given a little soup and one piece of bread, but this was hardly enough for one person. Moishe was constantly yelling, 'I'm hungry, where is my bread?' We would give him some of our own, but he was never satisfied. My mother was getting very thin because she was giving Moishe all of her portion. I saw her do this and I pleaded with her to stop. 'What would happen to this family without you?' I needed to find a solution to our problem.

Across the river, which was now flowing rapidly, there was a bigger village with a butter factory. I discovered it was possible to buy the milky water, the run-off from the butter-making, which my mother used to make soup. It was not much, but it was more nutritious than water alone. Still, this was not enough to feed my family, so I continued to explore.

One day I followed the curve of the river around the peninsula and along the banks, further than I had gone before. I came across something that could only be described as a floating sidewalk. I had never seen anything like it. I hopped onto the boards and made my way further along. Eventually I came across two Russian boys in a small, narrow boat. They were spear fishing. In my broken Russian I asked them if I could join them, and they told me to come back at night.

In exchange for a cigarette lighter we still had from Kalisz, these two boys showed me how to catch fish. We steered the dinghy not over the river itself, but to where the river had overflowed from the melted ice. The water was only a foot or two deep, and I could see the sturgeon sitting like pieces of wood beneath our eyes. The fish were huge, maybe four feet long! The Russian boys stood above the fish with an iron spear and lunged expertly, catching one at almost every attempt. They showed me how to do it correctly, not stabbing it in the tail because then it could bite your hand, but near the head. Soon I was also catching fish. I brought home three or four and the whole house ate. Thus we solved our problem of hunger.

We stayed in the homestead for only a few weeks, still waiting for the river to thaw completely. In that time the great socialist holiday, May Day, came and went. I was excited to see how May Day was celebrated in a Russian village, in this cradle of socialism. I went out with some other people to the village across the river. There were a few drunken boys and that was it. They were singing hostile songs, trying to instigate a fight with us: 'Above the Polish palace, above the Ottoman leaders, our Red swords are slashing!' It was quite a disappointment.

Naftali came to me one day and said it was time to go. He hated the forest, as we all did. The Russians had made a mistake with us. An average Polish person put into the forest loses his head. With the average Russian this was not so. A Russian, be he a professor, a doctor or a farmer, could be thrown into the forest, given an ax and he would already be adjusted to the lifestyle. The Russians were a multi-talented people, able to adapt to change and withstand terrible hardships, but we were not Russians. I agreed with Naftali that I would go. My family agreed that I should go first and find a job and an apartment before they came down. What sense would there be to leave such a place before these things were settled?

I bought a Polish military backpack from our religious friend Gostinsky and prepared to leave. My mother was crying over the situation, asking me where I intended to go. She knew it was a luxury that we were all living together peacefully in that homestead and I had trouble convincing her that it was best that I leave. I reasoned with her, telling her that Russia must have great things to offer us, just not in the forest.

We left on a Sunday, the Russian day of rest. We figured we could travel a good distance before anyone discovered we were gone, hopefully not until Monday. I led the group to the floating sidewalk – no one else had ventured this far – and we followed the flow of the river to a village called Choltskaja Zapan.

In this village the profession was raft-building, a dangerous occupation. Men would stand on floating logs and guide like-sized logs together using a long stick with a hook called a *bagor*. When there were enough logs, another man would tie the bundles together with metal wire. This had to be done quickly and correctly, otherwise the logs would bunch in the river and dynamite would be needed to blast the jam free.

We came across a group of our people there, Jewish refugees from Poland. We told them we were leaving the forest, going south to Cerepovec. When I explained to them what the Jewish officer from Moscow had told me, they were shocked. No one knew they could leave the forest. Many of them joined us, including Shloime Ackerman, with whom I would become great friends.

We continued to Koniewo where a few of us, the professional people, were left behind by Yastrobov. I found Bronich Shanker and his wife the German teacher. I entered their home and found Mrs Shanker standing there without a dress! I asked her why she was walking around in her underwear and she told me her *yubka* had been stolen at the *banja*. I asked them if they had heard from Hella, the girl I took to the hospital that night. They had not. I let them know our plans to leave the forest, but they were not ready to go at that point.

We went down to the port in Koniewo, hoping to find a boat to Cerepovec. There was a white ferry going to Cerepovec, but it was run by the Cerepovec Forest Trust Company and was filled with men from their management and members of the NKVD. I was sure they would arrest us, but they did nothing. So, with the little money we had, we bought tickets to Cerepovec.

There was a buffet set up on deck and Sinek jumped at the sight. He had the money, so why not? Those who had the money joined him and started to feast on the boat. I had very little money. I ate a little bread and a few pieces of smoked fish my mother had prepared. There was *kipjatok* ( readily available, almost boiling water from a cauldron) and salt, and this was enough.

Most people, like me, slept on the deck since the cabins were very expensive. I stayed awake a long time, looking at the beautiful villages that had come to life since the winter. The sparks from the chimney rained down and the smoke encircled the boat as we slowly churned along the river. This was a riverboat, with wheels powered by a wood-burning engine. The sound of the paddling combined with the smell of the engine filled me with a sense of wonder – I was happy we decided to leave.

In the morning we arrived in Chaika, where our tributary fed into the great Sheksna river. We had to switch vessels, leaving the riverboat for a more substantial craft named *Dzambul*, after the pro-Stalin Khazak poet. We came to Beloz Orsk and made our way through the series of locks in the river. It was amazing how the locks lifted us up and let us down, passing through effortlessly yet moving thousands of tons of water.

As we approached Cerepovec we saw a great deal of activity on the river, which by that point was enormously wide. There were hundreds of vessels, some involved in industry and some for peasants. There were tugboats pulling bundles of timber as long as city blocks. One cable was hooked onto a floating house made of twigs where a raft-man dwelled. His responsibility was to get the logs through the locks, unhitching then re-hitching the bundles one by one. What an endeavor! In addition, he had to put lights on the bundles at night. It was quite a sight.

Finally we arrived in Cerepovec. We disembarked and began walking up the hill to the city. The streets were made of cobblestones, which made walking very difficult. I was used to trains, deep snow, floating sidewalks and boats. Now I had trouble walking on a normal street!

We passed a white building on the left. This was a nursing school my future wife later attended. We went to the only place we knew, Dom Krestianina. We registered and were given the same spiel: we could stay three days and no longer. This was instantly divisive: who would stay in Cerepovec and who would ignore the restriction of our documents and continue traveling outside the province?

*Note*

1.  In order to keep out the cold I took a blanket, made a hole in it, put it over my head and then tied it at the waist. By cold I am talking about minus 40 degrees celsius and the Polish undershirts were not suitable for working in these conditions – they were too long and when you started to cut the trees they got in the way and tore. The sleeves were also too long, and as we worked they got wet and then froze.

# 11 On the river

Most of the young men wanted to continue south towards the Ukraine. I had told my family I would be in Cerepovec, so I had to stay. In addition, I felt we should find work here since we could do so legally. During our allotted three days at the Dom Krestianina, I searched everywhere for a job – with a job you could get an apartment – but I found nothing. The two brothers, the 'hungry angels', found work making the upper parts of shoes. They were given a room in an apartment, but their landlady would not even let me keep my backpack there.

Our three days were up and we were forced out of the Dom Krestianina. A group of us headed to the train station. We were not well organized, and as days went by people simply disappeared – some took trains and some found jobs. We spent our days at the Dom Krestianina and our nights at the train station, but our prospects did not improve. I found work one day digging holes for the foundation of a building, but this was just one day. What little money I made I spent on tea and bread. Things were desperate.

I was offered a job hauling trees out of the river and to a building site. I followed the man who hired me to the city stable where I rented a horse, then I made my way to the river. I was given no instructions and consequently I made many mistakes. To haul a tree out of the water, you had to put the heaviest end on the trailer near the horse. I had this backwards and the horse could not move. Instead of helping me, the Russians laughed at me; it was incomprehensible to them that a boy my age should not know how to handle a horse and trailer. I was so frustrated that I walked away, dropping the reins and leaving the tree.

Another time two brothers from a carpentry cooperative approached a boy named Tovya and me about available jobs.

We went with them to the cooperative, but there was only one position available. I let Tovya have the job. I had a family, but he had nothing. I walked to the station miserable and hot, with the winter boots still on my feet, feeling like a failure and heartbroken.

There was another lost soul like me left over from our exodus from the forest – a refugee from Lodz named Zalma. Together we sat and talked, but it was not really a friendship. A man approached us one day and told us they were hiring people at the port. Zalma and I went down to investigate. The port was like a separate city, complete with hospitals, repair shops, restaurants, *banjas*, everything. The river was filled with apartment barges, like houseboats. Why, with all the space in Russia, did these people live on the water? But in Russia, you learn to stop asking why.

We walked up to a barge where a man and his two beautiful daughters lived. He was not too friendly, perhaps we looked a little shady, but he spoke frankly with us. I explained in my broken Russian the situation with my family and he warmed to me a little bit. He showed us where the personnel office was located and wished us luck.

A man in a white suit, Kowalow, greeted us at the office. I explained our situation and he said with enthusiasm that he needed us both and he had jobs for my family. I did not want to believe him, I know what liars some Russians can be, but what choice did I have? He told us we would be working on a tugboat and he would get my parents an apartment soon. I saw this as a miracle, that God had helped me again. I wanted to kiss Kowalow's hand.

We were promised new clothing, the beautiful white outfits the river workers sported, and we were given meal tickets and a place to sleep at a nearby inn. We were to start work the next day. I asked him for paper to write a letter to my parents since I would not have time to see them before I left. He gave me a beautiful piece of stationery and an envelope with the cooperative's letterhead. This was amazing because paper was very hard to come by in Russia.

I went to a market and sold my winter boots for 800 rubles. I bought myself a pair of horrible shoes for 100 rubles – we were getting new outfits, after all – and sent the remainder to my parents in a letter explaining the situation. I kissed the letter and sent it to the homestead. Zalma and I took our meal tickets to a cafeteria and ate like kings before heading to the *banja*. We slept at the inn and returned to Kowalow in the morning.

I was shaved, washed and well groomed, ready and excited to work. Zalma, as was his nature, stood in front of Kowalow hunched over like a tired, depressed horse. We were told to take one of the big ferries, like the *Dzambul*, to the first lock and wait for another boat to pick us up. We did this, and we ate heartily again at the buffet on the top deck.

We waited at the first lock for the entire day, but no one came for us. It started to rain a little, but we stayed where we were told until well past midnight. Finally a small rowboat from a nearby vessel came over to us calling out, '*Kolchoznica! Kolchoznica!*' This was the name of the boat; a name derived from Kolchozin, a collectivized farm. Zalma was a clumsy person, and he was afraid to get into the rowboat. He finally managed to do so, but he was even more afraid of climbing the rope ladder hanging off the side of the boat. A young man on deck looked at him like he was crazy and offered no help. Our first impression was not a good one. These were rough characters and showing fear and weakness at the outset was not a good idea.

The boat was larger than the ferry that carried us to the locks. It was made of wood and was powered by two wheels. The whole structure shook from the wood-burning engine. There were approximately 40 people on board, Captain Chistiakow and his family on the top deck, the officers – the aristocrats of the boat – on the second deck and the crew in the hull.

Zalma and I were taken into the hull and given bunks. We understood we were to go to sleep, so we did. A couple of hours later a man shook me awake and took me to the top deck. It was raining steadily as he explained my duties, which I had difficulty in understanding. I deduced from his gesticulations that I was to carry wood from a pile on the deck and send it down a metal chute to the boiler room. Later I learned to re-stack the wood I had used and roll ballast barrels from one side to the other to correct the balance of the boat. Every hour I had to ring a bell and await a signal from a man in the steering house. Finally, I was responsible for the boat's *kipja-tok,* using water from the river – the same water into which our toilet emptied.

I worked hard that night, albeit inefficiently, partially destroying my clothing with the combination of rain and my poor technique. At the end of my shift I was exhausted and filthy, ready to sleep again. Zalma took over after I explained his duties and I went to bed.

The next day we stopped by the riverbank to pick up wood. There were two planks stretching from the boat to the shore, one for bringing an empty wheelbarrow to the woodpile and one to bring a full wheelbarrow to the boat. Walking without carrying anything on these planks was difficult for Zalma and me, but the Russians were zipping back and forth like it was a natural thing. When Zalma's turn to carry back a full wheelbarrow arrived, I knew disaster was imminent. Sure enough, the planks wobbled and his legs gave out causing him to crash into the water. He was bleeding, he had really hurt himself. The Russians laughed at him and let him thrash in the water for a while. The wood floated away and the wheelbarrow sank, but still no one helped him until eventually the captain told the others to fish him out. At the next lock Zalma was sent to a hospital and I never saw him again.

I was left alone on the boat and the Russians were very hostile towards me. I knew I could do any job they asked me to do, only I had to learn how to do it. On the boat there was no training, just doing. As the days went by my technique improved, but by that time I had already destroyed my sweater and earned a reputation as a klutz.

I was not like the Russians, I was not a drinker or a dancer, I could hardly speak their language and I was dressed in horrible clothing. They brought everything with them: soap, preserves, dried bread, salami, cheese, dried vegetables, everything they needed for the long trips. I had nothing. I was eating only what scraps Leeza, the captain's wife who was the cook, gave me after the meals. If I had money I could have bought fish along the way – the men who lit the bundles of logs also sold fish, usually trading for bread or vodka – but I had given everything I had to my family.

I washed regularly but I did not have soap. Soon I was infested with vermin. I washed my clothing with ash, as we had done in the freight train, but this did not help. The Russians only laughed at my misfortune, especially the head mechanic, Kniazew, who was the boat's party leader. He took great pleasure in putting me down, never missing a chance to tell me that the banks of the man-made Rybinsk Sea were lined with Polish *kykes*, prisoners because they were refugees. Without Zalma on board, there was little rest for me. When it was time to load wood, there was no stopping. If the locks were opened for passage, it meant a 30 or 40 hour shift for me. It was miserable! I was the lowest wretch on the boat, so I was constantly asked to do small chores, like fixing parts of the engine and crawling into small spaces to retrieve things. I never received thanks for anything, nor was I given proper clothing or soap. It was a floating prison.

I made one friend on board, the captain's son Pavel Chistiakow. He was also an outcast on the vessel because of his rejection from the Red Army. This was a major embarrassment for any Russian. Acceptance into the Red Army was always a step up. The boys toiling in the fields in a village were not given passports, they were kept in their region for their entire lives. In the Red Army, if you survived, you had an unrestricted passport and an honorable reputation. I believe his eyesight was too poor for him to serve. He showed me better techniques and helped me adjust to boat life a little better. In addition, I was given a name – Genasha.

I sometimes saw handfuls of peasants collecting hay on the banks of the river, but there was very little activity for most of the trip. As we entered the Rybinsk Sea, however, I began to see the strangest things. I saw entire villages float past our boat. The peasants had dismantled their homes and made rafts from the lumber. Entire families sat on these makeshift vessels next to stacks of bricks from the chimneys, along with their cows and chickens. The Soviet government was in the process of making the Rybinsk Sea and would inform villages when their homes would be flooded. What else was there for them to do?

The Rybinsk Sea led to the mouth of the great Volga river. This was where we unloaded our wood and other vessels carried it to various destinations, like the Caspian Sea. There were hundreds of boats in the mouth of the Volga, large and small, and there was an aviation factory nearby. After days on the quiet Cheksna river, the racket of all this activity was a pleasant distraction.

When we had unloaded the wood and the work was finished we were given the most beautiful bread, white bread. I felt like I was holding two pieces of the sun in my hands. This short time to rest, to drink tea and eat this bread, was heavenly. I was doing this for my family and I would survive, I thought, and this kept my spirits alive.

Coming back from the Volga river one night, the crewmembers were talking passionately about something. They were agitated and concerned – they had just heard about Molotov's Law. This decree was imposed on the Soviet people in June 1940. It stated, simply, that no one could leave his or her job. If you quit, you were sent to prison. If you came to work late or drunk, you were sent to prison. In effect, all the Soviet people were turned into paid slaves.

This was the worst news I could have heard. I saw how many refugees were now prisoners serving sentences of hard labor and I knew my parents would not have heard about the law. It was a trick to get people like my father arrested and sent to places like the Rybinsk Sea. I could do nothing to warn them, their fate was out of my hands. I worked on that boat with the belief that I was helping them, now it felt like I had abandoned them. It was too much for me to handle and I broke down and cried. I sat down in the stern of the boat, lost like a child. I missed my family so much and I felt like a failure. I wanted to die, to throw myself into the river. I curled up next to the woodpile and sobbed.

I heard footsteps behind me and a gruff voice ask, 'Why

are you crying?' It was Afanasief, one of the boiler room workers. He was a Volga Russian, huge and full-bearded. He said, 'You are not a Russian, Genasha, Russians do not cry. What's the story?' I did not know what to tell him, so I told him everything and he listened. I cried to him unashamedly, I could not keep my despair or my anger inside me. He looked at me, assessing me with his hand on my shoulder, and said, 'Genasha, don't worry.' He then gave me such a hug, like my father, with strong arms and the smell of sweat.

Afanasief left for a moment and came back with black bread, honey, smoked ham and real tea. 'Genasha, sit down and eat', he ordered. I protested, but he forced me to dine as he explained his situation. He told me he had a Jewish wife and three children, but he did not know where they were. He had been a civil engineer working in the oil fields near the Caspian Sea when he was arrested for sabotage – they arrested thousands of people for sabotage. He was released for a short time, but discovered he was to be arrested again so he fled, taking a job in the boiler room of this vessel. He made me feel like an equal, like I had a friend on that ship. I had not felt this way with any Russian, or any Pole for that matter. Afanasief supported me and I felt better.

A week later a director of the shipping company made his way to our boat by way of a little skiff named *The Dictator of the Proletariat*. He called a meeting to explain Molotov's Law and how beneficial to the Russian working class it would be. There was always a convenient spin to be put on such treacherous legislation. When the meeting ended, I noticed Afanasief speaking with the director while both men looked my way. He was explaining my situation, how I had no soap, no clothes, no reading material and no decent food. The director came up to me and asked me if this was true. He was so sympathetic, so good, that I started to cry again. He assured me things would improve. His assistant came from the skiff and handed me a bag of clothing: black pants and a black shirt, a white hat, underwear, beautiful shoes and socks. He also gave me soap, strange bars with intricate patterns. I was so grateful to Afanasief.

The director took the head mechanic and Captain

Chistiakow aside and scolded them for their actions. They were so small at that moment, the whole crew was so small. Only Afanasief and I were big.

Things changed completely for me after that. I was no longer the dirty worm they could mistreat, but a member of the crew. I was learning to do everything on the boat and I became very useful to the captain. He nicknamed me Golubchik, Little Dove. I had transformed my living quarters into a comfortable place, using the tricks I had learned from our trip from Poland. I had hay tucked away in the corners giving off a sweet aroma and I kept everything so clean. I even had flowers decorating the small, circular window. 'Golubchik, you are an example for the others', said the captain.

To earn the personal acceptance of the crew, however, there were a few things I had to suffer. One was tattoo day. I ran to Afanasief and pleaded with him to help me avoid this desecration of my body; it was against my religion. 'It is also against your religion to get yourself killed', he said. He opened his shirt and showed me myriad tattoos of eagles and anchors and all sorts of things. 'You have to show that you are with them, Genasha, otherwise an iron might fall on your head one night.' I saw that he was right, so I had an anchor tattooed on my right hand. Apart from drinking more vodka than I would have liked, this was the only sacrifice I regretted in earning the safety of comradeship.

We made runs up and down the river, what they called a *race* – there were plenty of English words in their language. We rarely stopped in Cerepovec for longer than a few hours. I spent my free time reading books given to me by different members of the crew. Many had stashed their favorite novels in their belongings and were happy to share them with me. This helped me understand and learn proper Russian, not just the vernacular of the river. I would often climb into the rowboat near the back wheels of our vessel and rock in the water as I read page after page. Otherwise I spent my time worrying about my family, I had no idea how they were doing.

I was loading wood on the top of the deck one day as we

headed towards the Rybinsk Sea when I heard somebody calling my name from another boat. I turned to see the *Dzambul* and the whole Bubis clan waving over the side railing towards me. I saw little Peretz – he wanted to jump into the water and swim to me! I wanted to tousle his hair and hear him curse one more time. Blima looked beautiful. I felt a longing to hug her, to sit by the fire and tell her stories again. It filled me with joy to see familiar faces. We yelled our greetings to each other, and they told me they were going to the Ukraine.

I never saw them again. Everyone in the Ukraine was slaughtered when the Nazis overtook the territory and I assume they were too. This family was so important to my family, especially so to my mother. Their charity and humility saved us in those cold winter months.

We came to the first lock one day and the captain disembarked to make his customary call to head office. This was the only communication any of us had with our headquarters. He came back and told me that my parents were waiting for me in Cerepovec. I exploded with happiness – they were safe! I did not know how they had managed to get out of the forest, or why, but I was delighted to know they did. I asked the captain when we would next be in port and he told me two weeks.

I was so excited to see them. I had gone through some horrible times on the boat, but with Afanasief's help I was now settled. Leeza gave me two bowls of soup at mealtimes, I had plenty of soap and I wore a beautiful uniform. The positive things I wrote to them in that letter had come true after all. The two weeks dragged on until, finally, we came to port.

My entire family was there, along with some of our new friends. I was a hero to them. I gave my brothers the white Rybinsk bread and my mother the intricately patterned soap. I was a big-shot. We hugged and kissed like it was a miracle, which, in a way, it was. My family had come to Cerepovec after receiving the letter I sent. My sister, smart girl that she was, managed to convince the boys in the fishing boats to organize a flotilla of refugees and guide them to Konevo. With the letterhead on the stationery, she was able to get an apartment at 10 Niekrasowa Street. How had she grasped the system so quickly?

I was given one day's leave, so we went back to the apartment. The house was the last on the street, abutting the fields. Every house in this section of Cerepovec looked the same, modeled after the old village style. The street was made of dirt and flanked by wooden sidewalks. Behind every house there was a garden which provided the residents with much of their food in the warmer months. There was no electricity apart from the loudspeakers situated at both ends of the street, which periodically blared out propaganda and official announcements.

My family rented one large room and one small room and we shared the heat from a large stove. My mother kept the smaller room clear in case refugees arrived in town with nowhere to stay. Already a husband and wife had stayed with them for a few days. My mother would not accept their money, but she asked them to supply the household with firewood – a symbolic rent. When I arrived for the first time they had already gone.

I enjoyed my day off so much; it was wonderful to relax with my family and to discover they had not only avoided the treachery of Molotov's Law, but used the subtleties of the system to acquire an apartment. I was proud of them. There was only one problem – my father wanted to work on the boat with me.

I tried to dissuade him from taking a job on the river, but he was certain he should do it. I asked Afanasief for advice and he came up with a solution. We persuaded Kowalow to let my father join us, unpaid, for one race up and down the river. If my father accepted the job officially, he would be tied into it as I was. This gave him an escape clause.

He was put into the boiler room with Afanasief. They gave him a pair of shoes to protect his feet from burning embers and he spent his days stoking the fire with wood. He hated it, as I knew he would, complaining continually about thirst and being covered with smoke and soot. At the time the river was experiencing a plague of mosquitoes, sometimes swarming so massively they would block out the sun. We had to smoke our room to keep them away. My father got the picture – work on the river was not for him.

Afanasief, my father, and I talked about our situations. It was clear working on the boat was not our calling, but Afanasief and I had no choice. My father could leave, but what else was there to do? Afanasief pointed out the simplest thing, something that had not occurred to us: 'You are a butcher. Why don't you join the cooperative at the meat factory?' And so he did.

Captain Chistiakow gave me eight hours' leave when we returned to Cerepovec. I believe he granted these hours to me because he felt I had established connections in the party – perceptions of power in Russia went a long way. My father and I went to the meat factory, the slaughterhouse, which was situated near our apartment on the other side of the fields. There was a guard out front.

'This is my father, a master butcher from Warsaw,' I said. You had to lie a little to get inside the door. The guard picked up a line and invited us to enter. We were introduced to the director of the factory, Saharov. I explained to him that my father was a master butcher who needed a job, so he led us to a storage room with hanging meat. 'Show me what you can do,' he said.

My father's movements were poetry. I could see him growing in size and prestige in front of my eyes and the eyes of the Director. He displayed his strength while moving the carcasses, his efficiency with the quickness of his incisions and his craftsmanship with the resulting cuts of meat. 'What kind of cut would you like?' he had me ask the director. He did not know. In Russia, you learned to do everything, but in Poland you became a master of one thing.

To embellish a little, I asked my father to assess a cow. He grabbed one by the neck and by the haunches and predicted its weight. They put it on the scale and he had missed by one kilogram. 'You're hired', he said. He led us to meet his wife, the head of the canteen. We ate a nice meal and were given a dozen *pilmenis*, Siberian ravioli. My father took these to my mother who subsequently gave them to our landlady – this was always a good idea.

With my father employed and my family settled, I returned to the boat and continued the *races* up and down the Cheksna river. In time my sister enrolled in an accounting school and Nuchem went to work for the electric company. Moishe attended school and my mother transformed our home into the neighborhood center, a place where refugees came to eat, drink and laugh with one another. Even the landlady respected my mother, though it did not hurt that my father brought back so much meat from the slaughterhouse on a regular basis.

The boat did not always stop in Cerepovec during our normal *races*, only when we returned from the Volga with barrels of oil. I missed my family so much when we were on tour and I resented every minute I was stuck on that boat. From time to time we were given longer leaves, which I cherished. When I knew we were coming to Cerepovec I would save the white bread from Rybinsk and anything else I thought my brothers might like. I knew when I came into port Nuchem would be waving to me from the dock.

Through the spring, summer, and autumn nothing much changed for us. Our neighborhood, which was initially designed for peasants who had moved to the city, still had a rural feel about it, the residents were not totally dependent on the Soviet system. Our Russian neighbors grew their own food, made their own clothing, and held on to their Russian language. There was a rejection of the Soviet language, which was differed by using shortcuts, making it efficient and ugly. We had food from my father, but we did not have crops. We spent many hours waiting in line for the Soviet to 'give' us our vegetables.

On our street there lived a few refugee families, including the Perlers from Warsaw and the querulous Zielberberg family. Mr Perler worked on an egg farm and would bring us broken eggs at the end of the day. Mr Zielberberg, like me, worked on a boat and despised it. With the other refugees we shared a sense of camaraderie. Apart from not knowing what was happening to relatives we could not contact, we were happy.

We had plenty of Russian neighbors too. There was Maria, a beautiful Russian woman who, like many of her generation, was an outspoken anti-Soviet. She was a strong, blonde woman with perfect teeth that gleamed when she laughed. She reminded me of a wolf. She was tough, brazen and a little anti-Semitic. My father started getting a Jewish newspaper delivered to our home. Maria was talking to the mailwoman (in Russia there were no mailmen) and noticed the paper. Soon she was telling the whole neighborhood that we were not Polish, but Jewish. Rumors began to circulate, but nothing came of it. The most ridiculous rumor was that we had blown up a bridge, that we were saboteurs.

We paid no attention to this. Instead, my brothers and I went out of our way to help her, bringing her water from the well, which was two blocks away, and carrying her packages when we noticed her returning from the center of town. Eventually she warmed to us, probably because she saw how much we helped each other. I went with Maria to the river to do our laundry, asking her for instructions. 'What? A man doing the laundry in Russia?' She showed me how to use the ribbed paddles and how to rinse the soap out properly. She laughed at me the whole time and I laughed too.

Overall it was a pleasant place to live, only we could not stop thinking about our missing relatives. We tried to contact our extended family by writing to the designated meeting points, like Minska 57 in Baranavicy. We wrote a letter to Latvia, to Sonia's home, the wife of Uncle Shloime Gerszon. We had tried to contact them before, but we never received a response. Finally an answer came in the mail: they were in the forest, further north than we had been, and Shloime Gerszon had broken his arm. He had been arrested and therefore could not leave. My mother put together packages of potatoes, dried vegetables, grains and smoked tongue (for which my father had developed a process). She sent these packages regularly to our cousins who were living nearby. On the one hand we knew they were alive, but on the other hand we knew a prison term in Russia was like a death sentence. We could only send what we could and pray for a change.

Up and down the river, up and down the river, this was my life and I hated it. With the first signs of autumn I became restless; I needed to find a way off the boat. I treasured the time on shore, but we were making such quick *races* to beat the cold weather that we rarely stopped at home. I missed my family.

We received word in Rybinsk that we would be stopping in Cerepovec on one of the next runs. On that trip we were given pieces of cake. I was so excited with the prospect of giving the cake to my family that I was afraid to touch it, but I did. I would hold it up to my nose and smell its sweetness, though I did not eat a morsel. We were also given two loaves of the special white bread, but these started to gather mold.

I wanted to preserve the bread for my family so I thought I would toast it a little on the pipes leading out of the engine room. As I placed the loaves on the pipes, the boat shook violently. I lost my balance and landed with my back on the hot pipes. I was badly burnt, but I shrugged it off, figuring it would go away.

Sometimes the wood in the chute would jam. When this happened I had to climb into the space and free the logs. At other times the workers would purposely block the chute to take a rest. The burn on my back made the clearing extremely painful and difficult for me. In a few days, having not properly cleaned the area or protected it from mosquitoes and filth, I had developed a terrible infection. The captain dropped me off at the first lock and I was taken by boat to a wooden hospital in Cerepovec, staffed mostly by women doctors.

I was treated quickly in the hospital, but I had to stay there for a few weeks as they monitored my progress. I was determined to use this misfortune to my benefit, I hoped to get off the boat. The head doctor, Uglielnov, was of Bulgarian origin and would sometimes stop by my bedside. We chatted in Russian and I found him very friendly. I believe he took an interest in me because he would ask me personal questions, such as whether I was a boxer on account of my well-toned muscles. In the end, I took a chance and asked him if he could help me off the boat, if he had the power to release me from

Molotov's Law. I told him I wanted to study and be with my family.

'You Jews!' he yelled. 'None of you wants to work! You just want to take what we give you and get an education!' He was so hostile! Where did it come from? I did not want to remind him that he had an education, but he was neither Russian nor Jewish. He told me I would never be released from the boat and walked away. I did not bother telling my parents about this, what would have been the point? I was in the hospital for almost two months, time for which I was not paid. To receive benefits from the cooperative one had to have been working for at least a year.

By the time I came back to work the edges of the river had begun to freeze; winter was rapidly approaching. Our boat was fitted with a series of wooden beams jutting out from the bow to act as an icebreaker. Someone would have to balance on these beams and continually immerse a measuring stick to keep the captain informed of the river's depth. I was excellent at this because I was small and able to move easily around the framework. Still, despite our efforts, we sometimes found ourselves beached on sand. When this happened, we would weigh the anchor on the other side of the river and winch ourselves free. The final days were treacherous, but we stayed on the river for as long as possible.

We headed to the winter port on our very last run. It was extremely cold. We could see the river freezing in front of our eyes. As the water splashed against the hull, more and more ice would remain attached to the wood. The captain needed someone to cut this ice off the vessel while the others went into a village. He nominated Afanasief and me. We were given iron rods and left to defend the boat from the elements.

The iron bar was heavy and my shoes gave me little traction. I jabbed and jabbed at the ice  and the effort of lifting the bar wore me down. I took a big swing at a block of ice, slipped of the boat, and tumbled into the water. The iron bar was fitted with leather straps for the hands, which held me to the bar as it sunk rapidly to the bed of the river. Afanasief fished me out, but my hands were already blistering from the cold. I could not move them at all. I was taken, once again, to the hospital.

Uglielnov, the same doctor, took care of me. I knew he would not help me get off the boat, but I asked him anyway. Predictably, he refused. My hands improved, but in Russia they sometimes kept you in the hospital for a long time. I spent my days thinking about what to do. I decided to write a letter to someone who could help me. I wrote 20 pages on notebook paper provided by Henya and mailed them to this address: Moscow – Kremlin – Comrade Stalin.

I described our entire history, from the Polish hostility to our life in Cerepovec. I glorified the Soviet system, praising the way it took us in and provided so much for us. I was learning the game – I knew what to write. There was no chance of the letter reaching Moscow, but who knew who would read it? The worst that could happen was already the case: I would have to continue working on the boat.

A few days after I mailed the letter, two people from the Communist Party's provincial office in Vologda came to see me in the hospital. I could sense they were wary of me right away. Once again, in Russia if there was a perceived connection to something authoritative then there was power. They asked me why I did not want to work on the boat. When I told them I wanted to finish my education, they said they would send me to a school in Leningrad where I would learn to be a captain. This was not for me, I needed a release from Molotov's Law in order to study an academic subject, not a trade.

The Soviet Union was like a giant spider's web, in the middle sat the Kremlin. By sending that letter I jiggled a tiny piece of the web, yet it reverberated far away. The men from the Vologda provincial office felt they needed to dampen the tremor, which was to my benefit. Two days later the men came back and told me I was released from the boat, even paying me for the time I missed.

I came home, free from Molotov's Law but unsure what to do next. My father's job at the slaughterhouse was a godsend for us. With the food he brought home and his status as a working man, I did not have to hurry to find a job to feed us or keep the rented rooms. I began taking night classes and living what was a more normal life for a recently turned 19-year-old.

Despite having been in Cerepovec for so long, I still had not spent a lot of time with people my age, certainly not Russians. By the time I moved back home, our house was already a social center. Russian boys were interested in the refugee girls and would convene in our street on a regular basis. Russian girls took notice of the refugee boys as well, though less candidly. There was much socializing going on, but I felt awkward. First, I had spent most of my time in Russia, up to this point, living in a cubbyhole on a boat. Second, I brooded over the international situation and the different episodes of human betrayal I had seen. Third, I was different, more reserved than the Russians were. In Russia the boys dance with such enthusiasm and athleticism and it was a marvel to watch, but I could not dance. How could I see myself dating a Russian girl?

In truth I was happiest staying at home. The house always smelled of good food. My mother filled the cows' stomach linings with potatoes and flour, cooked the tongues and brains and found a way to use everything my father brought home. The door to our home was always open and no visitor was ever turned away. My father and Moishe learned and sang Russian songs together and I sat in the chair reading books and newspapers. These were precious moments for me. Despite my mother's urgings, I preferred the home life to socializing with my peers.

I studied Russian, literature, algebra and German. I enjoyed being a student again, but I felt I needed to work if my family was to live comfortably. With Shloime Ackerman, a friend I had met at Sholksa Izappan when walking out of the forest, and Yakov Zielberberg, the oafish son of the querulous Mr Zielberberg, I searched for temporary employment. Together we went to the electric power plant.

The plant was in the old section of Cerepovec, nestled between the two rivers that ran through the city, the Cheksna and the Yagoba. Like everything in the area, it was fueled by wood. The building was very old with a chimney billowing out smoke at all hours, reminding me of the Mueller factory back in Kalisz. In the back there was an enormous tower, used for cooling the water that had been heated by the turbines. It was a major operation.

The director was out sick the day we stopped by, but a younger man discussed things with us. I told him that we sought temporary employment because we were not yet established in the city. He laughed at this and said, 'You're talking like a *kolchoznik!*[1] You just want to work a little while and then hurry back to your village?' I explained to him that I was studying and therefore needed to find work I would be able to leave when I completed my education. He accepted this answer and he accepted us.

We cut wood for eight hours a day, using large, extremely sharp bow-saws. We learned to push and pull the saws rhythmically, helping each other, and soon adjusted our bodies to the physical exertion. The logs from the river were hauled to the plant and placed on sawhorses. Depending on what size firewood was needed, a log would take five minutes to two hours to cut. We settled into the job nicely. Combined with night school, this became my life.

Our supervisor was named Spiritow, an elderly Russian and a throwback to the czar's time. He spoke a different kind of Russian and wore a blond fur coat with matching gloves and boots. He seemed so out of place, almost ironic. Because my Russian was better than Yakov's or Shloime's, I was the one to approach Spiritow with our requests. One time he said, 'I have seen you reading during the breaks. I think you will not be a worker in Russia, you will be a Commissar.' From that moment we became friends.

Spiritow and I spoke about the international situation frequently. He allowed me to go into the guards' quarters to listen to the news and report what I had heard to Shloime and Yakov. I also attended *referats*, meetings set up by the party to help explain the international situation and answer any questions. In these meetings various party members would insist that relations with Germany were splendid and that the Soviet Union was not amassing troops on its western border. When I told Spiritow this, he shrugged and said, 'Don't believe it. I know who the Germans are and I know who the

Soviets are. These politics can only lead to war.' He was right. The war would change our lives again and again.

*Note*

1. A *kolchoznik* is a forced member of a collective village (*kolchoz*) where all members are forced to give their private property (including farm animals and tools) as well as their own labor to the collective.

# 12 Return to defenses

Late 1940 and into 1941 was a year of prosperity for the Soviet Union; the country was at peace. The government was calling the victory over Finland a great success, though in truth it was an embarrassment to the armed forces. Talk of taking over Finland completely faded away, probably because Finland received its armaments from the Germans and the Soviets feared getting in too deep, so the campaign ended. Territorial expansion to the west continued, lining the pockets of the party elite and any number of foot soldiers fortunate enough to be on the front lines without getting killed. The Molotov/Ribbentrop pact had kept the Soviet Union out of the war with Germany and Stalin's propaganda machine had elevated him to God-like status.

There was a holiday atmosphere in Cerepovec and everything was peaceful. The city parks, named Culture and Rest like every park in the Soviet Union, were filled with returning soldiers, sailors and boys from the nearby infantry school. There was much singing and fighting when the vodka came out, but it was of a festive nature. Songs like *My Beloved Town* and *The Blue Handkerchief* were popular among the youth, as were Soviet tunes describing the destruction of the enemy in the form of a dark cloud.

The refugees had settled themselves nicely in Cerepovec. There were many marriages and children were born. We were not exactly living a Soviet life, but we enjoyed the prosperity of the times and found our niche on the perimeter of Soviet society. The Russians did not accept us yet as members of their community, but this did not matter since we were not too keen on being Russians.

For the first time it was possible to get almost any product from the stores and there was no need for bread cards.

Because of our past hardships, both the Russians and the refugees knew to take advantage of the situation. If there was a rumor that the next day the government would be 'giving' out shoes, a queue began to form the day before. Whether or not shoes were needed did not matter, everyone knew at some point such an article would be of great value.

Another couple moved into the spare room in our home and stayed with us for a few months. The husband (if they were married) worked as a porter carrying sugar for the Autotransport Company. He said he knew how to escape Cerepovec and eventually he did. Nor was he alone in this desire, it was almost a universal sentiment that life would be better outside of Cerepovec, somewhere further south, and gradually people disappeared. The Perlers went to Krasnodar near the Black Sea and the 'hungry angels' went to Ivanovo, a historical textile city to the north of Moscow.

The Viernik brothers had much success in Ivanovo because they had been professionally trained in Poland. It was an identical situation to my father's at the slaughterhouse. One of the brothers was a master textile worker in Lodz, which was the second largest textile center in Europe (behind Manchester in England). He wrote a letter from Cerepovec to a *kombinat*[1] in Ivanovo and was accepted as a worker. In no time he was a big-shot. He wrote a letter to my family telling us that there would be a great life for us there. Although things were settled for my mother, we agreed I should take a trip to see if he was correct. Unfortunately, tickets for the train were given first to soldiers and party officials leaving only 20 or so tickets for the general public. There was a black market for these, but after I had failed to buy one in four attempts we decided that it was not meant to be, so we stayed in Cerepovec.

Although there was a general level of contentment, Molotov's Law kept many people in jobs they did not wish to do. Two refugees, Yakov Zielberberg's father Yitele and a shy boy named Chikavitch, were stuck working for the Cerepovec Forest Trust Company. When they were still in the forest they read the letter I had sent my parents and were under the illusion that it was a good job. They soon understood how

194

miserable it could be, so I explained to Chikavitch how to be released. He appealed to Kowalow, saying that he wanted to study, and a few days later he was free. Yitele Zielberberg, unfortunately, was too old for this excuse and had to continue working on the boat. Chikavitch somehow arranged for a ticket to Crimea and left a suitcase with us at our house, intending either to return or to send for it when he was settled. We never heard from him again.

In time we were the last remaining family in Cerepovec from the band of refugees who had arrived on the freight train from Kovel. There were numerous single people and wartime couples remaining, and they often came to our home to enjoy the atmosphere of a Polish–Jewish home. My mother was like the matriarch of the refugees and our home was filled with love. I knew how fortunate we were and I made an effort to pray every day at a little Jewish cemetery near our home. It was across from an old Christian burial ground, which was vandalized horribly and filled with drunks, urinating and lying among broken headstones and garbage. It pained me to see a holy place so desecrated, and it amazed me that the Jewish cemetery was untouched. I did not know any formal prayers, but I created my own. I needed to give thanks for our good fortune.

My mother was a master at helping other refugees without hurting their pride. There was a barber from Warsaw who had lost the use of his legs. Instead of giving him charity, my mother had me make a highchair for him so refugees could go to his home for haircuts. He had a sickly wife and a small, redheaded child who reminded my mother of her niece, Chaya Sura's little girl Liebe Rifkah. My mother became so attached to that girl that sometimes she visited them three times a day. The barber, like barbers everywhere, liked to talk and eventually this got us all into trouble.

We were constantly in the bazaar, finding things to send to Shloime Gerszin and Sonia. Along the sides there were stalls set up by artisans where you could get your shoes and clothing mended, buy books, newspapers and propaganda placards, or get your photograph taken. Often I would peruse the newspaper, *Pravda* (truth), while my mother looked for dried goods to send away. It infuriated me that the Soviet press, which hailed the accomplishments of the Germans in France, portrayed the British and French in a negative light.

We were often at the health clinic nearby the bazaar because my mother still suffered from the ulcer on her leg. They gave her an ointment that resembled motor oil and caused her much pain, it stung sharply. One day I sat her down near the photographer in the bazaar because the pain was so great. She cried to me in Yiddish as I tried to wash away the thick ointment. The wife of the photographer came over to us and asked if we were Jewish. We told her that we were and a conversation in Litvak Yiddish and Polish Yiddish ensued.

We explained out situation, how we came to be in Cerepovec and what we had escaped from in Poland. She and her husband had no idea what was happening to Jews there and were totally shocked. My mother started to cry as she described to the woman the ghettoes and the relatives we had left behind. The photographer asked me about my mother's leg. I told him we had no luck finding an effective treatment for her ulcer and it had been bothering her since before the war. He said he would help me. I did not know it at the time, but I was speaking to the unofficial Mayor of the Jews in Cerepovec. My mother and I had stumbled upon something like an underground *kehila*, a closely guarded network of exclusively Russian Jews.

He sent me to Rosa Luxemburg Street, to the headquarters of pharmaceuticals in the region. I was to speak with a woman named Rosa and to tell her that the photographer had sent me. I left my mother with them and went to the warehouse. I met Rosa, such a beautiful, elderly Yiddish woman. I described my mother's wound and she gave me an entire kit of ointments, fluids, bandages and powders, along with instructions on how to use them. I told her we had no soap, so she gave me soap and a little alcohol. I cleaned and dressed my mother's wound back at the bazaar and immediately it felt better.

This was completely illegal, but this was how the small group of Jewish citizens survived the Soviet times. After this initial encounter, my mother and I used the underground

Jewish network to help other refugees, but we never told anyone where we received our materials – not even my father or my siblings. This society made no room for the Jewish refugees and we were lucky to have penetrated it. Through their help my sister was able to get gold caps for her teeth from a deal I made with a watchmaker and a Jewish dentist. There were maybe 50 Jews, factory directors, doctors, dentists and tradesmen, interconnected and helping each other, set apart from the rest of society.

In addition to cutting wood on the sawhorses, we had to retrieve the logs from the river and other locations and bring them to the power plant. In the winter of 1940–41, this meant cutting the logs out of the ice and snow with axes and picks. It was hard work and it was extremely cold.

We began working in brigades, ours led by Nikolai Rezin. In addition to Shloime, Yakov and myself, there was a mother and her two sons, a nice older boy and a devilish younger son named Filya. There was also a father, Volkov, an outspoken anti-Soviet, and his son Mitja. Mitja was not crazy, but a little backward. The other Russians used to make fun of him, asking, 'Mitja, have you had a woman yet?' A scrawny teenager named Volfka also worked with us. He had the face of an old man, covered with freckles and full of worry. He would squat on his haunches during the breaks and smoke cigarettes, not saying a word. I always wondered what went on in his head, whatever it was it could not have been good.

I began taking fewer classes and my attendance waned, instead I worked the night shift. On very cold nights, when I could smell the frost, I was permitted to enter the boiler room to warm up. The workers there would allow me to feed wood down a rolling chute that led to the ovens. The amount of wood I sent down depended on the temperature gauge above the workstation. I was earning a good name because I was genuinely interested in how the entire operation was executed and I was polite. This was in contrast to most Russians, who cursed three times in a sentence – even the women!

Next to the boiler room there was a restricted area where

only the head mechanic worked. This room held the turbines and was covered with a rubber floor. I became friendly with the head mechanic and we discussed things openly, which was interesting because he was considered to have a standing well above the workers. I said to him, 'If you are so smart, why do we still cut the wood with our hands? Why don't you make a mechanical saw?' He said he would think about it.

Would you believe he designed a saw? It did not have a tread, but it had a moving blade that shortened the cutting time considerably. Because of this there was a buzz about us, the refugees, throughout the plant. The young man that hired us let Yakov, Shloime and myself into the officer's canteen to eat and eventually introduced me to the director, Comrade Ribinkow. Amazingly, he had the same tattoo as I had – he too had spent time on the wretched boats. We were friendly with each other immediately, though I was quite shy on account of his position. He would walk with me through the halls of the office and show me propaganda placards, perhaps trying to convince me to join the party.

There were good-looking girls in the office, and they too became interested in us. Primarily because we had good reputations and also because we were gentlemen. We would go every week to collect our wages and enter the office with our hats in our hands, as we were taught. This mannerly behavior intrigued them and was in stark contrast to the rough tongues of the Russian workers. Although the attention was nice, nothing came of their interest.

Work occupied most of my time as we went further and further away from the plant to retrieve the timber. I stopped going to classes altogether. The director of the school, who was also my algebra teacher, was an elderly woman named Vinogradiva. She came to our home to enquire of my where-abouts; I was a good student despite my patchy attendance record. She was such a beautiful person, so caring and sincere. She reminded me of my former teacher in Kalisz, Pani Sikorska. When I told her that I had no time to study, she offered to come to our house to teach me! For some reason the lessons never materialized, but it was a kind gesture.

Our brigade received word that the Soviet government

planned to construct the Volga strait, and part of Cerepovec would be flooded. There was already construction started on the other side of town, building homes for the soon to be displaced persons from that area. Our job was to cut down all the trees in that zone and transport them back to the power plant.

My boss on this project was an ethnic Pole born in Russia named Masikevich. He liked us because we were from Poland, though I do not know if he had ever been there. He was fun, energetic and dexterous and I liked him a lot. The foremen of the project were two Jews, Milchen and Rubinstein. Both had been active in the wood business in the time of the czar. Rubinstein spoke with a strong, guttural, Jewish accent. His supervisor was an anti-Semite named Zapituchen. '*Rhhh*rubinstein!' he would yell to the delight of the other workers, 'you motherfucker!' I did not find this so funny – was this not the way Lenin spoke? Rubinstein, red-faced with thick glasses, would reply softly 'Tell it to me from the grave.'

I tried to befriend Rubinstein because I wanted to know more about the history of the Jews in Cerepovec. We started to talk about the past, and at first he was very open. I asked him about the time under the czar and about the little cemetery near my home. This made him uneasy. He told me he had nothing more to say and that I should ask the photographer these things. So I did. The photographer described a nice Jewish community in Cerepovec under the czar. It was a wealthy community mostly on account of the logging business, but also from the butter factory. 'Those people were wealthy,' he said, 'those people are now lying in that little cemetery.'

Our brigade was taken off the Volga straits project and sent to various villages and towns in the surrounding area to retrieve wood. This was good in one sense because we were paid fairly – our wages reflecting the hours we worked – and we worked many hours. Problems arose because we were camping together and there was no escaping the traditions of the Russian worker. We were paid on Friday and immediately they would send out for vodka. In Russia, vodka is more than food. We could not go against this, not if we wanted to be comrades or even safe. The Russians could be so bloodthirsty, so dangerous when they drank so we had no choice. We ate plenty of crabmeat and cucumbers while swilling down large quantities of vodka.

We were sent to Torovo on the Cheksna river to retrieve wood near a railroad bridge and a prison camp. It was like the North Pole, like a frozen desert, white without end. We took our breaks inside the camp in the free workers' section, adjacent to the prisoners' canteen. I stared incredulously at the number of prisoners, some of whom looked like they were sleep walking, and wondered, again, what could they all have done wrong. The Russians in our brigade occupied themselves with arguments and laughter, completely oblivious to the plight of the prisoners. Were these not Russian people? How could there be such callousness?

On these trips our general hygiene declined considerably. We were sleeping in villages and most were getting drunk. One night I ate cabbage and pork soup, although I did not know it was pork – it was the first time I had eaten it – but it tasted so good. Then I got sick. I was covered with boils filled with pus and very painful. A doctor told me that my condition was the result of two things: poor diet and poor hygiene. I bought yeast and began making tea with pine needles, but there was nothing I could do about my hygiene and there were very few vegetables to be found. One night a drunk fell on me. The collision burst one of the boils, causing it to weep and throb with pain. I was furious and kicked him so hard he fell out of the door. Despite my condition, I was not released from work. Eventually I felt better.

As the ice and snow melted, we no longer had to trek into the fields or up the river to collect the wood, it floated down to us. We would balance on floating logs and retrieve the timber with a *bagor*; the long stick with a hook I had seen used on the Cheksna. The best at negotiating this task was the wily Russian boy named Filya. He was a bandit. He was skinny, tall and blond, with a knife on his belt and a competitive nature. He took issue with the favoritism I was shown by the senior men and consequently tried to push me as far as he could. He was not a bad person, but this was his nature. After weeks of his bullying, I had had enough. As we both stood on floating logs, he prodded me with his *bagor*, trying to make me lose my balance. I could no longer accept his behavior, so I took one big swing with my *bagor* and knocked him into the water. I waited for him to retaliate, but nothing came. From that point on, he no longer bothered me. My reputation among the Russians probably improved after the incident.

Soon it was May Day, 1941. I was curious to see what kind of celebration Cerepovec would have. There was not much to remember from May Day in 1940, but I guessed this was because of the small size of the village we were in. Shloime, Yakov and I went to the power plant expecting to see political demonstrations with flags and speeches. Instead we saw a few drunken workers and few women walking around the plant with gas masks. The women were on duty, guarding the plant against sabotage. We went with a few other workers to the headquarters of the Communist Party, sang the *Internationale* and other songs and returned to the plant. The government was 'giving' out biscuits, but that was it. This was the workers' holiday! And they all called themselves communists.

Around this time the police contacted my family. It was time for us to replace the temporary passports we were issued in Kovel with official Soviet passports. Privately I wondered why we needed Russian passports, were we not Polish citizens? Of course I did not question the police. In official matters too many questions could lead to imprisonment. We went to the photographer for passport pictures and he agreed with me that it was strange. At the police station we filled out our forms. There was a space for our nationality, not our citizenship. I convinced my family to write 'Jewish' instead of 'Polish', but most of the refugees wrote 'Polish'.

We were given five-year internal passports with the same restrictions as our temporary papers. We were still classified as Article 53: socially unreliable. We could not live in big cities or near borders, and we could not leave Vologda province. Our province was where the czar had sent scores of prisoners and where the Soviets did the same. I wondered if Article 53 existed in other provinces.

Our situation had improved considerably since our arrival in the province, but our official status had remained the same. In a way I was disappointed that we were not given passports without restrictions, not knowing that almost everyone had some sort of restriction placed on them. In truth the new passports did not change our lives at all. My father continued working for the slaughterhouse, my brother for the electric cooperative and my sister continued studying. My mother was as giving as ever, tending to the barber's redheaded daughter, cooking for the neighborhood and our landlady and sending packages to family members. We had what we needed.

May passed into June and the weather continued to improve. In spring we had some very hot days. Unfortunately I overdressed on one of these days and suffered from a tremendous thirst while working by the river. Normally I did not drink the river water unless it was boiled, but I saw the Russians lowering their faces to the surface and I could not resist. I drank the water and I became horribly sick. I suffered from terrible dysentery and there was blood in my stool. I was taken to the hospital for infectious diseases.

I received great treatment from the doctors and nurses there, and by the next morning I was already eating a little rice. For a while I thought the nurses were ignoring me, but I soon realized something was going on outside the hospital. Then I heard an announcement. This was Sunday 21 June 1941: the Soviet Union and Germany were at war.

It hit me like a lightning bolt on a sunny day. It was so unexpected and so horrible. I remembered all of our tragedies in Poland and the fear of repeating them caused my stomach to churn and my heart to ache. In the hallways of the hospital the women cried and the doctors hurried here and there in disarray. I looked out the window and saw a lot of movement. The infantry school was just down the road and already the boys were mobilized to action.

The hospital dismissed all the patients who were not contagious, including me. The streets of Cerepovec resembled an agitated beehive; swarms of people passed from one place to another with fear and sometimes hatred in their eyes.

Everyone was on guard. In a land where so many were arrested for conspiracy, people believed saboteurs existed everywhere. I ducked into the little Jewish cemetery and I prayed: 'Dear God, put your hand above us again and help us through this new period of evil.' I prayed in Yiddish as I always did, I do not know why.

At home my family was huddled around the radio listening to the official reports. The landlady and her daughter were very upset, the husband and father was a colonel in the army. Maria, our neighbor, was grinning to herself. You could see in her eyes how happy she was that the Soviets might be defeated. Eventually Molotov came on the radio. With a shaky voice he explained that the Germans had broken the pact. He called them double-crossers, and he asked that all of us fulfill our obligation to the Soviet Union. 'Our side is the right side. The enemy will be destroyed and victory shall be ours!'

My father's first reaction was to remind us that the Soviets had double-crossed the Polish by demobilizing their army, which could have been fighting the Germans on the Bug already. Still, we believed in the might of the Soviet army, despite the embarrassment of the Finnish war, because the alternative was unthinkable.

The city was in a state of confusion. We had already run out of bread and kerosene by the second day. I still felt a bit sick but I went to the power plant for work. Half of the workers were already drunk, many of them had been mobilized. There was fire in their eyes as they sang wild war songs and hugged each other goodbye.

The regular delivery of wood stopped completely and most of the plant's vehicles – trucks, boats and tractors – were taken away for the army. This was a power plant; it needed to stay running. Spiritow made most of the women responsible for hauling and cutting what little supply we had remaining, while the rest of us, including a few women, were sent up the river in a dilapidated rowboat to the forest to retrieve the barges. In essence, I was back to my old job.

The boat was huge but powered only by oars. It had been stored outside on sawhorses for a long time, and as a result there were many holes in the hull. The application of tar to the bottom of the vessel was not enough to keep the water out, so two or three people continually bailed while the rest of us rowed like Vikings. We were told the water would soon cause the wood to expand and seal the leaks, but this never occurred. The flies swarmed as they had before, so we lit fires throughout the craft to cover ourselves with smoke. Shloime and Yakov had a terrible time and, although I was already an expert on the river, it seemed to me we had been sent 500 years back in time.

For four days we rowed until we came to a landing holding stacks of pre-cut wood. Because of the shallow water, we were only able to load a small amount on the barge. I asked the skipper if he thought we should push the barge into deeper waters and build a bridge to it. He thought that was a great idea. The Russians, able to do anything, threw a perfectly arched bridge together in no time! We stacked the logs neatly until the barge was filled. The women with us prepared the meals, but otherwise they worked alongside the men. It took us about five days to finish the job.

We left the barge for another vessel to push downstream and headed back to Cerepovec. It was easier and faster rowing with the current and we arrived home in three days. We carried the remaining provisions and materials back to the power plant, hoping to head home shortly thereafter to get some rest. Unfortunately, we were stopped at the plant and told that we had all been mobilized for defense work.

We were given one hour to return to our homes to collect clothing and eating utensils. We were to reconvene at the port where boats would take us away to help with the national defense, that was all we knew. Yakov, Shloime and I ran home.

My family already knew I was to be mobilized. My mother did not have bread, but she made half a dozen pancakes from raw grains for me to take. She gave me a metal cup, a knife and a satchel to hold a gas mask. In that short time my family told me what horrors were happening to the Soviet army. I could not believe that the Germans were already beyond Minsk, I was sure they would have surrendered by now.

The minutes slipped by and I had to leave for the port;

Yakov and Shloime waited for me outside. Having no idea how long I would be gone worsened the familiar pain of separation. I did not want to leave my family again, but there was nothing I could do. I tearfully said goodbye and ran off with my friends. On the way we stopped at the little cemetery and I said, 'Boys, say a prayer.'

Not everyone at the port was selected for defense work; they sent about half of us home. Yakov, Shloime and I were taken, along with members of the water department and other cooperatives and put onto one of the big ferryboats, like the *Dzambul*. We headed to the Rybinsk Sea, which had changed since last I saw it. It looked completely different, bigger than before. This artificial sea was massive, covered with white-crested waves. From time to time you could see the steeple of an old church sticking out of the water. These were the last remains of hundreds of towns and villages.

A few nights later we reached a meeting point, a prisoners' camp, where we were combined with units from other cities along the river. In no time people were drunk. They were not drinking vodka, but aftershave, Kölnisch Wasser, which they forced me to drink too. It was awful, especially combined with a pickled cucumber. People were getting sick from the concoction, but I did not have too much, just enough to show my camaraderie. We slept on top of our belongings and woke to commands from the carriers.

We were loaded onto trains, thousands of us, and sent one after the other in the direction of Valdai. We passed through old towns like Bologoje and Biezeck, where very little had changed for centuries, and I thought to myself that Napoleon must have seen these same scenes. On the way we were passed by echelon after echelon of soldiers, sitting in their summer outfits and wearing pilot hats. After many days and nights we finally came to Valdai, the Switzerland of Russia, famous for its pristine lakes, virgin forests, monasteries and mountain resorts.

Many trainloads of people from other cities arrived in Valdai around the same time. From a transport from Jaroslav, I saw the brother of Buresh Weinstein, the boychik who had disappeared. We had a short conversation, but he did not know of his brother's whereabouts. His wife was a famous communist in Kalisz and had taken part in many hunger strikes while in prison. She was released when the war began, but, like our friend Yanik Stulman, she did not find her past endeavors helped her in any way in the Soviet Union. He departed with his echelon and I never saw him again.

We moved away from the train depot to a huge lake. I knew I had to take advantage of clean water whenever possible, I had had enough problems with hygiene in the past. I bathed in that lake, rubbing sand against my body to get as clean as possible. A few others followed my example and I told Yakov and Shloime to do the same. Shortly after, we were on the move, penetrating the forest and finally arriving in a huge meadow near a stream. Our first action was to dam the stream to create a water supply for our echelon.

We were divided into brigades. Ours consisted of workers from the power plant, the water department, the greenhouse and the staff of Cerepovec's newspaper, *The Communist*. Our head brigadier was Pytroff, a real Russian bear, filled with inner hatred and constantly wearing an icy smirk. He did not work. He was given orders from the planners and he made sure we fulfilled them.

We were supposed to build anti-tank trenches with a slanted front and a vertical back, stretching from one lake to another, but not penetrating the lake. The area around the trenches was to be mined so that with the first explosion the trenches would fill with water, stranding the tank brigade in the open meadows. On paper, the idea was brilliant, though why the Germans had to come through this particular meadow was beyond me.

We did not have tools initially, which was no huge surprise, but eventually we were given a slew of shovel heads – no handles. Without even thinking about it, the Russians cut off tree branches, shaved the ends and created handles for every shovel. Still, after all this time, I was amazed to see how capable the Russians were. We dug trenches the rest of the day in a zigzag fashion under Pytroff's supervision. We also made pillboxes out of wood and dirt, some holding cannons and some not.

The women from the greenhouse were responsible for our meals. The first night we convened around the huge cauldron and had a meeting. Looking around the meadow I could see perhaps 20 of the same meetings, the fires underneath the cauldrons glowing orange inside the circles of men. A young politruk, the head of the defense work and, in my estimation, a louse, gave us a fanciful speech describing the nobility of our work and our ultimate objective: to build a graveyard for the advancing Germans. Just as he was telling us what a foolproof strategy the planners had concocted, a German plane flew overhead and dropped a bomb near our campsite.

We scattered from our meeting and Yakov accidentally knocked over the cauldron. We scattered all over the place, but the plane disappeared and did not return. We reconvened and the politruk wisely decided we should spread out – a closer bomb would have taken out all of us.

Pytroff took us far away from the other brigades and ordered us to dig again, this time for our sleeping quarters. We did as we were told, but not too far down water began to fill the dugout. Instead of picking another location, we made a floor out of wood and little slots in the walls of the dugout for sleeping. We made a roof from branches and went to sleep.

For days we dug trenches, sticking to the plan by the letter. If a tree was in the way of our trench, we would dig out the tree. If the trench began to collapse, we would make a retaining wall out of branches. I thought our work was very impressive and we learned how to dig all day without getting tired. There was a rhythm shared by all of us. It had to be this way since many times the dirt from the trench would be passed up from the bottom, to someone in the middle, to someone at the top.

Removing trees was a danger because there would inevitably be a colony of red ants somewhere near by. They devoured us! They attacked so quickly, biting our genitals and getting into our hair. The only way to combat them was to jump into a lake. An attack from those ants hurt like hell.

On a day trip, Pytroff took us to the town of Valdai to build a pillbox. The town was abandoned, but the radios on the streets were blaring. When we finished we walked back to the forest through a village called Yimlgore, where a few residents still remained. They did not like us – they called us 'Defense Workers' in such a biting tone. Almost everything had been stolen from them since we had arrived, so it was easy to understand their contempt, but that was how it was. Outside the village was a lake with a beautiful monastery sitting on an island. I thought the scene was breathtaking, so I asked Pytroff what it was. He told me not to look over there, that it was the most horrible prison, the place where executions took place.

There was a hierarchy in the defense work, and on the bottom rung were the diggers. We slept in the dugout and survived on barely adequate provisions, but our situation was way below the politruk and the military personnel. They had a canvas tent equipped with lighting, into which the politruk invited the prettiest of the greenhouse girls to work as secretaries. The highest level, however, was that of the food supplier. The bakers and deliverers lived in a nearby village, stealing what they wanted and not coming near the hard, physical labor we undertook in the fields. The director of the food supplying operation was the head of the mill in Cerepovec, but he offered nothing but the minimum for the diggers in the fields. There were two refugees, Jewish boys from Lodz, working in a bakery out there, but when I approached them for something they also gave me nothing. Perhaps they were unable to help.

For two months we worked in the fields building the trenches and pillboxes, shifting from site to site depending on the planners' whims. By the end of August we had dug miles and miles of trenches, stretching as far as the eye could see. The nights were horrible because we could see the fire of burning villages steadily getting closer to where we were. We were very close to the action, but there was no front. From what we could tell, the Germans were approaching from every direction.

With miles of trenches, it was easy for German planes to spot us from the air. At night they would drop their bombs and all we could do was pray. Yakov, like a *misiganah*, would run into a lake when he heard the bombs coming. He really believed the Germans were too smart to bomb a lake. One night he ran straight into a toilet.

August turned to September and the situation was bad. It was turning very cold and not just at night. The tatters our clothing had become increased our discomfort. We had only been given one hour to prepare for our trip and we had not known we would be gone for so long. It was inevitable that we were not adequately supplied. We questioned everything about the defense work. Why did we do all this digging? Why did we do it here? Why were we shifted from place to place for seemingly no reason? To many of us, nothing made sense. Russia was enormous, we could make 300 miles of trenches and the Germans could still pick another route. It seemed clear to many of us that the planners had no idea what they were doing.

Hunger became an issue. We were given a piece of bread and soup, which was not nearly enough for the exertions we suffered through. It was crazy, but I cut my bread into three pieces to be eaten throughout the day. If we had eaten ten times as much bread we would still have been hungry, but I learned in Moraviny to challenge myself to keep my head above the horror. Unfortunately someone started to steal my bread. I would keep it in my pocket as I slept. In the morning it would be gone. Who was doing this? I slept near my friends, was it they? Did it fall out when I tossed and turned? I did not know. I felt sorry for whoever had sunk to that level, but I did not try to discover who it was.

An old man worked next to me in the trenches; he was over 70 years old. I never understood why they would pick such a man for this type of work. He was a good worker, like a machine, but he suffered from a lack of tobacco. I used to approach the army units that passed through our area and ask for pinches of tobacco, which they would give me with pieces of newspaper. I gave these cigarettes to the old man and in return he gave me his bread. I did not want to take it, but it would have offended his pride had I not.

I needed to do something about our hunger. I found out from the soldiers who laid mines that there were some abandoned fields from a local *kolchoz* filled with carrots, cabbage and potatoes. The problem was the fields were mined. A soldier told me I should take my first two steps very carefully, but after that I could walk normally; only the perimeters were mined. Once I got the idea into my head, nothing was going to stop me. I do not know how close I came to the mines, I only know we had vegetables in our soup from that day on. With my daily collection of vegetables and the now frequent robbery of the local villagers, we managed to eat enough.

An alarm went off at night and we were forced to relocate once again. It happened so fast that I did not really know what was going on. One of the women cooks had a satchel filled with stolen ingredients she had been hoarding. She, like the rest of us, was taken by surprise by the quick relocation. Her satchel was so heavy that she started to throw out ingredients one by one to lighten her load. Shloime was calmly putting them in his pockets as we walked behind her. That made us laugh.

We were stopped on the road by a supervisor from another group. 'Be quiet', he said, 'and lie down. The Germans are right in front of us.' Eventually we continued, but we all felt nervous, knowing that civilian defense workers were now interspersed with advancing German troops.

We cut down trees and left high stumps as we passed through untouched forest. I wrote with a pencil 'Hitler kaput!' on the exposed stumps. The Germans, in a similar vein, dropped leaflets from planes that read: 'Kill the Jews and commissars and come over to our side!' and 'Stupid girls, don't dig the trenches! our tanks can go through those holes!' If the Germans saw a bayonet stuck in the earth, they knew it to be the sign of defection and would let us in. Pytroff told us that anyone picking up a leaflet would be shot.

We shifted camp every few days and frequently came across Soviet soldiers in the forest. Whether or not we were still following a specific plan or if Pytroff was simply trying to keep us alive, I did not know. The Germans had penetrated the forest, but we did not know how many or if they knew about us. It was a nerve-racking time for me. I worried so much about the Germans that I did not sleep. In addition to my worries, I had a vermin problem again, making rest almost impossible. Instead I spent my nights exploring the villages and talking to Soviet soldiers in our area. Trying to analyze and understand the situation helped me deal with my fear.

My clothing was in tatters at this point, and my shoes had fallen apart from the shoveling. Fortunately I had been wearing peasant's underwear when I left Cerepovec, my regular trousers had disintegrated and they were all I had left. One night I asked a soldier if I could buy his coat. I saw that he had two, a short jacket underneath his greatcoat and that it was slightly shabby. He sold me the short coat and his trousers! In the morning Yakov and Shloime were stunned at the sight of my outfit. With a little mending and wire around the trouser legs, I was finally warm. I thanked God for protecting me again.

My shoes were so bad that I could no longer push the shovel into the earth. I told Pytroff that I needed to take a break from shoveling to try and fix them. I was wrapping metal wire around the bottoms of one when a civilian supervisor with a rifle came over to me. He pointed the barrel at me and asked why I was not working. I told him what I was doing, but he kept his gun trained on me. 'Do you have permission from your supervisor?' He asked. When I told him I had, he finally moved on. He reminded me of the *Volksdeutschen* in Moraviny. I wanted desperately to knock his head off with my shovel.

We were building a pillbox on the side of a lake near a railroad when a Russian officer wearing two pistols came over to us to ask how things were going. We told him we were getting cold, to which he replied that we should dig our dugout deeper. He came to us in a black car, the kind only the senior officials drove. When he left, someone told me that he was a Jew. We watched as he drove off. Out of the sky came a German plane, which dropped one perfectly aimed bomb, destroying the car.

This last attack finally prompted our leaders to withdraw the civilian forces from the area. We were divided and told to reconvene at a village called Big Nails. We came across a cow as we walked through the forest. Pytroff ordered us to grab the cow and bring it to the *banja* in the nearest village where we cooked it in an enormous cauldron. Eating the meat was magical, but I stupidly drank the water from a nearby lake. Immediately I was stricken with dysentery again.

The next day I tried to stay with the group, but Pytroff said I was slowing the group down. He was right. I was too weak to keep pace with the others and the sleet and snow had started falling. He sent me back to the *banja*, telling me he would mark the trees with three lines to indicate their path. If I survived, he told me, I could rejoin the group.

The *banja* was warm, which was nice, but I did not care. I was sure I was going to die soon, if not from the sickness then from the Germans. In the morning I felt awful, but I made myself search for food. I figured if there was a village nearby, there were probably crops. Sure enough, I found a field of carrots. I dug out a few and washed them in the lake. I felt almost immediately better; they must have fortified my stomach. I stayed one more night in the *banja* before I searched for my group. On the way I had an urgent bowel movement, after which I felt healthy. The next day I found them in Big Nails, and Yakov, Shloime and I had a nice reunion.

My stomach felt better, but I was terribly hungry. A carriage carrying bread from a local village came to our campsite. A stupid impulse came to me – why not steal a loaf of bread? When the drivers were occupied with the horses, I sneaked behind them and stashed a loaf under my jacket. You could get a bullet for this! I knew it was a death sentence but I did it anyway. I walked off and found a private place where I finished half the loaf in one sitting. I had not eaten bread for almost a week and my body was trembling. A few hours later I finished the rest. I saved my life while endangering it, but these are the things we do when we are hungry.

For some reason our next move was to the front lines. Once again our faith in our organizers was anything but firm. In no time we found ourselves huddled in trenches as a German bombardment and Soviet counter-offensive ensued. I saw, for the first time, the Soviet weapon called a *katiuszas*. It was a device that hurled a walking wall of fire, produced a menacing roar that alone would scare any enemy. I had no idea how well the army was doing; I was too afraid to ask. Around midnight, however, came the order: 'Save yourselves any way you can!' It was a full-scale retreat.

I stayed close to Pytroff because I figured he knew how to survive. I carried my shovel as a weapon as we headed down a main road. For some reason the Soviet trucks in front of us were hurling bread, shoes and clothing into the road. I picked up a pair of shoes and continued running. Pytroff turned into the forest and I followed. Many others came with us too, but not everyone from our brigade. For a while we stayed quiet, not moving from our cover in the forest.

Eventually we moved through the forest when the noise of the attack had diminished. We came to a village and saw the aftermath of destruction, which had left every bridge, every home and the railroad station in shambles. Initially I thought it was the result of German bombs, which it may have been, but then I remembered Stalin's speech from mid-July. Over the loudspeakers in the fields we had heard him so clearly, with that thick Georgian accent and quiet, broken voice, appeal to the Russian fighting spirit. He called us brothers and sisters as he recounted the horrible things that had befallen us. He told us Hitler wanted to destroy Russia, but it was up to us to stop him. He wanted villagers to burn their houses when they retreated, to destroy the equipment left behind and to take their cattle with them. He encouraged us to form guerilla partisan units to fight in the forest. We listened so attentively we could hear the clink of his glass when he took sips of water. Perhaps some of the destruction was a result of this appeal.

We moved quietly through the forest from village to village, until we came across an untouched, populated village. The inhabitants were from an old religious sect called the Old Believers. We asked them if they were not afraid of the Germans. They said the Germans would not touch them. They were very friendly to us, letting us eat their food and drink from their cups, but we could not stay in their homes at night. While in someone's home during the day I came across a mirror. I whirled around to see who was behind me, but realized I was fooled by my own reflection. I looked crazy, like an animal. I found some soap and washed myself and I shaved with a knife. It was not the greatest grooming job, but at least I was clean.

We left the village the next day and walked through the forest, keeping our brigade parallel to the train tracks. The destruction became less massive as we progressed, though there were still pockets of strategic demolition. We came across a railroad station called Radionofka, which was also the name of a man in our brigade. A German bomb had just hit the station and they were still fighting the flames when we arrived. We retreated again to the forest, but we were sure we would soon jump a train heading back to Cerepovec.

Around this time I asked Pytroff why we had not formed ourselves into a guerilla movement to fight the Germans in the forest. I sincerely wanted to do something like this. He was angered by the suggestion, calling me stupid and naive. He said our cooperation with the Red Army would be the worst thing, even as guerillas. 'Once they put their hands on you, Genasha, you are no longer a person.' It was true. Even if we fought independently we would eventually be absorbed into the Red Army, which amounted to a death sentence.

We continued walking through the forest and sleeping near the tracks. One morning we heard the vibrations of a train. We came out of the forest to see a Soviet two-man, hand-powered rail car on an inspection pass along the tracks. They were as shocked to see us as we were to see them. They trained their rifles on us, not knowing if we were spies or saboteurs. Ultimately we convinced them that we were a lost civil defense unit, searching for transport away from the front. They continued down the tracks and we returned to the forest, just as a German attack started a short distance away.

Through the dirt roads of the forest passed a convoy of treaded, Soviet transport vehicles new from the factory and carrying scores of soldiers. We saw the German planes destroy four of these mammoths, it was horrifying. We scampered down the line of the railroad still under the cover of the forest, but there was a feeling that our luck would soon run out. The attacks were getting closer and closer to our brigade.

Later that day we arrived at Biezec station, a historic town fairly close to Bologoje. It was filled with people stinking of hunger, dirt and fear. There we waited for hours. Finally a military transport train rumbled into the station, carrying infantry and tanks. It was heading towards home. Pytroff somehow arranged passage on the train for our brigade. Snow had begun to fall heavily, so I found a sheltered place underneath one of the tanks. Shloime and Yakov sat separately to lessen the odds of both being blown up by a German bomb. We thought we were heading home.

I thought we would be safe for a while because the Germans would not be sending bombers into the air in such heavy snow. It was a stupid thought, just like Yakov's belief that the Germans would not bomb a lake. Immediately after this false realization I heard screaming and I saw people scattering away from the train. The Germans were right above us. I jumped out from underneath the tank and ran off the train onto a road, trying to get into the forest. There was so much confusion with the snow falling, the roar of the planes, the whistling of the bombs and the yelling of the passengers, that I found myself tangled up in some fallen telegraph wires, staring at the sky. I was praying, 'Shema Ysrael! Shema Ysrael! Shema Ysrael!' as I watched the planes systematically bomb the train wagon by wagon. I saw an officer with a pistol and a few soldiers with rifles shooting at the sky. They were cut down quickly. I freed myself and ran into the forest. The others were still close because we were surrounded by wetlands, there was nowhere to go. We attempted to stay out of sight and fortunately the planes left after destroying the train.

We followed the tracks to Bologoje station. There were so many refugees there, a repulsive scene so typical of war. Some people had been waiting for days. No one knew when the next train would come, or if there would be space for refugees to board. We waited together for a day and a half before a train pulled into the station. Pytroff again got us on board and we headed towards Rybinsk. It occurred to us that the river might freeze before we caught a ferry back to Cerepovec. It was already snowing almost daily in Bologoje and we were heading further north. By train, the return home would be slower and longer. At the rate the Germans were pressing into Russia, this would be a dangerous journey.

In Rybinsk Pytroff showed our documents to some military personnel and he was able to procure some soup for us. Still we were hungry, so I went out to find something to eat. There was a restaurant near the port, where officers dined with tablecloths and fine silverware. A waitress came out of the restaurant and caught a glimpse of me. She asked me if I wanted some bread. I looked at her like she was an angel, like she was today offering me a fistful of diamonds. Of course I said yes and followed her to the back of the restaurant. She gave me a whole bag of torn-up bread. I gave half of the bag to my brigade and sold the other half. I returned to her with the money and bought some more. I purchased four loaves of beautiful bread. Shloime, Yakov and I ate one loaf immediately and saved one to share later. The last two, I insisted, were for my family.

Thanks be to God, the last boat came in, already equipped with icebreakers. Just as we were about to board the ferry, the air-raid siren sounded and we threw ourselves to the ground. Fortunately the planes never came, so we entered the boat with just the bread and the *kipjatok*. We saw no more planes on the trip back to Cerepovec. We arrived at night, exhausted and hungry, but safe.

Shloime, Yakov and I made our way to Niekrasowa Street. The city was dark; the electricity was shut off at night as a defense against the German planes. The streets were filled with soldiers but very few civilians. The cold and the darkness, combined with hostility and fear, made Cerepovec seem like a wild animal's lair. We cautiously continued home, stopping by the little Jewish cemetery to say a prayer of thanks.

I had walked out of my house months ago, not knowing where or what I would be doing, and here I was at my family's door. Can you imagine our reunion? It was so emotional for me to find that everyone was still at home and safe. My mother and sister had been going to the power plant every day to ask when I would return. They were told I would come back shortly, so my family actually expected me. It was only by chance that I returned at all, but I saw no need to tell this to my mother.

I was beyond dirty. I was filth-ridden and covered with vermin. I lied to my family, telling them I was not used to sleeping in beds, that I preferred the floor. I was very afraid of infesting our apartment with parasites. I had lice and gnats everywhere – in my armpits, my ears and my eyebrows – everywhere. In the *banja* I shaved off every bit of hair I could, but still I was infested. Rosa at the pharmacy gave me a powder and some ointment, which finally cleared things up. When I did try sleeping in a bed, I could not sleep!

I did not have many days of rest before I was enlisted into more civil defense work, this time for the city of Cerepovec. The German front continued to press forwards, it was only 100 miles away. All able hands were called upon to dig trenches around Cerepovec. It was freezing, exposing your face was dangerous and digging a trench a near impossibility. We had to light fires to warm the dirt enough for our shovels to penetrate the ground.

This cold was brutal, but the Germans also had to deal with it. They were experiencing some minor setbacks during the winter, but the issue of Leningrad was already settled. As we dug trenches, I could see in the distance huge transport planes flying low over the horizon. They were bringing food and supplies to Lake Ladoga, and they returned with thousands of women and children, refugees from Leningrad.

As far as the refugees were concerned, our greatest worry was whether or not we would be drafted into the Red Army. The perception was that everyone died in the army, which was not too far from the truth. We questioned whether they would select the refugees, since some of us were listed as Jewish and others Polish. In addition, there was the issue of Article 53; would they select socially unreliable citizens? As it happened, our questions were answered when a mobilization card came for me.

I half expected the card, but I was still devastated, it was like a loaded gun taking aim at me from afar. I did not let my family come with me to the military base, which was nicknamed 'the Meat Grinder'. As I waited for my name to be called, I made friends with two refugees, Shimon Pelta, a Jew from Lodz and the younger brother of the two Jewish bakers from the defense work and Dolgovitch, a Catholic Pole from Vilna. Dolgovitch looked like a greyhound, he was skinny and tall with a long, distinguished nose. He was a good runner and an excellent thief. We spoke guardedly in the waiting room; each of us knowing the atmosphere was heavy with potential death.

We saw men go into the selection room and come out with their eyes glazed over. When a man was selected for the Red Army, his natural defense was to detach himself from the reality he knew. Women were wailing outside the building and I was getting increasingly nervous about my interview.

Of the three of us they called me in first. I was first brought to a doctor, then a military officer and finally a political commissar, who looked at my documents and saw the Article 53. He asked me suspiciously how and why I had come to Cerepovec. I saw something dangerous in his eyes and was unsure how to respond. I went to a map on the wall and showed with my finger the path we had taken, but he did not like that. He told me he was selecting men for an elite paratrooper force and that I should wait outside with the others for now.

Selection into a paratrooper squadron was guaranteed death and none of us wanted anything to do with it. I told the other two and somehow they managed to perplex the commissar as well. The three of us were sent home and told to return the next day.

We returned every day for the next three days, which was incredibly hard for my family until eventually I convinced the recruitment staff to call us when we were needed and not to have us return every day. They placed white tickets into our military books and we went home. We were officially in the reserve forces,the bullet had been successfully dodged.

As far as the power plant knew, I was officially mobilized and therefore freed from Molotov's Law. Although I began work there under the agreement that I could leave, I had not dared to try before now. Since I stopped attending classes and worked as many hours as the full-time staff, I had assumed any earlier attempt to leave would have been met with resistance. I had not been paid for a long time, so I figured I would pick up my final check and say goodbye to the staff. I placed a copy of Stalin's book, *The Questions of Leninism*, under my arm; the girls in the office were impressed by what I was reading. I met the director and picked up my check, not mentioning that I was only in the reserves.

I did not really know what to do next, but Dolgovitch, the thief, knew where to go. He convinced Pelta and me that we should get work at the fire department. His reasoning was simple – they did nothing and they were given bread. 'Why not?' we thought, and agreed to meet the next day.

*Note*

1. A *kombinat* is a factory that makes many different kinds of products, rather than just one. For example a bread (*cheleb*) *kombinat* made all kinds of food products, not just bread, but was still called *chelbo kombinat* (literally the bread combination factory).

# 13 My Soviet life

In the morning Dolgovitch, Pelta and I went to the fire station. It was not far from the Sovietski Prospekt, a short walk, in fact, from the headquarters of the NKVD. The station comprised a series of brick buildings, probably built in the 1920s, and looked to be as solid as any set of structures in Cerepovec. We walked into the garage housing the fire trucks and the big engines, then through a leather-insulated door opening into the main office. I thought the leather must have kept the office quite warm in the winter, as well as quiet when necessary.

Inside we introduced ourselves to the secretary, Dusha Samsonova, and the bookkeeper, Maria Gregorgivna Kusnyetsova. When we told them, in our heavily accented Russian, that we wanted to work in the department, they broke into laughter.

The situation at the fire department had become a joke to them. In years past, generation after generation worked in the station; it was a tightly knit collective of family members and friends. Retired firefighters stayed on the payroll as wood stackers or custodians, while their sons and daughters took on the responsibility of fighting blazes. Our arrival, three clearly foreign and disheveled men from the street, epitomized the state of affairs at the station. It had become a halfway house for promising young men awaiting their call-up from the Red Army and was staffed by inadequately trained firefighters and military cast-offs. We were humorous to them not only because our appearance was diametrically opposed to the prototypical firefighter of old, but also because they knew they were going to hire us.

The fire department was under the umbrella of the internal security force of our district, the NKVD. At the time of our arrival, the fire chief had been mobilized and so the station was under the local supervision of one of three shift leaders, a man lacking the authority to hire new personnel. A call was made to the NKVD headquarters, specifically to the fire inspector of the whole district, Rabinin. In time we were given applications to fill out, but since I was the only one who could even moderately write Russian, I filled one out for all three. This sufficed, and we had new careers.

We toured the facility and learned what we could of the system in which we would soon work. There was always a crew on duty. Each shift lasted eight hours and was supervised by a shift leader. Dolgovitch, Pelta and I were put on different shifts; a man named Vesilovsky led mine.

The garage occupied most of the first floor of the central building. On one side there was a large common room and an eating room, on the other was the office, a small library and an auditorium. On the second floor there were living quarters for officers and married firefighters. Two dormitories flanked this building, one for single men and the other for single women.

The epicenter was the office, in which an instrument built by the German company Siemens and Halska was situated. When a fire alarm was sounded somewhere in the city, this device alerted not only the shift on duty, but also the two adjacent dormitories, the NKVD and the water department. A ticket discharged from the machine with the fire's location and the engines roared to the scene. Other stations in outlying cities still relied on the eyesight of a surveyor atop a wooden lookout tower, or a telephone call from a citizen – the Cerepovec station was state of the art.

The first few weeks were difficult for me because there was so much to learn. What Dolgovitch had thought, that we would have very little to do, was totally wrong – there was much to do and much to learn. Still, I loved it. Every day I knew I understood more and more of the processes of fire fighting.

My shift leader, Vesilovsky, snarled at me during drills and kept after me at all times. He was rugged, with missing fingers and steely eyes, and I learned of his habits of womanizing and drinking. In the first few days he made me do countless menial tasks, like standing guard for hours after my shift had ended and bailing out the basement where a steam heater had burst. One day during drills, someone had to climb an old church and be lowered down by ropes. Vesilovsky volunteered me. He made the others stop my descent a few times, once while I dangled upside down. He did not know that I had done much more treacherous things off the side of the boat during storms. He asked me with a wicked grin how I liked the drill, to which I replied 'It was nothing special.' I had little respect for him, but this did not worry me, his pushing made me learn all the more quickly.

Assigned numbers designated duties at a fire scene. Initially I was number six, the liaison between the crew and the leader. At all times I had to remain close to Vesilovsky with a storm lamp, ready to dash away with a command for the firefighters manning the hoses or inside the building. Later I learned all the duties.

One evening a warehouse caught fire on Sovietski Prospekt. The blaze was easy to control and soon we were assessing the damage. The firefighter, including Vesilovsky, stole things, and he told me to take something. Even though I knew this could get me in trouble I took a packet of wooden matches. Vesilovsky did not know that the NKVD had sent an inspector to the warehouse on a motorbike. He had witnessed the thievery and called his superiors. When we returned to the station, Rabinin was there. He lined us up and came directly to me, demanding that I empty my pockets. Seeing the stolen matches, he asked who had instructed me to take them. I told him I had acted alone. Assuming that the matches would have been soaked by the firefighters and of no use to anyone, I took them for the storm lamp I carried even though they did not belong to the department. Because I did not incriminate anyone else, the others accepted me. Still, the thievery was known and written up, mostly comically, in the fire department's newsletter, *The Alarm*.

Overall, it was a very good situation for me. I continued to live at home, but I was given bread and soup at the station. This was a relief for my family, since I represented another mouth to feed and supplies continued to dwindle because of the war.

The station was filled with nice, young people, clearly raised as Soviets and very patriotic. The women were very well educated and very friendly to us. In addition to the secretary, Dusha Samsonova, and Maria Gregorgivna Kusnyetsova, the bookkeeper, there were three younger women. Maria Gregorgivna's daughter Vera, her niece Rima and Nina, a telephone girl unfortunately in love with Vesilovsky, who treated her badly. Vera had studied to be a doctor and Rima a teacher, but the war had forced the closure of both their schools.

The boys were aggressive and rough, but polite. We did not get to know many of them because they were pulled into the Red Army so quickly. Those who remained were often crippled and bitter. In the evenings, when a shift was over and the engines had been cleaned, the young people would sit around the common room singing and dancing to Soviet music. When the occasional Russian tune was played, you could sense a change in their demeanor, a lessening of the tension in their eyes and I felt that this was the way they really wanted it.

In my free time, I sought refuge in the little library tucked behind the office. Nobody, it seemed, ever went in there apart from the cleaning staff; the room was not even heated. To me it was a gold mine. There were periodicals, like *Pravda*, dating back to before Russia's entry into the war. It was comical how different the party line had been then. In a matter of days, the British and French evolved from slime to honorable comrades, while it suddenly became clear that the Nazis had committed horrible atrocities throughout the occupied territories. It was all so transparent.

There were countless technical manuals and fire-fighting journals, which I studied over and over again. There were lists of statistics and performance records from different stations in the region and different individuals. I devoured any information I could about fire fighting, including the mechanics of the trucks, the different materials needed to fight different fires and the necessary precautions every warehouse, home and factory needed to take for preventative action. In time, I knew more than the shift leaders and more than the crewmembers. Vesilovsky could no longer answer my questions.

Ivan Ivanovitch Karavyeff was the utilities and supply manager for the station, as well as being in charge of the alarm system. He walked around the station with a book under his arm, looking like a good Jew heading to the synagogue. I asked him to show me what he was carrying. It was *The Short Course on the History of the Communist Party*, with Chapter Four written by Stalin. I was familiar with the book – Chapter Four had been smuggled into Poland on cigarette paper. Karavyeff could not understand theoretical Marxism, nor could he fully grasp the ideas of enacted Marxism. I asked him for the book and I studied it. It was a compilation of falsified information, a revisionist history book not even mentioning Trotsky or Bukharin. The book glorified Stalin and made me sick. Still, I explained everything to Karavyeff in a simple way and he was flabbergasted. News about this spread throughout the department. My stock was rising.

We were deep into the winter of 1941–42, the coldest on record. There was not yet a marked deceleration of the German advance – their delays had been attributed to the cold rather then the Russian defenses. Life was cheap in the Soviet Union and people treated each other poorly and without respect. We were surrounded by death and dismay, but still my family did what it could to help others in the neighborhood.

We tried to take care of so many households whose fathers and brothers had been mobilized. We were still a complete family unit and thus a haven of normality among the refugees; just being around us helped some people deal with their situation. In addition, and more importantly, we had an easier time getting food because of my father's job at the cooperative. We shared all we had with our closest friends, among them the family of Shloime Ackerman, who had been mobilized in the early winter.

Before he was mobilized, Shloime had brought his two brothers and their families to Cerepovec. His brother Shoal was a midget and a butcher and my father helped him join the butchers' cooperative. Shoal, who was not very clever, was caught stealing and sentenced to six years in prison. My mother tried to take care of his wife and daughter in his absence.

Unfortunately Shoal's wife went mad. She suffered from a disease none of us had seen before, her skin turned black and her body and mind wasted away. One night my father went into their apartment and took her child. Subsequently, Shoal's wife climbed our woodpile and banged on our window, demanding we give her back her child. My father went to her and said, 'Go home, woman, the girl stays with us.' It seemed callous, but it was the only way to save the girl. Within a few days she had died, her skin covered in blackness.

I tried to report her death to the authorities, but I never worked out where to go. The war had brought so much disorganization to the city administration and people were dying so rapidly, there was no way to keep track of all the names. We had to take care of her body properly, so I put her on a little sled and went to the general cemetery.

The scene at the cemetery was ghastly. There were so many people, hundreds, lying dead and stacked on top of one another. Mostly these were refugees from Leningrad whose health had been ruined before they escaped the city. They were so malnourished that the act of eating was such a shock to their systems, it killed them. Their clothes had been rifled through and anything of value had been taken, even the fillings from their teeth. The ground was too frozen to bury them, so they would remain there through the winter.

I saw a man digging a grave on the other side of the cemetery. He had made a fire and thawed the earth enough to break through the frozen layer. I went to him with a bottle of vodka my mother made me bring and asked him if he could make the hole big enough for two. He did, and in this way we gave her the best burial we could. In time her young daughter went to live with another relative.

Things continued to worsen for all of us. The bread supply for Cerepovec was cut off entirely. Instead, each citizen was allotted a certain amount of raw grain. The queues for food were insane with people sometimes being trampled to death. When I was on the day shift, I was able to get into the queue at three or four o'clock in the morning, taking not only my family's bread cards, but a handful of our neighbors' as well. The grain was not passed out until nine o'clock, but such was the struggle. I learned to stay about ten feet away from the doors. Closer than that and you would be pushed to the side by the onrushing crowd. The trick was to situate yourself so the crowd would push you right in. It was mayhem every morning. The young punks would climb onto the crowd, literally walking on the tops of peoples' heads to get to the grain. One morning I wore a low-quality blue, Russian sweater. Despite the cold, I sweated so much in the crush that my body turned blue!

Were our neighbors happy with the grain I brought back for them? On some level maybe, but you would not have thought it from the bickering I put up with upon my return. It got so bad – 'He got more, I got less' – that I built a set of scales.

We tried anything to procure food. My mother and I had the idea that I could take vodka, sewing needles and buttons to outlying villages and exchange them for food. I made snowshoes out of wire, wood and rope and headed out with a satchel. In the first village I was able to trade some vodka for some potatoes, but most of the houses did not need what I carried. I came to a second village and knocked on the door of a house. Three drunken, burly men sat at a table and peered at me with murderlust in their eyes. Fortunately I was wearing part of my fireman's uniform and thus looked partially official. I asked, trying to hide my accent, where I could find the head of the *kolchozin*. They believed my lie and gave me directions. I retreated from that village and headed home, telling my mother when I returned that this was not such a good idea.

Cerepovec resembled a front-line city most of the time. Alarms rang out a few times a week, alerting the local defense units to their stations. When these rang, I would have to run to the fire station, while overhead cannons fired at German planes. The noise was deafening and then it would be gone. By the time I arrived at the station, inevitably the alarm had finished and I would sleep in the common room until my shift.

At the station, in the city and in the homes there was general gloom. The number of casualties listed daily never seemed to decrease, as names of deceased husbands, cousins and brothers were returned to the residents of Cerepovec. The tragedy was personal, people, like the custodian at the station who lost her husband and niece on the same day, carried a depression born out of internal anguish, not just collective misery.

Every day at the station we had a political hour in the auditorium, put together by a politruk sent to us by the Communist Party. Her name was Olga Ivanovna Pavlova, an evacuator from Leningrad. She had dark skin, almost black eyes and a long, birdlike nose; to me she looked half gypsy. She read from the daily newspaper and marked the progress of the German army with red pins on a large map on the wall. The front-line correspondents, Ilya Ehrenberg for instance, wrote about the atrocities the Nazis had committed on the citizens of the Ukraine, like leaving the tortured and lifeless body of a suspected arsonist, a young girl, in the center of a small town for three days to set an example. The Ukrainians, some of whom greeted the Germans as liberators with flowers and bread, had felt the sting of Nazi cruelty and knew their freedom was lost. These stories, the horrible conduct of the Nazis and the very real threat to their survival impelled the Russians to look at the Red Army less as an instrument of Stalin's aggression and more as the fighting soul of the Russian people.

I had been in the Soviet Union a long time, yet only recently had I been able to discuss freely my past experiences with the Nazis. During one of the daily sessions Olga Pavlova asked us to make comments. I stood up and told my story. No one had heard such things, no one at the station knew what I had gone through. I did not tell them what troubles we had at the border, nor would I. Instead I stuck in a barbed comment: 'Thanks to the Soviet Union, we are alive.' That Pavlova noticed me and she reported me.

The girls in the office had seen me reading in the library and they knew I had helped Karavyeff to understand Chapter Four, now they knew my past and they started to be very interested in meeting me. I was invited to a birthday party at Maria Gregorgivna's house, where Vera and her cousin Rima also lived and would be in attendance.

I was very nervous as I dressed at home, this was the first time I was to be inside a Russian's home as a guest, not as a refugee. They lived in an apartment on the top floor of a large wooden house. It was beautiful. It had electricity, wallpaper, a leather sofa, old books and journals from the czarist period and nice lamps. I was fascinated by the books, but I let the girls occupy my attention. In addition to Vera and Rima, there were Vera's two younger sisters, Tanya, the baby, and Nadya, a real Russian beauty, not in appearance, but in her temperament. Rima flirted with me quite a bit, calling me Ghenrik, instead of my Russian name Genasha, because she thought it sounded more sophisticated – she would have called me Henrik, but in Russian there is no 'h'. I had a nice evening, even though I was laughed at because I could not drink with the Russian men.

Later, on a trip to the cinema set up by the political and cultural activity commission, I sat between Rima and Vera, unaware that they were already fighting over me. In truth I was curious about Vera. We had had a few conversations about Poland and current events and I had found her very warm and caring. Still, how could I consider a relationship with a Russian girl?

The station still lacked a fire chief. The shift leaders, like Vesilovsky, did their best to maintain order, but they enjoyed some privileges. Rabinin came to the station infrequently, usually sitting in the fire chief's office and meeting with some of the staff. On one of his visits, I was called in to meet him.

I had never been inside that office and I was immediately fascinated by the map on the wall indicating all the water points in the city of Cerepovec. Rabinin was seated at the desk and motioned for me to sit across from him. For a man in charge of so much, he struck me as very sympathetic and mild-mannered. His gray hair, soft eyes and gentle smile made me feel comfortable. There were portraits of Stalin and Lenin on the walls, as well as pictures of the head of the NKVD, Lavrenti Pavlovitch Beria – Stalin's most notorious henchman. Rabinin pointed to Beria's picture and asked me if I knew who he was. I knew how to answer these questions, so

I told him who he was and how well he ran his organization. Of course, I thought he was the biggest bandit in the Soviet Union next to Stalin, but I kept this to myself. Rabinin told me that they had heard a lot of good things about me and that it was time to make me a leader of a truck.

I did not know how to respond other than with honesty. Of course I wanted the promotion, but I did not know if I would be able to do it. I was afraid my Russian would not be sufficient in a time of emergency. Rabinin assured me that with all the reading I had done and with the help of the office girls, I would be fine.

He kept me talking for more than an hour, asking me about Poland and my social background. I told him that my father was a butcher who had organized a union, not, however, that he had owned his own store. I felt compelled to tell him everything about the Germans, the forest, the boat, being released to study and my happiness with my new job at the fire department. He said that the Soviet Union was built by people who wanted to learn, study and work; it was built by people like me. He wrote out an order: Genasha Josevitch Skorupa is now a leader of a truck. It was my first promotion.

With this promotion, albeit resulting in only a minimal increase in stature, I became even more desirable to Vera. I sensed how attached she had become when the entire station was mobilized to defense work. She came to me in tears, telling me she would pray that they did not select me. I was lucky – Dolgovitch, Pelta and I were not enlisted. Upon our return, Vera came to me again in tears, this time of happiness. It was strange to me, this Russian sentimentality as I was under the impression that there was no room for it in Soviet life. I was confused and touched by her emotion. I was feeling something for her.

Two shift leaders, including Vesilovsky, were mobilized for defense work. I was chosen to replace Vesilovsky and so in just a matter of days I had been promoted again.

Finally our station was sent a fire chief, a man from Vologda. He was a military man, very strict and in love with the pistol he carried on his belt. He was also a drinker. These two passions of his came together disastrously one evening, resulting in his shooting out all the lights in his upstairs apartment. We reported this to Rabinin and the next day he was gone.

It was a strange process, getting a new fire chief. For some reason, a man in that position would not get punished or demoted for his actions, but moved to another station instead. There was always a period of curiosity when a new chief came. Where was he before and what did he do? Our replacement fire chief was a man named Aleksayeff and he came to us from Beloz Orsk. He was a womanizer, that was his crime.

I liked Aleksayeff immediately. He was small and energetic, like a rabbit, constantly moving around the station with a smile and a lot of enthusiasm. He lived with his wife and two children in an upstairs apartment and they all helped bring a new spirit to the station.

Aleksayeff understood the psychological toll the war was taking on most of the staff and designed programs to alleviate some of the grief. One of the first things he did was ask Maria Gregorgivna to put together a theatrical group. Soon we were all acting, including Aleksayeff, which was a much-needed distraction. He also reinstituted the practice of citywide preventive fire fighting, something I had read about but never experienced.

Preventive work consisted of inspecting residences and commercial spaces, determining if structures met the fire code, giving instructions as to how to bring a building up to standard, and returning later to ensure compliance. If somebody did not make the necessary changes, we had the right to levy a fine. This, in monetary terms, was no big deal, but to have a record of negligence was not something a factory director ever wanted.

As a shift leader I was responsible for not only the performance of my crew during drills and actual fires, but also the preventive work for certain geographic areas of the city. We three shift leaders signed an Agreement of Socialist Competition. It was a friendly challenge to see who could accomplish the most within a month. I wanted my shift to do the best work and we did.

Galina Yefimiva was assigned to my shift. She came to the fire department at the same time as Aleksayeff, though through different channels. Her parents had both died of hunger during the siege of Leningrad while she was lucky enough to escape on a train for the wounded. She was enlisted in the army but, when tuberculosis was discovered in her knee, she was released to the Communist Party and subsequently sent to our department in Cerepovec. She was a tall girl with slightly slanted eyes and pockmarked skin; I thought she looked half Mongol. She was ugly and she smelled badly, but she was incredibly bright and a genius at painting and drawing. I pitied her, but her thinking intrigued me. She was unwaveringly patriotic, perhaps the only true Soviet I had met.

Both Galina and I latched on to the challenge and worked tirelessly to make our shift the best. Her maps were impeccable and I inspected factory after factory, mostly during the hours we were not on duty. At the end of the month we had a party to celebrate what we had accomplished and we discovered our shift was far and away the most productive. Aleksayeff was thrilled. He declared he was opening an office for Galina and me to continue our efforts.

In a short while I had written pamphlets, given lectures and evaluated almost the entire city's propensity for fire. I kept a list of how many ladders, shovels and water bottles were stored in each house and I began sending memos to the NKVD describing how the city could better protect itself against a massive fire. I had found my strength and Aleksayeff continued to encourage me.

Vera and I, meanwhile, were becoming more and more involved. I am not really sure when it started, I do not have any recollection of deciding it was a good idea, but somehow we were together. She was happy with the recognition I received for the preventive work, but she was jealous of the time I spent with Galina. I told her not to worry because I did not have the slightest interest in Galina. She explained that she was not worried about me.

Nuchem worked diligently for the electric company, performing maintenance on the propaganda loudspeakers and learning more and more about the profession in general. He was very talented in this area. Unfortunately this made him an ideal candidate for the Red Army's mobile radio personnel corps. It was a tragedy for the whole family – our most beloved Nuchem was mobilized.

He was enlisted and immediately sent on a 70-mile march to a training base in Kushchuba. This was indicative of the state of the Red Army at that time; there were no vehicles available to transport them. We did not know were he was, only that he had been mobilized. Finally a letter arrived describing the march and including one sentence in Polish: 'I haven't seen Helfgott for some time.'

We were heartbroken. Helfgott was one of the bakers from Kalisz and Nuchem was telling us that he was starving. We decided that I would go to Kushchuba, carrying with me breads and meats, to see how he was getting along.

Aleksayeff gave me permission, probably because I had been such an excellent example to the others up until now. Going to see a younger brother at a training base for no other reason than to give him some food could have been seen as an unpatriotic action. I was lucky he was so friendly. My mother gave me a full satchel of things my father brought back from the cooperative and things she saved from the family supply. It contained salami, bread and the pancakes she made out of raw grain. I took this, kissed them goodbye and went to the train station.

I could not get a ticket. Every train headed in that direction was for military use only. I wondered why, if that was the case, they had not transported Nuchem by train. When I got one of the guards alone, I gave him some salami and he let me sneak between two cars. Thankfully the train slowed down at Kushchuba and I was able to jump off without injuring myself.

I walked to the training base carrying the letter my brother had written. I was stopped immediately by two guards. They demanded to know what I was doing at the base. I showed them the letter and asked if I could see my brother. In return, they asked what was in the bag. There was plenty of food and they wanted food, so they told me to wait in the guardhouse until morning. For this, I gave them each some meat.

The guardhouse was cold and filthy. Because I had the satchel of food, I was forced to fight off mice and rats throughout the night. I prayed that I would be able to see Nuchem in the morning, which never seemed to arrive.

Eventually the guards returned and brought me through the base to meet my brother. When I saw him my heart sank. He looked worse than he had done in Moraviny. His cheeks were sunken and his neck was frighteningly thin. There was so much space between his tunic and his skin. I gave him the food and we talked.

He told me how horrible the conditions were at the base. They had very little to eat and what they did have was of poor quality, making his stomach burn through the night. The officers were mistreating them and they were learning to fight with wooden rifles. What would happen on the battlefields was a huge cause for worry.

Something had to be done; I could see how he would die in the Red Army. I was going crazy thinking of plans to get him out of there. I considered stealing him out at night and running away, but this would surely end in our deaths and our family's imprisonment. I wanted to switch places with him, but this he would not do. I told Nuchem I could get him false documents from a firefighter's school in Uzbekistan, demanding, by order of the NKVD, that he return immediately. Nuchem was not ready for this, he could not play along with any deceit.

In the end I left him there. There was nothing I could do. I sneaked between two cars on the train and slumped down, a defeated and destroyed person, and sobbed heavily. I feared I would never see him again. One month later he was taken to the front.

Home was not the same any more. My mother cried all the time, a slow, but constant sob causing a perpetual tear to stream down her cheek. She was so upset, we all were. My father walked through the house dejected and ashamed, somehow blaming himself for the tragedy. Henya and I had to play the role of the optimistic Soviet during the day, but crumbled when we went home.

I was in two separate worlds: one in which tragedy and

history tore out my heart and one in which I learned and lived something totally new and exciting every day. Vera clung to me at the station and I appreciated her affection.

We walked the streets of Cerepovec at night. The city was blacked out and silent, but it was perfect for us. We could talk openly with each other and cry if the suffering of the war became too strong. I missed Nuchem so much, but she helped me deal with my anguish. At work we wrote each other letters written in Russian with the Yiddish alphabet – it was our secret language. We were becoming very close.

Vera took her little sister Tanya to the villages one week to visit relatives and bring back food. On just her second day gone I received a letter from her telling me how much she cried from missing me. She asked me to meet her at the train station on the day she returned. I was touched. I met them and walked to their home. Her mother, Maria Gregorgivna, was not happy to see me as she was against our relationship for all kinds of reasons.

The next day, sitting alone in the office, Maria Gregorgivna told me a story about a friend of hers who had dated a German engineer before the war. Eventually he was arrested and taken away, but the KGB questioned her family for weeks. They wanted to know why they let a German into their home and why they thought a German deserved to have a Russian woman. She was hinting to me, none too delicately, that I was a stranger and she did not approve of my dating her daughter. These were legitimate fears, and I was inclined to agree that it was not a good idea, yet something kept Vera and me together.

When I explained to Vera that I would probably never fit into her society, she broke down in tears. I knew that she had had arguments about me at home and I could see how much she really cared about me. Still, Russia was like an ocean, everything dissolved in it. I told Vera I could not become Russian, but she was totally unable to accept this.

Aleksayeff, meanwhile, was building my confidence. I was given more and more responsibility and I was climbing the hierarchical ladder of the department. He sent me to Vologda from time to time to take courses on fire safety. Without these courses, it was impossible to advance. At night I trained a corps of civilians in basic fire-fighting techniques and I organized a rapid response unit for the night-time German air raids.

As the Germans changed their weapons, we had to change our techniques. A man from Vologda came to Cerepovec with a few of the new magnesium bombs the Germans used. These started fires that could not be extinguished by water. Instead, we learned from the instructor, and from handbooks printed in England, how to control the blazes with sand. After an attack, we would inspect all the areas hit and cover the wreckage with tons of sand. We were very thorough.

In my shift I had plenty of trouble with the drivers who resented me for my quick rise through the ranks and were unwilling to take part in any activities outside of caring for their vehicles. Most of them refused to train new recruits because, once we had replacements, they knew they would be mobilized. Not all were like this. A driver named Aronoff, who drove the five-ton water tanker, loved to work on separate projects. Together we designed mechanical garage doors, which I am sure he could have built, but he was mobilized before it could have been done. Still, the bitterness of the drivers was something I would have to deal with, not to mention the problems caused by my relationship with Vera.

In dealing with the pain of my brother's mobilization, I threw myself into my work. I read incessantly and proposed a number of changes to Aleksayeff. My efforts did not go unnoticed. In time Aleksayeff appointed me deputy chief, second-in-command; I was in charge of training and learning. I was responsible for designing plans for the week, accounting for every hour and designing plans for the year. I gave the charge of basic training to the shift leaders and asked them to come up with schedules I would approve or disapprove. I changed the entire operating system and I had only been there a few months. In addition, the politruk asked me to give the daily political lesson from time to time.

I often thought about the boat crew and especially Afanasief. I wondered if he had been mobilized and if he was still alive.

I was so grateful for his help on the boat; I wanted to help him if I could. Already I had gained enough power at the station to keep Dolgovitch and Pelta safe from mobilization. I sent them to training courses and put them in positions that were seen as indispensable in the fire department. I hoped to do the same for Afanasief if I could find him.

I last saw Afanasief at the end of the long winter. In the Russian north, spring comes quickly and violently. From the last frost to the first week of warm weather, the river was the best show in town. People would line the banks and watch the titanic battle between solid ice and the roaring current. I, too, loved watching the awesome power of nature.

On one of these days I saw my old boat on blocks being painted by the crew. The upper-deck personnel had not yet arrived, but there was Afanasief. We had a big hello, hugging and kissing in good Russian style, though I was still not used to it. He told me how the crew still talked about how I beautified my quarters on the boat and read in the little dinghy. He was full of life and laughter. I asked him why he had not come by our home for a visit and that my father would very much like to see him. He told me he did not think that was a good idea. What did he mean by that? It was a friendly meeting, but it was the last time I ever saw him.

I had the same idea for my father, that he should work at the station, but he would not do it, he was a butcher and that was that. Of course this left him open to mobilization and for a while he did avoid the Red Army's clutches. The situation in Russia, however, continued to worsen and soon they enlisted anyone with two legs. A mobilization card came for my father and a second horror filled our world.

I went with him to the recruitment office, explaining to him how he had to play the role of the stupid Pole if he was to escape. I wanted him to pretend to speak no Russian at all and to act confused and dumb. But his eyes were vacant, I could tell he was lost already. To play that role he had to be very focused, which he was not. They took him and we had lost a second member of the family.

Imagine the tragedy. My mother ran to the cemetery with Moishe and Henya and prayed. I felt like I was split in two, like a schizophrenic. It felt like my life at the fire station, no matter what I accomplished, was an empty shell and my life at home was disintegrating. I, too, prayed at the cemetery. I asked God to give me the strength to continue because I was nearing a breakdown. I was dealing with all this horror at home and at work I was consummately visible – I could not afford to show weakness.

For a while, work became academic. The systems were in place, so the station ran smoothly, but my heart was not in it. I suffered my grief internally while displaying a smiling face to the outside world. The truth was, I was having an identity crisis. Was I a proud Soviet, or a poor refugee? I did not know anymore, only that I was Jewish and I needed to keep that part of me, my very soul, intact.

I was pressured to become more of a Soviet by my superiors and more of a Russian by my peers. Rabinin called me into his office one day and asked why an energetic officer like me did not belong to the Komsomol, the Communist Youth. I tried to say I did not really understand the role it played in society, but he did not believe me. I was, after all, substituting for the politruk and teaching Chapter Four. I agreed to join; if I had refused I would have become the enemy.

Vera and Maria Gregorgivna were excited that I was joining the Komsomol. They both recognized my unwillingness to let my Jewish life dissolve in the Russian ocean, but they saw this, despite its being a Soviet organization, as a step towards Russification. I was invited to parties and functions with Vera, many times alongside Russian couples. I could see how different they were, how they kicked off their shoes, drank heartily and sang. When I spoke, their eyes narrowed and the mood shifted, I was so obviously a stranger. I could function as a Soviet, but not as a Russian. Still, Vera and her mother did all they could to change me.

Vera, in contrast to her mother, not only pushed me to become more Russian, but also more Soviet. She had been brought up in the Soviet system and knew no other. She urged me to get more schooling, seeing it as the only way I would be able to leave the fire department. She, after all, was going to be a doctor. Maria Gregorgivna, on the other hand, was fighting the silent battle all Russian parents fought at that time: the battle over the parentage of their children. I believe she preferred my Jewish background to one of a Soviet.

Aleksayeff, despite his generous and uplifting disposition, still indulged in some unglamorous behavior. One evening, drunk as a lord, he came to one of our theatre productions wearing only his underwear. Episodes like this were infrequent and mostly joked about throughout the station, but his drinking eventually got him in trouble. He crossed the line when he went on a week-long bender, locking himself inside the apartment of the wife of a mobilized driver. It was a disgrace and Rabinin sent him away immediately.

I was upset that Aleksayeff was transferred out of Cerepovec as he was in many ways responsible for my success thus far. I wondered whether I would receive the same degree of respect from the next chief, or if things would change completely. Personally I did not have to worry about mobilization because Rabinin liked me a great deal. Pelta and Dolgovitch, however, had only me to protect them.

The new chief was a man named Susin. He came to us from one of the three Vologda fire stations. After some research, we discovered he had been guilty of the same crime as Aleksayeff – he was a womanizer. In Vologda he had impregnated a young telephone girl.

Susin and I got along fine from the beginning. He lacked the enthusiasm of Aleksayeff, but he immediately recognized my value and hard work. This was probably because he was lazy, which suited me fine. I intended to become indispensable to him, and in that way have leverage if he wanted to send my friends to the Red Army. He was a good man, from what I could tell, and he looked after his people. In time he started calling me, 'my Jew', and left me alone to run the station. It quickly became clear to me that he was a party fatcat, too indolent even to check on my work.

After I joined the Komsomol, I was immediately offered a little wooden house next to the station. This was what happened when you joined the party, suddenly there were housing and food when previously there had been none. My mother cried when we moved out of the apartment, but it was better that she lived closer to the station now that my father and brother had gone. Vera organized everything for us and she treated my mother with such care. I tried to dig a basement for storing food, but the water level was too high so I stopped. It was not a great place, but it was convenient.

Susin saw this house – really it was a shack – and laughed. He asked me why on earth I had moved into such a hovel. Somehow it offended his pride that his deputy lived in such a place, so he moved my mother, Henya, Moishe and myself into a three-room apartment on the first floor of the station. Unfortunately this was the politruk Pavlova's apartment. Susin did not like her very much and took pleasure in moving her to a smaller apartment on the second floor. It caused some friction between Pavlova and myself, which was not a good idea.

I flourished under Susin and so did the fire department. Our clout in the city was heightened again and again, as was my personal reputation. I delivered a speech at City Hall, explaining the citywide fire-safety plan we had developed. It was well received and it increased the respect of our department even more. Power in the Soviet Union, as I have explained, was a question of perception. With Susin being so lazy, I became the representative from the fire department at most functions, I inspected most of the factories and I submitted the reports to the NKVD. As a party member and as a visible person of persuasion, certain liberties came my way.

I was in constant contact with the factory directors of Cerepovec. I performed most of the inspections and negotiated the use of various vehicles and water supplies for times of extreme emergency. We had a good relationship, especially those factories under government contract. No director wanted his factory to have a record of negligence, especially since the Germans were dropping bombs so frequently, so I was given special treatment when I made my inspection visits.

Zuyev, the director of the vodka factory, needed a clean fire-safety record because he supplied the army with the ingredients for Molotov cocktails. When I inspected his area, I always seemed to come home with a few bottles of vodka.

Naumov, the property manager of the grain depository, needed a clean record because his stockpiles could combust with just the slightest spark. After inspecting his factory, my mother never wanted for high-quality flour. The same pattern held for most locations.

I brought these materials back to our apartment, secretly, and gave them to my mother and sister to distribute to the refugee community. My sister brought the vodka to work, where her co-workers, waitresses in the restaurant, sold them on the black market. In this way, we made a little money to send to our relatives. Our apartment had two entrances, one to the garage and one to the outside. Members of the refugee community would visit my mother and leave with small satchels, all unseen by the staff of the department.

With Susin's permission, not that he cared, I continued to develop the role of the fire department in the community. We gave instructional courses, paid for by the factory directors, on fire safety. Directors from the entire district sent their people to our station for these courses. We even built reserve water basins in the most industrial sections of the city.

Many buildings in Cerepovec had been converted to hospitals when the war began. One of these, a former teachers' college, was a serious fire hazard. The kitchen, built so quickly, was made of wood and lacked insulation. It was crammed into a small section of the basement, between a room containing flammable cleaning materials and a laundry room. The property manager, a nice Jewish man, made all the changes I suggested, but still it was dangerous. Inevitably there was a fire, but we controlled it quickly, in part due to the preventive measures he had taken.

A little while later, when the kitchen was functioning again, I made a routine inspection. There was still more preventive work needed, and I told this to the property manager. He listened to what I said, paused for a minute, then asked if I wanted an extra job. In exchange for food and money, I would assume the role of the building's fire inspector. Why not? It was a simple enough job. Periodically, especially when I was hungry, I would inspect his building and make a few preventive changes. For this I was well taken care of. I told Susin about this arrangement and he called me a genius. He went and got himself a few of these jobs.

The laundry room in that building was run by a nice, smiling woman. She asked me if I wanted her to do my family's washing. I thought it was a great idea since laundry was still such a hardship for my mother. At night I went to that building with our dirty clothing to meet that woman. I was so naive; I did not realize that she wanted to have sex with me! I politely and awkwardly backed out of there and came back home. 'Mother', I said, 'no more laundry.'

We received a letter from Nuchem. He was at the front, in the north of Russia, serving as a radio operative. We were overjoyed to hear from him, to know that he was still alive, but somehow saddened as well. In that area of fighting the Soviet casualties were heavy. Yes, he was alive, but it was hard not to look at it as simply a temporary suspension of the horrible news to come.

Then another letter from Nuchem arrived, and our hopes increased. Shortly after, we received a letter from my father. Someone else had written it and the censors had crossed out all but three or four sentences, but it was still news that he was alive. My mother clung to these letters, and I started to believe they both might return.

Weeks went by without hearing any news from them and my optimism waned. Then another evil afflicted my family. My sister received a mobilization card. She was sent to Moscow to join the anti-aircraft squadron there, where she would fire cannons at the approaching German bombers. My mother was devastated.

Henya had been gone for a few weeks when, unbelievably, Moishe was called to duty. He was half-blind and slow – what could they want from him? He went to Bubyeva, to the forest not far from where the Germans had advanced. They tried to teach him to be a blacksmith for the army. He worked over there until he hit somebody in the hand with a hammer. They sent him home and I immediately hired him to become a firefighter.

In Moscow Henya fainted while firing the cannons. It was determined she had a heart condition and she was sent back to Cerepovec. This condition, which eventually claimed her life, was a blessing at the time. She began a new job at the railroad station, again as a bookkeeper. Our family was coming together again, but still we heard nothing from Nuchem or my father.

At the station I discovered Susin had put Pelta and Dolgovitch on a list for mobilization. Before this list was sent to the military authorities, I went to Susin to play my trump card, hoping that I had indeed become indispensable to him. I told him that the three of us had come together and we would leave together. I said that I would join them in enlistment or they would stay with me at the station. He capitulated and those two avoided the Red Army.

My mother invited Pelta into our apartment for meals and for prayers. He always seemed hungry and lost. I tried to set him up with a few jobs on the side, like the ones Susin and I enjoyed, but these never worked out. Because of this special treatment, I was very stern and officious with him in public, even standing at attention when we spoke. I hoped he knew I did this artificially, but how could I tell?

The summer came and went and winter was fast approaching, but still we heard nothing from Nuchem or my father.

As I was leaving the converted teachers' college one evening, I thought I heard the faint sound of Hebrew. I walked back and forth to make sure my ears were not deceiving me and I tried to locate its origin. It was the guard on duty, a Lithuanian Jew. He was singing the most beautiful music, songs I had not heard in years. I spoke with him a little, but I preferred to listen. It was so uplifting to hear Hebrew music. It helped me understand why the Russians clung so sentimentally to their traditional songs, there was something closer to truth in them.

Another evening by the bazaar I thought I heard Yiddish being spoken. Behind a cart there was a man in tattered clothing and tire-rubber shoes, lying in a heap and moaning softly to himself. I was shocked. I went to him and asked him what happened. 'I'm dying', he said. I picked him up onto my shoulders and took him to our apartment.

His name was Fishman. He had been arrested in Kovel and sent to prison in the forest, for what I did not discover. He had been released three days before I found him, and since then had not eaten a morsel. We kept him secretly in our apartment for a week, waiting for him to recover. This was highly illegal as every guest in our apartment had to be registered with the police. I wondered what I should do with him, so I went to the Jewish property manager for advice.

He was such a nice man, that property manager, and much more ingenious at negotiating the Soviet system than I was. He never told me his name, this being one of the tricks he used in case he needed to become invisible. Our negotiations, while on the surface official, were definitely only semi-legal. He provided a solution to Fishman's problems. When Fishman recovered, he moved into a room at the converted teachers' college and worked guarding the woodpile at night.

Within a few weeks his face had filled out and he wore better clothing. My mother was especially pleased with this. The property manager, however, was not so happy. That dunderhead Fishman was stealing the firewood! Instead of sending him to prison again, the property manager gave him a new job. Fishman escorted a bus full of wounded soldiers all the way to Uzbekistan, never to return to Cerepovec. Unbelievably, his wife and children, whom he had not seen since Kovel, were in Uzbekistan. He wrote to us describing their happy reunion. Fishman was a cursed and charmed man.

The refugee community heard of our kindness to Fishman and applauded our deeds. But, seeing now how accessible things were to us, our apartment was forever inundated with requests for help. My mother could never say no, and so I spread myself thin trying to comply with the community's requests. One of the worst errands she made me run was to the commercial supplier of the KGB and NKVD. This was a warehouse that gave these organizations their food, which was of the highest quality. The woman working there, Claudia Ivanovna, was like a pig – fat with small, beady eyes. To me, she represented all that was bad with the Soviet system. How could she weigh so much when other people were dying in queues for bread? She adored me and flirted with me incessantly. It was such a dishonor for me to suffer through her antics, even if it was the best food in the city. Eventually I refused to go and sent my mother instead.

My mother got very ill with the change in weather. She was coughing up blood and needed to see a doctor. With Rabinin's help, I was able to bring her to one of the party doctors, a Polish man. He gave her what I think was penicillin. It was a drug they were only giving to senior officers and it cured her quickly. While in his care, my mother formed a nice relationship with the doctor. When she was released, we had a new supplier of medical treatment for the refugees. This, in combination with Rosa at the pharmacy, helped the community a great deal.

Perhaps because we felt so badly about Nuchem and my father not being around, my mother, sister and I probably took too many risks in helping the refugees. I was walking a tightrope at work, not only because I was siphoning off the top – everyone was doing that – but also because I was channeling it outside of that elite clique. Still, I had the attitude that I was obligated to do whatever I could to help the others.

This backroom dealing was by no means limited to assisting the refugee community. Susin and I used the department's newly found clout to make everyone's life at the station better. We were given a certain amount of gasoline every week for drills, but instead we would write down that we did the drills and lease the trucks out to profiteers in the black market. We transported merchandise from one factory to another, and in return collected some form of payment. For example, we brought wood to the director of a clothing supply store and soon our firefighters had warmer jackets. We helped a rope supplier and a shipping company and soon we had organized a fishing brigade with new nets.

I became known as a man who could get things. When inspectors came to our department from Vologda, I supplied the social gatherings with vodka and food. Strangely, I was never invited to these parties. I was still an outsider to many of the bigwigs. This did not bother me too much, but it upset Vera a great deal. She overheard a lieutenant colonel discussing me to some of his cronies. She heard him say that I was not one of them, which was true, I was not.

Shortly after she heard this, Vera was called into the offices of Lieutenant Glebov, the unofficial head of the factory spies. He and I had become friends, but this was secondary to his Soviet responsibilities. Every week she had to write a report about my activities. In essence, she had to spy on me. She ran to me crying with this news, but I assured her everything would be all right. I explained that I would tell her what to write, and nothing would come of it. We discovered later that a girl from the Komsomol, Zorina, was also instructed to file weekly reports about me. I made sure the two reports tied in and tried to regard the whole business as just another part of a system I would have to get used to. They investigated everyone, not just me. Still, once you were caught in that spider web, it was very difficult to escape.

In the middle of winter the heating system at the fire station broke down. This was no small matter because in Russia it was impossible to get spare parts, especially during the war, and the winters were very, very cold. When it was determined that our furnace was irreparable, I suggested to Susin that we build stoves throughout the station. He agreed, what else was there to do?

He sent a request for money to buy bricks to the district offices and we waited for their response. None came and the situation was bad. I knew of a construction site on the other side of the Yagorba river where a building was only partially completed. At the outbreak of war they had ceased construction and there remained a stockpile of unused bricks. I tried to find out who owned the site, but I had no luck. I told Maria Gregorgivna and Susin about it and we decided to get the bricks.

Maria Gregorgivna wrote an official document for me, an order to take 2,000 bricks from the construction site, and she added an official department stamp. I went with a crew of firefighters, not telling them anything beforehand, and read from the document when we arrived. It looked very official, but it was theft.

Back at the station Tsvietaeff built our stoves. He was a fireman with only one leg, the other having been blown off in the Finnish war. Most of the time he was very bitter, and usually he talked like an anti-Semite, but with this project he renewed his sense of self-esteem. He built a number of stoves in strategic places throughout the station and we were all grateful. He was a hero for a while.

I found out later from Maria Gregorgivna that Susin had received money from the district offices to buy the bricks. She asked me if I wanted some of that money, but I refused. I started to consider all my illegal and quasi-illegal activities. Did Maria Gregorgivna know her daughter was filing weekly reports about me? Was asking me if I wanted some of the money a test? It was better, I thought, to err on the side of caution and be as 'by-the-book' as I could while working.

One of my worries, the politruk Pavlova's dislike for me, was settled. She was transferred out of Cerepovec and replaced by a young man who had returned wounded from the front. Before she left, however, she felt compelled to tell Maria Gregorgivna and Vera, not for the first time, that I was no good.

Alexander Vlasoff was the new politruk. He had fought in Kovel on the first day of the war. He told me that the citizens of Kovel were shooting down at the retreating Soviet army from their windowsills. He stayed with his unit until Stalingrad, where he was badly wounded in his face and in his foot. Where he lay after being hit, he saw soldiers burned alive by Molotov cocktails. Despite his wounds, he was still devilishly handsome.

As soon as Vlasoff arrived, I had a special assignment for him. We were running low on firewood. We had enough from our normal stack to heat selected areas of the fire station through the winter, but we were looking at running out completely in the spring. I organized a brigade of firefighters, equipping them with food, axes and clothing, and sent them to the forest. They would cut down the trees and when the spring came we would get the firewood with a barge. I stayed at the station and entrusted Vlasoff with the vodka, probably the most important duty of all.

A few days after they left, Pelta, looking half-dead, woke me in the middle of the night. He was supposed to be in the forest with the others, so I knew something had gone wrong. He told me hurriedly that Vlasoff had been stabbed. In the forest the brigade stayed near a small village. Vlasoff, supposedly in charge of the vodka, had got terribly drunk and had tried to start something with a village girl, thereby upsetting the village boys. They stabbed him repeatedly, slicing to pieces his sheepskin coat and covering him with blood. Pelta had brought him on a sled to Cerepovec – the cold kept him from bleeding to death. I put him on a truck and rushed him to a hospital, where he recovered, but he was fired as politruk. Strangely, he ended up marrying Nina, the telephone girl who had been so abused by Vesilovsky.

Our new politruk came to us from the converted teachers' college. His wife was the laundry woman. Now I had her smiling at me every day.

I did not want to admit it to myself, but the business about Vera putting in reports about me started to cause a little paranoia. This was not the only factor; I was also reading back issues of *Pravda*. Karavyeff, by chance, supplied me with a stack of issues from the years 1937–39, filled with the details of the trials that wiped out all of Stalin's competitors in the Communist Party. Everything was written from the Stalinist point of view, but I saw the true horror of the situation. If someone disagreed with the majority, he was declared an enemy of the people and he and his whole family were executed. The editorials in *Pravda* called for blood. Was this the sign of a healthy government? The list of names was astounding – I recognized so many former heroes, like Bukharin and Piatakoff.

Gradually my paranoia increased. I began to believe that I was in greater danger here than I had been with the Germans, at least I was able to run away from them. Here, I was at the whim of anyone who decided to declare me an enemy. I was still classified under Article 53, which I already considered a black mark against me. If someone reported me as an enemy of the people, I was sure they would take away my family and me. I started to see enemies everywhere. Karavyeff knew I was interested in politics, but why did he leave all of this for me to read? Was he testing me? What would happen if I got into a fight with Vera? If she told somebody the wrong thing, I would be finished. If Maria Gregorgivna really got tired of our relationship she could end it with a whisper in the right person's ear. I felt hostile stares in my back from people I had come to trust. This was paranoia, but this was also the truth about the Soviet Union.

I performed my duties as deputy chief exactly as they were written in the manual. For example, if a woman on guard had a conversation with a co-worker, I walked over to her and gave her a reprimand. This was a change and nobody liked it, certainly not I, but I was afraid I would be reported if I did not do it. This was how I had to conduct myself, I thought, if I was to avoid denunciation.

I mastered the art of playing dumb. If a subject arose that was even questionably anti-Soviet, I either feigned ignorance or kept my mouth shut. Karavyeff, one day, brought me into the room housing the Siemens and Halska instrument. I had asked him about it because it was from such a big German firm from the time before the war. While we were in there he turned a key to a clock. Out came some beautiful music. It was *Borgitz Veriakleny*, a famous hymn from the czar. I knew exactly what it was, but I asked him about that strange music. We both made no comment after that. Another time Dusha Samsonova, the secretary, described the death of her parents to me. They were *kulaks*, so how could I comment correctly?

Even if I kept quiet and toed the line perfectly, I could not avoid incidents of Soviet treachery. Once, on the night shift, I was summoned by the KGB. I went to their offices and followed their instructions to call and invite over a member of the fire department. Two agents waited behind the door with pistols. When the man came in, they seized him and took him away. I was told I saw nothing. This must have happened all the time, but it was the first time they used me to do it.

Another time I had to defend a member of the department who had purchased a herring at the bazaar. When you bought a herring that was all you got, there was no plate or bag to help carry it home. He went to the cart next to the fishmonger and bought the cheapest piece of paper there, which happened to be a small placard of Stalin. He used it to carry the herring. Somebody saw this and accused him of being counter-revolutionary. He escaped with a reprimand.

These incidents were nothing compared to the shameful treatment of the refugee community in late 1942. The KGB, looking to keep busy, decided to weed out the enemies of the people within our community. Of course there were no enemies of the people, but the agents had to justify their positions so the Red Army would not mobilize them. Their investigation focused around the legless barber we had helped into business when we had first arrived in Cerepovec, the one with the redheaded daughter.

Times were terrible for all of the refugees and when they came to get their haircut, they would complain. The barber, like barbers everywhere, had a big mouth – a visit to his house was an exercise in commiseration. He would say, with typical Jewish humor, that life was better when he was cutting hair under the German occupation, they may have wanted to kill him, but at least he would get his 5 Marks. His sister-in-law, Genya, had come to live with them and heard all of this chatter.

Smirnoff, a young, good-looking KGB agent, began taking Genya out to the cinema. Eventually, after much prodding, she told him that the barber had said these things about Russia. From this statement they made a complicated case against the refugees. The barber and his wife were taken away immediately and their daughter was sent to an orphanage.

My mother was heartbroken; she loved that child so much. Foolishly, she tried to retrieve the child from the orphanage and bring her to our apartment. For this, the KGB detained her for a week. I pleaded with them to release her, telling them that she was a stupid, Polish woman who still believed in the old ways. She did not know, I said, that the Soviet government took care of all its children. Having friends in the NKVD helped and she was released.

The conspiracy, however, was just starting. The KGB went on a quest to find the barber's cohorts. Every couple of days we heard of another refugee being taken away.

A week or so after the barber was arrested I came back to our apartment to find a Jewish girl from Lodz, Sonia, sitting with my mother. She described to us how bad a time she was having in Russia, and how she had been forced to run away from Vologda because the Soviets were mistreating her. I did not know it at the time, but she was a spy. I did know that I did not like that provocative speech. I was a Soviet at that point, at least superficially and I even had a picture of Stalin on my wall. Why would she say this to me? I told her that without the Soviet Union, we would all be dead, which was true. The hardships, I said, would end when the war was won. I wanted to kick her out, but I knew my mother was prepared to let her sleep with us. As it turns out, after hearing my little speech, she left.

Around the same time I performed one of my usual inspections of a hemp-manufacturing factory. I did not recognize the guard on duty, so I gave him a little test. By law he was not to let me pass if I did not give him the correct password. I approached him in an official fashion and demanded that he give me his rifle, but I never said the password. He gave me his rifle! I arrested him and brought him to the director of the factory, which was my responsibility. The director told me to go home. The guard was a spy from the KGB and he was Polish.

Sonia came back to our apartment another time, this time with a man in tow. They were speaking to my mother when I arrived. I took one look at the man and I could not believe my eyes: it was the false guard from the factory. I politely excused myself and walked outside. Did he not recognize me, or did he simply pretend not to recognize me? I paced for a few moments wondering what to do. Were they really after me? I walked back into the apartment and told them both that they would have to leave. This was a government house, I told them, and they were not registered to visit.

When they left, I told my mother that no one was to come into our apartment again. I knew how much this hurt her, but we were clearly at risk. I was right to be so strict. Other refugees were tricked into saying the wrong thing and wound up in prison. In the end, some 15 refugees were taken away.

We found out the barber and his wife had died in prison and the child had died in the orphanage. We assumed the worst for the others as well. The local KGB was so proud that they had infiltrated this Polish nest of counter-revolutionary activity, but in reality they only committed murder.

From that time I changed my methods of assisting the community. I no longer involved my sister or Moishe and I kept my mother's role to a minimum. I tried to be like a submarine, with watertight compartments. I did not want my family to know about my business, lest something should happen and they too would be incriminated.

The winter of 1942–43 was my worst time period psychologically. There was still no word about my father or Nuchem, I imagined everyone to be an enemy, and it looked like the Soviets would lose the war. The Red Army lost ground in the Crimea, surrendering Odessa and Sevastopol, and the situation in Leningrad was still dire. The Soviets kept one railroad open and used it to evacuate refugees, but these poor souls were dying with their first mouthful of food. Those who survived were like walking ghosts, and they were easily robbed of their clothing and food. There was such callousness, but it was to be expected. The Soviet system took away people's humanity and replaced it with the notion that the government would take care of everything.

Stalin had weakened his armed forces by destroying the leadership of the Red Army in the late 1930s and by collaborating with the Germans for so long. The generals in command now were fearful of making decisions without Stalin's consent and consequently led their forces poorly. Millions of Soviet soldiers died because of the military leaders' trepidation. Others, soldiers and officers alike, simply switched sides. We did not know it at the time, we only knew what they told us, but never in the history of warfare had so many soldiers abandoned their ranks to fight for the other side.

One the other hand, the Russian people started to personalize the war, shifting the purpose away from a glorification of Stalin to the greater goal of saving Russia. Stalin latched on to this wave of nationalism and used it to inspire the people. In his radio addresses he glorified the great military history of Russia, the fighting spirit of the Russians and the great achievements the Russians had given the world. Propaganda claimed the Russians had invented everything of progress in the modern world: airplanes, radios, telephones and so forth. Stalin minimized the role of the other states, declaring that the weight of the world and its future rested on the broad shoulders of Mother Russia. All of this, ironically, came from a Georgian who could not even speak Russian properly.

We did our part for the war effort at the station. We joined other fire departments in the region and purchased a tank for the army. This was part of a nationwide campaign; every collective and civic department tried to buy something for the army. I found out from Maria Gregorgivna that Susin did not contribute any money, claiming he needed it all for alimony. Such was the paradox. I also gave blood from time to time. I was type O negative – the universal donor. Sometimes, when the wounded came in quickly, I would be called down to the hospital to give blood straight to a person on the operating table.

My paranoia subsided slightly, but I still did everything rigidly by the book. I had friends in the Communist elite who would help me if I were in trouble, but still there was no safeguard against my denunciation. By the time the spring arrived, I was like an automaton in my official duties and in society. The department ran efficiently because of my hard work, even though it was staffed only by women and wounded soldiers. I needed everything to be perfect, other-wise I would worry too much about my enemies, whoever they were.

When the river thawed, I put together a unit to collect the firewood we had left in the forest. I went with them this time and I did not bring any vodka. An older Russian named Horkoff came with me. He was more than a jack-of-all-trades, he was a master-of-all-trades. If I gave him an idea, he would work out how to make it a reality. He built collapsible beds in the fire station after I had suggested we could use a few beds like the ones they used on the boat. He was a carpenter, a tailor, a shoemaker and a thief – my most valuable worker.

Horkoff represented the tragedy of the Soviet system. He was multi-talented, strong and clever. In the days before the revolution he was a *kulak* from another region. He probably had a family somewhere, or perhaps they had been killed. He lived in Cerepovec pretending to have always been a member of the Proletariat. One night at the station, during a party for the firefighters, Horkoff was belligerently drunk. He said to me, with savage eyes, 'Comrade leader, there will come a day when we will slaughter the Soviets.' He let the comment slip out and, when he sobered up, he tried to retract it. I told him that I never heard it and I let it slide.

The spring flooding made it so our barge could not get close to the stack of wood. This was why I brought Horkoff. In no time he built a bridge and soon we had filled the barge. I wanted to return to Cerepovec as soon as possible, so I went with a few others through the woods. It was about 30 miles, but this was much faster than traveling on the river. I felt a lack of control when I was not at the station.

When I returned I was called into the NKVD for a meeting with Lieutenant Glebov, the man to whom Vera gave her weekly reports. As I said, by this time we had become good friends, but still I feared him a little. He was, after all, the unofficial head of the factory spies – a career made from denouncers. We sat together at a political course given to active members of the party, and I had helped him to understand theoretical Marxism better. Why I was chosen to take part in that course, I did not know, my position was not at the same level as the others. It allowed me, however, to build relationships with some important people.

When I entered Glebov's office, he said nothing. He motioned for me to sit and slid a couple of documents across his desk for me to inspect. They were from the Red Army. It was the official news that Nuchem and my father had been killed.

A thunderclap hit me on the head, and for a few moments I was in a daze. I came back to reality and saw that Glebov was staring at me, seeing if I would cry. I remembered what Afanasief said about crying in Russia: 'Moscow doesn't believe in your tears.' Crying would show that I was not proud that my closest family members had fallen fighting for the Red Army. Somehow I remained composed and I left his office and walked into the street.

I had such a pain in my heart. It felt like everything had fallen apart, that the entire Russian experience was fraudulent. I did not know what to do or where to go. I did not want to go to the station, I did not want to go home and I did not want to see my sister. I went to that little Jewish cemetery and said what I knew of the Kaddish, and I cried. I cried so much, not only because they were gone, but also because I did not know who was with them at their moment. It hurt me so much to think of them dying in such a hostile environment.

I went to see my sister at the railroad office. She saw my face and knew exactly what had happened. She fainted, and when she was revived we cried. The women at the railroad office also cried. Everybody had lost someone close to them, and everybody understood our suffering. The pain burned so strongly in my chest then and it still burns now after 60 years.

We went home to tell our mother. As soon as she saw us she asked, 'Nuchem? Papa?' It was amazing, she was more composed than we were. Still, her eyes filled with tears and she beckoned us to embrace her. As we did she comforted us, telling us that life would go on. We wept together and prayed, knowing that all we had now was each other.

Nuchem and my father were both killed in September 1942. We received notice in the spring of 1943.

The responsibility of my family was now not only mine in practice, which, in effect, it had been since we left Kalisz, but also in standing. I knew that if I made one mistake I could jeopardize our survival. Everything I did, I did with steadfast adherence to what I believed to be the perceived principles of the Soviet system. My faith in Soviet life had, of course, disintegrated, but being a good Soviet meant acting like a good Soviet; my dedication to the ideal was a matter of other people's perceptions. Apart from a few zealots, like Galina Yefimiva, this was how everyone lived.

We had restored contact with Uncle Shloime Gerszin and his wife Sonia. He had been released from prison and was now living in Uzbekistan with my cousins. Through them we discovered that my cousin Esther, the daughter of the widower Josef Stockman, was living alone in Kierghizia. Her brother Gerszin had already died of hunger. My mother demanded that she come live with us. I registered her officially with the authorities and built a bed on our famous trunk, and little Esther came to live at the station. She was emaciated and sorrowful, but she improved under my mother's care.

In central Asia my cousins were having successes and failures living as tradesmen in the bazaars. At one point they lost all their money so I sent them 2,000 rubles. They sent a letter back, almost laughing at me. That money was worthless down there, it was an entirely different world. When times were good for them, Sonia sent us packages of dried fruit.

My mother was right, life did go on. Reestablishing contact with our relatives and having Esther come to live with us helped a great deal psychologically. Once again we lived as an extended family, albeit incomplete, but in the Soviet Union, one could never be completely in control of one's destiny. Despite the safeguards I had spent so much time building, I was still subject to the whim of the government. In 1943, an agreement between the Polish government in exile and the Soviet Union nearly destroyed everything I had accomplished.

The Soviet Union and the Polish government in exile had agreed to rebuild a Polish army, ostensibly under the command of Stalin. Thousands of Polish prisoners were released and sent to central Asia where they trained under the authority of General Anders, a Polish general. As soon as Anders was on his own, however, he took his battalions through Iran, into Palestine and beyond. They still fought the Germans, but they were no longer under the control of the Soviet Union. It was a major embarrassment for Stalin, but the reaction of the Poles, their real desire to fight the Nazis, convinced him to form his own Polish army.

Initially it started with the formation of the Association of Polish Patriots, an organization formed to help the Polish government in exile distribute food, medicine and clothing to Polish refugees in Russia. I was asked to join, but I sensed something peculiar. I did not want to enlist unless I knew I could get out. To decline, however, was borderline counter-revolutionary. I told the recruiter that I was a Jew and a Russian officer and I had nothing to do with Poland. I explained that due to the time constraints of my position I did not think it was possible for me to help, but if it was necessary my sister could assist them. In this way I believed I showed my loyalty without risking our necks.

Henya did become active in this; she started going to meetings all around the province. She helped distribute the products sent from England, where the government in exile based its operations, and she met Poles and Jews from all over the region. She ran into some familiar faces, including that devil Sonia, the KGB spy! She went to Vologda, Ivanovo and other cities, and I saw that the scale of the operation was too big for the Polish government in exile to support. Stalin was using the association to collect names for his army.

What I feared most had come true; mobilization cards came for Pelta, Dolgovitch and myself. My threat to Susin had become a reality. Susin and the politruk made phone call after phone call trying to stop my mobilization, but there was nothing that could be done. This recruitment had nothing to do with the Red Army, they were told, this was the Polish army under the authority of Stalin.

That was it, I was going to the army. From Cerepovec, only Dolgovitch, Pelta and I were mobilized. We were told to meet the next day at a recruitment office on Sovietski Prospekt. In the meantime, I frantically tried to assure that my family would be cared for while I was gone – which would probably be forever.

I did not trust Susin to keep my family in the apartment at the station. I saw how quickly he pushed out the politruk Pavlova for us, so why would he not do the same for somebody new? If he did, it was likely that my mother would end up living at the Communist Center for Widows. I went there and spoke with the administrators, but I was unconvinced that they would take special care of her should she be forced to move in. I spoke with Maria Gregorgivna about the situation and she promised to look after my mother should something arise. This eased my mind, but I was still worried.

I went to the recruitment office with Dolgovitch and Pelta. I took with me a half-liter of vodka and cash as bartering items; a necessity, I had learned, on any long trip. My family came with me, as did Vera and Maria Gregorgivna. We handed our documents to a Red Army officer named Popov and we were put behind an iron fence. Let there be no mistake, we were most definitely the property of the army.

In front of me, on the other side of the bars, stood my dearest loved ones. My sister and Vera were crying bitter tears, and I longed to comfort them, but I knew I was making an impression on Popov and therefore could not show any emotion other than pride. This ate away at me from the inside. Vera and I had been together for over a year, and we were in love; of course I felt the anguish of separation. My mother was like a stone, paralyzed in disbelief. She shed no tears, but her eyes were vacant, she already considered me lost. I told them that I would return. But how, after so many had left and died, could they believe me?

Outside of my family Pelta had few people who were close to him in Cerepovec. While Dolgovitch and I said goodbye, he curled up and fell asleep, such was his concern. Dolgovitch, on the other hand, had married a telephone girl at the station and they were expecting a child in the coming months. He was so distraught and unhappy his eyes filled with tears. The desperation of the situation and my desire to protect my family sent my mind off in a thousand directions hoping to find a way out of this predicament.

We were put on a train and escorted by Popov to Vologda, the central mobilization point of the province. Popov was a tough, wiry Cossack with a short fuse and happy eyes. His skull had been split at the front, and it appeared that you could see the pulsing of his brain. We had the same rank in the party so I immediately developed a dialogue with him on the train. I liked him a lot and I discovered that he did not like Poles.

Vologda was teeming with men, each of them part of a group escorted alternatively by a Red Army officer or a Polish army officer. It was amazing to see the old uniforms on the Polish soldiers, at once evoking feelings of boyhood pride and revulsion. We saw Polish gendarmes wearing their distinctive hats with the Polish eagle and the yellow sash – we called them canaries – leading queues of Polish military prisoners. How could soldiers have been arrested already?

We saw hundreds of *posioleks*, Polish citizens, like my Uncle Shloime Gerszin, who had been arrested and brought to the remote corners of the Vologda province to work with no leave. We saw hundreds of Red Army soldiers, clearly Polish, who had been released from one army to be enlisted in another. Even gypsies had been mobilized. Whole clans of these nomadic peoples camped outside the mobilization center, protesting the involvement of their loved ones. At the station I saw a train filled with women – they too had been mobilized.

We were taken to the *banja* and our clothes were disinfected. For three days we waited to be called to an echelon, all of which were sent to R'azan', the headquarters of the Polish army. Popov was to escort us the remainder of the way.

Eventually our echelon was formed. In addition to Dolgovitch, Pelta, Popov and I, there was a handful of Jews and many gentile *posioleks* on the train. In an instant the old hatreds flared. They yelled mockingly, '*Kykes! Moishka! Moishka!*' The intensity of their abuse increased as we continued our trip. The Poles living way out in the forest had not changed a bit.

Because of my fireman's uniform and my relationship to Popov, I was already seen as the unofficial leader of the Jews. I separated them from the gentiles. To my great disappointment, Dolgovitch went directly to the Poles. Knowing that Popov did not like Poles and thinking there was something to be gained there, I gathered the others and fought back after a round of abuse. Popov separated the groups, fuming. I used this as an appeal.

I told Popov that what he saw was just the beginning of what was to come. We were not Polish, we were Jewish. 'They will kill us', I said, 'before we ever see the Germans.' I explained how they had treated us for centuries in Poland and how they had handed us over to the Germans, if they did not kill us themselves, at the start of the war. I made sure he knew that we wanted to fight – I had to say this – but we wanted to fight in the Red Army. I begged him to tell someone about us when we got to R'azan'.

I went back to the Jews in the train and told them what I had said. If they wanted to be a part of my plan to leave the Polish army, then I asked them for money. If they did not, that was fine. I told them that if anything bad came of it, I would take all the blame. They all offered something and I gave it all, including the bottle of vodka, to Popov.

We disembarked at Divovo, a station heavily damaged by German bombs near the city of R'azan. This was the headquarters of the First Polish Division, symbolically named Tadeusz Kosciuszko after the famed Polish General. We walked into a large field filled with thousands of men. There were long tents brandishing the Polish Eagle scattered across the landscape. The epicenter of the operation was a derailed train car wherein Red Army and Polish army officials shared space. Popov lined us up.

As he was about to disappear with our documents, I reminded him of what I had told him on the train. He stopped and separated the groups himself, making separate lines for Jews and gentiles. I saw him pull our documents out of the pile as he went off to his commanding officers. He was going to try to help us.

As soon as he left Dolgovitch ran to me from the other line. He saw that I had accomplished something with Popov and knew that he had made a mistake. 'Comrade Leader', he begged, 'you can't let them take me! My wife is pregnant!' But what was there to do now? If he had come to me on the train I could have showed Popov his documents as well, but he chose to align himself with the *posioleks*. For more than a year I had protected him from the Red Army, but now his fate was out of my hands.

We waited for hours. In that time a Polish corporal with a Jewish accent walked past our line. I approached him and discovered that he was a redheaded Jew from Lodz. 'What is the situation for Jews here?' I asked. He leaned close to my ear and said in Yiddish, 'Flee!'

A Polish boy looking for money came to our group. He wore the nicest Polish boots, a style I had not seen for years. I made a deal with him, giving him money and my shoes for his boots. We were both pleased.

As the hours went by, I could sense the concern of the Polish gendarmes. We were just sitting there, waiting, surely this aroused some suspicion in their minds. I took our little group into the tall grass of the steppe where we were hidden from view. In time I saw them searching for us.

Many in the group were anxious and a little upset with me. The best we could hope for was a transfer from the Polish army to the Red Army. Was this any better for them? I stood to gain immensely. If I could get into the Red Army, someone from the NKVD in Cerepovec, I thought, could get Pelta and me out. Still, I believed I was helping the others and not just myself. I truly believed they would be terribly abused, if not killed by the Poles before they saw combat. I took the advice of the Jewish corporal as evidence.

From the tall grass we could see the Polish section of our echelon being taken away, along with them went Dolgovitch. This increased our worry. Were we supposed to go with them? Would the gendarmes really be searching for us now? Where was Popov? We could do nothing but wait, which we did through the night.

In the morning someone heard Popov approaching. He was yelling my name, 'Skorupa! Skorupa!' I went to him and he gave me some good-natured abuse for hiding from him. He told me I had an appointment in the derailed train car, so I followed him there and waited outside.

He was in there for 15 or 20 minutes in which time my nervous tension tripled. My head was spinning and my heart ached. Whatever I said, I had to put the right spin on it. If I were in any way seen as someone who did not want to fight, who knew what could happen to the others and me? I prayed to myself, '*Shema Ysrael. Shema Ysrael.*' Finally Popov came out and told me to go in.

There was a long table flanked by two benches. On one side were Red Army officers and on the other Polish army officers. I was asked to account for my troublesome request. I nervously, but calmly, explained that we had never considered ourselves Polish, but we were pleased to be part of the Soviet Union. I described the mistreatment of the Jews by the Poles historically and recently on the train. I could see the anger appear on the face of the Polish officers, and the wry smiles on the faces of the Soviets. I turned to the Red Army officers and said that my father and brother had already proudly given their lives to the Soviet Union, and if I were to fall, I would fall in the Red Army. With this I left.

Outside, my body was shaking. I had no idea what I had accomplished in there, but I knew there would be consequences, whether good or bad. I prayed again and waited for Popov to come out. When he did, he carried in his hand a sealed envelope. He explained that I had to take the envelope to Rabinoya, the next train stop, and get the documents officially approved. There was a field office where an officer would or would not give me a stamp.

I went back to the others and told them to remain out of sight. I then caught a train heading towards Rabinoya, clinging to a platform used for transporting weaponry. As the train approached Rabinoya, it slowed a little because of a curve in the tracks. I jumped off and looked about the little town; it was like nothing I had seen. Everything was made of wood, even the streets. I had seen wooden sidewalks, but never wooden streets. I asked someone where I could find the field office of the Red Army. I was standing right in front of it.

I went in and asked to see the officer in charge. I was led down a short hallway into a room with one desk and one portrait of Stalin on the wall. A very broad-shouldered man sat stoutly beneath the portrait and behind the desk. I handed him the envelope. He opened it, sniffled, grunted, shifted and with a small smile said, 'Good man.' He opened his desk drawer and pulled out a stamp. He shot one hot breath on its rubber end and *bang*! I was no longer enlisted in the Polish army. I snapped to attention and said, 'in the service of the Soviet Union', and I left.

I hopped on a train heading back to Divobo. Unfortunately the tracks did not curve at the station and I was forced to jump off the train at a very fast speed. I jumped poorly and landed on a railroad tie. I broke some of my front teeth and damaged my knee. Still, the exuberance I felt at being released from the Polish army kept me moving at a quick pace. I found the others and told them the news. Popov congratulated me and told me to gather the others – we were heading to Moscow.

I did not dare ask Popov where he was ultimately taking us. I wanted to show him how proud I was to be part of the Red Army, but I was wracked with worry. I was so affected by my fear that I only let myself think of the trip as far as Moscow, not beyond. If I did, my head would spin out of control.

Popov procured some military provisions for us, so we ate dried fish and bread on the train. At the station in Moscow we walked into an enormous celebration. I believe the Red Army had just recaptured Kiev. Loudspeakers covered the city with music and speeches, while fireworks shot across the sky. It was a huge party, but not for us. We were collected in a military roundup almost immediately. Our disheveled appearances must have violated a city ordinance because we were taken away for being unclean. The military police took us underneath a bridge, out of sight of the people, and made us perform menial calisthenics.

Popov was livid. He yelled at the military policemen with such venom that it caused his head wound to pulsate. 'You backliners! You cowards! Is this how you treat our soldiers!' I was afraid he would get himself in trouble. In the end they released us and gave us coupons to eat and see the exhibition in Gorky Park.

The exhibition was a collection of armaments taken from the German army. I saw the new German tanks, so big it seemed an apartment could be made of the interior space. I saw individual speedboat engines and new rifles and pistols. It was all very impressive, but whatever I had seen of the German war machine in the past had always impressed me. What amazed me was that the Soviets had held them off.

We were given food and icecream at Gorky Park. Popov was in a better mood, having cooled off from the confrontation with the military police. I asked him, in the most delicate way, where our next stop would be. He said curiously, 'Vologda', as if I should have already known. By law he had to return us to our place of origin, but I did not know this. The relief I felt was so strong that I almost fell over.

We came to Vologda. Most of our group went their separate ways, but Pelta, Popov and I stayed together – Popov was required to escort us all the way back to Cerepovec. There was a military telephone at the station. I asked Popov if he could make a call to the fire department to tell them that I was in the city. He said okay, and even handed me the phone when the connection was made.

I spoke with Major Nikikin, the head of the provincial administration of fire departments. I told him that I had been released from the Polish army and was put into his care. This was not true, but I put the responsibility immediately on him. He was so happy. He told me he was transferring my army status back to the way it was. He wanted to send a car to take me to one of the fire stations in Vologda, but I told him that was not a good idea, I did not want to get Popov into any trouble.

I walked to the fire station, leaving Pelta and Popov behind. Susin was there to greet me. He was in Vologda taking a refresher course. He probably needed it badly since he had actually been forced to work since my departure. He was ecstatic when he saw me. He told me he would get rid of my replacement and I would have my old job back – his laziness required that I get my old job back.

I made a call to the Cerepovec station. Vera answered and she started madly crying when she recognized my voice. I told her we would speak soon and I asked her to let me speak to my mother. I said, 'Mother, I'm coming home.' I wanted to tell her myself. Susin picked up the phone and spoke with Kopneen, the man brought in to replace me. He asked that a car be sent to the Cerepovec train station to pick me up.

The three of us headed to Cerepovec. Kopneen had not sent a car, but that was just as well. I was used to the frenzy of travel and being surrounded by thousands and thousands of people, walking in such a quiet city was a pleasure. I thanked Popov for his help and I promised to repay him somehow for what he did. In the future he came by with his girlfriend from time to time, and I wined and dined them. We became friends.

I walked into our apartment and saw my mother. She was so happy to see me, but the emotion of the situation forced her to open up parts of her heart that she had sealed. She collapsed in sobs. She finally allowed herself to grieve for the loss of our father and Nuchem. We cried together, but eventually we smiled. We were both so happy that I was back.

The reception at the fire station was generally warm, though I could sense some people's disappointment at my return. Vera was overjoyed. She had proven her dedication to me by taking such good care of my mother while I was gone. I was very happy to see her and I loved her for comforting my mother, but the lukewarm reception from Maria Gregorgivna made me think twice about our future together.

Within a few days, Susin returned from Vologda and demoted Kopneen from deputy chief to a shift leader. If Kopneen was upset at me for this, I could not tell. He was a good-natured man, with a smile for everyone. He and Pelta became very good friends, he even taught Pelta to drink like a real Russian. I was reinstated as deputy chief and I resumed my duties.

After this whole ordeal it was now more clear to me than ever that the only victory for us, the Jewish people, was to survive. Seeing the old Polish hatreds and being stuck in a society that rejected religious principles served to harden my resolve. I pictured the Jewish nation as a damaged tree and us as one of the few remaining leaves. I was determined to do anything I could to keep my family, friends and relatives out of harm's way so we could turn from tiny leaves into strong branches. My relationship with Vera, despite how close we had become, did not fit into this philosophy.

My mother thought of the same things and worried about my relationship with Vera. When I was gone, Vera had come to her frequently and was genuinely caring, even hugging one of my tunics whenever she left. This display of sentimentality frightened my mother. She asked me, 'Henrik, is this for you?'

'No, mother, it is not,' I replied, but getting away from Vera would not be easy.

# 14 Tension

I had only been back in Cerepovec a few days when I was called into the KGB offices on Sovietski Prospekt. I was to speak with Samosin, the head of the city's KGB, probably the most powerful man in Cerepovec. He and Gregoriev, the head of the NKVD, shared an apartment with a bathtub. Even the highest officials in Cerepovec had to register two or three weeks in advance to use the bathtubs in the city's *banja*, these two had one in their home. I was very nervous for our meeting.

Samosin was a huge man with an enormous belly. His gaze was like a snake's, even when he laughed a cold stare emanated from his coal-like eyes. I was never at ease in his presence and nor was anyone else. He was responsible for approving all the arrests in the barber's case and innumerable other acts of malfeasance. He not only had the eyes of a snake, he was a snake. Undoubtedly, he was the most feared man in the city.

I went to the offices, praying to myself as I entered. An operative, a KGB man in civilian clothes, walked around the waiting room. I announced to him who I was, but he already knew (they knew everything, the devils). I was told to wait, which I did, nervously. Finally I was asked to go into Samosin's office. I said one more prayer.

There he sat corpulently behind his desk. I sat across from him, transfixed by his stony eyes. He asked me if I had just returned, but of course he already knew. He said he would have stopped my mobilization had he known about it before-hand. It was another lie, but I politely thanked him and apologized for not informing him in time. He then asked me about my linguistic skills, specifically if I could read and understand Polish, Russian, Yiddish, Ukrainian and Czech. I told him I could read and understand all of those languages to a certain extent, but this was due more to their similarities than to my skill and education. He then handed me a letter in Polish and asked me to translate it. I did, and he compared the results with a translation done before. 'Very good,' he said, 'you are now the head of the Polish and Jewish division of the Censor Board.' I could not decline, it was simply not an option.

I was sent out of his office and down the hall. In the third room on the right I met my controlling officer, her name was Alexandra Dubinichovna. She told me to call her Sura. She was a very attractive Russian woman, with dark, smiling eyes. She explained to me immediately what I had to do. There was a bag of 50 or so letters, which I had to read and censor, marking anything anti-Soviet. Any mention of a lack of food, military information, factory information or aggressiveness to the regime had to be marked, and with particularly hostile letters I had to provide a full translation. These censored letters were then sent to a technical staff for further action. Sura told me no one was allowed to enter the office while I was working and I was not to touch a thing. If a light bulb needed changing, for example, I had to put away my work and inform the operative in the waiting room. She said she would call me whenever I was needed.

Once or twice a week at the fire station there would be a message that Dubinichovna had called. I did not need to call her back, I would just go down to the same office and find a satchel of mail. The letters came from almost all of European Russia, even some from the prison camps. The most hostile letters came from the Ukraine, written in half-Polish and half-Ukrainian, denouncing the tyranny of the Stalinist regime and the evil of the Jews. I saw letters written on birch bark and letters written in blood. Some enclosed pictures of Stalin, not all of which remained intact. The strangest letters I read, however, were from people I knew.

Through the letters I followed the lives of familiar names from Kalisz. It was amazing to read about their travails and it touched me to think that there were survivors from my own town living through the Soviet experiment as we were in Cerepovec. My father's friend Selig Zielberberg wrote the most loving letters home to his wife, from the front, who was living near Stalingrad. He was known as a Trotskyist back in Kalisz and he fought with the Red Army all the way to Berlin. I recognized a few letters from one of Nuchem's boyhood friends, also writing from the front. He was in the Polish division. Esther, our cousin who had recently moved in with us, wrote to Uncle Shloime Gerszin and Sonia about what a big-shot I had become. I had to pretend to not know about it, but a lot of what she wrote was not true! Still I never mentioned it. The most entertaining letters I read were from the father of a family Henya had met in Vologda during a meeting of the Association of Polish Patriots. He had left his wife in Poland but had an on-and-off again affair with a woman living in Uzbekistan. One letter would describe his infinite love for her and the next would call it off completely. In the end they were married in Poland, but then divorced.

After a few weeks of this, the confusion and worry I felt about my role – specifically whether I was hurting other people – prompted me to learn more about the censoring process. I became friendlier with Sura in an attempt to get more information from her. I smiled at her and asked simple questions, all very politely and gentlemanly. Unfortunately this backfired when she began to want to become more than friendly with me. She came into the office wearing lipstick and nice clothing, assuming we were to start an affair. I became very afraid; this was not what I wanted. I explained my relationship with Vera and luckily she respected this and kept her distance. She still held on to some of the principles that preceded the wartime immorality, and, if anything, seemed to respect me more because of my behavior. She was very forthcoming with information, explaining thoroughly my risks in the system of censorship.

Every letter in the Soviet Union had to have a stamp from a military censor before it could be delivered. Sura told me that the post office girls performed this function. Most of what I did was unchecked, but once or twice a month they sent a satchel to Moscow for inspection. So far they had been pleased with my work. From then on, Sura told me when they were sending the satchels to Moscow, which was important for me to know. I let a lot of the more hostile letters go through, thinking that I had saved these people from interrogation.

Sometimes an operative and another agent would come into the office while I was working. This was not supposed to happen, so when they did I covered the letters as best I could. The operative tried to become very friendly with me, even calling me by my father's name, Genasha Josefovitch, a very familiar thing to do in Russia. He would casually ask me about people, usually refugees, as if their names just happened to come up in conversation. It seemed the KGB was still after them and they were looking for my help. If he asked me about someone I knew, I never let on. I told him countless times that I had few friends among the refugees. When I had left the offices following these conversations I would tell my mother about whom they were asking. I left it up to her to inform them that they were in danger.

I officially worked at the fire station and I almost officially worked for the KGB, a concept that I could never quite grasp, but one I hoped would cause little harm. Using my mother I was able to warn members of our community about any potential danger they were in, but not frequently. If I were to be caught compromising my position in the KGB, there would be no question about my fate or the fate of my family. This was my second career for the remaining months of the war. It was not an ideal profession.

The problem with Sura and the laundry woman, their unwelcome advances, was not uncommon for me in Cerepovec. It had nothing to do with my appearance or my stature, but that I was one of only a few healthy young men left in the city and that the moral fiber of the nation had crumbled during the war. What was odd was my refusal to partake in that type of behavior, since everyone else seemed to acquiesce so easily.

Many factories and buildings had female directors and property managers. In the absence of their husbands, and with their hands suddenly in command of so much, their reputations around the city became infamous. A combination of their control over the access to certain materials, the lack of men in the city and the knowledge that their husbands had field wives at the front proved too much to deter their desires. Men like Rabinin, Samosin and Gregoriev – married men, family men – benefited from their unscrupulous behavior. The women, in turn, benefited from the status of these men. There was even a saying: 'After the war we will write everything off.'

Being one of the few healthy young men in town had additional consequences. At the fire department I was unable to assemble squads that were capable of handling a fire without my presence. The shifts were stacked with women and crippled men – who would be able to climb the ladders with a live hose without falling off? Rabinin reprimanded me for going into the heart of a fire once, but when I explained the situation to him, he understood. If I sent someone else, I would have sent that person to his or her death.

One of the more bizarre results of being fit came about a few months after my return from mobilization. The Department of Physical Education decided to put together a provincial track meet. It was a silly propaganda stunt, for whom, in Vologda province, were they trying to impress? A woman came into our station looking for fit young people. At first I thought she was crazy, a *misiganah*, but then I realized she was serious. I was chosen to represent our city in a distance race and I went with the Cerepovec delegation to Vologda.

I stopped in to see Aleksayeff who had been transferred to one of the stations in Vologda. He was like a bird with clipped wings. He was under the constant supervision of Major Nikikan, the head fire chief of Vologda province. His station was boring him and he complained to me bitterly. I slept next to his stove the night before the race. While at the station I saw the boy Susin had fathered with a telephone girl. It was amazing how much that little boychik looked like his father.

Before the race they brought us to a canteen where we were given soup made from ivy. I had never eaten such soup, certainly not before athletics. Not long after we ate, really a matter of minutes, we were brought out to the track. I did not have proper shoes to run in, and my knee was still badly hurt from jumping off the train incorrectly, yet I finished third. It was a joke. They gave me a certificate and I went back to Cerepovec.

Although I was desirable to many women in Cerepovec, Maria Gregorgivna still did not want me near Vera. We were at the point where I silently agreed with her sentiment, but there was nothing I could actively do to change the situation. She, however, could. With the swing of the war now clearly in the Soviet Union's favor, cities that had been under siege were now fighting to bring back the normality that preceded the conflict. Outlying cities, further away from the front than Cerepovec, began closing down temporary hospitals and reopening the formerly converted schools and factories. In Kazan a pediatric medical school was reopened and Maria Gregorgivna pushed Vera to enroll.

We put together a good political recommendation for her and stressed the fact that her father was in the army. She was accepted and soon she went to Kazan. I was relieved, but I was also saddened. She wrote letters on newspaper, telling me how hungry she was and how she lacked the proper paper to do her schoolwork. Maria Gregorgivna and I set about finding ways to keep her supplied. She and I both wanted her to stay in Kazan, and not just so she would become a doctor, only Maria Gregorgivna did not know that we agreed.

We were paid for giving blood, which I continued to do, so I sent this money to Vera. I also knew the city inside and out, so for me to locate paper was not a big deal. Getting that paper and sending it to Vera, however, was a huge ordeal. I had to take it from someone else, which meant I had to trade something for it.

On one of my inspections of the city theatre, I came across a storage room filled with paper, ostensibly to produce posters for shows. Since there had been considerably less activity in the theatrical world since the start of the war, there was plenty extra. An older Ukrainian actress, by all accounts still strikingly beautiful, ran the theatre. She, like many female directors in the city, had an infamous reputation. It was rumored that she had affairs with Gregoriev and members of the city council. I sensed this was true when she repeatedly refused to adhere to the preventive measures I required her to undertake, but never received a reprimand. On an inspection with the property manager, I was led to her bedroom, which was in an apartment that contained a beautiful piano above the theatre. I was admiring the piano when the property manager pointed to the bed and told me, 'That is her real instrument. That is how she gets things done.'

The actress and I spoke occasionally before Vera went to Kazan, but we became more familiar after a conversation we had when I inquired about the paper. She said she would give me some next time I did an inspection. I thought nothing of it at first, but then she started to call the fire department on the direct line. Susin and Maria Gregorgivna suspected I was having an affair, her reputation was well known. I assured them that I was not involved with her at all.

I went to the theatre for an inspection and she was there. She took me around the facilities, showing me the costume room and backstage, plus the paper storage room. She said I could take 200 kilograms of paper. This was more than enough, more than I could use in fact. She took me up to her apartment and disappeared into the bathroom. When she emerged, she was wearing a soft negligée. This was not subtle at all, but I played the role of the naive refugee. When she made advances, I withdrew. In the end I did not offend her, but I was worried that I had jeopardized the retrieval of the paper. I need not have fretted; she found my behavior endearing and was more than happy to supply me with the materials, some of which I sold for money to send to Vera.

A few nights later there was a performance at the theatre. I was there in the seat reserved for the fire department – we had such a seat at all major gatherings. Sitting next to me was a line of city dignitaries, including Gregoriev and a few members of the city council. The Ukrainian actress came up to me and took me by the arm, leading me out of the seating area. 'Come', she said, 'let's make an inspection.' The provocation was unbearable! In a world relying so heavily on perception, this was an awful thing for me to endure.

Maria Gregorgivna was supposed to be a modern Soviet woman, and in a way she was. Her husband fought for the Red Army, her children were educated and enlisted in the Komsomol, and she worked for a civil department under the command of the NKVD. Superficially, she was the proto-typical Soviet mother. Under the surface, however, she longed to be Russian. She desperately clung to some of the older traditions, many of which were decidedly anti-Soviet.

Long before I arrived in Cerepovec, Maria Gregorgivna had given Vera's hand away. It was an arranged marriage to Igor Bobroff, the son of the bread factory director. Under the czar one was born into the aristocracy, under Stalin the direc-tors created an aristocracy. The Bobroff family was part of it and Maria Gregorgivna wanted her daughter to be part of it also. Clinging to this out-dated custom was strange for a modern Soviet woman, especially for Maria Gregorgivna since she had broken the arrangement her parents had made for her when she was a young woman.

Vera showed no interest in Igor, but his mother continued to pursue the arrangement with Maria Gregorgivna. Once she came to the station to look me over. The two mothers sat quietly in the office discussing innocuous topics until I politely excused myself. When I returned the two of them silently observed my every movement. It was an awkward day. Oddly, I liked Igor's father quite a bit. I received a lot of bread from his factory.

Vera and her sisters constantly tested Maria Gregorgivna's limits. To her, it was so important for them to maintain their Russian culture, even when the state did all it could to pull them away from the old ways. She spent a fortune preparing Russian dishes for them and throwing parties with Russian people. She sold off, piece by piece, almost everything in their apartment to raise money for these things. The effect was strong. You could see it in Vera's sentimentality and in her sister Nadya's temperament. There was something like the Jewish soul in them, something old and wise that I did not see in the others. The Soviet system, however, pulled harder and harder every year.

Before she went to Kazan, Vera was invited to a conference

in Vologda for all the editors of the industry-specific newspapers in the province. It was a Komsomol-sponsored event, and therefore, in reality, it was a lesson in political indoctrination. She was taught how to structure a newspaper better to benefit the people by including stories about holidays, the party, factory production and, of course, Stalin. While there, the girls talked about hairstyles. Her beautiful, traditional Russian braids were considered a thing of the past. Upon her return, Maria Gregorgivna was devastated, Vera had cut off her braids without consulting her mother.

Vera's increasing enthusiasm about the Soviet regime frightened me; I started to agree with everything she said out of fear she would denounce me. In the past, when we took excursions to the river, or walked through the fields, we were simply a young man and a young woman, free of political undertones. Things had changed, however, and even alone I felt I could no longer relate to her. Any time we were in a group of young people, her readiness to agree with the most outlandish opinions, even if government-generated, sickened me. I saw how the Soviet culture had sunk its teeth into her and would not let go. I felt for Maria Gregorgivna. She fought a silent battle to keep her daughter Russian, while I had all but given up the fight for her heart.

The Soviet youth had been told, since conception, that black was white and right was wrong. They were blind to the most horrible cruelties because they were so committed to the regime. They became killers themselves, believing that they were doing good work. For all intents and purposes, Stalin had replaced God and there were legions of politruks ready to sell this line. It was easy for me to reject the absurd propaganda of the Soviets because I had a Jewish upbringing and exposure to a world of literature unavailable to Vera and her peers. In contrast, they had newspapers with Stalin's name written 200–300 times per copy.

No person better exemplified the tragedy of the Soviet system than Vasily Bilyeff. Before Kazan, Vera told me with excitement that the bravest and most outstanding boy from her class had returned to Cerepovec on a ten-day leave. She very much wanted me to meet him. Most classes have such boys, the best at athletics, the strongest, the brightest and, in the Soviet case, the most patriotic. Vasily Bilyeff was the shining star of Cerepovec. We went to the Communist library to meet him.

He was impeccably dressed, very good-looking and heavily decorated. I asked him what he had done to earn so many medals at the front, but I received only a mumbled reply. Later, I asked Vera the same question. She told me he was not at the front, but he was a warden of a prison. I froze with this answer, I knew how wardens got their medals. Only by killing prisoners were you recognized for bravery in the penal system, a system filled with upwards of 90 per cent innocent people. If a prison guard wanted a vacation, he would throw a prisoner's hat over the boundary line and order him to get it. When the prisoner crossed the line, he would shoot. This Vasily was the hero of the Komsomol. The fact that Vera did not see the inherent evil of his position and revered him like the others, caused me even more alarm. I did not even talk about Vasily with her for fear that she would sense something anti-Soviet in my speech.

With my job as a censor and still working tirelessly for Susin, plus the fact that our personnel was not entirely capable of fighting fires on their own, I was extremely busy. The good news was the success of the Red Army against the Germans. By the spring of 1944, we sensed that victory would be ours. As I said, the rise in Russian nationalism greatly added to the fighting zeal of the Soviet troops. There was a backlash to this movement, however, as minorities in Russia suffered the hatreds of old.

Wounded soldiers of central Asian origin, like those from Uzbekistan, were treated poorly by the citizens of Cerepovec and also by the doctors and nurses at the temporary hospitals. They called them *ulyuki*, dried fruit, and categorized them as secondary priorities. Anti-Semitism also flourished at this time, and not just among the proletariat.

We received a call at the station that a woman had committed suicide in the elite section of the city. I went there to find that the mother of a senior officer had thrown herself down a well. Before doing this she had neatly placed her slippers off to the side. I heard the whispers, they were saying it was okay, she was only a Jew. This was devastating for me to hear. The allegiance to the Soviet system was so absolute in people's minds – take the reverence of Vasily Bilyeff as an example – but the death of a Jew, a mother of a senior officer, still meant nothing to the Russians. I went down the well by rope and retrieved the body. Giving her to her son, I told him quietly to say the Kaddish.

Even Vera, on one of her visits from Kazan, began to regard my Jewish ancestry as undesirable. On a walk through the streets of Cerepovec, she complained to me that her friends in the Komsomol were calling her a Jewess. 'I am not a Jewess!' she yelled with tears in her eyes. 'But Vera,' I said, 'I am a Jew.'

There were other incidents, examples of how anti-Semitism was a stronger force than the fear of being anti-Soviet. In our station I had an ugly confrontation with Tsvietaeff, the man who built our stoves. I walked through the garage and saw Zorina, the informant from the Komsomol. She now worked at the station and sometimes stood guard at night. She was talking to Tsvietaeff, which was not allowed while she was on duty. Since I was doing everything by the book at that point, and especially because she was an informant on my activities, I approached her and gave her a reprimand.

Tsvietaeff lost his temper. He bounced around on his one leg, screaming the most horrible things at me. 'You *kyke*! You bastard! You cowardly backliner! You diseased Jew!' He fell down and continued to yell. Soon the whole station had come into the garage. I stayed composed, asking the shift leader to please remove him from the station. Later Maria Gregorgivna came to me in tears, telling me that they all loved me. I replied sarcastically, 'Yes, I know. You all love me. Even the Germans love me.'

People at my professional level and above still clung to the old hatreds. I was sent to the fire prevention school in Vologda that spring to complete an officer's course. It consisted of a lot of theoretical exercises, problem solving and the learning of new techniques. I enjoyed these courses because I learned so much and because I was away from Cerepovec for a few days.

A Ukrainian military officer and I were the best tacticians

in the course and we were in competition for the top spot. We got along very well and worked together for a lot of the exercises. Together we would go to the yard for the 15-minute smoking break. On one of these breaks, the men told jokes and laughed. Inevitably some of the jokes were anti-Semitic, most of which I considered cruel but harmless. 'What does CCCP stand for?' one asked. 'Three Jews and a Russian.'

The tone increased in its acidity as some complained about the fire chief from one of the Vologda stations, Lieberman. They called him a conniving Jew and joked that he was transferred from the last station because he had slaughtered all their pigs for himself. A climbing instructor, a young fellow who had been with a band of guerillas during the early part of the war and had witnessed the slaughter of some Jews, comically mimicked their panic in the face of the Nazi guns. 'Oy! Oy! Oy!' he whined, while dancing comically. The others laughed. I was reminded of Dobra when they lined us up against the wall, this was probably the same noise. We thought we were going to die. His mimicking infuriated me and I put a stop to it.

To file a complaint about someone, you had to inform that person before contacting the official channels. I walked up to the young instructor and told him my intentions and immediately they all shut up. I did not walk around claiming I was a Jew, there was nothing heroic in doing that, but I had reached my limit. I was fortunate to have stayed as composed as I did, my first impulse was to fight him. The next day I spoke to the politruk of the school and filed my complaint. You should have seen how they respected me then.

In the end I finished first in the course, which was almost a disaster. Major Nikikan called me into his office and told me I had been promoted to fire inspector in another district, like Rabinin in Cerepovec. I was mortified; I did not want this, I did not even want to be a fire chief. I felt that my family would disappear in another district. Most likely I would be sent somewhere deep in the forest where we would be surrounded by backward Russian peasants. How could we survive as Jews? I had nothing to lose, so I appealed to his Russian soul.

I explained our familial situation. I had a mother who spoke no Russian and could not physically survive the extremities of forest life and I had an invalid brother. As a bookkeeper, Henya would have trouble working in such a region and would most likely have to stay in Cerepovec. The separation would devastate my mother, especially considering that we had already lost my father and Nuchem. I told him that my whole life was dedicated to the well-being of my family and I asked him if he could somehow relieve me from the position. He looked at me for a moment and then told me he would not promote me.

When you touched their humanity, when you peeled away that artificial Sovietism, they could be so good. Yes, there was entrenched anti-Semitism, but there was also a desire to adhere to the better principles of socialism. I believe Nikikan was going to give me whatever I wanted after I had filed the complaint, a gesture of good will to counter-balance the offensive jokes. For this I was very grateful. I knew that refusing this promotion would go into my permanent file and reflect poorly at some point, but I also knew I was under the protection of Rabinin, Gregoriev and now Major Nikikan. The alternative would have ruined my family.

Throughout the summer and autumn of 1944, I lived my life as a Soviet citizen fairly resolutely. I performed my duties diligently and tried to improve the lives of the people at the station. I was able to procure an empty field for a war garden, in which we planted potatoes and cabbage. On one half every member of the department was given two rows of potatoes and on the other half we shared the crop. Inevitably the individual rows flourished while the communal side suffered from lack of care. I threatened to turn the whole garden into a communal plot if things did not improve.

Getting the potatoes for the garden was fun. I took Pelta with me by steamboat up the river to a place called Miksa, the home of a huge agricultural Kolchozin. You should have seen the way Pelta attacked the buffet on the ride there! It was an official trip, so we did have money to pay for the potatoes, but still I had to bribe a few officials with gasoline and kerosene.

We went to a few different places and finally succeeded in bringing back about 20 bags of potatoes. In one of the bags I smuggled back some horsemeat. With this we were able to eat cabbage and potatoes with salt, and we caught plenty of fish from the nets I had requisitioned before. Things were not so bad.

Most everything went smoothly at the station, apart from the antics of Kopneen. He had taken Pelta under his wing in the most deplorable fashion. The two of them were constantly drunk and the previously innocent Pelta started to chase the girls. Kopneen was a happy person, a real charmer, but he was also a thief. He wore the station's boots and coats as if they were his own and did the minimum amount of work. He had affairs with various women at the station. He impregnated one woman who was already a mother. She tried to give herself an abortion and died from the complications. It was a tragedy. I spoke with Pelta about it, telling him that he was headed down the same road, and he soon reformed his behavior.

Vera returned from Kazan from time to time, and these were generally happy visits. When I knew of her return, I would get my hands on some biscuits and sweets and head over to Maria Gregorgivna's home. 'Girls', I would yell, 'put on the *kipjatok*!' Vera and her sisters loved it when I did this and I did too. Whether alone or with her Soviet friends, however, Vera and I continued to hold different ideas about the Soviet state. Maria Gregorgivna and I continued to supply her with materials for her schoolwork and Vera brought back beautiful felt-lined boots for my mother, but these things were superficial. We were not going to last, only I could not be the one to break things off.

To make a little extra money, Maria Gregorgivna rented out rooms in her apartment to soldiers and officers passing through Cerepovec. When I visited Vera on her returns, I never knew what kind of person would be staying at their house. One officer, a commander of a small torpedo boat, came through the city a few times a year. He was very tall and very handsome. His clothing was English; made with wool we had never seen before. He was much admired, but he was a terrible drunk. He had an affair with the woman who ran the orphanage; the same woman, we discovered, who had reported my mother when she tried to take care of the barber's daughter. She was in love with him, but it was an unrequited love; he had affairs at every port. One night he returned to Maria Gregorgivna's apartment very drunk, looking as if he would fly into a rage. Everyone was afraid of him, but I knew that he had a sense of humor. I walked up to him and cautiously took off his belt. He was so confused that he laughed. He liked me immediately. A few hours later, after he had told me how stupid the woman at the orphanage was and how great a fighter he was, he gave me a gift. It was a beautiful, flat officer's pistol with one clip. This was unheard of in Russia, that a civilian should have a pistol. I should not have taken it, but I did. I did not tell anyone about it, not even my mother.

In the bigger picture, the Red Army advanced steadily through Europe. Each time a major city was captured, fireworks and Soviet music filled our skies. Official announcements were bombastic and cheerful – without a doubt the great Stalin was leading us to the finest victory of our history. Every now and then, if I listened carefully, I heard an underlying anti-American sentence or two during the announcements. I could already sense the propaganda machine gearing up for another malicious battle of defamation.

The cold weather returned to Cerepovec and life went on. My twenty-third birthday came and went with little fanfare, and soon we were deep into winter. Apart from a catastrophe or a denunciation, I had nothing to worry about. My connections kept my family and many of the refugees adequately supplied through the winter, and the war, we felt, would end soon. The Association of Polish Patriots was still active in the region, my sister included, and materials sent from abroad sometimes ended up in our homes. On one February day, however, my whole world fell apart.

Susin had gone to Vologda for an officer's course, leaving me responsible for the fire department. In practice this was not much of a change, but symbolically it was; I was accountable for whatever happened. I was at the cinema, in the seat reserved for the fire department, when I received the call. The power plant, where I used to work, was on fire. The shift leader had already dispatched the five-ton tanker. I told them to pick me up with the other truck, which was smaller but equipped with a hydraulic pump.

En route to the fire we overtook the tanker. The condition of the roads in Cerepovec was abysmal. The tanker had slid on the ice and hit a pothole, breaking its front axle. This was such a disaster. Not only had we lost one of our vehicles, but we had also lost precious time in the battle against the fire. If the turbine room continued to blaze, there would eventually be a major explosion. Every second was critical.

We arrived on the scene and backed our truck to the frozen river's edge. We were fortunate there had been a warm spell recently; cracks in the ice along the banks made access to water possible without chopping a hole. Because there was water in the hose already, the hydraulic pump was already primed. This would not have been the case if I did not change the operating procedures; priming a dry pump took upwards of ten minutes. This would have spelled the end of the power plant.

I had my crew spray only the turbine room as I put on fireproof clothing. They hosed me down with water and I entered the fire. I knew where the pressure valves were located because I had spent time in that room with the head mechanic. I was able to open up the valves and get out of the blaze in time. Soon we had controlled the fire and avoided an explosion. Major Gregoriev from the NKVD made us into heroes.

Trying to return to the station was a problem. Our truck was stuck at the river's edge; we could not get it up the hill. The earth was muddy and the pump, which was on the back, would have been damaged if we pulled it up with a winch. Some of my crew told me that we should take it out on the ice. There were still lumber-carrying trucks on the river, so clearly it could handle the weight of our vehicle, but I was still unsure. I sent my number six, the liaison, to Gregoriev to explain the situation and ask if we should risk the river. He came back and said that we should go on the ice.

The driver was a bitter man, a wounded soldier with a bad

stomach. He and I did not get along very well and he was one of those that never wanted to do anything extra. I told him that we would have to drive fast across the ice to lessen the chances of breaking through and minimize our time on the river. He told me he did not think it was a good idea to go on the ice at all. We pushed the truck back a ways and loaded ourselves in. 'Go! Go!' I yelled.

We were under way and moving quickly. We heard the ice cracking underneath us but we seemed to be clear of danger. For some reason the driver started to slow down. 'Keep going!' I yelled, but it was too late. The back of the truck dropped into a crack in the ice. We all ran to safety. The driver told me he thought he had seen a hole ahead of us, but there was none.

The truck was sitting on the ice with its back end close to falling through. Nearby a group of people repaired a barge. I sent my crew over to them to collect some logs and an anchor chain to make a winch. I thought we might be able to roll the vehicle out of the crack in the ice and pull it to shore.

As soon as we attached the chain the ice started creaking loudly. We fled quickly. I turned back from the shore and watched the entire truck drop and sink to the bottom of the river. It was surreal. Such a disaster could not possibly have happened. The driver and the rest of the crew moved to the side and had a laugh at the situation. I, on the other hand, felt a panic I had not felt since the cemetery. I was responsible for everything. I would get 25 years for this, I thought, and my family would be sent to the forest.

This was a total disaster. Never in the history of the fire department had such a series of events occurred. The five-ton tanker was disabled, the hydraulic pump truck was underwater, and all that remained was a small transport truck at the station. The city was helpless. I had reached my lowest ebb. I wanted to kill myself.

I marched a few crewmembers down to the port and commandeered a truck. I had already standardized the instruments during our preventive campaign, and it was within my rights to take it over in an emergency. I left them there to be on call. I brought the others back to the station and asked the office girls to call other stations to locate a broken-down tanker from which we could get an axle. There were no spare parts in Russia, so fixing the tanker looked to be a long process.

I went into our apartment and I saw my mother. I told her what had happened and she understood immediately what kind of danger I was in. There was no electricity because of the fire; the gray, gloomy atmosphere compounded my feeling of despondency. I packed a bag in preparation for prison.

Two hours later I received a call from the NKVD. I put on my boots and picked up my bundle of clothing. I reported to Gregoriev. 'How much will I get for this?' I asked.

'Stupid. Sit down. Tell me what happened.' He was calm and gentle. I explained everything to him. We both remembered that I had appealed for the construction of a new bridge in that area long ago. If a bridge had been there, surely this disaster would have been avoided; I had written many memoranda to this effect. Gregoriev said that he believed I did everything I could have done and saw no reason to reprimand me. There would be, however, an inspection delegation from Vologda coming the next day, as was standard with any kind of mishap.

I was mortified. As soon as they heard my accent, saw my papers and listened to the account of the driver, who had said it was not a good idea, I would be sent away. Gregoriev knew this and did something for me for which I have been eternally grateful. He sent me with Rabinin on an inspection tour of the outlying villages, at least a week-long trip.

We left that night by sled. It was cold, so I ran behind to keep warm from time to time. We came to a village inn. It was a dark and decadent establishment, more czarist than Soviet in its décor. The people inside sat like devils in deep chairs and smoked heavily. Rabinin had a girlfriend there and disappeared quickly. Someone heated up a room for me and I went in to sleep. A few moments later a girl came to my door. This, I understood, was standard practice for Rabinin on an inspection tour, but I wanted nothing to do with it.

We inspected various factories and trained groups of peasants in basic fire-fighting skills. The trip took us just over a week to complete and when we returned the delegation from Vologda had already departed. Gregoriev had indeed saved me. Of course, I was still facing some major dilemmas, not least of which was retrieving the truck from the bottom of the river.

Gregoriev asked me how I planned to get the truck back. I told him the first thing we needed to do was find out if it had landed on its wheels or not. For this we needed divers. Gregoriev called the commander of the military divisions stationed in Cerepovec for the winter and asked him if he had any divers. They did. By chance a flotilla had wintered in Cerepovec and was in possession of a primitive underwater breathing system. I went to meet the divers, picking up four cases of vodka along the way. I gave them some alcohol and they agreed to help us out.

The divers went under water and I was trembling. If the truck had turned over, it was lost completely; at best we could return in the spring and salvage some parts. When they returned to the surface they gave me great news. The truck was on all four wheels and the anchor chain was still attached to the front. If we pulled correctly, we could bring her right out of the water. But how would we pull it?

The people at the port gave us a portable winch on a sled. To use this required more manpower than I had, so Gregoriev supplied me with four German prisoners of war. Moishe guarded the Germans with a rifle. If the situation were not so serious I would have laughed. What kind of guard was Moishe? He was yelling at them, 'Fritz! Hans! Fritz!' We strapped the Germans like horses to the sled and sent them onto the ice. A diver went in the water to connect the two chains. Suddenly the ice cracked and the sled fell through, taking the Germans with it. Two of the prisoners drowned, though not many of us cared. Still, I had to bring them back to Gregoriev, dead or alive. It cost me another case of vodka convincing the divers to retrieve the bodies.

We needed another idea. I consulted with Horkoff, my labor brain trust. He suggested we build something called a 'priest'. We dug a hole about one-meter deep, wide enough to insert a sturdy log vertically. The log was stripped of its bark and we greased the end stuck into the earth. We drilled a hole and slid an iron bar through the top perpendicularly. I understood the name; it was a cross, made of iron and wood. With the help of the divers, we attached the anchor chain to the priest and slowly turned the mechanism. It functioned perfectly, but it was hard work and took a long time. As the men churned their legs, I came to them with small cups of vodka, giving them a boost from time to time.

We succeeded in bringing the truck out of the water, but we were unable to pull it to the road. We were in the same position we were in before, only this time I was not taking chances. I acquired a tractor from the agricultural Kolchozin. It had treads like a tank and was steel-protected. We had no trouble dragging the truck from the river's edge, though we did damage the pump a little bit. With this tractor we were able to tow the five-ton tanker as well. It was an exhausting day, but we had succeeded in our task.

As it happened, the day we pulled the trucks back to the station was the national holiday for firefighters. That evening we had a great party. The divers joined us – they had plenty of vodka – and we celebrated our accomplishments. Later I could not get rid of them – they came back to the station every day because they liked our girls. In time we arranged for both vehicles to be fixed and the whole incident was forgotten. It remained, however, in my permanent file. It was just something else they could use against me should someone decide to denounce me.

The German POWs sent by Gregoriev came from a series of camps that had been set up around Cerepovec. There were separate camps for senior officers, officers and enlisted men. The separation was probably a result of some Geneva Convention stipulation.

I went to the barracks of the senior officers once for an inspection. It was quite a way from the city. I was amazed to see the privileges they enjoyed. Each officer still had his personal weapons and there were attendants waiting on all of them. There were even flowers on the tables. By law, however, they had to stand up when I walked in. I made them stand up for a long time while I checked everything in their barracks. After some time I turned to them and said, 'Do you know who I am? I am a Jewish boy from Kalisz, near Poznan, you cursed Germans!' I accomplished nothing by saying this, but I felt like I had to say something.

The other two camps, for junior officers and enlisted men, were in what was called the Red Village, a place where they were put through a rigorous course of anti-fascist indoctrination. The intent was to make them communists, though I never believed such an action would work. There was a newspaper printed for them called *Freies Deutschland*, which glorified Stalin and made heroes out of the prisoners who had already proven themselves comrades. I found it laughable, the Germans were so arrogant, even as prisoners, but the city needed them as part of the labor force. Factories were taking 10 or 15 prisoners a day and the Germans were soon socializing with the Russian girls. They were everywhere. The people of Cerepovec were unhappy with the city crawling with Germans while their sons were somewhere at the front or already dead, but the manpower was needed. At times their anger could not be suppressed. I witnessed a woman shake a ladder used by a German housepainter. She was cursing at him and crying and she shook the ladder until he fell. Such was the relationship.

There was a fire in the disinfecting room at the Red Village one day, to which I brought a crew. Instead of risking anyone of my people, I set up a few prisoners with a hose and let them fight the blaze. They put out the fire, but later I was called into the military offices of the city because the prisoners had filed a complaint. They were already comrades, they claimed, why did I make them fight the fire? I spoke with a lieutenant colonel about the situation. I explained my history with the Germans, and I told him it was a joke to think that they were becoming communists. I would not be told how to treat the Germans. He never bothered me again.

There was a hospital for the POWs in the Red Village. Not many people came out of that hospital feeling better, they were dying left and right. I went there on an inspection once and opened up the attic. There lay many, many dead Germans, with rats coming out of their bellies.

The senior officers' camp was eventually transformed into a Red Army barrack for a wintering division. I thought the men were unlucky to have been put in a camp so far away from the city, but then we discovered the reason. This division was made up of criminals taken from prisons and was used for the most dangerous missions, they were known as the Wild Division. Everyone was afraid of them, even the military personnel in Cerepovec. No one could stop them from robbing the houses near their camp or stop them from raping the Russian girls.

To my horror, I received a report that there was a fire in the Wild Division barracks one night. I went there with my crew, only to discover they had started the fire themselves. They would not let us in, not even to see the blaze. They trained their weapons on us and threatened to shoot if we tried to enter. The men leered at the women of my crew and I grew nervous. I asked to speak to their commanding officer, which eventually I did. He was just like the others, with his hat cock-eyed and his great coat draped slovenly across his shoulders. I told him they would destroy their barracks for no reason and that we could help them build a fire somewhere nearby until a brick stove could be built inside. He listened to me and even agreed, but he knew the character of his men and was not about to do a thing. Eventually, when it became clear they would in fact burn down their barracks, he convinced some of his division to help. We built another fire and I brought back bricks for a stove the next day. This was my only run-in with the Wild Division.

Vera sent frantic letters from Kazan. In the Soviet system, each student was required to perform some sort of national service before advancing to the next year of coursework. In Kazan the students had to work in the forest. Vera was terrified to do this. She had heard terrible things about the conditions in the forest and rumors of sexual abuse from the Kazani supervisors. She did not know what to do.

Maria Gregorgivna decided to take her out of Kazan and send her to the newly reopened pediatric medicine school in Leningrad. It was not as easy as it seems. There was something like Molotov's Law in effect – she had to have an exceptional reason to withdraw from her schooling. We took a chance and sent official orders from the fire department, completely fabricated, calling her back to Cerepovec for special service. With these papers she received a release from the university and a train ticket home. It was perfect, only Vera foolishly forgot to get an exit stamp in her passport.

Maria Gregorgivna arranged a meeting for Vera in Leningrad with an admissions officer at the school. She had found enough money to finance her schooling and Vera was a very good student, but acceptance was contingent on having official residency papers from the city of Leningrad. Because the city was just getting back on its feet, any newcomer had to prove that he or she had at least 20 square meters of living space to be given residency papers. This, plus her passport not having the proper notation, posed some major logistical problems. Still, I was determined to get Vera settled in Leningrad because the alternative, her staying in Cerepovec, was unbearable.

I took her passport to the NKVD offices and entered the office of passport control. A friend of mine sat behind the desk. We were not too close, but I was hoping she would help me. I handed her Vera's passport and asked her for an exit stamp from Kazan and an entry stamp for Cerepovec. I was very nervous, if she thought this was strange, which it was, she could report me. If I was questioned the false papers we sent to Kazan could get a lot of us in trouble. Still, there was no other choice. Thankfully she did not even look at the name. She stamped the passport and everything seemed normal.

We decided that I would go with Vera to Leningrad to make sure she was settled properly. I wrote to a fire department there and asked to be enrolled in a safety course teaching the new British techniques of fighting fire with foam. They sent me the paperwork needed to get into the city, so everything was in order for our departure. I took with me a personal letter from a telephone girl at the station, promising to deliver it, and two suitcases of cakes my mother had baked for the trip. We knew that bribes in Leningrad usually included food – the city was still half-starved.

This was my first visit to Leningrad, a city I had read so much about. It was beautiful, more beautiful than any of the pictures I had seen. I marveled at the magnificent bridges over the canals and the splendid monuments on the Neva river. The siege, however, had left many gaping wounds in the city's façade. There were still trenches, partially covered, left over from violent battles with the Germans. Many statues were covered with wood, temporarily camouflaging the damage. Buildings had signs telling pedestrians to only walk on certain sides, as the structures were no longer solid. The people were thin and downtrodden and the city smelled of hunger and sickness.

We had specific directions to get us to the home of Maria Gregorgivna's cousin, Vinogradovna. Vera was to stay there while in school, even though her own space would amount to far less than 20 square meters. We took a trolley from the train station to Vesileff Island. The trolley was packed with people; the more agile clung to the back. We arrived at the apartment building and rang the bell a certain number of times. All the apartments were subdivided and each tenant answered a specific number of rings. Vinogradovna ushered us into the apartment.

There was only one room and it was tiny. In it lived Vinogradovna, her husband and her son. Vera would have to sleep in a chair. The family was not too Soviet-minded. Her husband was a waiter at an old-fashioned luxury hotel left over from the czar's time. Her son was a composer and pianist, but he had lost a hand in the war. He lived as a specu-lator on the black market.

Vera and I went to the meeting with the admissions officer of the school. She was a friendly woman, but very officious. I gave her some cakes, but still she said she could not accept her as a student. Without exception she had to have the residency papers from the city. Everything else, however, was in order.

We went to the Winter Palace Plaza, one of the most famous buildings in Leningrad. On the fourth floor sat the general who gave permission to people wanting to remain in the city. Vera went in to see him. We hoped she could persuade him to give her the right papers. Although she did not have 20 square meters of space, she did have an address in the city, a good record of party activity, a promise of acceptance at the pediatric medicine school and her youth. We were confident this would be enough.

The general was a stern, imposing man and Vera was terrified. I sat back and watched this proud, independent young woman turn into a puppy in front of him. She spoke like a child and he gave her no sympathy. She was refused papers and had 24 hours to leave the city. We stepped out of his office and she cried. She would have to go back to Cerepovec.

I went back into his office. I told him my position and asked if I could report to him. I explained how Vera was working for us in many different areas and had become an important asset to the NKVD. He knew exactly what I meant. He told me to come back with documents from the school and documents from the living quarters.

We left the Winter Palace Plaza and went to an exclusive area of town where I hoped to deliver the letter from the telephone girl. I could tell that these apartments were reserved for members of the KGB – they were too nice for anyone else. Vera waited outside. After some haranguing from the doorman, I was finally able to deliver the letter. I entered their apartment to find them drinking tea. Heavy aromas still hung in the air from what must have been an excellent feast. I stood soaking wet, as it always rained in Leningrad, and politely announced myself to them. They took the letter and did not even offer me a seat. Despite their rude behavior, I asked if they could help Vera with her situation, figuring they were heavily connected in Leningrad. When I told them the name of the general, they said they could do nothing. I sensed they would not have done anything regardless. I left feeling bitter.

Vera and I returned to Vinogradovna's apartment. It was getting late and the question of where I was to sleep arose. The family was not too sympathetic; they were not going to make room for me there. I left Vera and went to the fire station where I was supposedly taking a course. They gave me a sofa in the waiting room and stamped my documents, stating that I had taken the course. It was a lie, but there was camaraderie among firemen.

The next morning I returned to the apartment determined to

get Vera's residency papers and school acceptance. I sat for a moment in the kitchen they shared with other tenants. There was a Jewish woman making tea. 'Why are you together with a *shiksa* [an unmarried gentile woman]?' she asked. I did not answer her, but I did not know myself. We spoke for a while and she told me two wonderful things. First, the property manager of their building was a Jewish woman named Rosa. Second, that day was a Jewish holiday and I could go to the synagogue. There was a synagogue! I had not seen one in years.

I went to see Rosa the property manager right away. I brought her a bag of cakes and explained the situation to her. I asked her to write a false note stating that Vera had 20 meters of space in that building. She was sympathetic but afraid. She asked me how dangerous it was to give me such a document. I told her it was between her, Vera and me. She agreed to do it. I wanted to kiss her, Vera would not be coming back to Cerepovec.

We went from Rosa's office to the admissions officer and showed her the living-space document. Because Vera needed the official papers from the city the woman could not yet enroll her, but she typed a letter stating that she had been accepted. We took these to the general and Vera presented herself proudly. He issued the documents. We returned to the admissions officer and in a few minutes Vera was officially enrolled. Everything had worked out.

We both felt very relieved. The rest of the day was ours to enjoy. We strolled up and down the canals, looking at the beautiful city and stopping at famous sites, like Dostoevsky's house. We went to a celebrated pastry shop and waited in three queues, one to order, one to pay and one to pick up. Although the process lasted over an hour, it was pleasant. We walked to the synagogue. Vera waited for me as I approached the damaged building. Outside there was a sign thanking Comrade Kagolovitch for fixing the roof and inside there was another asking for alms to be put in a box and not given directly to beggars. I had tears in my eyes seeing signs written in the Hebrew. I said the Kaddish and put some money in the box. It had been so long.

I intended to leave that night, but I wanted to get my ticket early. We went to the station and waited in line. From out of the blue Galina Yafimiva stormed over to us, stamped her foot like a horse, yelled '*Nyet!*' then spun around and marched away. I was shocked. I had not seen her in many months, not since she had been transferred back to Leningrad. She had written letters to the station asking about the Polish boys, but I had no idea that seeing me with Vera would make her so upset. It was very strange.

In the evening Vera and I went to a film. Before the picture began, people danced. Vera wanted me to dance but I told her I was exhausted. In reality I did not feel like dancing, I never felt like dancing. In my mind I was never young, I was always overburdened with problems, real and imagined. I apologized and joked about how beautiful the men of Leningrad would find her.

After the film I needed to get back to the station. Vera wanted to join me, but the trams were over-full and the weather was dismal. I told her to stay. We kissed goodbye. This was the last time I ever saw her. In Cerepovec I continued supporting her financially and helping her family, but for the most part it was over.

I was selected to be a member of the jury for a series of trials that took place in the early spring of 1945. A man came to the fire station and asked for three people to serve as jurors. Susin chose Zorina, Moishe and me. Whatever laws written in the Soviet constitution about the procedures of trials were loosely followed, this was universally known. I was skeptical and afraid of what role we were expected to play.

The trials were at a jailhouse, not a courthouse. We were seated in a booth near the back of a small and dark room. Three older men, a troika of judges, followed us into the room and sat at a table facing the entryway. An older man was brought to the front. He reminded me of the man I had worked with and had given tobacco to during the defense work. One of the judges stood up and told the man that he had been accused of anti-government activity and described in some detail his offense. He had been drunk and raised a glass, pronouncing that he was drinking to the third czar. There was no defense. They did not ask him any questions.

The troika withdrew for five minutes and returned. A different judge stood up and told the man he had been found guilty and sentenced to 15 years in prison plus the confiscation of his property. The old man fell to his knees and crossed himself. They took him away. We sat in our booth, scared to death.

The next person brought in was a woman. She was a resident of the part of Russia that Finland had occupied during the Finnish war. In conversation she had said that the Finns were nice people and that life, if they had stayed, would not have been that bad. She was sentenced to six years.

Another woman was sentenced to six years for stealing bread from the bread factory in which she worked. The guard suspected she had done it before. When they took her away she cried, 'My children are starving!'

Finally a skinny, frightened boy was brought into the room. He could not have been more than 12 years old. He had been mobilized to a vocational school as Moishe was for a short time. He ran away and was caught. He was also sentenced to six years.

With this we finished and were led out of the room. It was an absolutely horrifying experience. Why were none of the defendants allowed to speak? Their despair was palpable and their grief overwhelming. I thought of the barber and all the refugees who had been sentenced to prison. How empty they must have felt, how defenseless. I was consumed with anger over the injustice I had seen, but I had no outlet for my emotion. With whom could I speak of such an evil corruption of justice?

A few days later the same man returned to the station. His name was Lieutenant Lefkovitz, a Jew. He brought me something to sign, a document officially condemning these people to their sentences. This was the role of a juror in that crooked Soviet system.

I had pledged to God that I would not put myself above others, yet if I signed these papers I would be doing my part to destroy four innocent peoples' lives. My heart and my head would not let me attach my name to their demise. I told Lieutenant Lefkovitz that I would not sign. He was flabbergasted. Who in the Soviet Union refused official duties? He told me it was just a technicality and that their fates were already determined, but still I would not sign. I appealed to his Jewish sensibilities, telling him about my life at Moraviny and explaining my deal with God. He understood that I would not sign even if it meant my own death and at this he departed. I did not know what would happen next.

I saw my mother after our meeting and I told her what had happened. She knew we were in grave danger, but she was proud of me. 'Let it be, Henrik', she said, 'this was the only decision.'

A few days later Lieutenant Lefkovitz returned to the station. He was there to inform us that the next trial was to take place within our reading room. I looked at him with inquisitive glances, but he acted as if nothing had happened. I began to panic. What if I was to go on trial in my own station as an example to the others? I finally caught Lefkovitz alone and asked him what I should expect. He told me to relax. He had signed my name for me and there was nothing more. Lefkovitz, like Mr Staszik, the Schwartzer Yankel, Afanasief, Gregoriev and so many others, had become one of my angels. I felt like the hand of God still rested over my head.

On 9 May 1945, there was an announcement over the radio in the middle of the night. The loudspeakers shook throughout the city with the amplified bass of Comrade Levitan's voice. The Soviets had won the war. Cerepovec was drunk.

At the station we had bread and cranberry juice, sweet beer and vodka. Susin was tippling. He decided he and I should fly the Red Flag above our city hall, just as it flew over the Reichstag in Berlin. On the roof we discovered that the flagpole had rotted, but this could not stop Susin. We rigged a makeshift pole by wedging the existing pieces between two ladders. Then, with more pride than grace, he triumphantly hoisted the flag. That night I discovered that Susin also had an illegal pistol, because it fell out of his pocket and landed on my head!

In Moscow a massive parade rolled through the streets and into Red Square. It was a cavalcade of massive machinery and proud soldiers led by Marshal Zukov riding an enormous and beautiful white horse. With pride and sentiment, the Soviets threw German flags at the step of Lenin's Tomb. The glory was intoxicating, the confidence of the nation was dangerously high. After the parade a dark and heavy rain fell on Moscow. The older Russian women called it a bad omen.

Before the war ended we heard the names of those familiar Polish cities: Baranovici, Warsaw, Lodz. I was over the moon on hearing those names. Now that it was over I wondered if I would see those places again. I went to the train station from time to time and I looked at how shiny the tracks had become from all the movement. I hoped those silver tracks would take me back to Poland some day.

Soldiers across the vast expanse of the Soviet empire sent back packages filled with looted materials. Maria Gregorgivna's husband sent a package with clothing still marked with pink triangles and yellow stars. Maria Gregorgivna had no idea what these denotations meant, but, since I had worn a yellow arm sash, it was not difficult for me to understand.

Soon waves of soldiers returned to the city. They were exalted and covered with medals, but they were simply not ready for normal life. To get up, go to work and return home while adhering to the strict code of the Soviet system was a near impossibility. The streets were crawling with drunks by day and by night. To counteract this, the press downplayed the role of the soldiers and increased its glorification of the party. Placards lined the streets: 'If you do not work for the people, your medals are worth nothing!' POWs, returned from German prisons, were sent directly to Soviet prisons. We saw trains wrapped with barbed wire roll through Cerepovec. They were charged with desertion and their families were prosecuted as well. Even men who had fought as guerillas, having been somehow cut off from their ranks, were treated as deserters. The KGB prosecuted thousands, dropping another bureaucratic blanket over the whole of Russia. Stalin feared the glory of the Red Army would supersede his own.

With this readjustment came a general uneasiness among the people. The infidelity during the war had to cease, but these patterns were not easy to break. Reunited couples celebrated then bickered, sometimes cyclically. A return to relative normality, oddly, strained their fragile relationships.

Compounding their problems were massive shortages across the Soviet Union. How, we wondered, with all the territory acquired during the war could we still be suffering from lack of food? One answer was the end of the Lend–Lease program, which the Americans terminated after Stalin's aggressiveness at Yalta and Potsdam. Stalin refused to recognize the Polish government in exile; he had his own plans for Poland.

The hospitals in Cerepovec changed from short-term to long-term units as the front moved across Europe. Now at the end of the war many of the converted schools and factories were reverting to their original uses. I was on the city's Commission of Health and Security; I inspected these buildings before the original occupants moved back in. I was surprised to discover that the special treatment rooms were still intact and sealed off. The Jewish property manager at the teachers' college told me they were keeping them ready in case there was a war with the Americans. The confidence, the spirit of nationalism, was so high that they believed they could do anything.

The end of the war brought changes to my family and the refugee community. Personally, I was freed from my job as a censor and, with the return of the soldiers, I no longer had to perform so many duties at the station. My time was occupied mostly with inspecting buildings and training the new recruits, but I joined Henya at the various meetings held by the Association of Polish Patriots. I had come to the conclusion that it was safe to join this organization and I did not try to hide my involvement. We held meetings in our apartment from time to time, where we would pass out materials sent from abroad and discuss our futures. We all wanted to return to Poland, but the opportunity had yet to present itself.

To my mind the political climate in the Soviet Union was getting worse and I was nervous about our fate. Stalin continued to present himself as a god while downplaying the role of the other allied forces during the war; this despite the fact that western materials, even after the termination of the Lend–Lease Program, kept much of the population alive. I wondered when he would turn on the refugees, since his patterns of glorification seemed to coincide with the vilification of other groups. With shortages of food and machinery so widespread, not helped by the continual strain of having to use the power of the bayonet to bring the Soviet system to newly occupied territories, I was sure Stalin would either throw us all into prison or force us to return to Poland. I prayed for the latter.

The Association of Polish Patriots printed a newspaper called *Free Poland*, which was Stalinist in its perspective but still talked about repatriation as early as the summer of 1945. No official actions, however, seemed to take place and as the summer left and autumn began, we were still unsure if and when we would be able to leave. We had a meeting at our apartment in the middle of the autumn not only to discuss repatriation, but also to distribute clothing. It was at this meeting that I met my future wife, Shelly.

I recognized her as she had been at a few of the previous meetings, but I remembered seeing her before. She was in the same car as the Zelver family on that long train ride from Kovel to the forest. She stood, so vulnerably, on the hard packed snow as we disembarked in Cerepovec. I remember thinking how beautiful she was and how, like a precious flower, she needed protection in that environment. Later in Cerepovec, she sold juices from a kiosk outside the *banja*. My father used to buy cranberry juice from her on the walks back home. Recently I had seen her at the funeral of Marszalkovitch, one of Cerepovec's most famous doctors. She remembered seeing me as well.

As the others huddled around the clothing, we talked at first haltingly, then comfortably about literature, politics and Poland. She had gone to *gymnasium* before the war and had studied tirelessly since coming to Russia. She knew more about literature than I did, which, to me, was magic. I asked her about her family and she started to cry. I was so touched by her tears. I saw in her a symbol of Jewish purity, something that had survived untainted by the Soviet experiment. This was a revelation for me – she was so pure that I was afraid to touch her. My first instinct was to protect her.

At the end of the meeting I asked her if I could meet her again to continue our conversation. We agreed to see each other at the library a few days later. Foolishly, I did not specify which library. I went to the komsomol library and Shelly went to the city library. We did not meet and I did not know where she lived. In my mind I thought that maybe it was for the best. I still had the situation with Vera to tend to and I did not want Maria Gregorgivna to find out. In my heart, however, I was very disappointed. Talking with Shelly was the truest sensation I had felt since we had set foot on Russian soil.

A few weeks later there was a pot-luck party for all the refugees at the Tempchins' house. Shelly used this as an excuse to come over to our apartment, ostensibly to ask my mother what she should bring. I was home when she arrived. She was a little flustered, not really sure of what she was saying, but in the end she asked me why I had not gone to the library. When we discovered our mistake, we were both overjoyed, I already felt love for her.

It was a good party, full of life and laughter. We were facing another winter in Russia but we could feel a spring-like wind blowing from the west. Although Stalin had taken no official action to repatriate the refugees, the feeling was that a move was imminent. Our mood was light and our hopes were high. Shelly and I talked through the evening and when the party finished, we walked home together with my family. My mother and I had a moment alone and she asked me, 'Henrik, is this for you?' I said, 'Yes, mother, it is.'

We fell in love but it was not easy. She asked me about Vera and I told her everything. I told her that Vera was not for me but it would take time before the situation was healed and in the meantime I was still pretending to be with her, it was awful, but I had no choice. Shelly did not understand the danger I was in, nor did she know my past dealings, which made it difficult for her to trust me, but she did, and for this I considered her an angel.

We knew we were in love. There was something absolutely correct in our togetherness. I believe we both agreed that our personal happiness was secondary to the struggle of our people. We knew we were the seeds of the new Jewish people and even if we were forced to go through a heartbreaking time, we would work things out.

I desperately wanted to return to Poland. My involvement with the Association of Polish Patriots was not secret in my professional circles, but my most heartfelt desire was. I carried on a two-faced play throughout the final months of 1945 and into early 1946. On the inside I was in love with Shelly and awaiting official instructions from the Soviet government to repatriate, while on the outside I was waiting for Vera to return and trying to carve a niche for my future family in the Soviet experiment. If Maria Gregorgivna entered our apartment, the picture of Vera needed to be on the wall. If Shelly was there, the picture was hidden in a drawer.

Shelly was a nurse in the temporary hospitals in Cerepovec. With their closure, she was out of a job. Henya took her to the restaurant and found her employment as a dietician. This was a meaningless job, but one that needed to be filled since it was Soviet-created. She did nothing all day but watch party fat-cats eat with silver cutlery on white linen, while outside the hunger persisted. She could not stand the position. Eventually a long-term care hospital opened in Sokol and Shelly was offered a job as a nurse. She accepted the position.

We went for a walk before she left. She wore a light dress with a floral print and as she walked I wondered whether her feet were actually touching the ground – in my eyes she was floating. She was beautiful to me and she amazed me with her modesty. After we had passed through the bazaar I noticed that we were on the same street that Vera and I used to walk, at the same spot where Vera and I fought about my Jewish heritage. The situations, however, were incomparable, I found comfort and trust with Shelly and I knew, undeniably, that she was my future.

When Shelly left for Sokol, I went through every day gritting my teeth. I did not want to drink one more glass of vodka, I did not want to praise Stalin one more time and I did not want to attend one more party where everybody touted how wonderful everything was. I was sick of it, but I was forced to keep my intentions and feelings bottled up.

The paradoxical rhetoric of the Soviets made my head throb and my heart sink. There was an election to the Supreme Soviet in which the only candidate was a woman from a kolchozin, Markeliva. I voted alongside many others who carried flags and placards like it was a celebration. It was a farce, yet afterwards I was required to explain to the fire department staff how the Soviet constitution had provided a glorious and free election for the people. The hypocrisy was killing me. In my imagination I could smell the fresh Polish air, but in reality I was choking on the exhaust of the Soviet machine.

Finally, at the end of January, *Free Poland* published instructions for repatriation. As a group, the refugee community was overjoyed. It was, at this point, almost unthinkable to remain in Russia. We had created in our minds an image of Poland in springtime, with flowers and trees in bloom and opportunity in every city. In contrast, Russia had become a sea of gray and dust, a land where no Jew could live well. Still, we knew the reality of the situation was a far cry from what we imagined and we were fearful of what we would find upon our return. According to the state news agency, our only source for information, Poland was a wasteland. People were dying of hunger and we were to be sent back in the hundreds of thousands. Did we survive this long only to return to another famished land, perhaps more perilous than our situation in Russia? We would know soon enough – nothing would deter our return.

Shelly returned from Sokol and registered for repatriation in Cerepovec. She talked openly with the doctors in Sokol about her decision, telling them that she was nervous to return. Doctor Durnievsky, the head doctor of the hospital, told her he would climb into her suitcase if he could.

I faced a different set of problems. I could not talk openly with my colleagues about repatriation because I pretended not to want to go. I told everyone at the station that I was unable to convince my mother to stay in Cerepovec, and thus was forced to register. I told them I would go with my family as far as Vologda and leave them there if I was convinced they were in good hands. I told many other little lies, each one a justification and regret for my imminent repatriation.

I met with officials from the Association of Polish Patriots and showed them my old documents from the Kalisz Chamber of Commerce. I was listed as a carpenter, a classification I had not possessed since the first few days in Moraviny. Moishe, Henya and my mother all registered as well. We had no trouble with the association, but to leave I still needed permission from the fire department, and thus the NKVD.

The way I saw it, the NKVD was to review my file and decide whether or not I would go to prison or Poland. They would review everything I had done at the station from the book of matches I had stolen to the submerged truck disaster. They would see my patterns of avoidance when it came to service in the Red Army and the Polish army. They would question my patriotism when they saw how I continually helped the refugee community, a known anti-Soviet breeding ground. They would see how I behaved like the party elite by accepting bribes and privileges, skimming off the top, to better my own situation. They would see all of this and decide whether or not I should be allowed to leave. Everybody had a file and anybody could be arrested at any time, but my file was decidedly heavy.

I waited for my meeting with the NKVD by keeping busy. In preparation for our journey, we went through the usual rigmarole of collecting biscuits and breads, rope and nails, potatoes and vodka. My mother sold everything she could at the bazaar. I made a deal with my friends at the station to look after our furniture if I returned or to keep it if I did not.

A flood of refugees descended on Cerepovec, many of whom came to our apartment. We were the unofficial headquarters for refugees wanting to register for repatriation. Henya was an organizational marvel, helping countless strangers gather their documents and speed through registration. We had so many at our apartment that I asked permission to use the fire station's truck to transport them to the point of registration.

I received a telephone call from Gregoriev, the head of the NKVD. He told me to come to his office to pick up my documents. I wondered if I would be greeted not by him, but by two armed guards waiting behind doors.

'You want to go to Poland?' he screamed. 'They will cut off your head!' He paced through his office, back and forth, seemingly exasperated. I did not know what to say, and so I remained silent. 'You are our man, Genasha,' he said as he pulled out a list of all my borderline activities. 'You have made such a success of yourself here.' He tried to convince me further, telling me that to believe in a democratic Poland was naive. 'We hate the Poles, and they hate us. They will kill you there.'

I was shocked by his passion; I did not expect to see such an outpouring of emotion. I knew he had fought the Poles in 1920, but I did not know his hatred remained so poignant. I told him that I did not want to go, but I was subject to the will of my family. I was aware that the Soviet Union had saved my family and had given me the opportunity to achieve success, but my priority was always going to be my family. Surely he could understand my position. I asked him if he would give me my repatriation papers.

He looked at the list in front of him and he pondered his options while I stood silently, my eyes set proudly. Gregoriev walked towards me and embraced me in a massive bear hug. He handed me my papers and said, 'Good luck, Genasha.'

I was walking on air.

14 Henry, age 14

Henry sent this photo to his cousin, Moshka, who was fighting against the dictator Franco in the Spanish Civil War. Moshka served in the Polish Brigade, *Dambrowski*, which was named after the Polish nineteenth-century general who became the inspiration for the Polish national anthem.

15 Hinda Boms Skorupa, Henry's mother, age 43, 1938

*My mother was the soul of the family, and its sun. Everyone gravitated to her. She had kind words and practical help for everyone who needed help. Her cousin Sarah was very poor and lived in a basement apartment not far from our house. Every Friday, before the Sabbath, my mother and I always went to visit Sarah and her children, to give them blessings and a bundle of food for the Sabbath – challah (bread), fish, meat, vegetables, everything to make a beautiful and festive meal. And my mother always found a subtle way to invite Sarah's children, Chayaleh and Gershon, to eat at our house for the entire week. Sarah's husband, Yosef Stokman, was a glazier, who was unfortunately chronically without work. My mother always reminded us that we should behave nicely to them, and never make them feel humiliated.*

*I stuck always to my mother like glue, and I always tried to make her happy.*

16 Miriam Boms, Henry's cousin, age 20, 1939

*Miriam was the daughter of Aunt Rivka and Uncle Herschel, my mother's brother. Miriam was a sweet, gentle girl, and she was very smart and very kind to others. But she suffered greatly under the domination of her very religious mother, who did not allow 'frivolous activities' such as socializing with us, her less religious cousins. When Miriam wanted to wear prettier clothes that were less severe and more stylish than what her mother would allow, she kept these dresses and matching feather hats called kapelusz at our house. So did her brother Joseph, who wanted to wear clothing that was more European and 'less Jewish' than what his mother permitted.*

17 Welcher Family Portrait, Lublin, 1938. Bottom row (left to right): Mincea Weizer (Sheva's maternal grandmother); Esther Bracha Welcher, Sheva's mother; little sister, age 5; Israel Welcher, Sheva's father; little sister, age 8. Top row: Sheva's eldest sister, age 18; brother Chaim, age 17; Sheva (Shelly), age 16.

*This is my wife's family. You will see my wife, Sheva's (called Shelly in America) grandmother, Mincea Weizer, in the picture wearing a sheital (head covering, a wig that religious Jewish women wear after marriage) but you will not see her grandfather, Nussen David Weizer because he was so religious that he wouldn't appear in a photograph with women – even women from his own family! Nussen David's only occupation was to study Torah, and to teach yeshiva students. Being almost blind, he knew the holy texts by memory. Tragically, when the Germans started to liquidate the Jews of Lublin, he ran with his wife to the Jewish cemetery, where they were killed. As you can see, Esther was a modern woman. She is not wearing a sheitel, like her mother, Mincea.*

18 Uncle Herschel Boms and his family in the Wartha Ghetto, in western Poland, annexed by the Germans in 1940. Seated (left to right): Aunt Rivka; youngest daughter Dvora, age 7; Uncle Herschel. Top row: Cousin Ratza, age 21; Cousin Miriam, age 23; Unknown; Cousin Shifra, age 22. Three brothers, Yosef, Ichi and Shlomo Nissin, escaped to Russia and are therefore not seen in this family photograph.

*Uncle Herschel used to come to our house every Sabbath so he could spend the day reading. He loved to read everything, especially Jewish history, and at our house, he could read undisturbed. The family business was a dairy store, located on the corner of Czasna and Nowa, which sold cheeses, butter, eggs, milk, bread and rolls. Both parents and the children worked in the store. I remember when my cousin Yosef, who was a talented carpenter, built a modern icebox out of wood and metal. It was so heavy that my father had to help him carry it and install it. Henia, my courageous sister, tried to rescue them, but Aunt Rifka refused to let anyone come with us 'to the unholy Bolsheviks!' With this decision, Rifka sealed the death sentence for herself, her husband and my wonderful cousins, Miriam, Shifra, Ratza and Dvora.*

19a Hinda Skorupa (née Boms), passport photo, 1941

*This is my mother's passport photo, when we were forced to have Soviet passports in 1941. At the time, my mother was 43. Until this time, we had only temporary documents giving us the right to live only in Wologda Province, located in the north, in the direction of Leningrad. Later, in 1941, we were forced to take Soviet citizenship with Statia 53 from the Criminal Code, describing us as 'Socially Unreliable'. With this status, we had limited mobility.*

*I was secretly thinking that we should not take these Soviet passports, but I kept these thoughts to myself, because I did not want to endanger the life of my sick mother, for fear that we would be sent away immediately in punishment. In constant discussions with other Jewish refugees, I insisted that we write in the passport that we were Jewish, not Polish, because if we were going to be punished or singled out, I wanted to stand up as a Jew. The majority of the others wrote 'Polish' as their nationality, because they thought it would be safer. However, my 'Jewish' designation, ironically, later saved my life.*

19b Yosef Skorupa, passport photo, 1941

*My father, Yosef Skorupa, born in 1894, was a study in contrasts. He was known for his strength and also for his quick mind. By trade, he was a butcher. By inclination, he was a scholar. He loved to learn, and one of his greatest pleasures was listening to his children reciting their lessons. My father was also very active politically, as a leader in the Workers Zionist Movement, the left faction of the Polizion. Throughout his early adult life, he was a strong supporter of the socialist system, but he was shattered when he saw the cruelties of the real Soviet system.*

19c Henia Skorupa, passport photo, 1941

*My sister Henia, born in 1920, was by nature a real rebel. When she was not able to continue her studies because of the strict quota system that severely limited Jews studying in Poland, she joined the Communist Party, which was illegal in Poland. By doing propaganda work for the Party, she was arrested and sentenced to seven years in the juvenile offenders system. After she appealed to the higher court in Posnan, Henia received a parole, thanks to the efforts of an excellent, high-priced lawyer that my parents could ill afford. However, to help their children, they would do anything. For this terrible trouble brought onto the family by my sister's recklessness, I witnessed the only time in my life that my mother slapped my sister's face. Financially we were ruined.*

*When I was in hiding (because I was already supposed to be dead from the cemetery shooting), Henia took over my family function of trying to save people's lives, by alerting them of danger and helping them escape to Russia with us. It was a very dangerous situation for Henia to return to Kalisz to try to save lives, but she could not do otherwise. Sadly many of her efforts failed, because relatives and friends were already dead, or refused to leave.*

19d Nachun Skorupa, passport photo, 1941

*My brother Nachun, born in 1923, was a dear, talented boy. He was gifted in many fields, especially in electronics and other technical things. He was also very talented with the needle and could have been an excellent tailor. In fact, we wanted him to apprentice under a tailor, but the war started and he never got the chance. Nachun was also a very good sportsman, especially in soccer and ping-pong. At that time, ping-pong was like an epidemic – everyone was playing it – and my brother was very, very good. He had many friends and was always so well liked. After the German occupation, I tried to protect him, as a big brother should. After we were caught and sent as slave laborers to a German estate, I tried to protect him with my life. When the Germans started to beat us, and forced us to beat each other, I refused – even if it meant they would kill me. I told them, 'This is my brother, and I will not beat him.' I expected to die for my refusal, but instead, I was mercilessly beaten until I was no longer conscious. When the Gestapo returned us from the slave labor to our hometown in Kalisz, to dig a huge pit in the Jewish cemetery intended to be our own grave, in the turmoil, I succeeded to push my brother out of the danger so he could run away.*

20 Henry Skorupa, age 20, in the uniform of the Fire Department of Czerepowietz in the state of Wologda, northern Russia, 1942

*I was the Assistant Chief of the Fire Department, and I was in charge of all the training and fire prevention activities. We had to do constant training to keep the firefighters at readiness, especially since many firemen were mobilized to the Red Army. As a result, the majority of firefighters left were women. I devised drills to give them practice before the real emergencies. We had instruction books from the Moscow headquarters, on which I based my drills on their instruction. The Fire Department was a part of the NKVD, Narodni Comisariat Vnutrinicht Dyell (National Minister for Internal Affairs), and it was a sister organization of the KGB. It was under the direction of infamous Lavrenti Pavowich Beryia, who still makes me shudder.*

*When I was mobilized to the Red Army, they challenged my loyalty since I was born in Poland and not on Russian soil. For three days, they tried to decide what to do with me. Finally the political commissar (head of the local Communist Party) made the decision not to put me in the army, but rather he directed me into the Fire Department.*

*I had no choice about the matter. I had to go where I was sent. I felt G-d's hand on me, because I was the first member of my family to be mobilized into the army. We believed that to be in the Russian Army was like being in a meat-grinder. From one side, they put in soldiers. From the other side, they took out dead people. At this time, the losses in the Red Army were astronomical. That's why I felt G-d's hand protecting me, and putting me into the Fire Department, instead of the Army.*

*I sent this photo to my best friend, Shaya Kawa, imprisoned in the Gulag. To encourage him to hold on in a prison so brutal, a place without options, I sent him this picture of me in my uniform. On the back I wrote: 'As long as you have life, don't lose your hope!' I learned today that my best friend Shaya died, on the eve of Rosh Hashona 2005 (5766). Even in grief, whenever I think of him, a smile comes to my face because he was so mischievous and so much fun.*

21 Skorupa family, in Czerepowietz, northern Russia, 1943

First row (right to left): *My heroic sister Henia, mother Hinda (née Boms) Skorupa, and myself, Heniek.* Second row (right to left): *Esther Stokman and my brother, Moshe. In order to get this picture taken, I had to order electricity. There was a shortage of electricity in the town. There was lack of wood to heat, but by this time, I was already a personality in the town. As the Fire Department official, I wielded a lot of power in the town. And I was able to order electricity for half an hour in the section of the town where the photo studio was located – that's how we got this photo taken. The photographer – his name was Lebyedyev – was a big anti-Semite, and as he was photographing us, he was mumbling under his breath that the Jews can do everything. Reluctantly, he took the photo. Esther is the daughter of Sura Stokman, who committed suicide in Poland. We brought Sura, my mother's cousin, special food every Friday because they had so little. She came to Russia with her father Yosef, sister Chayaleh, brother Gershon, according to my instructions.*

Everyone but Esther and Gershon were killed in the terrible attack in Byelayazterkov (which means 'The White Church'), when the Germans attacked Russia in the Ukraine. Esther and Gershon escaped to Kirgestan, where Gershon died of hunger. Henry found out about Esther, and after enormous difficulties, he was able to bring her to the family.

*As you can see, Moshe's eyes were not normal. Notwithstanding, he was mobilized by the order of Stalin to learn a trade in a factory. Being half blind, he hit another worker on the hand with a hammer by mistake. He was released and I right away put him into the Fire Department to protect him.*

22 Boms family cousins, with group of refugee friends in Kazakstan, 1943

*My cousins are seen here: Yosef (seated, extreme right), Shlomo (standing, behind Yosef, extreme right), and cousin Yitzhak, nicknamed Itcheh (standing, extreme left). My dear cousin Shlomo is the last survivor of the three brothers. They came to Kazakstan under the terms of the agreement signed between the Sikorski (Polish) government in London and the Soviet government under Stalin. This agreement freed former Polish citizens who had been imprisoned in Soviet labor camps, and as a special provision of the Polish government, allowed these freed citizens to form a Polish army under General Anders. General Anders, a big Polish general, was a rampant anti-Semite, who personally intervened in many cases to make it difficult to accept Jewish men who wanted to serve in the Polish Army. Anders was also vehemently opposed to the Soviet leadership of the Army, and escaped – together with his entire army – to the Western Front, to fight with the British. Among the Jews fighting in General Anders army was the famous future Israeli politician, Menachem Begin. Menachem Begin was released like my cousins, in the treaty, but instead of staying with Anders' army, he went to Palestine, and became the leader of the underground military movement, the Irgun Tzawa Leumi [National Military group]. The Irgun was hunted by the British, and also hunted by the Jewish authorities for their violent attempts to free Palestine from the British Occupation.*

23 Henry Skorr, returning to Poland, 1947

*This picture was taken the first time, since 1939, that I wore a regular civilian suit. I returned to Poland in 1946, and as a gesture of gratitude to me for helping him establish his photography business and atelier when I was working as leader of the Artisan's Guild in 1947, Mr Pinchus Rosen took this first official photograph of me. In fact, everything I had was a gesture of gratitude, even the suit I wore. There was a known conspiracy in the Chamber of Artisans in Dzierzoniouw (pronounced D-jer-zho-nee-youf) Poland, which was to prevent Jewish artisans from working. I used my position as a leader in the Guild, under the auspices of the Communist Party, to establish and to legalize Jewish businesses, such as butchers, bakers, shoemakers, tailors, barbers and, of course, photographers. As I look at this photograph, I remember how difficult it was for me to enter a normal life. After my strenuous years of struggle in the Soviet Union, constantly facing dangers and constantly trying to avoid these dangers, I could not adjust easily to everyday life. It felt abnormal to me, to get up in the morning, to go to work, to come home and to lead a normal family life. I felt like a drug addict, constantly tuned to the 'highs' of the wartime danger which I was used to avoiding. In a way, after so many years of living with danger, I almost needed the danger to feel alive. I suppose that is why, during all my post-war years in Poland, I involved myself in the dangerous work of the Communist Party. I realize, however, that my efforts to help people were the motivating influence of my Communist activities: I was desperately trying to use the power of the ruling Communist Party to protect and help people.*

24 Ziska Weizer Szpeter, Shelly's aunt from Paris, holding Esther, age six months, in Dzierzoniouw, Poland

*My wife, Shelly (called Sheva Welczer in Poland) had an aunt who was a big moral and political inspiration, both to my Shelly, and to many others. Because there was rampant anti-Semitism in Poland, especially in the universities and the high schools, Ziska was not able to continue her studies after her first year at Warsaw University, because of the vicious physical attacks against her by Gentile anti-Semitic students. Their usual tactic was to attach razor blades to long sticks, and to brutally slash the faces of Jewish students. Because Jews had no protection from such vicious attacks, in order to protect her life, Ziska left Warsaw University in 1935. She was unwilling to leave her studies, so she found a way to continue her education in Paris, which was much more liberal than Poland in their attitudes toward Jews. However, before she left Warsaw, she worked with the esteemed Janusz Korczak, famous Polish-Jewish doctor, radio personality, author and leading educational reformer. Before the war, he organized orphanages for the children of Warsaw, and during, when Jews were pushed into the ghetto, Janusz Korczak went with them and organized a special orphanage for the many Jewish children left without parents. His orphanages, replicated throughout Poland, were organized on the principal that in order to create future leaders out of these children, they had to have experience in being leaders. Therefore he created 'children's republics' where they ruled themselves (with adults helping). Ziska worked with Korczak for about a year, before she left for Paris, where she remained for the duration of the war, until she was deported to Treblinka in 1943. At Treblinka, she became part of the underground leadership of the resistance for the whole camp. Her close friend was leader of the Polish Socialist Party (PPS), Cyrankiewicz, who became first prime minister of independent Poland in 1946. Both Ziska and Cyrankiewicz were integrally involved in organizing and leading the famous revolt in Treblinka in 1943. They succeeded in burning down one crematorium, but the cost was very high: many people were killed. Under the Germans, if you didn't succeed in escaping before they caught you, you can die like a hero; you can die like a victim; you can die like a traitor; you can die like a martyr; but only one thing is certain: you have to die. Ziska was an idealistic communist, believing that the communist ideal of 'To each, according to his needs; from each, according to his ability' would bring social justice to everyone. She, together with her husband, Jacques, was active in the French Communist movement before the war. During the war, Jacques, who used the pseudonym RAVIN, was the leader of the Jewish Resistance in France. In this picture, Ziska and her husband are visiting Poland to report on Jewish life after the war, Stalin's offensive against the atom bomb, and also to visit an international exhibition in Wrotslaw, also known as Breslau in German. Breslau/Wrotslaw was the capital of Lower Silesia, until today. At that time, Breslau/Wrotslaw, called the Western Territories, had the largest concentration of Jews after the war.*

25 Wedding Celebration of Henry's sister, Henia Skorupa, to Oskar Zalcberg, Dzierzoniouw, Poland, 1947

*My sister's marriage to Oskar Zalcberg was a match arranged by our friend, Mr Reichman, a Lithuanian businessman who married a woman under our care. During the war, when accommodations were at a premium, my mother kept a spare room, just big enough to fit a bed, in order to help those who had no where to go. One of these families was Mr and Mrs Gdalie Scharf, and their baby son, who came to live with us in the room in 1942. Soon, however, Gdalie Scharf was mobilized to serve in the Red Army, and no one ever heard from him again. My mother continued to help Mrs Scharf, who was desperate after her husband disappeared. Eventually, when we returned to Poland in Dzierzoniouw, she met and married a dignified, elderly businessman in his sixties, Mr Reichman, who had lost his wife and children in the war. When he married Mrs Scharf, who by now had two children, Mr Reichman recreated a second family. He took gentle and good care of his new family, and it was Mr Reichman who made the match between my sister Henia and Oskar. My brother-in-law, Oskar Zalcberg from Bielawa, was a businessman in textiles and tailor supplies with his brother Josef. There was an interesting story about how Josef's wife, who had several sisters, wanted Oskar to marry one of her sisters. However Oskar resisted and resisted, and explained that he wanted to marry Henia instead. Oskar was very energetic, very active in the Zionist movement and such a nice man. When Henia and Oskar got permission to leave Poland, they already had a little boy named Yoshi (named after our father, Josef). Although Henia and Oskar were ecstatic about getting permission to go to Israel, for me, their decision caused problems with the Communist Party. Now I knew I also had to leave.*

26 Moshe Skorupa, age 20 in Dzierzonieow, Poland, 1946

*My youngest brother, Moshe, was born blind, and all his life he suffered from an assortment of illnesses. In fact, even when he was born, it did not go so easily because instead of coming out with his head first, like it should be, he came out backwards. Because of his blindness, Moshe was always bumping into things and having many accidents. In addition, his head was covered with sores that were constantly oozing pus. My mother was always taking him to the Jewish Health Clinic for treatments. They would put him on a table, put him glasses on the eyes, and turn on quartz lamps to dry the sores. They fed him fish oil, which I still remember, had a terrible smell. When they were doing repairs in our town, they opened the sewer pipes. Poor Moshe fell in the sewer. Another time, he was walking in the street, and it was slippery from the ice, and he fell and broke his arm. We carried him around in our arms, in winter in a sleigh, and always in our hearts. On account of his illnesses and his frail health, he was the dearest to us, and especially to our grandmother, Brandle Boms. On the day of our departure in 1939, when we were escaping the Nazis by running to Russia, her last words to us were, 'Take care of Moshe.' And conversely, Moshe's last words to her were, 'Baba, come with us.' Being partially blind, he had very good hearing. And he had, together with my father, a beautiful voice. On the first day of the Occupation of Kalisz, the German soldiers were walking and singing their military songs. So Moshe stopped me as we were walking because he wanted to listen to the singing of the soldiers, not taking account at all of the danger of the situation. So we stopped and listen, all the time I was nervous that we would be caught. Moshe, despite being so sick, was a little Jewish philosopher. He was always questioning the events around him: Why did the Germans occupy us? Why did Poland fall? In truth, although we were running to Russia to save our lives and, by this time, we were already in Bialystok, somehow my little brother's words changed our course of action. He spoke so much about our beloved Baba, whom we had left behind, that it was impossible to continue. My mother began to cry for her mother. Moshe persisted that we should turn back to save Baba. And ultimately we did.*

27 Members of the Bursa (Orphanage), Dzierzonieow, Poland, 1947

*The Bursa was a youth home for orphaned children who lost their families in the concentration camps, in Russia or in other ways during the war. It was named after David Edelshtat, a progressive poet from the United States. He was a leading Jewish American communist, and the Bursa was established by the Jewish Committee, and was lavishly subsidized by the Joint Distribution Committee, based also in the United States. The 'Joint,' as it was called, was a philanthropic organization that helped Jews in need. Often we hear about the Joint helping immigrants coming to America get settled. Astoundingly, it even functioned during the war to help the starving Jewish population in the ghetto, by organizing ghetto soup kitchens, illegal schooling and workshops in conjunction with ORT, whose purpose was to train people in professions. The members are wearing heavy coats, which were surplus from the British Army. To cover up the British green, we died them black. These coats were so warm, we were comfortable even in the frigid Polish winter. I was the leader of this group. Just after we arrived in Poland from Russia, at a time when we were still sleeping on the floor of the local school, which was administered by the Polish Repatriation Office for the benefit of the poor, my friend Zelig Zilberberg approached me. Zelig Zilberberg was a pre-war Jewish communist who was a prisoner in the Polish concentration camp called Kartuz Bereza, which was the first political concentration camp established in 1938 by the Poles. It was organized in the German style on the territory that the Russians had occupied. Zelig was the head of security and he came to me with a Soviet-style directive: you must become the administrative head of the Bursa, which they were organizing. In fact, I did not even know of what he was talking. Since I was already well used to following orders, I did not even think of disobeying. They put us – my mother, wife and sister Henia – into a big farm carriage, pulled by huge Belgian horses, and took us to the Bursa. There they gave us a beautiful apartment. That is how I became a 'boss.'*

28 Ziska and Jacques Speter, Shelly's aunt and uncle from Paris, c.1962

*Ziska was my wife Shelly's maternal aunt. She and her husband Jacques were enthusiastic, naïve communists, believing in the theory of Marxism. There were big leaders of the French Communist Party, in the Jewish Department. During the war, Jacques was the leader of the Jewish guerilla fighters in France (the Jewish Underground), known under his pseudonym of 'Jacques Raven'. As a Jew, Ziska was arrested and deported to Treblinka, where she participated in the prisoner revolt against the Nazis. At the end, when they saw the brutality of Stalin's regime, they were heartbroken by the betrayal of their idealistic dreams. Jacques died of Alzheimer's and after that, Ziska, not wanting to live without him, committed suicide.*

29 Molly Picon's visit to the Bursa, Dzierzonieow, Poland, 1946

*Here is a picture of the enormously important visit from the famous actress Molly Picon. She appeared in 'Yiddl mit a Fiddle' [Jew with a Fiddle], 'Greeneh Felde' [Green Meadows, Green Fields] and a variety of other Yiddish productions. She was also a star of English-speaking stage and screen.*

*Here she is seated in the middle of the front row, with her husband on the right. Near her is the (unofficial) Jewish governor of the province of Lower Silesia. His name was Egged (whose family started the famous tourist business in Israel, Egged Tours), and it was universally agreed that he had more power and influence than the official governor.*

*This visit to the children of the Orphanage was seen as very significant because of its intrinsic message of solidarity with us. She was coming to give us support, and bring our message to the Jews of America, and people of the world. However, when she arrived, she did not see us as regular people, equal to anyone else in the world. In her eyes, it was clear that she saw us as exotic animals, similar to what you might find in a zoo.*

*Although she was a great actress, she could not hide her true feelings. In her smooth face of one who has not suffered, she didn't realize that the only difference between her and us was that she was lucky enough to have parents who left Europe in time to escape Hitler. She could not relate to us as people, and we were deeply hurt that we could not bridge the divide. In any case, it was still very significant that she came to see us, and I never forgot the excitement of her visit. And her visit always gave us the sense that we are not alone anymore.*

30 Summer home of the Bursa, in the village of Rosciszow, Poland

*I took the whole Orphanage on vacation in the summer to a beautiful little village in the Sowie Gura (meaning Owl) Mountains, located ten miles from our town of Dzierzonieow, Poland. The village had been abandoned by its peasant farmer population during Hitler's times. I organized, in Soviet style, at the Bursa, a self-help food operation. We raised our pigs until they grew up, to supplement our food supply. We gave the pigs their own names, like Kubusz and Janek. We even took the pigs with us on vacation in Rosciszow. We didn't know how to handle the pigs but we had, among the orphans, a boy who had been hidden with a Polish farmer, so he knew what to do. He was responsible for the care and feeding of the pigs, and we named a pig after him. Once the pigs were grown, we sold them to get kosher meat. The Bursa was organized according to the principles of the progressive Polish-Jewish educator, Janusz Korczak. He believed, as did I, that to teach children about responsibility, you had to give them responsibility. To teach children about leadership, you had to give them a chance to lead. But with these children who had gone through the horrors of the Holocaust, we had special difficulties. A few of the teenage girls lost their minds, when they lost their parents, and they spent the whole night crying. Some of the teenage boys were so demoralized that they began stealing from each other, hiding the bread in their beds, and accusing everyone else of stealing the bread; they even accused me. When some of the older kids returned late at night, they would pound on my door at midnight, demanding food. (I was the only adult in the building because all the other staff – the kitchen help and the teachers – went home at the end of the day.) To make things easier for everyone, I assigned, on a rotating basis, someone to set out fresh coffee, bread, margarine, etc. every night until midnight, so the kids could eat at will, even after the kitchen was closed. I knew how much they suffered, almost like martyrs, so I treated them like saints. I had to tend to their emotional wounds, like a doctor, but I was not equipped. The children were so damaged that sometimes they began fighting with each other, because they didn't know how to express all their anger. And, sometimes there was just a natural conflict between the children, because of the vast difference between those who had been in the concentration camps and those who came back from Russia. Plus, don't forget, these children came from different backgrounds and political views, and as you might expect, they had political disagreements as well, especially between the dominating Communist Party followers, and the Zionist supporters, who only wanted to go to the holy land of Israel. Let me add, by the way, that their fighting was strictly with words, not with fists, because we didn't allow physical fighting. My intention was to teach them professions, so they could go out in the world and work. In addition, we gave them education for their studies. As life became more normal, the older girls and boys, who were 18–20 years old, began to fall in love, marry, and start new lives. We encouraged their marriages so they could establish a new life, and leave the Bursa. The majority left the country and went to the Displaced Persons Camps in Germany and Italy, and from there, many of them made their way in the illegal immigration to Palestine.*

31 Esther Skorupa, my only child, age 9 months, April 1949

*After so much suffering and hardship, Esther was the treasure of our lives. But because of the pressure of the Party and what they demanded of me, I didn't get home, usually, until 2 or 3 in the morning. So it was very hard for families, when the schedule was like this – constantly meetings, meetings, meetings, and it was mandatory that I attend. Once when I came home at 2 a.m., I went to Esther's little bed to kiss her, as always when I returned home. To my shock, I found that she had no hair. I asked my wife, Shelly, "What did you do? Did you cut off all her hair?" The answer became clear when we turned on the light. Esther had simply turned herself around and it was her bare behind, not her head that I was kissing! This has been a family joke ever since.*

32 Henry Skorr, his grandsons and his great grandson, 2005

Pictured (left to right), Henry with his physician grandsons, Josh and Benjamin, and his great grandson, Joseph, named after Henry's father, who, Henry asserts with a glint in his eye, 'may yet grow into a future physician, like both his father, his uncle and both his paternal grandparents!' Missing from photograph is great granddaughter Kayla Bleier.

*When I thought there would be no one left of my family, I dreamed of one day being free again. Now, with my wonderful grandsons, Josh and Benjamin, and my beautiful great grandchildren, Kayla and Joseph, the circle is complete. From the past, when I was a young boy in the pit, surrounded by the dead and dying around me, I thought that in five minutes no one would even know I existed. But I am here, and the miracle of life is victorious. The chain of immortality continues, and will continue forever, G-d willing!*

*Part IV*
*Poland and Israel*

# 15 Return to Poland

In our final days, Cerepovec experienced a flood of Polish/Jewish refugees from the outlying villages and smaller cities in Vologda province. They came to register for repatriation papers and to catch the trains back to Poland. Decorated soldiers from the Red Army, wounded men, emaciated women, some healthy families, they all descended upon our city and many came straight to our apartment. The reputation that our home was a safe haven for Jewish refugees had spread throughout the province, but it was a nightmare for me to see so many come to us for help so close to the day we would depart. In the family we all had our papers, but we still resided in a government apartment. If just one of these returning refugees turned out to be a wanted enemy of the people, what would stop them from accusing us of harboring criminals?

Henya, the organizational marvel, sent scores of refugees first to the Dom Krestianina then to the proper agencies for procuring repatriation papers. She limited the flow of refugees in the apartment to only a few, thus allowing my mother and me to tend to our family's preparatory needs.

We had learned from experience that to begin a journey involving trains in Russia without extra provisions and plenty of money was to invite unneeded hardship. In addition, we understood Poland to be dying of hunger; it was all that the government had told us. Facing the long journey and believing I was taking my family into a war-torn wasteland, I began to have second thoughts. Still, I prepared diligently. My mother made packages of black bread, biscuits, potatoes and grains, while I gathered rope, nails, small tools and anything else I thought might come in handy on our trip. We went together to the bazaar in order to sell items we no longer needed, or thought might fetch a good price.

While at the bazaar I went to see the unofficial mayor of the Russian Jews, the photographer. He had returned from the army, but his son was still mobilized. I told him I had some reservations about returning to Poland. It was supposed to be a wasteland and, despite my fear of denunciation and Soviet injustice, in Cerepovec I could presently provide for my family's needs. 'Don't be so stupid', he said, 'Poland is no good, the Poles are no good, they hate the Jews. But from Poland you can go to Palestine or America. I only wish I could go with you.' This blew me away. Maybe he was right, maybe we would be able to leave Poland if things were not livable. Surely we would be citizens there, not refugees limited by Article 53 or ensnared by the Soviet spider's web. I was reenthused and continued with our preparations with added zeal.

Back at the fire station I had to conceal my eagerness and play the part of the reluctant defector. There was an official ceremony conducted in my honor, a changing of the guard almost, during which the politruk and the fire chief each read prescripted texts and improvised something nice for me. I gave a very emotional speech, telling my friends that my family and I would never leave them, that we had left the blood of my father and brother with them and that because of our shared sacrifices we would be joined forever. Many of the women were in tears and some of the men hugged me strongly. I gave Maria Gregorgivna a letter to give to Vera. I still kept up the false pretense that I was dedicated to her because, in my mind, I was afraid to change any pattern so close to our departure. I wrote something conservatively heartwarming, consistent with my previous letters, knowing that Maria Gregorgivna might read it herself. In it I told Vera the same thing I was still telling Maria Gregorgivna and the chief: if I could assure that my family was in good hands at the border, I would return. Although the money would have helped us, we did not sell any of our furniture before we left. Instead I told Maria Gregorgivna that she could use it only if I did not return – as far as she was concerned, a most unlikely prospect.

In late February the day of departure finally arrived. There were two trains in Cerepovec station waiting to take the refugees back to Poland. I had obtained the use of one of the trucks from the fire station and transported refugees from the Dom Krestianina to the train station. Again there was a collection of refugees spilling out of our apartment. Many had procured their papers previously and had only now come to Cerepovec – straight to our home. People were sleeping on our beds, on our floors, everywhere. It did not worry me any longer, I felt nothing would stop us from getting on those trains and leaving this drab, deceitful Soviet life.

I went with my mother, Moishe, cousin Esther and Henya to the little Jewish cemetery for the last time and we prayed for my father and Nuchem. I said my final goodbyes to the staff at the fire station and we went down to enter the train. We loaded my famous trunk filled with extra provisions and we sat together with Shelly and her friends Tosia and Katia, also nurses from Sokol.

I carried the pistol in my pocket, which I knew was a stupid thing to do, but something inside me would not let me throw it away. Of course seven bullets could not protect us from whatever we would find in Poland, but it was a symbol of our changed attitude as Jews – this was our journey to freedom and no one would try to harm us again.

Soviet officials glanced over our documents, but I did not see anyone get turned away. It was easy to get the proper papers since so many of us had registered with the Soviet government in Kovel when we arrived – why else would we be in Cerepovec? A Polish document of some sort was required as well, as this designated to what part of Poland you would return. The Soviets were not too strict with the distribution of documents since, in their minds, we would be returning to Poland as their Jews and their Poles. Politically it made sense, as there was still some debate as to the future of Poland. Of course, with the Soviets forcibly taking over Europe as far south as Bulgaria and Yugoslavia, in my mind the fate of Poland was already sealed.

There were quite a few of us settling into the car when an

old pattern recurred. Bronek Shanker, the same man who started bossing people around on our trip into Russia, began dictating orders again as if he were the appointed leader of the refugees. This hurt my mother so much; it brought back memories of my father and how he shut Bronek up with a little squeeze of the fist. I saw the pain in my mother's eyes and I had a talk with Bronek. I did not have the strength of my father but I had the respect of the others and after a few words he quietened down.

The train rolled out of Cerepovec and in so doing closed a chapter of our lives. The emotions I felt were complicated. I had come to the conclusion that we had won the battle of life. Hitler had been unable to destroy us and the Soviet regime was unable to change us. Of course the price we had paid was high, but we survived. We were going back to Poland without our father and brother, without the Bubis family or the Perlers, but we were victors. In my heart I knew that we carried the souls of the lost people with us on that train. The barber, his wife and child, the others indicted in the KGB investigations, the countless, nameless refugees forced to fight and die for the Soviets, were all with us as we progressed out of the city. And yet in Cerepovec I had achieved so much for an uneducated boy who spoke poor Russian; I wondered if I would ever be so successful again. And, for some time, I was in love with a Russian girl. This had been my first love, no matter how much it troubled me, and it would always be special.

Privately my thinking about Vera was not entirely resolved. We had had conversations about what would happen if I was to return to Poland, and we agreed that she would come. Now I did not want her to come to Poland for so many reasons. First, there was my relationship with Shelly and second, Vera would be an anchor to the Soviet system I did not want. I pictured a life of misery, being told by others whether I was a good person or not, living a life of theft and lies all in the name of a greater Soviet society; it was a nightmare to imagine. I would continue writing to Vera, but I would not encourage her to leave Russia, even if it meant I had to lie.

We came to Vologda, the central meeting point of trains

heading to Poland. Thousands of gentile Poles had come from the outer reaches of the province, the areas where most of the prisons lay. The Association of Polish Patriots efficiently moved groups of people from one train to another, according to their final destinations, and consolidated people to limit the number of trains necessary for the voyage. We were not moved from our places, but there was an influx of gentile Poles into our car. We found ourselves side by side with a number of former prisoners, forest workers and factory workers. The frost between us was felt immediately. The age-old loathing returned, but we were not nearly as affected as we had been before the war. The gentiles were dealing with a different sort of Jew now and they were afraid to touch us.

The Association of Polish Patriots sent one representative to each car. Our representative was Stefan Zmiko, the provincial head of the association in Vologda. He was a very nice man, equally sympathetic towards Jews and gentiles, but his wife, a beautiful woman with a noble presence, was very cold towards us. His wife's attitude did not bother me, I hoped it to be a relic of the old Poland, one that her husband had already abandoned. Stefan signed our papers and communicated with the organizational staff along our route, never once treating the Jews differently.

Our train took over four weeks to get to the Polish border, and with every mile I felt a layer of the Soviet armor peel off me. The difference between our journey into Russia and this trip was like night and day. We were not the same people any longer. Yes, we were refugees, but we were not leaves blown by the wind. We were experienced people, stronger from the Soviet experience and looking forward to freedom. We demanded clean quarters and adequate food. Every time the train stopped for a day or so, we insisted that we be brought to a *banja*. Provisions were provided by the Association of Polish Patriots, including condensed milk, canned meats and blankets, which we shared equally with the gentiles. Pelta loved that milk – we would give him our empty tins and he would not leave a drop.

As we progressed through White Russia, the snow and ice began to thaw. We moved through previously occupied territory and former battlegrounds. Rising out of the snow we could see dead German soldiers with their rifles still in hand, seemingly ready to shoot. These were remote Russian landscapes, but I was still surprised to see these corpses untouched since the end of the war. Some forests were charred or nearly destroyed from artillery fire and many bayonets were stuck into the ground with helmets on top to mark the dead. Dead horses lay next to dismantled tanks and cannons and newly built fortresses, a defense against guerilla movements, dotted the landscape near train stations. It was getting warmer, a welcome change, but the cold had previously concealed some of the most horrifying sights.

Echelons of returning Russian soldiers passed through the same stations and sang boisterous songs about their conquests. One song described the beauty of Bulgaria, Romania and other nations, but declared no place was more beautiful than Russia. There were also trains filled with prisoners and POWs, undoubtedly slated to stand trial for desertion back in Russia. These men screamed anti-Soviet and anti-Semitic sentiments from their confines.

Inside our car the feeling was generally good and our optimism was high. Our interactions with one another reflected our attitude and confidence – there was a lot of flirting. Pelta started to sleep nearer and nearer to a girl named Sonia Tempchin, though her mother would not allow him to get too close, and Katia was flirting with a boy named Lolek. Where at the beginning of the war these relations seemed somehow false and cowardly, now there was a certain innocence to them, humility and dignity seemed to have returned. We wanted to restore our own cultural norms and we were doing that. Once, as the train sat at a station, I stumbled upon Shelly, Tosia and Katia preparing to relieve themselves. They saw me coming and ran away. 'Where are you going?' I yelled, 'I can turn around.' I guess I was still in the Russian mode.

My mother on the whole was doing well, but she would have moments of great depression whenever she thought of returning without my father and Nuchem. She felt the loss of these two so strongly and so personally; that millions had died in the war was of little consolation to her. She was still sick, at this point she had lost nearly 80 kilograms, but we had a medical kit from Rosa and the constant help of the nurses. Shelly, especially, took tremendous care of her.

The train cut through the Russian countryside, stopping at stations outside big cities like Kiln, Smolensk and Minsk, but mostly our pauses were in small, still intact stations. Falling into old habits, I explored these places whenever I knew there was going to be adequate time. Eventually we came to Baranavicy, the city I had dreamed of before the war. We stopped at the station and we were told there would be a few hours before the train would set off again. I decided that I would find Minska 57, where I had sent the letters from the forest and where my friends and I had agreed to meet before the war.

I was hit with a flood of memories, like tracing the path of the train from Kalisz to Baranavicy on the map displayed outside the bookstore. I could still hear the accents of Milsza and her mother at my father's butcher shop, and I remembered how fascinated I was with her and how exotic they seemed. I recalled meetings with my friend Mendele and others and how we thought Baranavicy would be far enough away to rendezvous. This was my first real look at what had happened to my past in Poland and I was excited and terrified.

I disembarked into a station filled with Polish women selling various foods and crafts, exactly like the Russian women in previous stations. Although this was now part of Russia, it was a Polish city in its recent history and as a result the people acted more like Poles than Russians. Along with that came a more cynical and outwardly hostile anti-Semitism.

It should not have been a surprise, but I was startled when one of the Polish vendors said to me, '*Zydki*, do you know where the *Zydkis* from Baranavicy are?' '*Zydki*' was a derogatory nickname for a Jew. I looked at this fat, grinning woman and wondered what she would tell me next. 'Up there, in that forest, the *Zydkis* were slaughtered.'

I felt sick to my stomach, not just because I knew she was telling the truth, but because she had such a look of satisfaction on her face. I was staring at evil. I wanted nothing more than to take out my pistol and put a bullet between her wicked eyes. I could feel that anger swell inside me again and it was all I could do to continue walking. I dismissed her comment as one that came from a damaged woman in no man's land.

I left the station and found Minska 57, which was in the former ghetto. Barbed wire and pulverized buildings were all that remained of most of the area. Minska 57 had no windows left and the walls had crumbled. Not a soul walked near the area – I was alone looking at what was left of Milsza's past. I saw a path leading out of the ghetto towards the forest and I imagined the mother with her two beautiful daughters marching out to be shot. I wanted to go out there but there were signs warning of mines. I improvised the Kaddish and I went back to the train. I did not tell my mother what I found, only that I was unable to locate their home. This was my memory of Baranavicy.

From Baranavicy we traveled south and west to Brest-Litovsk, the Polish–Russian border. This was the first station we came to that we had seen before. The difference was alarming. What was once a tremendous, fortress-like station was now a decrepit, ramshackle depot crawling with KGB agents and Soviet soldiers. There were mountains of empty shells, which with the destruction, proved evidence of an enormous battle. The bridges that spanned the length of the station, separating the Russian and Polish-style tracks, had fallen or were only partially intact. I remembered how low I felt at this station when we passed through on our way to Kovel, how I had sat on one of those bridges contemplating suicide, and I felt a sense of accomplishment and elation at having returned.

Zmiko organized us well. He told us we would have to go through a little inspection, but when that was over we would get into trains on the other side of the station, trains in Poland. Four or five soldiers came into our train and went through the documents handed to them by Zmiko. They started looking around the car and I began to feel extremely nervous – I still had a pistol in my pocket.

But the soldiers did not search anyone. They did not even

look into our trunk, which was filled with food. It was very strange, but it was a miracle to me. One of the soldiers ripped our exit visas, keeping the Russian portion, and handed the Polish portion back to Zmiko. That was it. We gathered our things and transferred to the Polish trains.

The trains were smaller than the Russian ones, so we could not all sit together. I wanted Shelly to sit with my family and me, but she chose to sit with Tosia and Katia instead in another train. They were insulted that I wanted to split them up, and that I felt entitled to sit with Shelly. They were all mad at me for the way I dawdled with the Vera situation. I knew I would be able to explain myself later, but I did not want to try to do that until I could be assured there would be no repercussions. (Inevitably, almost 60 years later Shelly is still mad at me.)

I was so used to the knocking, bumping and pulling of the Russian trains, that I was sure the landscape was moving as we first pulled out of the station. We were all overjoyed to leave that colorless Soviet life behind and the movement of the train was our first indication that life would be smoother and more civilized back in Poland. It helped that spring had begun, as the air smelled of the awakening earth.

As we glided through the countryside, peering out the window at lovingly manicured fields, we continued the ongoing conversation of our journey: what we would do in the future. The younger people were set on building a new Poland with socialist ideals, but the older Jews were determined to go further than Poland. My thinking was still partially controlled by the Soviet mechanism; of course I agreed with the younger crowd because I was afraid to contradict such a sentiment.

The train staff was made up of Poles, but they still wore German railroad outfits; only the swastikas had been torn off. As we pulled into the first station in Poland, I saw one of these men working near our car. I asked him in Polish how things were going. He said, 'This is not our Poland. The Jews are back and they brought the Soviets with them. "Bad is that bird who makes a mess of his own nest".'

I do not think he knew I was Jewish, or else he did not care, but I knew his words to be the true sentiment of the Polish people. Only officially was Poland an ally of the Soviets; it was only a matter of time before the Jews would be blamed for the misfortune Poland would suffer at their hands. This was a shot to my heart, but my optimism did not wane. He had no idea how lucky I felt just seeing a Polish railroad worker again.

The countryside continued to astound me. The peasants composed a picture of history, seamlessly blending into the landscape as they tilled the earth in their traditional white shirts alongside strong horses. What we saw seemed so natural and harmonious, especially in contrast to the heavy machinery and bitterness of kolchozin work and workers. Near train stations we slowly passed through small villages, many of which had not been destroyed during the war. These small houses with whitewashed fences and flower boxes along the windows did not make us miss the gray of Soviet Russia. Before the war we understood Poland to be not so nice, but now it looked like a paradise.

As we moved further into Poland the liveliness of the train stations increased. Instead of just an official presence with a few women selling wares, each stop was a hive of activity. Polish boys carrying scales asked us if we were selling gold or jewelry and paperboys marched up and down the platforms with all the old newspapers in their satchels. The most amazing things were the kiosks set up at every stop by the Polish Repatriation Department.

We would show the workers at these booths our papers and they would give us food, clothing and money depending on our needs. The organization was so beautiful to us, so generous and so friendly. Again, the difference between the Russian reality and this was unbelievable. I never thought that I would see a government agency handing out white bread, coffee and fruit, but that is what the Polish Repatriation Department did.

Near the provisions there would almost always be an information stand, helping refugees find family members lost during the war. We poured over these lists, sometimes finding names of old acquaintances, but we did not find any immediate relatives. Those who did were overcome with emotion. The knowledge that someone in the family had survived was one of the most beautiful gifts God could give.

At one station a Jewish boy was selling newspapers, the *Arbeiter Zeitung*, my family's old paper from before the war. I thought it was a dream, like a time warp or something. I spoke to him in Yiddish, asking how the Jews were doing in Poland. He told me that the Jews were living in western Poland on kibbutzim and the majority of them wanted to move to Palestine.

I read the paper from cover to cover, so excited to read something not written by Soviets, but by Jews in Poland. The articles still had the same spin, the same political angles. It was a treat. At the back of the paper there was a classified section combined with community notes. In that section I saw an advertisement:

> *Ziska Weiser from the family Welchers of Lublin is looking for members of the Welcher family including Shelly Welcher. Our address in Paris is …*

Shelly was in the other train with the girls, still very mad at me, but I ran to her just the same. I showed her the advertisement and she began to cry. It was her favorite aunt. The discovery of a close surviving relative was a burst of the purest elation for Shelly. At this point in our lives we assumed that most of the people we had loved as children were dead, murdered by the Nazis or Poles. This great news helped to push away our own problems and we celebrated her news together.

We sat down on two outdoor seats and enjoyed the beautiful countryside and warm shining sun. We talked so much, so freely as we had on our walks in Cerepovec. We discussed the future, our love and the fate of the Jewish people. She teased me about Vera and how I had said to the fire department that I did not want to leave Russia. She was amazing and I was enraptured. In Warsaw we would send a telegram to Paris.

The significance of Ziska's survival was clear to me; I knew of the important influence she had had on Shelly's life. It was not just a case of Shelly discovering a surviving relative, though this alone was a miracle, but of her finding her mentor and the person responsible for her survival.

Shelly came from a beautiful family. Her father was a businessman of some standing in Lublin, known for his generosity to the community and his pious ways. He had businesses supplying broken glass to glass factories, importing bottles for pharmacies, distributing wholesale shipments of coal and selling vinegar (a government concession), among others. Their household included Shelly's parents, grandparents and three sisters. Her grandmother worked making bedspreads, employing two assistants, while her grandfather spent his days in the synagogue teaching and praying. This life was something of another stratum compared to my family's life in Kalisz. These were highly educated, noble Jews, of the sort we used to admire greatly.

Ziska was not only Shelly's favorite aunt, but the treasure of the family. She was a nurse who also worked with Janusz Korchak, a famous child psychologist and storywriter who chose to die at Auschwitz with his beloved children instead of handing them over to the Nazis.

Ziska was a dedicated Communist, determined to change the world and eager to be involved in the worldwide Communist movement. She filled Shelly's head with ideas of immigrating to countries that allowed Jews to study at universities and were forming great communist parties. Ziska herself left for Paris to study, but continually sent Shelly letters and left her in the care of a group of young women also eager to bring communism to Poland. Ziska married a man from Rovno in Paris, a functionary of the Comintern. Back in Lublin the family wondered whether he was Jewish and if a rabbi had performed the wedding service.

Shelly often considered leaving Poland to study, but she did not want to upset her family. When the war began, Shelly's *gymnasium* had closed. This was the final impetus for her decision to go to Russia. She moved with one of the young women to Vlodava, the home of an uncle so pious he would not even look at Shelly because she was a woman. The Bug river divided Vlodava; one side was under German control, the other under Soviet control. Her family was very much against her leaving, but she was determined to do so. On their second attempt, Shelly and her friend were able to cross the river, paying a peasant for transport, and get through the Russian border.

Initially she went to Rovno to live with Ziska's husband's family, but when refugees were required to register she went to Kovel. Like us she moved to the forest, but while we were transferred to Koniewo, she was sent to Beloz Orsk. There she did what she could in the forest industry, which was not much beyond picking up stray branches, and lived through that first winter with the help of her supervisor and the Russian teacher with whom she lived.

In the spring she returned to Cerepovec and registered with the Komsomol. After a few ill-suited jobs, like selling beverages from a kiosk, her wish to study nursing was granted and she began to follow in the footsteps of her aunt. By the time we left Russia, she was an accomplished nurse and well regarded at the hospitals.

The advertisement in the *Arbeiter Zeitung* warmed Shelly's heart and created a new sense of devotion for both of us. In all likelihood Ziska was the one person most responsible for Shelly's survival. She desperately wanted to see her and thank her, and to renew their old familial relations. It was especially pleasing for me to share such a moment with her after all the half-lies I had been forced to tell.

As we approached Warsaw, there were very few towns and villages untouched by the artillery of the war. In fact, the area in and around Warsaw was like an open wound. The mood inside these stations changed as well. No longer was there a celebratory feeling of renewed hope, but instead a sense of the horrible conditions under which our compatriots had lived. We entered stations, registered with the Polish Repatriation Department and departed. In this way, by minimizing our contact with the downtrodden, we maintained our optimism.

We came to Warsaw. The main railroad station was nearly pulverized and the destruction throughout the city was equally dramatic. We stayed in Warsaw for a day, and we could feel the hostility of the Poles in the air. We made our way to the Central Jewish Committee in the Praha train depot, which was less damaged than the main station. My heart sank as I thought of Dolgovitch. We had heard that he had fallen here while in the army.

When we entered the offices of the Central Jewish Committee, the staff, to my surprise, implored us to be quiet. I did not think we were talking loudly or boisterously, but their irritation was clearly evident. One of them asked, 'Why are you speaking Yiddish so loudly?' I was shocked by their behavior. In their eyes I could see the fear we all had under German occupation. How long will it be, I wondered, before Jewish eyes are freed from that expression?

Through the Central Jewish Committee we registered our names and the names of our lost friends and relatives. At every station from Warsaw to our final destinations there were registration lists created by this committee, providing the most important tool for the reunification of lost loved ones in Poland. Also at the committee offices, Shelly and I sent a telegram to Paris.

From Warsaw the group split up. Many of us were traveling to western Poland, to the recovered territories where most of the Jews were shipped, but those who had discovered family members or relations in other parts of Poland took their leave from the main group. Pelta, who had received a letter months ago from a surviving brother in Lodz, departed on a separate train. We were so happy for him to have found real family, but it pained us greatly to go our separate ways. In many ways he had replaced Nuchem for me, but in the end I was happy that he could live with his own brother.

By now we had been on trains for almost two months. We were used to it, conditioned to it. We had lost the measure of time and knew only the rhythm of the tracks and the world that passed by our windows.

We departed Warsaw and arrived at Poznan, a city almost totally destroyed by artillery. Hitler had ordered his troops to fight to the death there and the results were disastrous. Poznan was historically a controversial city. It was sometimes in German hands, sometimes in Polish hands and sometimes in both. The railroad workers still wore German clothing, and to me they remained German in their attitude and their thinking. As a result, the railroad was run beautifully and professionally. We spent hours watching the trains back up, pull forward, attach to different engines and right their courses efficiently and smoothly.

We registered with the Central Jewish Committee, where there were a few people moving around like mice, and returned to the train. It was already April and the weather was gorgeous. The mornings were cool, but the sun shone brightly during the day. Taking advantage of the warm day, I took Moishe to a pump near the trains and gave him a bath. The Poles had a laugh at that.

From Poznan we continued southwest into the recovered territories of Lower Silesia, or Niederschlesien. This land, we were told, had been evacuated by the Germans and would be Jewish country. Here was where all the kibbutzim had been established. Along the way we saw countless German farms, old structures with red stone roofs and whitewashed walls. If Polish farms were nice, the German farms we saw were heavenly, like postcards. And these farms, along with industrial complexes and whole villages, were mostly empty.

In contrast to the peaceful, beautiful landscape and the promise that this land was to be ours, the railroads were protected like we were entering hostile territory. The Polish railroad police guarded the tracks with heavily armed guards seemingly on high alert, as if in a state of war. We were unaware of the sheer number of underground guerilla movements sympathetic to the fascist and anti-Semitic rhetoric of the Germans, and so felt alarmed at their posture. Of course the official press in Russia would not have told us about guerilla movements, so it was a slight shock to discover we were still in some danger.

Our train stooped in Legnica, the headquarters of the Red Army in Poland. There were quite a few guards patrolling our train and by this time we had heard of a number of guerilla attacks on trains in the area. We were not terribly nervous; we were, after all, in the seat of the Red Army and protected by the Polish police, but there was an uneasiness that had not been present earlier on in our journey. At night we closed our doors, as we were instructed, and we went to sleep.

There was a knocking on our door in the middle of the night. It was unmistakably the sound of a gun barrel on wood. We opened the door and faced two Russian soldiers, both obviously drunk. One pointed an automatic rifle at us and the other threatened to toss a grenade specifically designed to expel shrapnel. We were packed in like hay, unable to move and terrified.

There was a Jewish man in our echelon who had been a highly decorated member of the Red Army. We gave each other a glance, not knowing if we should try to overpower them. We both knew it was too much of a risk. The pistol throbbed inside my pocket, but I knew I could not use it. If the soldier with the gun pulled the trigger, 32 bullets would fly into our car. With no other option, we pleaded for mercy.

The two officers only cursed at our pleas and took a Russian girl, the wife of a Pole, by the arms. In front of us, they raped her. We were powerless to stop them.

With no other option remaining, I pulled out some vodka from our luggage and gave it to the soldiers. Instantly they were friendly. They asked us if we had any watches (every Russian soldier had an armful of stolen watches), and we gave them our watches. Finally they fell asleep.

During the entire situation, an armed guard from the Polish police was marching back and forth, certainly cognizant of our situation. When the thugs fell asleep, I removed the gun and went to the policeman, asking him to take care of his comrades. He told me that the two soldiers were our comrades, not his, and that I should call the Russian commandant at the Red Army base.

Using an emergency railway phone I called the commandant, but he only accused me of being a provocateur and a liar. In the end we waited for the two soldiers to wake up and depart. Nothing was done to them and the poor Russian woman was left with only our reassurances that it would not happen again.

I was crushed. Had we left the frying pan only to land in the fire? The sense of innocence that we tried to reclaim was shattered. We were still refugees, unwanted guests in a new Poland and we now knew we would be treated as such.

During the next day, still in Legnica, we went to the center of town. This was a historic city, a former capital of one of the Silesian–Piast principalities and home to a glorious Polish victory in the 1400s. It held the first university built in the province and had been a cultural center for centuries. Now, after being horribly damaged by the war, much of its countryside was being rejuvenated by the creation of kibbutzim.

There was an aggressive advertising campaign for the Zionist ideal. Banners and placards with Hebrew writing adorned many buildings and façades. This was so alien to us; never in our Poland would there be such an outspoken, pro-Jewish, pro-Zionist movement. We visited these kibbutzim and were delighted by what we saw. Many of us decided to join a kibbutz at the earliest opportunity. It was an inkling of what was to come.

The city was crawling with Russian soldiers, even in the Polish part. The Red Army had not only a base in Legnica, but an entire section of the city into which only Russian soldiers could pass. We were happy to have seen the kibbutzim, but anxious to depart.

We came to Dzierzoniow, though it was still called by its German name at the time, Reichenberg. Nothing had been destroyed in this medieval, walled city. The roads were made of cut stone and the gothic architecture seemed to have been caressed by time, not abused. This was our last stop and throngs of people lined the tracks in anticipation of our arrival.

To our surprise Blankrod, an old friend of my father, and his boy Nathan, a good friend of Nuchem, greeted us as we stepped onto the platform. This was amazing. While working as a censor I had intercepted a letter from Nathan, who was serving in the Red Army, to his father in Stalingrad. I wrote to Blankrod telling him what happened to Nuchem and my father. Later I intercepted another letter from Nathan telling his father that when he heard of Nuchem's death he fell to his knees and cried. It was wonderful to see them in

321

Dzierzoniow. They saw my mother, how emaciated she looked, and once again they felt the pain of war. They cried, we all cried, and then celebrated our meeting.

They took us by carriage to a small town called Pietrolesie. Along the way we saw perfectly manicured German farms with their enormous horses looking like elephants on the landscape. These farms, however, were partially unmanned; the Germans were in the process of evacuating the region. At Pietrolesie we were lodged in communal apartments.

Across the way from the apartments was a large orphanage for infants that primarily held Jewish children. Tosia immediately went over there to find work. We were exhausted and spread ourselves on the floor to sleep. Before we did we were given American matzos; it was already Passover.

The next day we went out to explore. The first thing we did was to go to the city hall to register. Some staffers there showed us around the town, asking us which apartment we would like. The apartments were not only fully furnished but also filled with clothing and some supplies. We tried to determine which ones most interested us. They were also giving away stores. We happened upon an old friend from Kalisz in one of these. His name was Zeidel and from our conversation I could already tell he was into a little shady business.

Blankrod took me on a bike ride to another village not far away from Pietrolesie to a nice apartment where he was living. His wife gave me some shirts and a pair of trousers. Later we all returned to Pietrolesie and Blankrod's wife and my mother relived their tragedies.

Early the next day, Shelly and I went for a walk. Her elation felt at discovering her aunt was alive had subsided and in fact put her in a most depressive state. She was angry with me again for the entire Vera situation; she had not yet come to terms with it. She was determined to leave for the regional capital Wroclaw, formerly Breslau, with her documents and register there as a nurse. She clung to our family, though not by her own admission, but was still unsure if I was a good man or not. She wanted to go, even if it were as a symbolic gesture, yet she did not even have socks on her feet.

I told her everything about Vera. I explained that after

spending so much time together I at least owed Vera an explanation, just as I had to explain everything to Shelly. I had done
nothing dishonorable, I had simply had a relationship before
I met her. In any case I knew that Vera was not right for me,
nor would anyone else ever be. There was only Shelly and I
felt in my heart that we had so much time to spend together
in the future, I implored her not to pile pain on top of pain.
This calmed her down a little and she agreed to stay at least
until she found some clothing.

The rest of the day we spent together, walking through
fields and gazing at the mountains. During that walk we
recovered some of ourselves and began to build anew. I
believed that nothing would separate us again. We went back
to my family, I was eager to select an apartment.

When we returned, an old friend from Kalisz, Zelig
Zielberberg, was waiting for me. 'Henrik is back!' he yelled,
and gave me such a hug. I had intercepted a letter he had
sent to his wife, telling her of his regiment's impending push
into Berlin, and I had written to her myself. I never received
a response and assumed he had been cut down. He discovered that I had returned from the repatriation lists at the
Central Jewish Committee. He came to Pietrolesie as soon as
he heard.

Zelig was already a big-shot. He was the head of local
security in the district Communist Party. Everything had to be
guarded against attacks from the underground armies. Every
factory and every institution had their own force. Zelig was
responsible for coordinating them all. He told me that he had
a job for me and that I had to take that job. It was already like
Russia, which did not surprise me a bit. I asked him what the
job was and what it entailed. The Communist Party had
organized a dormitory, a youth home, in Dzierzoniow for
children from the concentration camps, children that were in
hiding and other orphans. They needed me to run this. Zelig
said there would be a house for the entire family and assistance from a woman named Moraviecka already working
there. Not that I had a choice, but I agreed to the job. It could
have been a lot worse.

The next day my mother, Henya, Moishe, little Esther and I moved into a residential apartment in the children's dormitory. It was a former German trade school now called the David Edelstat Dormitory after the progressive American writer. The school was situated on the outskirts of Dzierzoniow, next to a textile factory we used for training the older children. Behind the dormitory was an expanse of fields followed by a Red Army field base. The doors and windows were fortified with iron bars, but I wondered why there was not an armed guard. Everything was financed from the United States, from the socks on our feet to the education of the children. It was a mini-paradise compared to Russia. We had stockpiles of food, enough for a siege, an enormous professional kitchen and a staff of teachers, doctors and cooks.

The dormitory was full of children and young men. Concentration-camp survivors slept in bunks next to children who had been hidden during the war by kind-hearted Germans. While the former could be described as half-normal at best, the latter refused to believe that they were Jewish, some even crossed themselves every night before sleeping. There were children from Russia and Poland, as well as young soldiers from the Red Army with nowhere else to go. In all, over 200 children lived in that dormitory, each one carrying a burden unbefitting their years.

The building consisted of three floors, a basement and an attic. Our supplies were in the basement, classes and communal living occupied the three floors, including a dining room and a conference room, and the attic held old Nazi supplies. The supplies were fascinating. There were pictures of Hitler with the caption: 'The hand that rules Germany', an armory of placards and propaganda and a few bayonets from the Hitler Youth movement adorned with the Iron Cross. There were also manuals describing the mechanics of automobiles and textile machinery and a host of other trade school-related literature.

The youth house was officially under the control of the communist government and I was their representative. The woman running the daily operations, Moraviecka, was like a mini-Stalin, she drove everybody crazy just going through the daily routine. I was brought in to supervise in an effort to alleviate the aggravation she caused the staff and the children. I was like a property manager in the Soviet style, only I did not have a clue as to how the dormitory should be run. I answered to a board of directors, made up of not only communists but also representatives from the varying political parties in the area as well, including those from the Bund and the Poalei Zion. Together we would make a Jewish life for these children within a Polish democracy.

I tried to analyze what it was that I had to do. Being a master of preventive measures, I immediately asked about the security of the building and how we received our supplies. Being on the outskirts of town left us susceptible to attacks from any number of underground groups in search of provisions. And, since most of the children were Jewish, what would stop them from attacking the dormitory itself? I went to the Jewish Committee to make some inquiries.

The Jewish Committee was housed in an old, elegant building that had belonged to the Jews before the war. Next to the building was a synagogue, untouched by the Germans. At the meeting I discovered a wonderful thing. Unlike Russia, where no opinion other than the communist opinion was tolerated, the committee was made up of members of the Bund, the Poalei Zion, other Zionist parties and the communists – just like the youth house. Perhaps because of the financing from the United States this was a requirement of the committee, but it warmed my heart just the same. We discussed the security of the dormitory.

The committee agreed to give me one armed guard, but I implored them to give me more. I told them I needed a telephone connection and a small arsenal. I asked them for a machine gun, a few automatic rifles, ammunition and some grenades. They were a bit taken aback by my requests and sent the head of the Jewish police to the dormitory with me to devise a defensive scheme.

In the end we had one official guard outside, four rifles set up on the first floor, and a portable telephone which I would carry with me everywhere I went. Russian soldiers would be called to man the rifles if an incident should occur. I was satisfied with this plan.

I put Moishe and Esther in the dormitory with the other children, while my sister, mother and I used our apartment. Shelly had moved into another apartment with Katia and Lolek, who were fast becoming an unpleasant couple. Tosia stayed in Pietrolesie at the orphanage. Lolek renewed contact with a former lover, Palinka, and continued his womanizing on the side. Palinka's family had already opened a factory and had accumulated some wealth which Lolek and his father saw an opportunity to seize. Katia was in love with Lolek and grew more and more distraught every day.

My mother did not like Shelly to be under  Katia and Lolek's influence. She asked me if I intended to marry her, and I told her I did. 'Then bring her to us, Henrik. If you do not marry her then I will have another daughter.' Shelly moved in and was given her own room.

Shelly's nursing credentials were not accepted in Wroclaw. It was the first example we saw of the Polish government's hostility to the Russian–Jewish repatriates. Even though Shelly carried documents proving the completion of her studies, the administration in Wroclaw found reasons to refuse her. They refused doctors and other professionals trained in Russia as well. Their reasons were varied and unconvincing. In the end Shelly was given temporary permission to work as an orderly nurse in a hospital in Dzierzoniow. Each day I would take her by bicycle to work. She never got used to riding on the handlebars and I used to find it so endearing to feel her tremble.

In Dzierzoniow the roads were in great condition, perfect for riding bicycles. The Germans had left so many bicycles that every new family had at least one and it was the primary mode of transportation. I explored Dzierzoniow whenever I could, trying to bind myself to the city, to fall in love with the quaint stores decorated with little stones, the beautiful city hall and the small streets that snaked this way and that. On the one hand it was heaven on earth compared to Russia, but on the other hand it was still under Stalin's umbrella. It was a struggle to remain optimistic about our future in Poland, in my heart I knew it would become much like Russia, but I was determined to try to make a life here. And so began our second Polish life.

# 16 A new beginning

The Germans steadily evacuated the recovered territories. They had started this process at the end of the war and were protected by guards from the United Nations. It was so strange to see the lines of people and carriages leaving the city. It was exactly what had happened to us, an exodus we were not happy to witness again. We knew what being a refugee meant and it gave us no pleasure to see them leave so sadly.

Almost all the Germans eventually left the recovered territories, but before they did they continued working in Dzierzoniow with us, the new arrivals. There was an old German woman who worked in the youth house for a while. She kept everything very clean and orderly and was very stern with the children, but you could see how much she cared for them. There was still a German grocer in town when we arrived and his store was impeccably run. To my knowledge there were no violations  nor any acts of random violence or vandalism against the Germans still living there – a considerable contrast to the way we were treated when we were pushed out of our homes.

I did not feel great about the Germans leaving, but I believed it was a just process. The Germans who remained in Dzierzoniow were nice people, very friendly to us, but I was not convinced of their sincerity. They were afraid that we would harm them, with some reason. We did nothing to them, nor would we have, but psychologically we were not prepared to intermingle just yet. It was simply too soon for us to get over our contempt for the German people.

The money from the United States kept pouring in and with it we were able to create a very positive atmosphere at the youth house. Film stars and famous musicians came to the dormitory and performed for us, professionals and tradesmen taught the children new skills and our supplies were abundant and of high quality. Still, the morale of the children and much of the staff remained low. These were broken people whose psychological struggles caused me great pain.

We checked the children every night for stolen supplies and invariably discovered whole loaves of bread stashed between some of their blankets. The children from the Russian side were the worst, stealing things that could be of no use to them just for the sake of stealing. I asked one boy, who had accumulated over half a dozen British great-coats, why he had to steal when we had enough for everyone. He countered, 'You all steal! Everyone steals!' He had grown so cynical.

We taught them agricultural engineering, photography and textile work among other professions, but learning these skills did not calm the nervous nature of their damaged psyches. At night frictions between the groups of children would flare and the staff, dealing with their own issues, had a terrible time keeping order. Other nights they would act as one, demanding food nearly at midnight. What could we do? We gave them what they wanted.

A teenage girl, a survivor from a camp, hardly slept. Instead she paced up and down the dormitory mumbling to herself. Other children had terrible sexual problems, behaving like predators. I did not understand these things at the time and found myself at a complete loss in trying to bring these kids back to some kind of normality. Thankfully, a psychology teacher came to the dormitory and helped the children and me a great deal.

The staff had their own problems. One of our agricultural engineers, a man named Yad, brought back a Russian wife with him. Together they frequently rode through the countryside on his motorcycle, but on one of these trips a drunken Russian soldier pulled his truck out of a restricted street and struck the couple, killing Yad's wife. Yad could not get over his grief and shot himself. It was a tragedy for us all – he was a great teacher and friend to the children.

Yad's funeral brought me to the Jewish cemetery in Dzierzoniow for the first time. It was so beautiful, more like a museum than a cemetery thanks to the caretaker, Springer, a good-natured German man and friend to the Jews. Looking around at the staff and other friends who had come to the funeral, I sensed a general feeling of detachment. There was a vacant look in their eyes, an unhappiness with their current state. It was no secret that they felt Dzierzoniow was not a suitable place to make their homes. Mothers with fatherless children, Polish Jews with Russian wives, former professionals with greater ambitions; they had nothing invested in the city of Dzierzoniow and were almost all soon to leave Poland.

Many Jews had already begun fleeing. At night trucks drove down quiet roads and stopped to pick up people wanting to emigrate to Czechoslovakia and beyond. This was semi-illegal because the Russians and the Poles looked away, the Poles in particular wanting to be rid of the Jews anyway. The Czechs, for their part, were very friendly to the arriving immigrants.

A further factor increasing the desire to leave Poland was a renewed hostility towards the Jews and communists by the underground forces. They were now regularly stopping trains and executing Russian soldiers and Jewish people. But the violence did not come from the underground alone. In July we heard terrible news from Kielce. There was a pogrom by the police, the army and Polish citizens who had killed over 40 Jews and left over 100 injured. It allegedly started because a Jew was accused of cutting a Polish boy by the throat in order to take his blood to make matzos; a rebirth of one of the oldest and most vile myths. This began a chain of smaller pogroms throughout Poland. We avoided a disaster in Dzierzoniow because the head of the secret police was a Jew. His forces successfully squashed any such movements.

Smaller attacks, attacks on households at night, plagued our region. We heard of marauders killing husbands and stealing jewelry from homes and even mutilating pregnant women. We knew the youth house was a prime target for these groups, as we were both Jewish and mostly communist, and in the end our defenses were put to the test.

One night the armed guard called up to my room, telling me there were visitors outside the gates. He was instructed not to let anyone in at night unless I gave him permission. From my window I called down to our guests, asking them who they were and what they wanted, to which they replied that they were from the police and needed to run an inspection. 'The police do not inspect us at night', I said. In response a bullet whizzed by my ear.

We went on high alert. All the children were moved to the second floor and instructed to lie down. Some staffers manned the four rifles and aimed at the intruders. I told Shelly to hand me my pistol and to call the Russian soldiers and the police. I shot down at the group from the window while Shelly tried to telephone for help, but they had already cut the telephone wires. Shelly handed me a grenade and I lobbed it outside the gates. As it exploded I heard one of the attackers yell, 'Jesus Maria!' After that the bandits fled.

A guard from the textile factory ran to us shortly after the melée ended, asking us what had happened. I told him we had been attacked though we did not know by whom. We found a bloody shirt and a trail that led through the woods, but otherwise we knew nothing.

A few weeks later Russian soldiers robbed us. They had cut through the iron bars on the windows and had raided our supply room. In departing they left a trail through the fields to the Russian field base, so there was no question who was to blame. I filed a report with the Jewish Committee, which was at the time an internal storm of political bickering. The committee's bookkeeper was a Zionist, and I was a Communist. He officially decided that we had stolen the supplies ourselves and sold them to the Poles. They made a political mess out of the situation to the detriment of only the children.

Shortly after these incidents, about half of the children ran away. It was probably the correct decision as over the next few years the violence in the recovered territories became increasingly unpredictable.

We desperately wanted the Jewish experiment to work in Poland, and in many ways it did. We had created, in a short time, something unthinkable back in Russia: a Jewish life. We had  theatre, writing, music and commerce, all created and fostered by the large Jewish community in the recovered territories. The Jews in the Polish Workers' Party (Poland's Communist Party) needed such an experiment to thrive in order to maintain popular support and remain in charge, it was a *quid pro quo* arrangement.

In truth, fleeing Poland was not an option for me at the time. The infrastructure for emigration was not as carefully constructed as it would later become, after the inception of the state of Israel, and I did not dare haul my mother on another long journey. People who had tried to leave had returned. Elderly people with little strength left after the war fell victim to the demoralization of their compatriots at displaced persons camps; their belongings were stolen and they were badly treated. One boy had actually reached Palestine, only to return to Poland, where he lived with us at the youth house and recounted what a terrible state Palestine was in. The local government made a hero out of him in an effort to dampen the enthusiasm for emigration created by the Zionist parties.

Things were getting better and better for the community. Lost friends and relatives slowly returned to Poland, melding with our newer acquaintances to form a community with a strong resolve to make Poland our own. The Jewish Committee supplied us with everything we could have needed, and those who had started businesses were thriving. With every wave of departing emigrants the recovered territories were left with a higher percentage of people willing to stay and see what would come.

In the region we had leaders educated in the Soviet system and plenty of communist repatriates from France. Mostly these beret-wearing, friendly countrymen occupied the farmland, staying away from city centers and enthusiastically embracing this new Poland. Outside our region, however, things were very different.

Poland was a country divided. As the government made changes consistent with the Soviet ideal, the Polish people resisted. The introduction of agricultural cooperatives, like the kolchozin in Russia, was a totally foreign concept to the Polish peasants, whose methods of farming had not changed for centuries, and they struggled to grasp it. It amplified their anti-Soviet and anti-communist sentiments and prompted an increase in underground agitation throughout the country.

The concept of national political holidays in Poland was a joke to which no more than lip service was paid in every region but our own. As the armies marched and bands played, the people looked on with disgust or indifference. We, however, felt differently. Most of our children were already in communist youth movements and lined the parades wearing their white shirts and red neckerchiefs. We had our own holidays, like the raising of monuments in former ghettoes and the celebration of ghetto resistance. These were all government-created, but the outpouring of Jewish emotion helped these holidays take hold. During these days I really felt that our experiment might actually work.

I was dedicated to my family, Shelly and the children at the youth house, but I was doing a little of what I had done so much of in Russia – findings ways to help the Jewish community through my position. Many of the people who had arrived with our echelon had settled in Dzierzoniow, but not all had found a niche wherein they could provide for their families. For some of these people I found jobs through my connections with the party, for others I gave bread for them to sell (we had too much at the youth house). One said to me, 'You're in Poland less than a year and you're already a boss!' It was not true, but I had had plenty of experience in negotiating a communist system.

The Central Jewish Committee listed all of our addresses, which helped friends and relatives track each other down. Some of the visits were unexpected and pleasant. One man, whom I had saved from enlistment in the Polish army under Stalin, came to Dzierzoniow just to thank me. He was also under the impression that I was already a boss. Other encounters were not so pleasant.

Shelly discovered a cousin in Wroclaw, Shloime Koenig. He was a delicate man in the Welchers' class of people: wealthy, educated, religious and business-oriented. I thought he was very nice, but I did not know that he wanted to marry Shelly. In the end she told him that she had only one man in her life, referring to me. His subsequent jealousy was difficult for me to handle, but it subsided in time. Later we did a little business involving some gold coins.

My mother kept asking me about my Uncle Shloime Gerszon and his wife Sonia. I had no luck finding them. Even though I poured over the lists at the Central Jewish Committee and asked everyone who was newly arrived in Dzierzoniow if they had seen them, she still felt I could produce the answers out of a hat. Our last contact with Shloime Gerszon had been a letter he had sent us in early 1946, agreeing that they too would leave Russia for Poland, but we had no idea whether they had succeeded or not. I ventured outside of Dzierzoniow, visiting the Jewish committees in neighboring cities and asking returning repatriates if they had seen them. Finally, someone told me that he had met a man named Blitzblau in Zomkowitca.

I went to find them. I wore my Russian uniform to appear official and I took my pistol with me. In truth I was a little vain when it came to Russian clothing. Zomkowitca was a small city connected to the rest of Poland by a separate railway with narrow tracks laid by the Germans. It was crowded with Jews, but there was no listing for Blitzblau at the committee. I asked around and somebody told me they had moved to Zembice. The train to Zembice did not depart until the next day and I had nowhere to spend the night.

I went to the railroad station and prepared to sleep, but I feared bandits. I began to rethink my decision to wear Russian clothing – it made me a target not only for robbery but also for political reasons. I went into an empty room and pushed a chair in front of the door so that I would hear if anyone tried to enter the room. At night someone did come into the room and walked right up to me. I did not move until he was right above me, shining a light in my face. Meeting his gaze was the barrel of my pistol. He silently backed away and left the room.

The next day I arrived in Zembice and found Shloime Gerszon's address. Sonia answered the door and saw a man in a Russian uniform. She said to Shloime Gerszon in Russian, 'What does this military man want here?'

I removed my hat and said, 'Aunt Sonia, don't you recognize me?'

'Oh my God, it's Henrik!' she screamed.

After our initial reunion we talked about moving them to Dzierzoniow. They agreed that it would be better for them there and I even took their two young daughters with me, putting them directly into the youth house with Moishe and Esther. A couple of weeks later I returned with a borrowed truck and moved Shloime Gerszon and Sonia to Dzierzoniow, to an apartment with a piano in the center of town. My mother could not have been happier.

Friends and family from our old community continued to appear. We read and recognized more names on the lists at the Central Jewish Committee than we would have ever thought possible. Still, for every name we read, we knew of 20 who had perished.

Moshko, Shloime Gerszon's oldest boy who had fled to Spain to avoid prosecution under the old Polish government, sent a letter from Britain. He was a diplomatic courier for the new government and was, by all accounts, a big-shot. He was a decorated captain from the war in Spain and had changed his name from Moshko Blitzblau to the more Polish Mietek Skorupinsky. Eventually he moved back to Poland and we saw what a great man he had become. He had all the connections, he was even given a villa in Warsaw, but he was still a good boy, unassuming and polite.

Henya became the head bookkeeper in a large factory and began helping the returning refugees as much as she could. Incredibly, she employed an old acquaintance of ours from Cerepovec, the infamous Fishman. He had returned with his family from Uzbekistan and settled in the recovered territories. We joked with my sister not to let him out of her sight for fear that he would steal again. In truth, we were all happy to see him.

Shelly and I started to think about getting married. I did not want to live in the youth house with a wife, so I looked for a new apartment. A friend of mine, Kleter, knew just where to go and just what to do to get an apartment. He and his Russian wife spent many evenings going into empty apartments and removing anything of value. He took me to a cul-de-sac with six maisonettes, most of which were empty. I picked out an apartment in one of the maisonettes and thanked Kleter.

He said, 'Why aren't you taking both apartments? You will soon be married and you have your mother still. You should take both.' So I did. We moved into 5 Novagutska, apartments one and two.

We bought some furniture from a German woman who was evacuating her apartment in the same cul-de-sac. We looked over her furniture and asked her to name a price. We did not have to do this, she was leaving without the furniture whether she sold it or not, but it felt like the right thing to do. She named a price and we paid it. She was grateful for our honesty and presented us with some beautiful ceramic pieces, decorative plates and sugar bowls, to show her appreciation. We still have these plates.

I was completely dedicated to Shelly, but to my horror the situation with Vera had not yet been resolved. Maria Gregorgivna wrote a letter to me describing Vera's recent completion of medical school and transfer to Brest-Litovsk. This was on the Polish border – she still had not given up on me! The situation in Russia was not very good. Maria Gregorgivna and I had agreed on code words for our letters before I left. If I were to write, 'The cranberries are sour', it would mean Poland was no good and I wanted to return to Russia. In her letter she wrote, 'Our cranberries are sour and there is no sugar to sweeten them up.' Perhaps she thought Vera might have a better life in Poland.

Later I received a letter from Vera. She asked me to receive her greetings from a friend in Legnica, the daughter of a general stationed at that base. I decided to meet her, but I kept everything hidden from Shelly, though I believe she knew something was going on.

I stayed with some old acquaintances from Kalisz in Legnica and went to the army base in the morning. I showed Vera's letter to the soldiers there and waited for her friend to meet me. The base was officially part of Russia, so I was not able to enter beyond a certain point and Vera's friend was not able to leave.

We talked politely for a short while and through her I sent

Vera and Maria Gregorgivna my regards, but I said with conviction that there was no future for us in Poland. I asked that Vera not come to Poland and I gave her a few presents: a nice watch, a pair of shoes and some chocolates. With this I ended my Russian connection. Later, when I became a father, I sent them a photograph of my family, hoping at least to remain friends. I never heard back from either of them.

Shortly thereafter, I asked Shelly to be my wife. In October 1946 we were married in Uncle Shloime Gerszon's apartment. It was a Tuesday, a lucky day, and his apartment was filled with Jewish nationals, communists and old friends. Shelly insisted on a religious wedding, which was not too rare but certainly not the predominant fashion at the time. When I broke the glass, I could hear the sneers and chuckles of the communists in the room. It was a simple affair, they got me a little drunk and Shelly and I took a few days off to honeymoon at our apartment.

Our wedding was a joyous occasion, but it was touched with sadness. Since arriving in Poland, Shelly had discovered what had happened to her family in Lublin. Her father had been killed in their backyard and her mother was forced to buy back the body to give him a proper burial. Later her mother and sisters were executed after being made to sit for an entire day at a mass grave while the Nazis waited for more ammunition to arrive. Our wedding was like a balm for Shelly, a dose of happiness against the persistent gloom. I told Shelly that I had asked the souls of the dead from her family and my family to be present at our wedding. Perhaps they were.

In 1947 the board of directors decided to move the children from the dormitory on the outskirts of town to another building in the center of Dzierzoniow. This was done mostly for security reasons, as there had been an increase in the frequency of violent attacks in the region, but also because the Jewish faction of the Polish Workers' Party wanted to make some changes to the youth house.

As it was, we ran the youth house entirely on Jewish-American dollars and tried to teach the children their Jewish roots and responsibilities. There were other youth houses which focused on a communist education and upbringing that were home to mostly gentiles. When we moved locations, the Jewish leaders, in a cowardly move no better than any single deed performed by the *Judenrat*, forced us to accept scores of gentile children.

I saw this as the beginning of the end of the Jewish life we had created in Dzierzoniow; it showed me that the recovered territories were nothing more than a Polish ghetto. It made perfect, horrible sense; first they put us all in one place, then they took away our right to be Jewish. The Jews in the party leadership had been nothing in Russia, but now, living in the recovered territories, they were drunk on their own importance. They knew in time the funds from the United States would dry up and that Poland would be under Russian control. They showed no sympathy to their own people, even after the tragedy of the Second World War, and worked only to please Stalin.

This disappointed me greatly because I knew that accepting gentiles would dilute the character of the youth house. The atmosphere we had created was almost holy, as if the children's suffering somehow sanctified them. How could we maintain that tight-knit feeling when the children of our enemies slept alongside our own? I complained to the board of directors and to the Jewish leadership of the party in Dzierzoniow, but to no avail.

I felt that we personally had failed these children and the Jewish people by not keeping the youth house a holy place. In response, I actively sought out responsibility in the Polish Workers' Party. I thought that I had a better chance of protecting our Jewish life by getting further involved with the party leadership. Shelly and I began going to city committee meetings and I was soon appointed party leader for the Brush Makers Cooperative, a thriving collective filled with good workers and strong believers in communism. I even put Moishe to work there.

Being party leader for the Brush Makers Cooperative was something I did in addition to working at the youth house, but it was a party position and I knew it could lead to others. I felt that my days at the youth house were numbered, first because I did not believe in the direction it was going, and second because I was more ambitious than my position. I would wait and see, however, what the party had in mind for me.

I was disillusioned with the changes at the youth house but I still loved the children. On the weekends I borrowed trucks from the factory where my sister worked and took the children out to the countryside. Through a lot of organizing and a little luck, I was able to arrange a retreat for the entire summer of 1947. We took over the operations of a country estate abandoned by the Germans – it was a great adventure for the children.

We marched the entire group out into the countryside to a small village called Rasciszow, which was still half deserted. There were pigs, chickens and horses out there. The Polish boys and the Jews who had been hidden by Poles tended expertly to the animals. Shelly and I shared a small house near the children and enjoyed the whole summer in the country air. Other youth houses came to visit us and there was a summer camp nearby for young Zionists. The summer was filled with Indian wars and other games like 'Capture the Flag'.

In the middle of the summer my old friend from child-hood, Shaya Kawe, the son of the monument maker, came to visit us. He had been imprisoned for most of his time in Russia, but had been granted amnesty and had recently returned to Kalisz. I was excited to see him, but I almost did not survive our first encounter. While looking at my pistol, which he could not resist holding but did not know how to use, he accidentally fired a bullet that just missed my chest, screamed through the mattress and lodged itself into the iron bed frame.

Shaya Kawe told us of a recent phenomenon in Poland. If you could claim that a home or building belonged to a member of your family, whether that person was a close or distant relative, you were entitled to ownership of that property or money for its value. Shaya Kawe had already made this his industry and had accumulated some wealth. He asked me why I did not do the same. I told him I would give it a try.

At the end of the summer, we needed to march the children out of Rasciszow and back to the new dormitory. We heard from the police that there was a roving band of Ukrainian guerrillas in the area, so we surrounded the children with armed staff members and walked through the woods to Dzierzoniow. When we arrived, I took a few days off and went to meet Shaya Kawe in Kalisz to try my hand in the housing market. According to my mother, my relatives had houses in Warta and Sieradz.

This was the first time I had returned to Kalisz after so many years and it was surreal. I had run away to the east and now I returned from the west; it was like a ring of life. We pulled into the station and I felt light-headed and uneasy. I could see the fields I had run across after escaping from the cemetery, and I could still see German bullet holes from 1939 in the water tower on the horizon. I experienced a flood of emotions as I took my first few steps on the platform, but I righted myself and walked through the streets of Kalisz towards Shaya Kawe's home.

I traversed the entire city, seeing old neighborhoods and the evidence of destruction caused by the war. Remarkably, I came across familiar faces along the way. The first person I recognized was Janina Mrozinska, a former classmate of mine at Mikolai Reja; she had been an excellent student in our Polish literature classes and thus was my competition. I saw her walking with a child and I wanted to greet her. To my surprise, she shot me a frosty look, turned her child around and walked off in another direction. I could not believe her hostility.

Further down the street I met another classmate from Mikolai Reja, Woloszczyk, who was extremely friendly to me. We hugged and kissed and told each other of our lives. He named so many people who had fallen in the war and afterwards to the underground armies. Still, he was upbeat and asked me to return the next day to meet some more old friends. This cheered me enormously as I longed to be friendly with the people from my past.

The next set of faces I recognized belonged to Drytkiewicz and Muszynski, two young Polish men dressed in almost military fashion. They were the children of members of the

Polish police before the war. Given the way they were dressed, and noticing the scowls on their faces when they recognized me, I got the feeling they were part of an underground movement so I kept my distance.

Finally I came to the Jewish section, or so I thought. Looking around I felt like I was on the moon. Almost everything was gone, physically removed. The Jewish buildings, the synagogue, the *mikvah* and the shops had all been demolished. Some of the residential streets remained, including Ciasna Street, but there were no Jews. With the debris, the Nazis had filled in the river and created a park. This came as a complete shock to me – our past had been totally wiped out.

I met Shaya Kawe at his home, which was a house still owned by one of his relatives. He was so dear to me, like a brother, and finding him living and thriving in Kalisz made me happy to have returned. He was following in his father's footsteps; he had a monument-making business for which he employed one ethnic German engraver. He also was making a fortune through real estate and, as was the norm, he was doing a few shady deals on the side.

He explained the situation in Kalisz to me. First of all, unlike the recovered territories, the people here did not embrace the Soviet ideal. They resented the Jews for bringing the Russians with them and made sure they knew it. The Kalisz Immigrants Association from New Jersey supported those few Jews who did live in Kalisz. They had sent a representative named Arnold to start up a tailoring cooperative, which was thriving, and they housed the Jews in a building protected by the police (following two night-time attacks). Some Jews, like Shaya Kawe, worked independently. In short, Kalisz was like most of Poland, barely tolerable for Jews.

The following day I went back to meet Woloszczyk and a couple of other friends from school. Again, I learned that many of my Polish friends whom I had admired and respected had been killed. One, Smolencki, was an orphan living in barracks outside Kalisz who had been brought to our school by a socialist teacher named Kowalcki. He was half-wild, but he took to the socialist teachings and always joined the Jewish boys from the Poalei Zion when we fought the boys from the Endeki.

Another, Staszik, worked for the Polish KGB and had just been killed by the underground. Still, it was nice to see my classmates.

I spent the rest of the day visiting more old friends and acquaintances. First I went to visit the school director from Mikolai Reja, Browislaw Mjorkowski. The last time I had seen him he had been in a terrible state, shoeless and disheveled, and I wondered how he had endured the war. Sadly, our reunion was more awkward than cheery. He was very detached and cool towards me, and I left in low spirits.

I then stopped by the home of the woman who owned the building where my father rented the butcher shop. This was much more pleasant than the visit with Pan Browislaw Mjorkowski, first of all she was happy to see me. The last time I had seen her was when I had given her back the keys as she lamented ours and Poland's fate. This time she cried when I told her about my father and brother. She was an emotional person and I enjoyed seeing her, but I left fairly quickly. I was still not comfortable in a Polish home filled with icons and religious decorations.

Together Shaya Kawe and I set about claiming real estate for our families. He was already an expert. I went with him to a small village called Blaszky where he was suing the local government for building their city hall on his great-grandfather's property. Ultimately the town had to buy back the land from him and he made a small fortune.

The biggest estate in my family was in Warta, owned by a distant cousin of mine, Mayer Mirowicz. There were four or five other houses in that little city that belonged to my family, but I was not interested in getting all of them just yet. We took a train to Sieradz then a bus to Warta, catching its one daily trip.

In Warta I went to visit my father's old friend, Szymon. During the war he had hidden a Jewish woman and now they were married. He was the mayor of this little hamlet and she owned a store. He remembered my father and my uncles from the time of their youth and offered us a place to stay.

We told him of my intention to reclaim the estate for my family and his face filled with concern. Taking me to the window, he showed me a little house that had belonged to my uncle years ago. After the war about 20 or so Jewish boys from the concentration camps had settled in that house. Out of the forest came a band of Poles who stormed the house and executed all the boys. It was a warning to other Jews planning to settle in Warta.

He told us that during the day Warta belonged to the local government, but at night bandits took control. He warned me that if someone recognized the fact that I was trying to reclaim land, there was a chance that they would want to kill me.

I wanted to leave right then, but the bus did not return to Sieradz until the following morning. Shaya Kawe convinced me to pursue the estate anyway. We would finalize the paperwork during the day and stay with Szymon that night, which we had to assume was safe, then take the bus back to Sieradz in the morning. In his thinking we would never have to return to Warta because we could sell the estate through lawyers. It made sense to me.

Hastily we went to meet the town's record keeper, an ethnic German man named Nieman. He was a nice fellow and he knew the entire history of Warta. It was easy for him to connect the deeds of the estate to my family, he knew exactly who had owned the estate and when. We had sufficient evidence in no time.

We spent the night with Szymon and, although I was nervous, nothing happened. In the morning we took the bus back to Sieradz and hired a lawyer. He made the arrangements for a hearing and organized my evidence in the proper fashion. His fee was calculated in terms of wheat, not zlotys – there was no faith or value in Polish money.

In Sieradz I knew of a few homes which I could have claimed for my family, but I was not inclined to do so. I felt that I was not suited for this business, which, in my opinion, was tainted with greed and cynicism, not to mention danger. In time I discovered it had the potential to pit relative against relative, and this during the period of Jewish reawakening.

After a home or estate was reacquired, an official announcement was made and the new proprietor had to wait six months before he could sell it. During that time challenges could be made to the claim. There was a separate industry for people who waited for these announcements and then forged a family tree to prove they were closer relatives, and so it happened with Mayer Mirowicz's estate.

I received a letter from Lodz from a relative claiming to be closer to Mayer Mirowicz than I. I went with Shaya to Lodz to meet her and her husband, thinking they would at least cover my expenses since I was a relative. After all, I had put together all the paperwork and I was prepared to follow the word of law and relinquish my claim to the estate. They proved to be cruel people who said they would take the estate and not give me a penny, despite the fact that I had done all the work. When I asked if they felt ashamed of what they were doing to their relatives they seemed not to care.

I tried to claim that estate because I wanted to help Henya. She was engaged to be married and we needed some money for the occasion. I did not want to steal or get involved with too much shady dealing, so not getting a dime from the estate was very disappointing to me.

While in Lodz, Shaya Kawe and I decided to try and visit Szymek Pelta and his brothers, plus a few of my relatives. We visited a close relative of Lazar Komincki, Karo, at her apartment. At first she was very happy to see us, but then she was reminded of her children and became terribly upset. She had been forced to give her child away to the *Judenrat* in the Lodz ghetto, and in doing so, she was convinced she had saved her own life. I believe she had a nervous breakdown right in front of us as she wailed loudly and pulled the hair out of her head. We tried to comfort her, but it was of no use – she was too damaged – nothing we said could help her forgive herself.

I was very affected by Karo's behavior and I took the memory of her torment with me back to Kalisz. I went for a walk when we arrived. I thought about all those who had suffered, from the children in the youth house to the sinister couple in Lodz, and I came to the conclusion that there was holiness in our anguish. Some of us were forced to give each other over to death to save ourselves, we were stripped of our humanity, we were driven out of our homes and our pasts were erased. What more could we sacrifice? How much more suffering could God want from us?

Kalisz seemed like one long grave to me and, as when standing at the headstone of a loved one, I was contemplative and peaceful. I was no longer angry with the couple from Lodz because I did not know what they had gone through and thus what prompted their behavior. I let it go and decided to refrain from making other property claims, I did not want to see that side of people again. I only wanted to help heal the Jewish people.

I wondered how long we would continue forging a Jewish life in the recovered territories before our momentum was stopped, then reversed. Would we become like the Russian Jews in Cerepovec, an underground society with a vague recollection of the way things used to be? The signs were already there. In my heart I knew the experiment would fail and we would be swallowed up whole by the communist government, but something inside me felt I should continue striving for my people here in Poland and resist the temptation to flee.

I returned to Dzierzoniow to terrible news. The violent attacks had increased and there had been a horrific triple murder in the town. Two boys wearing masks had killed three butchers who sold horsemeat. The police caught them and they were sentenced to death. Their deed cast a pall over the city, it was an indication that the violence in our region came not only from the underground but from normal people as well. We increased the security at the youth house and I worried about my mother and Shelly when I was not with them.

The brutality of these boys and the continued savagery of the guerrillas reawakened the desire for many Jews to leave Poland. The state of Israel had yet to be established, but the infrastructure for emigration was sound, or at least much safer than it was. Entire institutions like the kibbutzim left Poland for Palestine, while others simply left Poland. Tosia, for instance, moved with the orphanage from Pietrolesie to western Europe. Henya and her fiancé, though they both held good jobs, had determined to go to Palestine after they were married. Theirs was the opposing conviction of the Jews in the recovered territories, one that I understood and respected.

From my trips to Kalisz and Lodz I brought back with me a

determination to leave the youth house and fight for our Jewish life in Poland through my connections in the party. Before I even intimated this to other members of the party I was offered a job. Unfortunately it was nothing that I had wanted or was prepared to do – I was asked to join the Polish KGB.

They called me into their offices and told me that I was an ideal candidate for the position. They had reviewed my past, very much in the Soviet style, and assumed I was willing to be a partner in their treachery. I was asked all sorts of questions, like if I was capable of arresting and even shooting criminals. I hedged, saying I was extremely happy at the youth house and more suited to that type of work. I insinuated that I was not inclined to shoot people and, by some miracle, I talked myself out of the job. It was a harrowing experience, one that brought back my former paranoia from the Soviet system. Was my refusal now going to put me under their surveillance as an enemy of the people?

I had returned to the youth house for only a couple of weeks when the party approached me with another offer and this time I took the job.

At that time, the beginning of 1948, the Jewish faction of the Communist Party had come to the conclusion that there was an anti-Semitic conspiracy in the Department of Labor. They assumed that the Polish guilds, with the help of the department, were hampering Jewish trade in the recovered territories as they had done for centuries in Poland. I believed that there may have been an element of self-interest in this accusation, using it as a ploy to procure more power in the economics of the region, but there was a historic conflict there that probably deserved some inspection. The party asked me to oversee the activities at the Department of Labor, buttering me up by praising my Polish language skills and my intelligence. They intended to pull me out of the youth house to do this.

Although it was what I wanted, the prospect of leaving my position saddened me much more than I would have expected. In fact, despite my conviction that I would be of better use to the Jews in Poland away from the children, I had second thoughts about leaving. I had seen many of the kids grow from damaged children to functional young adults. I saw how they began flirting with each other and how some of them had run away to Palestine. Sometimes this was the best thing for them, and unofficially I encouraged some of the older children to leave. Also, my feelings for the children may have been increasingly sentimental because my dear Shelly was pregnant.

In the end I accepted the job at the Department of Labor, mainly because I did not think I could decline a second job offer without hurting my standing in the party. In addition, if there were a conspiracy I would be doing Jews a better service by discovering its roots. Of course, like joining the fire brigade in Cerepovec, I did not have a clue as to what I was to do. I was told to clean up the office and introduce the party and Jewish line. How I was to go about this was a mystery.

The office in Dzierzoniow acted as the local and regional center of the Department of Labor. The provincial office was in Wroclaw. The regional director was a man named Tadeusz and the secretary of the guilds was Ludwig Holdonowicz. These two, along with a staff of clerks, ran the office in Dzierzoniow. I went to this office preparing to establish myself as office manager.

As I walked into that office I felt like I had stumbled into an enemy camp. The walls were adorned with religious pictures and icons and an old-fashioned Polish Eagle wearing the crown – this particular eagle was illegal at the time. I absorbed the sideward glances from mistrusting eyes and walked around the office as if I knew exactly what I was doing. I looked on the whole venture as a game of wits in which I would have to convince the staff that I was more knowledge-able than I was to have any hope of gaining their respect.

I spent a few hours looking over ledgers and books trying to get a handle on the processes of the office, all the while acting as if I were an expert. While doing this I said two things that hinted at my purpose for being there. The first statement regarded the religious pictures and the Polish Eagle, saying these things belonged in private homes, not in government offices. The second regarded the lists of names in the ledgers. Jews, I noticed, were listed by their nicknames, like Moshko instead of Moishe. I asked why their official names were not listed.

There were excuses made for both of my assertions, but they knew I had the power of the party behind me and did not argue too ardently. I left the office, taking with me an enormous volume of Polish industrial law and telling them I would return in two weeks. I had a lot of studying to do if I hoped to discover any illegal or conspiratorial practices.

The primary complaint of the Jewish leadership had to do with the Department of Labor's practice of allocating the abandoned German shops to skilled laborers. As it stood, stores were given only to members of the guilds. These men were masters of their trades and proven qualified to run their own businesses. The problem was that Polish tradesmen from outside the region were given these stores much more frequently than Jews within the recovered territories. The reason Jews were slighted was not because of any overtly anti-Semitic practices, which were no longer legal, but because they lacked the proper paperwork to prove their competency and thus join the guilds.

Skilled Jewish tradesmen were forced to work in cooperatives or in unsanctioned businesses if they did not produce their old documents, most of which had been lost in Russia or taken away in concentration camps. To receive new papers, the Department of Labor told them they had to redo their apprenticeship, their three-year understudy and their master's examination. This was not only absurd but impossible.

For two weeks I poured over the industrial law book, learning all I could about the Department of Labor and trying to find a provision for tradesmen who had lost their papers in the past. The laws in that volume stretched back to the sixteenth century, surely there were fires or wars that had resulted in similar situations. Finally I discovered Article 146, a provision for laborers who had lost their papers. To be issued replacement documents, a tradesman must present two witnesses to swear on his behalf. That was it. Why, if this was such a simple process, were the Jewish craftsmen told they had to repeat their training? This proved that it was a conspiracy.

I brought my discovery to the Jewish leadership. Since I felt so uncomfortable in that unfriendly office, I thought the Jewish leadership might do me a favor and send me back to the youth house. I thought this was fair since I had uncovered the deception they had suspected. They were pleased with me, but they wanted me to stay in the Department of Labor. Reluctantly, I returned.

I met with Tadeusz and explained that the Department of Labor had not given some of the tradesmen an accurate assessment of their situation. I did not imply that there was an anti-Jewish conspiracy, in fact I did not mention the Jews at all. I simply pointed out that a mistake had been made. Tadeusz insisted that he would have known about such a law if it existed, but he agreed to contact the office in Wroclaw to ask the provincial director.

The provincial director came to Dzierzoniow a few days later. I showed him Article 146 and he feigned surprise. He agreed that it was a law, but he told us that the witnesses' statements had to be stamped by a public notary. A public notary in Poland was a big deal. Having something notarized meant paying a lot of money if you were lucky enough to find one who would grant an appointment. Nowhere in the industrial law book did it say witnesses had to have their statements notarized. I pointed this out to the director, telling him that I was capable of verifying witnesses' statements since I was an employee of the Department of Labor and a member of the Polish Workers' Party. This reminded him who really had the power in that room. He agreed that I had the authority to verify the statements.

After this change in procedure, Tadeusz left his position and moved to Warsaw. Holdonowicz became the regional director and I was promoted to secretary of the guilds. A steady flow of Jews came into our office with their two witnesses. It was like a mini-revolution, we were undermining what the guilds were trying to do.

I verified witnesses' statements and helped tradesmen fill out their paperwork before sending it off to the provincial offices in Wroclaw. The staff in Wroclaw, in turn, processed their paperwork, officially making them members of a guild, and sent the resulting papers to the local governments. The local governments then sent the tradesmen their guild papers and trade cards, which allowed them to take over an abandoned shop. It was generally a two-week process.

For the first few weeks, the papers I sent to Wroclaw never made it to their destination. Every batch was mysteriously lost in the mail. I began hand-delivering them, letting them know I was not going to stop working for the repatriates, and soon the problem went away. It was not the only time I would have trouble in that office.

Months went by. Ludwig Holdonowicz and I had a good relationship, which made my daily life pleasant, but the elders, the representatives from the guilds, did not like me at all. We were engaged in a political fight. They were old Polish tradesmen, longing for the way it used to be when Jews were not allowed in their guilds and they monopolized government contracts. I was working to level the playing field, adhering to the principles of the Polish Workers' Party.

The elders had longstanding connections in the Department of Labor, and they used them to harass me. Inspectors sent from the provincial office continually paid surprise visits to our bureau. They would take a look at my record-keeping and try to find evidence of corruption. I used the same techniques as Holdonowicz, not changing a single process, and so I was never in trouble. Still, the hostility was tedious.

One evening, as Shelly and I made our way out of a Jewish playhouse, I noticed from the streets that the lights were on in the conference room of our office. I had a key, so I went upstairs to see what was going on. The elders from the guilds were having a meeting. Every meeting had to be registered and, as secretary of the guilds, I was required to be at all engagements. I walked in and asked what was going on. After hearing no reply apart from mumbled excuses, I walked out.

They knew I could have them all investigated, if not arrested. Most of the elders were involved in countless illegal activities and could not afford to be exposed. I represented the government and though they thought they could pull the wool over my eyes they still feared me. Discovering their meeting gave me a lot of leverage. Simply put, for them to stay in business I had to keep quiet.

These struggles at the Department of Labor, the clash of egos, the deception and battle of wits, reminded me so much of life in Russia. The innocence of our experiment in the recovered territories was fading. At the youth house it felt like we were working towards something good, but at the Department of Labor I could tell we were not. How long, I wondered, before a cloud of Soviet deceit covered Dzierzoniow?

On the other hand, my work at the Department of Labor brought me much acclaim within the Jewish community. I quickly became known as a man who could get things done, which was not unwarranted. I helped a lot of Jewish artisans start their own businesses and I was repaid with innumerable favors. This allowed me to help people in much the same way as I did in Cerepovec, seldom were the times when I could not find an apartment or work for a needy Jew. These activities increased my stature within the party and I was given more responsibility. By the spring of 1948 I was a well-known and well-respected member of the community in Dzierzoniow.

The party leadership sent me to three cities in preparation for the 1948 May Day holiday. I went to these communities to ensure that adequate plans were made for extravagant celebrations throughout the recovered territories. Symbolically, May Day was never so important for the Jewish leadership as it was that year. In April the British began the slow withdrawal from Palestine, thus ensuring the creation of a Jewish state. There would inevitably be throngs of Jews, the Zionists at least, leaving the recovered territories for Israel soon and the party leadership hoped to stem the tide by tapping into whatever enthusiasm for communism still existed.

I was not terribly pleased with the party at that time, because Shelly, who was eight months pregnant, received a lot of criticism for skipping meetings. Also a new directive had been sent to Dzierzoniow from the central committee. In our meetings we had to go through a process called criticism and self-criticism. A man would stand up and say all the things that he was doing wrong, like believing that there could be individual peasantry within a socialist government. The others would then tell him of his other shortcomings. He would then declare that he understood his mistakes and accepted his criticism. It was preposterous.

Also, the international situation worsened for the new communist nations. Stalin was unhappy with the discrepancies between these governments and took measures to ensure closer adherence to Soviet patterns. The Comintern was liquidated and the Communist Information Bureau (CIB) was formed in its place. Directives from this bureau included the criticism and self-criticism sessions and the forced collectivization of the farms. Every Sunday, as part of the new directives and in grand Soviet style, we all went to the fields to bring in the harvest. The people of Dzierzoniow did not like this too much.

The CIB forced the consolidation of the Polish Workers' Party and the Bund in an attempt to quell dissenting voices. The new party was called the United Polish Workers' Party, though the influence of the Bund was severely muted. We were told to be very hostile with former Bund members and we were encouraged to find anything that might allow us to deny them entry into the party. Our liberties as people and as Jews were fading.

The day before May Day, 1948, the leader of the Jewish Committee, Orlin, shot himself in the head. He was under investigation by the Polish KGB because of rumors that he had been an informant for the Polish government before the war. This was a clear symbol of the changing times. That cloud of Soviet deceit, which I so feared, was rolling ominously over the horizon.

On 14 May 1948, David Ben-Gurion announced the establishment of the State of Israel. No Jews would be restricted from entering Israel's borders. Life in the recovered territories was going to change.

# 17 The experiment fails

Poland and Israel made a series of immigration agreements designed to facilitate the transfer of the thousands of Jews remaining in Poland to Israel. The Comintern in the Soviet Union saw the emigrating Jews as torchbearers for communism, a force of influence that could secure ties to the communist states instead of the western powers. The Poles, for their part, were glad to see the Jews go. The Zionists were the first to leave, registering en masse for the return to the homeland.

Our family was divided. We had grown up with the ideology of the Poalei Zion but had become communists in order to survive. I knew I could not leave Poland because of my position in the party and because of Shelly's pregnancy. Henya, however, could. She and Oskar, a few months after their wedding at Shloime Gerszon's apartment, registered for emigration and left for Israel.

Henya's departure was very hard for my mother and for me, but we knew it was what they wanted to do. It was wonderful that she and Oskar would be living my father's dream of life in Israel, but it pained us to not be there with her. My mother especially suffered, but nothing in the world would keep her away from the birth of our child.

One night in June Shelly began having labor pains. It was late and there was no public transportation, so we walked together to the hospital where she was employed. Shelly went into a room and soon I heard her cries from the hallway. She asked the nurses, her colleagues, to close the door so I would not hear her pain. I stayed there for a long time, but the nurses told me to go home as it would be a while before she would give birth. I went back to our apartment and slept, waking early the next morning to a heavy downpour.

I walked hurriedly through the rain to the hospital and

was met by the nurses. They told me I was the father of a beautiful daughter. This news affected me greatly. Instantly I realized how much I had wanted to have a son. I walked out of the hospital and did not open my umbrella. 'Now it can rain on me', I thought. My distress was rooted in my love for my father and Nuchem and I had envisioned our child as a living testament to their sacrifice.

When I saw our daughter for the first time, all of my disappointment faded. I felt such an overwhelming sense of love and pride for her and I recognized her birth as the miracle it was. The silly idea that she should be a boy was erased when I saw her beautiful face and curly blonde hair. She would be a Jewish mother, what better memorial could there be?

We decided to name her Esther. After two days both mother and daughter returned from the hospital. From that point on, Esther became the source of all our happiness. Her sweet squeals sounded like laughter to us and her temperament was angelic. The love for her in that apartment was irrepressible; sometimes Shelly and my mother would fight over who would bathe her. Friends and relatives also loved little Esther and their constant visits made the atmosphere in our home one of happiness and celebration. Despite missing Henya, we had never been so happy.

Shortly after Esther's birth, Shelly's Aunt Ziska and her husband came to visit us from Paris. They were on assignment for a Jewish newspaper in Paris, *Die Yiddishe Freier Presse*. They were instructed to write about all the wonderful things the Soviet system had done for Poland. This was incredibly important for Shelly as, apart from her cousin Shloime Koenig in Wroclaw, she had not seen any of her family members. While the birth of Esther greatly helped her depression, in fact it made her a different person, the visit from Ziska was almost equally important.

Their visit started out so wonderfully. Shelly was finally able to mourn her lost loved ones with someone who shared her memories. Their reminiscing reconnected Shelly to her past and brought some peace within her soul. For that I was extremely grateful. In time, however, the couple's politics grated on me and we had some serious disagreements.

Ziska and her husband were still innocent theoretical communists living in the French reality. They had not seen the deceit and inequity of Soviet, and now Polish, communism. They spoke with official slogans and acted as if the recovered territories were a paradise. Shelly could see that I was irritated, but she begged me to keep quiet if only to make their visit pleasant and uneventful. For a while I kept my mouth shut, but soon I was forced to tell them the truth about communism.

One evening three Jewish tradesmen came over to our apartment to ask for my help. Two were witnesses and the third lacked papers. I took down their information and told them that the new papers would arrive in a couple of weeks. Ziska was shocked to see me working from my home and, suspecting I was involved in something illegal, asked me what I was doing.

I told her the truth. On many occasions similar groups would come into the office hoping for my verification of witnesses' statements, but would be turned down because there was something questionable about their stories. In front of Holdonowicz and even the typists, I was forced to walk the straightest line. By verifying these statements at home, I was able to go into the office early the next day and finalize the paperwork before anyone else arrived. I explained to Ziska that it was extremely difficult to help Jews within that office because I was surrounded by extremely perceptive gentiles.

Ziska was offended and said, quite arrogantly, that this sort of activity should not go on in a communist society. I was incensed. I asked her if she knew what really went on in this communist paradise, what the 'dictatorship of the proletariat' really meant. She gave me the standard responses. I could not resist setting her straight.

I told her that the 'dictatorship of the proletariat', in Russian terms, simply meant the killing of innocent people. I asked her if she thought it was a crime not to be members of the proletariat, and if she had ever heard of a capitalist government slaughtering their own people. I told her that I had witnessed the imprisonment of Jews, Poles and peasants in Russia for no reason and knew that they were worked until they died. I told her about the KGB and the constant threat of denouncement. I told her that in the end the new aristocracy would have everything and the rest would not have a pair of shoes; they would have hospitals and the rest would not have a doctor; they would have luxury and the rest would starve. Was this to be the future of the world?

She was lost, unable to respond. She could only ask me, if it was so terrible, why I was a member of the party. She did not understand that there was no other way in Poland, that to protect my family and the Jewish community I had to be a member. I did not know that my diatribe, the closest to the truth she would get from a party member, was exactly what she wanted to hear, though not for her newspaper articles.

She did not tell us that the communist leadership in France wanted to send her and her husband to the recovered territories to be big-shots in the party. They did not want to leave France, but if they stayed in Paris they would have their Polish citizenship revoked. If this happened they would be illegal aliens and unable to work. They had two children who were for the most part French, one had been hidden by French friends during the war and the other born after the war. It was a major decision.

I do not know how much my speech influenced their decision, but I am sure it had some effect. They returned to Paris and ultimately became French citizens. I believe Ziska felt bitter towards me, but regarded what I had said as fact or at least an honest and knowledgeable opinion. Years later we visited them in Paris and had a warm reunion.

My relationship with the elders of the guilds remained antagonistic throughout these months. It was a small victory for me when Esther was born because, by tradition, I was entitled to a gratuity from each of the guilds. Some of the elders shook with anger, but they had to give me the money. They were afraid of me and, as yet, I had proved untouchable by their friends in the government.

The party was pleased with my work at the Department of Labor. They wanted to utilize me in other areas as well. As a result, I ceased being the party leader of the Brush Makers Cooperative and became the new political supervisor of the Department of Taxation in Dzierzoniow.

At the Department of Taxation I discovered quickly that Jews were paying higher taxes than Poles. The head of the department was an old Polish man who was simply afraid of me. I approached him with the problem, never once mentioning Jews or Poles. I plainly said that the government needed more money, but the taxes had to be spread out evenly. I presented him with two carpenters, one Pole and one Jew, with virtually identical assets. The Jew had paid four times as much tax. This, I told the old man, was anti-government.

I succeeded in leveling the taxes in Dzierzoniow because I made a political, rather then a Jewish, argument. I did not threaten to expose any 'enemies' in the department, but this was what they most feared. The Jewish artisans were delighted with what I had accomplished and brought me shoes, clothing and money as tokens of their gratitude. I knew, however, that it was a hollow victory since theoretically there should be no private industry.

To appease the directives from the Comintern and still maintain a level of privatization in the region, I supported the idea of assistance cooperatives. In this system the supply side was centralized, taking away the stigma of private enterprise. Merchants would receive their materials from the government and sell their products privately. This idea caught on and there were soon voluntary assistance cooperatives springing up.

These were victories for me, but I knew they were dangerous. With every success I had, the party wanted more and more from me. Eventually, I feared, they would ask me to do something I could not do – I still maintained my pact with God. As it was, they were getting closer and closer to crossing that line.

I came to my office one day to find a friendly Polish man waiting for me on the steps. He said that he was from Polish security, which I took to mean the Polish KGB. I invited him in and asked him to sit down. I could only imagine what he wanted with me. I had turned the Polish KGB down before, if he asked me to work for them again would I be allowed to say no?

They did not want me to work for them, but they wanted

to use our office for interrogations. We had a small room on our floor with doors both to the kitchen and to the hallway. He asked me if I was willing to lend him a key for the hallway door so he could use the room for private meetings. If, he said, the doors to the kitchen were closed, he would be in there with somebody. Otherwise the doors would always remain opened.

I accepted his offer because I was powerless to decline. The janitor of the building heard our exchange and said to me when the man had left, 'Uh-oh, it's just like the Soviets already.' I told him to keep his mouth shut; I did not know whom he represented.

The Polish KGB man periodically showed up at the office, sometimes with somebody and sometimes alone. He was very friendly with me and we had long conversations about politics and things. During one of our conversations he asked me if I knew anything about a certain Jewish jeweler. I knew the man well, I had even done some business with him. In response to his question, however, I told him I only knew about his status in the guild and, according to the records, he always paid his dues on time. That afternoon I went to see the jeweler and told him he was under investigation. The next day he fled to Germany.

This became somewhat of a pattern, but it was not the only way in which I helped the Jews in Dzierzoniow. Jewish tradesmen set to leave for Israel were required to have their luggage inspected by a representative from the Department of Labor. Within the laws of this friendly immigration there were certain Polish rules designed to protect the Polish economy. No new tools or tools designated as essential to the Polish economy were allowed to leave the country. I performed these inspections but I was under strict orders to not let the departing Jews rob the Polish economy.

The problem was, we did not know what was needed in Israel. There existed a whispered propaganda about the conditions in Israel. We understood them to be so awful that people were dying of hunger. We also heard that the Israelis would not let you in without a pair of rubber boots. People spent their last pennies on supplies that ultimately proved useless, but with such misinformation channeling into Poland, what else could they do? They discovered after they arrived in Israel that the best thing would have been to convert all of their money into US dollars and hide it in their luggage.

A Jewish watchmaker approached me as a representative of the Zionist organizations. He asked me if I would be liberal with my inspections since the arriving Jews' ability to practice their trades was essential to the success of the State of Israel. I agreed to help them, but I wanted to know how I could tell if a tradesman was a friend of his or simply a provocateur. He told me that people would say the watchmaker sent them.

I traveled to different towns, going to shops and performing the inspections. I went through entire stacks of luggage following the Polish guidelines to the letter. When I finished the inspection I declared everything ready for transport. Then I went to the bathroom for five minutes, maybe longer. When I came out, I did not look inside the luggage again. Instead I wrapped the bundles and sealed them with a Department of Labor stamp. These packages were considered inspected at the border and were not searched again. In this way, carpenters, blacksmiths and others arrived in Israel prepared to practice their trades.

Esther's enjoyment of life was contagious and her presence brought so much happiness into our home. In the winter she loved to take sleigh rides; it was her greatest pleasure. I sat her on the sled and pulled her through the streets of Dzierzoniow while her cheeks glowed and her eyes sparkled. When I tried to take the same route back she recognized the streets and yelled 'No!' until I picked a new route. We could tell she was very bright even before she could speak.

She had such beautiful blonde hair. One night I returned home late and went into her room to say goodnight. The lights were out and I did not want to wake her so I reached into her crib and lightly touched her head. 'Oh my God,' I thought, 'why did they cut your hair?' I asked Shelly why she did this and she started laughing. I did not know that Esther was sleeping on her stomach, I had accidentally touched her behind!

There were gentile children living in some of the

maisonettes in the cul-de-sac. One of the boys, Anuszka, was the same age as Esther and also very blond, they looked like twins. By the end of the summer of 1949 they were both old enough to walk and talk. They loved to play outside and they were inseparable, enjoying each other's company enormously. One day Anuszka and Esther disappeared from the little yard out back. We ran around the neighborhood with Anuszka's mother until we found them by a school having a good time next to a group of Polish boys. We were so relieved to find them, but when Esther came home she asked me a horrible question: 'Daddy, are you sure I'm *Zyduvka*?' She could barely talk and already she was asking if she was Jewish.

As my familial roots grew, so too did my influence in the community. I continued aiding tradesmen in the recovered territories by monitoring their taxation and ensuring fair labor practices and I continued helping the emigrating Zionist with my inspection techniques. The party noticed the respect I received and asked me to attend various meetings and give speeches on their behalf. Somehow, either because of my reputation or from the help of someone like Shloime Gerszon's son Mietek, I was noticed in Warsaw.

I received a letter from the State Department asking me to come to Warsaw for an interview. I did not know what sort of job they had in mind for me, only that if they liked me I would have to take it. On the one hand I was terrified not knowing what was in store for me, but on the other hand I would almost certainly be leaving the Department of Labor, a place I had grown to detest.

Shelly and I went to Warsaw together, leaving Esther with my mother. This was at the time of the Korean War and at the railroad station in Warsaw there was a delegation of North Korean officers on a state visit. Even though this was at night there were thousands of people demonstrating on their behalf. The North Koreans wore Russian-style clothing. I did not like that scene too much.

The next day I went to the personnel office at the State Department and filled out countless forms. The following day I returned and did the same. On the third day I met with an officer who told me they wanted to move me to Stockholm for diplomatic work. He told me that my class and family origin was perfect, as was my Russian experience, including the deaths of my father and brother. With this position, however, I would have to leave my family in Poland. This was a safeguard against defection.

I could not decline the position – one did not decline such a position in a communist nation – but I despaired at the thought of leaving my family behind. I kept talking to the officer, asking questions and answering his. Thankfully he asked me about my sister. When I told him that Henya had left Poland for Israel he was shocked. 'How could you let her go?' he asked.

I responded defensively, telling him that it was not I who had let her go, but him – his department had signed the agreements with Israel. I told him that I had tried to dissuade her from leaving, which was not true, but there was nothing I could have done to stop her. The man accepted my response and told me that our interview was finished. I was to return to Dzierzoniow and await his call, which I knew would never come.

I left the personnel office and found Shelly waiting for me outside. 'Shelly,' I said, 'it's time to leave Poland.'

It was decided that we would move to Israel, but doing this would be an incredible challenge. I was utilized in many ways by the Jewish leadership in the party and they would be loath to let me go. If they suspected I intended to leave, I was sure they would have me arrested. Symbolically it was better for them to put me in jail as an enemy rather than allowing me to leave of my own free will. As it stood, the steady flow of Jews leaving the recovered territories severely crippled their hold on power in the region. They needed people like me, a respected member of the community, to stay if they hoped to remain in control for any significant length of time.

When I returned from Warsaw I did not know how I was going to register for emigration. The first step, I decided, was to extricate myself slowly from party jobs and thus limit my contact with people who would benefit from my downfall. The first thing I did was to resign from my position at the Department of Labor. To do this I utilized the letter I received from the State Department.

I told Holdonowicz that in six months I was to begin a job in Warsaw for the State Department. To prove this I showed him the letter. For a month I trained my replacement, after which I walked away from the Department of Labor forever. By doing this I no longer had contact with the elders and the Polish clerks, thus severing my connection with one set of enemies, the sympathizers of the Polish underground. The bigger problem would be breaking from the Jewish leadership in Dzierzoniow.

After I left the Department of Labor I went to see an old friend from the youth house, Nusom Pariser, about a job. He was the director of the Shoemakers Cooperative. I told him I had quit my previous job and would be leaving for Warsaw sometime within the next six months, I had to keep the story consistent. Nusom gave me a job with no trouble, making me the secretary of the cooperative.

I immediately saw all the bribery that had transpired in order for the cooperative to exist. Hundreds of shoes were sent to the members of the party in the recovered territories, for which no payment was received. Feeling brash, I cheekily sent them a bill. A few days later I received a bristling letter telling the shoemakers that they should be thanking the party for helping them organize their cooperative. Of course, they never paid.

Shortly after I began working at the Shoemakers Cooperative, I received a telegram from the district offices of the United Polish Workers' Party in Wroclaw. They asked that I travel to their headquarters for a meeting. While I was there they offered me the position of secretary of the city party committee of Dzierzoniow. In this position I would be responsible for the factories, the police, the civil administration, city hall, defensive units and the KGB in Dzierzoniow. Additionally I would be a part of the district leadership. In short, everyone in Dzierzoniow would have to report to me.

There was no way I could take this position. If I did I would not be able to leave Poland, I would instantly be a partner in their crimes and I would be culpable for all wrongdoings within the party in Dzierzoniow. I told them that I did not think a Jewish person should hold such a position because of the anti-Semitism in Poland, but they said that was not an issue in the new Poland. I told them that I was too young for the job and it was unfair that I, a little horse, should carry a load suited for a tractor, but they told me I would be surrounded with help. Finally I said that I could not take the position because I could not guarantee I would be in Dzierzoniow in the coming months, alluding to the fabricated position in Warsaw and not to my planned emigration.

This upset them very much, they had heard about the letter from the State Department and assumed the offer to be legitimate. It was all of their dreams to work for the party in Warsaw, as it was with most of the aristocracy. They accused me of arrogance and of wanting to abandon my comrades in the recovered territories. This touched a nerve and I said to them, 'Why shouldn't I go to Warsaw? Do you believe the blood of my father and brother was not red enough for me to be entitled to go to Warsaw?' With that, I put my hat under my arm and I walked out.

From that meeting I went straight to Lolek Orgon's house, Katia's old boyfriend from the echelon. He was living in Wroclaw like a king, womanizing and spending all of his money on luxuries, he even had Polish servants. He was the head of propaganda for the entire district and was, by all accounts, a regional big-shot. I went to him hoping he could help me dissuade the district committee from giving me this job.

He looked at their offer in a completely different light from me. Where I saw the position as a sort of prison, locking me into a life of deceit in Poland, he saw it as a way to gain influence and power, two things that could make life a lot of fun. When I told him it was not a job for me, he insisted it would be great. He could not understand my desire to remain untethered, he really believed in the party. In the end he did not help.

I returned home and continued working at the cooperative. In a few days I received a letter from the district committee approving me for the position of secretary of the city committee of Dzierzoniow. They gave me the date when I was to begin my new job. I did not answer the letter and I did not go to the new job. The date came and went while I remained at the cooperative helping Nusom.

I expected something from the district committee, a telegram or a letter, or even to be put under arrest, but for two weeks nothing happened. Could it be that they were afraid of me because of the letter from the State Department? I waited another two weeks and still I was not approached. I assumed that if they had not tried to force me into the secretary's job by now, they had given up all together. Now, I thought, it was time to register for emigration.

I decided to use white lies similar to the ones I used in Russia. As far as anyone in Dzierzoniow was concerned, only my mother and Moishe were registering for emigration. Secretly I had Shaya Kawe register Shelly, Esther and me in Kalisz under his address. Our cousin Esther did not register with us, because she had married a young man she had met at the youth house, a carpenter named Pinkas. This was disappointing to me because I wanted her to marry Moishe, but my mother was against this.

Once registered, we had to submit a series of documents to the Polish government to receive permission to emigrate. The documents stated that we were released from our jobs, that we had paid all our taxes and that we had given up our apartment. With this permission we could be issued a Polish passport. After getting the passport, the final step was permission from the Israeli government, which was simply a technicality – the embassy granted all Jews permission and helped them with the logistics of the voyage.

It would be a nightmare getting the required documents together for me because I would have to do it from a different city and without letting the Jewish party leaders know of my intentions. With my reputation and my political connections I was sure they could find a thousand reasons to arrest me.

I wanted to move to Kalisz, bringing Shelly and Esther with me. I left the Shoemakers Cooperative and for a couple of weeks stayed in Shaya Kawe's apartment with Shelly and Esther while my mother and Moishe remained in Dzierzoniow. Shaya Kawe had already received permission from the Israeli government and was awaiting notification of his date of departure. I assumed if I did not find a place before he left, we could take over his apartment.

Getting the documents prepared for my mother and Moishe proved fairly easy. It was no secret that they were moving to Israel, so no tricks were needed to get their tax records and Moishe's dismissal from work. The apartment in Dzierzoniow was in my mother's name, so those papers were also easily obtainable. For Shelly, Esther and myself it was a different story.

Getting our tax records was easy enough. I showed the old man at the Department of Taxation the letter from the State Department, telling him I needed our records for processing in Warsaw, and he gave me what I needed. Having our official residency in Kalisz, however, proved troubling. First, our possessions had to go through customs in Lodz as opposed to Wroclaw. Second, I did not have a job or real residency in Kalisz. I feared our applications would seem suspicious.

Officially we were living in the apartment owned by Shaya Kawe, but for more convincing documentation, and to keep clear of Dzierzoniow, I felt we needed our own place. For weeks, however, I found nothing. Kalisz was entirely different from the recovered territories; no one here wanted to help a Jewish member of the United Polish Workers' Party.

I spent the majority of my time in Kalisz, sometimes with Shelly and Esther, sometimes with my mother and sometimes alone. I tried to get a job at a Shoemakers Cooperative, just as in Dzierzoniow, but I was met with a hostile, antiSemitic reception. Jews worked in the Arnold Cooperative in Kalisz and that was it. I did not want to work there because I wanted to remain as anonymous as possible. I had enough money from all the gifts the Jewish artisans had given me, but a job would have helped me procure an apartment in Kalisz.

When I was in Kalisz and my mother was in Dzierzoniow, I would call her at the post office every day at five o'clock in the evening. A clerk would answer and I would ask her for Mrs Skorupa, who would be sitting outside her office. One evening, my mother said to me in Yiddish that some men had followed her and were listening to her conversation. I knew then that the Jewish leadership in Dzierzoniow were after me.

From that point on I never went straight from Kalisz to Dzierzoniow. Instead I went to two or three towns and registered with the police at each stop. It was a law that citizens had to register whenever they came to a new town, allowing the police to keep tabs on every one. By registering in different places I kept a steady stream of misleading information coming to the Dzierzoniow police. At times I thought my paranoia was unfounded, that I did not have to go through all of these precautions just to visit my family, but proof of my concerns surfaced one day in Dzierzoniow.

I had arrived by train and walked through the streets the Russian army used to occupy, arriving at our apartment late at night. I went straight to the basement to sleep and in the morning came up to our apartment through the back. Not five minutes later there was a knock on our front door. Shelly answered the knock as I hid behind the door. It was two plain-clothes policemen asking for me. I did not know what they wanted me for. Perhaps they had discovered that I had lied about the job in Warsaw, or that I was helping Jews smuggle illegal equipment into Israel. Really it could have been anything. I stood terrified listening to them question Shelly.

Shelly began to cry and, seeing her mother in such distress, Esther cried too. The policemen felt bad for her and asked her why she was crying. She told them she had not seen me for so long and that she did not know where I was. They told her not to cry – she was a pretty woman and she would find another husband. They stopped asking her questions and left. I immediately returned to Kalisz.

Shaya was set to leave in two weeks' time, so I arranged a meeting with an old classmate, Vranszak, who worked for the city's housing authorities. I hoped to persuade him to give me Shaya's apartment, but he did me no favors. The two weeks went by and still I did not know where I was to live. I went with Shaya Kawe to Warsaw, helping him carry all the possessions he hoped to take to Israel.

In Warsaw we discovered that he would not be able to take a Czech sewing machine he had just purchased with him. We left it with Mietek Skorupinsky instead, hoping that I could work something out later. Seeing Shaya Kawe off was very emotional for me. He was my closest friend, like a brother, and he had helped me so much. I knew we planned to see each other in Israel, but I was very skeptical about my chances of actually getting out of Poland.

I never found my own place or a job in Kalisz, but I was too anxious to wait until I had done so. I submitted all of our documents and hoped for the best. Every day that I spent in Poland I was tempting fate, the party would eventually find me.

For two weeks after Shaya Kawe left, I slept in his old apartment on a bare mattress. I spent my time during the day buying everything we had heard that we needed for life in Israel and making short visits at night to Dzierzoniow to drop off these things. We heard that it was important to bring salami and pig fat to Israel, that these were very valuable there. The apartment in Dzierzoniow looked like a butcher shop, with salamis drying everywhere. The pig fat was stored in long metal casings inside wooden boxes.

In the middle of the night I went to a carpenter from Dzierzoniow, a Jew I had helped to get papers, and asked him to construct two wooden trunks for me with secret compartments and holes for US dollars. One trunk was for Shelly and me; the other was for my mother and Moishe. Slowly we were getting the necessities together.

One day I went to Poznan to buy raincoats and rubber boots for all of us. It was a sure sign to the merchants, since I was buying these particular items, that I was a Jew. They gave me icy looks and I felt uncomfortable in the city. By the time I had finished my shopping it was late and I had missed the train back to Kalisz. I did not want to stay at the station because I feared bandits; the violence had not subsided and I was loaded with merchandise which meant I carried money.

A leather merchant with a truck was parked near the station. I chatted with him for a while and discovered that he was going to Kalisz. He said he would give me a ride. Halfway to Kalisz his truck broke down. I was forced to walk for an hour or so by the side of the road, carrying my bundles and fearing for my life, until I reached a small town called Nowydwor. I found the post office, thinking a government building was safest, and waited until morning. Eventually the postmaster gave me a ride to the train station and I made my way back to Kalisz. I walked the length of the town only to find that Shaya Kawe's apartment was no longer vacant. I found myself homeless and extremely tired.

I had very few friends in Kalisz because I had kept such a low profile. Thankfully one of the Blankrod brothers had moved back to Kalisz and worked as a tailor. I went to his house and asked if I could rest for a while. He was extremely gracious. He could see how exhausted I was and how I shivered from the cold. He put me in his own bed and let me sleep through the day. When I woke he said I could stay with him on his couch. He took my jacket and sewed a US$100 bill into the lining. I was to deliver it to his brother in Israel.

Shortly after, thank God, our permission arrived in Kalisz. The emphasis on residency, we discovered, was a recovered-territory phenomenon so our application had not been closely scrutinized. The fact that our registered home in Kalisz did not belong to Shaya Kawe or me proved inconsequential, though this would have been a problem in Dzierzoniow. Miraculously, the permission for Moishe and my mother arrived the same day.

It was time to apply for our passports. All of us went to Warsaw together. In Warsaw I felt like a second-class citizen. The Polish office workers who handled the paperwork involved in the issuing of passports treated us rudely, making us feel like we did not belong there. When they discovered my mother had forgotten a piece of paperwork, they seemed to take pleasure in telling us that her passport could not be processed.

I was so angry with her that I raised my voice. She calmly told me not to speak to her like that and I was instantly ashamed. It was the first time I had ever treated her so disrespectfully and it hurt me terribly. I was angry and afraid, the tension I felt had turned to desperation and I took it out on my mother. My fears were not unfounded; there were people in Warsaw from Dzierzoniow and from Kalisz. Those who approached me I told I was helping my mother, but those who did not, I worried, could report that they had seen me trying to flee.

I sent Moishe and my mother back to Dzierzoniow while Shelly, Esther and I remained in Warsaw. I had US$500 but I was afraid to stash it all in our trunks. We had heard rumors that some luggage arrived in Israel in pieces and I was afraid the money would be lost. While waiting for Moishe and my mother to return, I heard that the Hartwick International Transportation Company, the same company that would be shipping our luggage, was selling 100-kilogram bags of sugar. If you had US dollars you could buy these bags and receive them in Israel. The Polish government wanted US dollars because the economy was so poor. Why this was not widely advertised, I did not know. Since we had heard that sugar was scarce in Israel, I decided to buy two bags in my name. I had to convince the clerk there that, although I lacked a passport, I would soon be in Israel. It cost me US$400 and it seemed like a wise investment. If it worked out, I would be able to put a down payment on an apartment in Israel.

After three days Moishe and my mother returned. The paperwork was completed and we were told our passports would arrive in Dzierzoniow and Kalisz in a few days. We returned to our respective cities and waited. Thankfully, the passports did arrive.

Our plan was to leave together from Dzierzoniow. This way it would seem, with our combined luggage, that only my mother and Moishe were leaving and Shelly, Esther and I were simply going to see them off. Before I went to Dzierzoniow, I took a last walk through Kalisz knowing it was unlikely I would ever return.

I walked past side streets I had taken to escape the Nazis and others where I pretended to fix my carriage while delivering bread to our relatives. I stood outside the former homes of my friends from the Poalei Zion youth group not knowing if they had survived the war. I walked by the filled-in river where the bridge used to stand, picturing the Black Hands smiling and rough-housing. I wondered if I would ever see such a show of Jewish strength again. There were no Jews on these streets, all that remained was their blood and tears.

The bookstore where I had first charted my imaginary route to Baranavicy and later read the Nazi propaganda was now a communist bookstore. The map on display was of Korea, showing the territorial gains of the North Koreans in the war and the little hope the United States had at the time. This was before MacArthur turned the tide.

I felt like I was walking among ghosts, through the spirits of martyrs and the innocent who were killed for no other reason than hatred. I stopped by my first home, 21 Ciasna Street, and saw only Polish children playing in the back. I remembered my father lifting the big piece of iron and the Yeshiva boys fighting the Pole by the well, but nothing like that would ever happen there again. When I walked through these streets as a child I was recognized by almost everyone. The only one to recognize me now was our Polish neighbor Sczepen, who yelled, 'Butcher!' when he saw me. He was so kind, the only one, and I felt better having seen his big mustache and twinkling eyes.

I said the Kaddish one last time and left Kalisz. It was the last time that I ever set eyes on the home of my youth.

The tension I felt in Dzierzoniow equaled that of my attempts to flee the Polish army under Stalin. I tried my best not to be short with my family, asking them to do things instead of ordering. My anxiety was high because I was sure I would be arrested at any moment and all our plans would be lost. We successfully gathered our things and made it to the train station. On the platform we waited for what seemed an interminable amount of time, but eventually the train came and we headed to Wroclaw.

In Wroclaw I was nervous that someone from the party would see me, but I needed to help my mother get her luggage through customs. Again I was extremely lucky and we finished our business unnoticed and boarded a train for Lodz.

On the train there was uneasiness among the people. They complained about the government bitterly and cursed the Stalinist influence. I did not know what they were talking about, but soon discovered that the Polish government had substantially devalued the Polish zloty. What was 100 zlotys had become one. Later one zloty became three. Prices, we discovered, had also been raised. It was a disaster for the Polish people and a clear attempt by the government to make them dependent on the state.

We arrived in Lodz at night and went through customs. At the last moment I removed a number of gold coins from the secret compartments in my trunk. The only gold we were allowed to take out of the country was wedding rings and I did not want to risk being arrested as a smuggler. Also, with the devaluation of the zloty and not knowing how long we would have to wait for our transport out of Poland, I figured we might need some liquid assets in Warsaw. All we had was our smaller bags with clothing and the provisions for the journey. The trunks and bigger bundles would be put in storage until we were assigned to an echelon leaving Warsaw.

I had plenty of money, but the devaluation of the zloty did affect my plans. I had heard that it was possible to buy a portable house from the Swedish government, one that could be shipped to Israel and be ready to move into when we arrived. These houses were said to have insulation, and be equipped with plumbing and electrical fittings; amenities we heard were scarce in Israel. I planned to get permission to buy this house from the Soviet ambassador, using my service record and the fact that my mother was a Red Army widow to do so. Then I would go to the Swedish embassy to pay them and arrange for the house's transport. With the devaluation, this plan fell apart. My greatest hope for any kind of financial security rested with the purchase of the Hartwick sugar.

We came to Warsaw unsure of when we would leave. We were one group registered from two different places so it was unlikely that we would get assigned to the same echelon. I was terrified that my mother and Moishe would have to make the journey without me. I was also afraid of what would happen to Shelly and Esther if I was to be taken away at the border.

I went to the Israeli consulate to finalize our travel plans. The atmosphere inside that building was electric. Everything was painted in Israeli blue and white and pictures of kibbutzim, soldiers and barrel-chested fishermen adorned the walls. Unfortunately, seeing half a dozen or so people from Dzierzoniow muted my excitement. I had no choice but to approach them and tell them lies. I told them my mother and brother were going to Israel, and, despite my pleading, I could not convince them otherwise. It was the same old spiel, but I felt I had to keep up the myth. I also saw a man named Goytl Skurka from Kalisz, whom I ran into on the boats in Russia. I told him the same lie – it was getting ridiculous.

I asked the clerks at the Israeli consulate for an appointment and was soon granted one with a man named Barzelai. He was a real kibbutz-type Israeli, with an unbuttoned shirt and long, curly hair. I was so impressed with his attitude and his confidence that I did not hesitate to ask for a favor immediately. From the reception I had received from the people of Dzierzoniow in the foyer and the documents I carried, he was convinced that I was what I claimed to be – a big-shot in political trouble. I asked him to expedite my arrangements and to put my mother and Moishe on the same echelon as Shelly, Esther and myself. I did not want to brag, but I told him of some of the things I was doing to help Jews in the recovered territories and how this had put me in danger. I told him I could not walk around Warsaw for long as people from Dzierzoniow were already taking notice of me and soon word would get back to the Jewish leaders. I feared I would be arrested before I was able to leave.

He pondered my situation for a few minutes, looking over all of our passports and documents. Then he made a few calls and took the documents out of the room. I was terrified. He returned and said he had helped. I do not know how he did it, but he had arranged for all of us to be on the same echelon and even waived the transportation fee. 'Mr Skorupa', he said, 'the Joint Distribution Committee has covered your fees, and you and your family will leave tomorrow.'

# 18 Coming home

Barring any unforeseen difficulties, my family and I would leave Warsaw in the morning and be out of Poland by the afternoon, but I began to worry. Just as in Russia I was obsessed with the idea of denouncers, enemies who would recognize me, say something to the party authorities and have me arrested. Much of this was fantasy, and I recognized it as such, but the paranoia and the anxiety felt real. I wanted to hide somewhere until the minute our echelon departed, but there were last-minute preparations to be made.

I walked around Warsaw all afternoon selling gold coins and various trinkets, steering clear of anyone I recognized. I was able to accumulate US$20, which I stashed inside my shoe, and a bundle of Polish zlotys. I am sure I could have gotten a much better price for the gold outside Poland, but I wanted to minimize the easily detectable contraband before we went through customs.

As a normal Jew I could have left Poland with little trouble, but as a party member, and a minor big-shot, there would be suspicion of corruption and I could be treated as a defector. I wanted to get rid of my party documents before I crossed the border. If someone saw me destroy or hide the documents, however, I would be in serious trouble. I felt that Warsaw was too dangerous to try to do anything with them, so I kept them in my pocket.

We spent the night in a Jewish family's home in the Praha district of Warsaw. There were a number of Jewish families who rented space to émigrés set to leave for Israel. The accommodation was not great, my bed being the top of a table, but we were thankful not to be disturbed during the night. In the morning we gathered our things and walked excitedly to the train station.

We waited for our echelon to be called. There were people from Dzierzoniow and there was Goytl, from Kalisz, waiting for the same train. I still had them thinking I was only there to escort my mother and brother to the border. I was anxious and I appeared that way, but I tried to conceal my agitation by keeping active. I moved around the station looking displeased and authoritative, trying to carry myself as the big-shot they knew me to be, but inside I was crumbling.

On one of my walks I went into the toilets and discovered the walls covered in graffiti. The slogans were shocking: 'Down with the Jews! Death to the Russians! Long live the Polish Underground Army! Shit, Pole, Shit! It's all you can do without punishment in Poland!' I went to the other toilets and found the same type of writing, so I brought it to the attention of a Polish railway worker. I told him that Warsaw was Poland's capital, its greatest city, and this was the city's most frequented train station. I asked him how those slogans, so anti-Semitic and so anti-government, could remain untouched. He shrugged his shoulders and said they were running trains, not toilets. Not much had changed in Poland and I was glad to be leaving.

At last our echelon was called and we settled into a train. Around us, Jews from different communities made themselves comfortable and prepared for the journey. I could tell how someone had spent the war years by his or her demeanor on the train. Those of us who had been on trains back and forth to Russia thought nothing of a short trip to Italy, but others were terrified. There was a young woman with a very small child, nervously looking out the window and clumsily trying to lodge jewelry into her seat. It was obvious that she had not been exposed to very much, that she had been hidden during the war. My mother spoke gently to her, telling her everything would be fine as the train rolled out of Warsaw and into the Polish countryside.

A man from the Israeli consulate joined our echelon as an escort. He asked us for all of our Polish money so he could pay the inevitable fines that the group would accrue at the border. It made sense since our zlotys were almost useless here in Poland and entirely useless abroad. I gave him all of our money, trusting and hoping he would facilitate the border crossing for us.

We tore through the countryside, knowing everything we saw would be our last glimpse of Poland. I thought of the cycles of our lives, how we were once again uprooted and at the mercy of the trains. This was the second time I was leaving a country in which I had learned to succeed; the second time I forfeited my status as an influential person in the hope of finding a better life for my family. I prayed we were making the right decision, we had heard such terrible things about life in Israel.

As the hours passed, I began to worry increasingly about crossing the Czech border. I still had my party documents and I feared the reaction they would cause if found by the border authorities. I decided I would mail them to a fictitious address in a town on the other side of Poland. It was my hope that the letter would circulate for a long time before anyone opened it.

In the afternoon we came to Zebrzedowice, the Polish–Czechoslovakian border town. We were to go through the Polish side first, train by train, and then the Czechoslovakian side. The representative from the Israeli consulate took all of our travel documents and handed them to a Polish officer. We disembarked and formed a straggly queue for our final customs inspection. As we waited, I slipped the letter containing my party documents into a mailbox. I felt such relief when I let them go.

The line moved slowly. The inspector was a surly man speaking heavily accented Polish. He treated the passengers as second-class citizens at best. I believed he was an ethnic German working for the Polish government. My mother, Moishe, Shelly and Esther went through without incident, but I did not like the tone of voice he used with them. Whether real or imagined, I could sense an underlying anti-Semitism and brutality in him, and I desperately wanted to show him that we would not be pushed around. I knew, however, that I had to keep my mouth shut – getting through customs was far more important than proving a point.

The Jewish people throughout the war and for years after were always unruly when going through customs. Everyone, absolutely everyone, was smuggling something in his or her luggage or clothing. As a result there was nervous chatter, pushing and a general unrest in the line. The inspector took exception and yelled, 'What the hell is going on here? Do you think you are in a synagogue and you can push each other like animals?' My blood boiled. I should have kept my mouth shut but I could not. I foolishly believed that I was still a big-shot and I said to him, 'What right have you to talk to us that way?'

He let me have it. He went through my luggage and found a reason to confiscate almost everything. For every item he took away I was given a fine. He tried to take my Russian uniform from me but I would not let him. 'That is the property of the Soviet Union', I said. 'I will call up the Soviet ambassador and have you arrested!' He did not take the uniform, but he told me to put it on over my existing outfit. In the end he had taken, among other things, our raincoats and rubber boots, the jacket with the US$100 and all of my clothing save the two sets of clothes I had on my back. It was a disaster.

All of my money, except the US$20 in my shoe, was with the representative from the Israeli consulate, who was nowhere to be found. I could not pay the fines. The inspector called in a border guard and told him to hold me until I came up with the money. With his gun pointed at my back I begged every person I saw for some Polish money. Many people from Dzierzoniow, finally realizing I was actually leaving with them, gave me some of their money, as did perfect strangers. After an hour or so I collected enough to pay the fines. At last the Polish border guards let me through to the Czechoslovakian side.

My family was in a panic. They saw nothing of what had happened and had little to do but wait in agony. When I saw them I told them that nothing had happened, that everything was all right, but I was trembling. With all my fear and worry about getting through the border, I almost sabotaged it completely by opening my big mouth. I felt so ashamed.

On the Czechoslovakian side we had no troubles, their officials were friendly and efficient. They kept our documents as a precaution against anyone running away, which made me nervous, but otherwise treated us politely and warmly. By late in the evening everyone had completed the border crossing and our echelon rolled smoothly out of the station and into the Czechoslovakian night.

We stopped a few times and picked up a few small groups of Czechoslovakian Jews, but overall the night's journey was uneventful. On leaving Russia I had felt that with every mile I peeled off a layer of Soviet armor. Similarly, with every mile we covered in Czechoslovakia, my mind let go a layer of tension. In the morning, when we arrived at the Austrian border, I was relaxed, even smiling. I could not remember the last time I had genuinely smiled.

There was only one Austrian official. He stamped our documents and sent us through. At this checkpoint I saw more Jews from Dzierzoniow who finally realized I was emigrating with them. They were amused by my ruse and together we laughed. There was a former owner of a café in Dzierzoniow, though he was really a carpenter, whom I knew quite well. I had been to his café many times with members of the Jewish leadership to discuss and plan the world revolution. He was shocked to see me and asked how I had managed to get out. I believed he, along with many of the people from Dzierzoniow, thought I was running away from corruption or other wrongdoings, after all, they had known me as a big-shot with a comfortable life. I did not care what they thought, nor did I wish to explain my actions. All of that was in the past.

We traveled through the day and into the night, stopping a few times to pick up more Jews. The spirit was good and our optimism was high. It was not like the blustery chatter of the ride to Russia, nor like the self-assured promises of a great socialist society we spoke of on our return to Poland. We did not know what awaited us and we accepted this. It was enough to know we were moving to a Jewish country, whatever hardships would be, would be. It was refreshing to be surrounded by realists for the first time in my adult life.

In the morning we went through Italian customs. Again, there was just a man stamping documents, nothing rigorous.

By mid-afternoon we reached Venice, the train's final stop. It was a Sunday and it was raining. We saw masses of Italians on bicycles holding umbrellas, it looked like a violent sea of black parasols, bumping into each other and moving in currents. The city reminded me of Leningrad with all of its canals, and I thought of how happy I was to be so far away from Vera and the communist world.

The rain stopped and we went to the docks, awaiting the call to enter our ship. Around us Italian peddlers in little boats approached us with a thousand different things to sell. I spent US$10 on a Siemens radio. The peddler said, '*Buono! Buono!'* I did not know if he was swindling me or not, I only knew that radios were said to be very valuable in Israel. It turned out to be a decent radio.

Finally we were called onto the ship; a large, white steamer called *Galilee*. The Israeli sailors did not look very Jewish to me. Their loose-fitting and unbuttoned shirts exposed bare chests, their hair was wild and wind-blown, knives were tucked into their belts and their muscles were bronzed. An argument between some Italians and a few of the Israeli sailors began shortly after we boarded. In an instant, fists were flying and the Italians retreated. I was so impressed – this was the display of Jewish strength my father would have loved.

The inside of the hull was framed with beautiful wooden beams and offered a wide-open space for the passengers. Our luggage, that which was put through customs in Wroclaw and Lodz, was down below where the ballast was kept. We departed from Venice in a misty haze but soon the weather cleared and the Adriatic seemed enchanting. The spirit generated by the fight between the sailors and the Italians set the tone for the entire voyage. We were on our way home, we were so happy.

Esther was a devil to the sailors, but they loved her intrusions. She ran around that ship like it was a playground, pulling at the Israelis' legs, asking all sorts of questions and not letting them work. She was adorable. She wore a brown jumpsuit that Shelly had made for her and she was so happy on the water.

Shelly and I became close to a Czech couple our echelon had picked up along the way. They were very friendly, as were most people on the ship, and they gave little Esther a few treats.

I ran into Goytl on the second day and he finally realized that I was not staying in Poland. He was not staying with the rest of the passengers because his son was a member of the crew – he and his wife stayed in his cabin. In 1930 Goytl's boy, a Zionist, left the family for Palestine, even though his parents were staunch communists. Now they were reunited on the journey to Israel. Through this connection I sent a telegram to Henya, hoping she would meet us at the port in Haifa. I was happy I did not have to go through the regular staff to do this as the language barrier would have been difficult to overcome.

The food on the voyage was not bad. We ate in shifts and waited for our unit to be called over the ship's loudspeaker. We normally ate as a family and with the Czech couple. Some people from Dzierzoniow joined us from time to time and we enjoyed these meals. The Adriatic and the Mediterranean seas were glassy calm, which put us in a relaxed and peaceful mood.

Midway through the voyage, Esther wilted like a little flower. She became feverish and suffered from dysentery and we were desperately worried. The Czech couple gave her oranges and things they thought might make her feel better, but nothing seemed to help. Thankfully, the first day of her illness proved to be the worst, although she did not recover fully during the trip. Shelly spent every moment caring for her, with my mother helping in any way she could.

It became clear that Esther was going to be healthy again in time, but it gave us a scare. The reaction from the passengers was heartwarming. Everyone said something nice to Esther and to us, and we understood this to be the spirit of community that would help us all in Israel. The sailors also sent their best wishes for Esther; they had really enjoyed her antics during the first days of the voyage.

The weather could not have been better. Apart from Esther's illness, everything was perfect. In the blue-green waters of the Mediterranean, we began to see dolphins swimming next to the boat, a magical sight! Over the loudspeaker the crew played Hebrew songs, which filled my heart with warmth and pride. It was glorious on that water. I felt that all the years of tragedy and pain had finally come to an end. I thought of my father and Nuchem and knew that they were proud and happy that we had fulfilled the old Zionist dream.

I went down below, hoping to find a toy or something in our baggage that would make Esther smile. I opened one of our trunks and discovered that somebody had stolen the canisters of pig fat. I was upset and unhappy that someone would steal from us on this type of journey, but upon further reflection I thought that maybe it was not such a good idea to bring such a thing to the Holy Land. I let the incident pass unnoticed.

On the fifth day of our voyage in the late afternoon a voice came over the loudspeaker. 'Soon you will see Haifa. Soon you will see Israel.' Everybody ran to the top deck and looked over the horizon. In the distance we could make out the shore and soon we could see Mount Carmel. Coming closer we could see the hills of Haifa and the flat-topped roofs. I stupidly said that the houses were not fully constructed, but someone told me that that was how they were designed. As more land came into view, I felt the holiness spreading over my eyes. Somebody began singing the national anthem of Israel, the *Hatikvah*, and we all joined in. Some of us cheered and some of us cried, but there was no second-guessing, no trepidation. It was Friday evening, the start of the sabbath, and we had come home.

We were not allowed off the ship until we cleared customs and had a brief medical examination. We reported to a German-speaking doctor that our daughter was ill. He told us that her illness was not serious in this climate and he would take her to a hospital. Shelly, however, would not let him take Esther away. She did not question his abilities as a doctor, she just would not be separated from her daughter. She asked if, as a registered nurse, she could accompany the child to the hospital. The doctor agreed and my wife and daughter left the ship.

The rest of us went through customs and disembarked. The Israeli officials laughed at me because I brought dozens of empty bottles to the customs inspection. I had collected the bottles during our trip, saving beverage containers, since I had heard of such shortages in Israel. There was no bottle shortage, nor, I discovered later, was there a sugar shortage.

By bus we went a few miles to Shar Aliya, the center for immigration. This was where all the immigrants were held until housing could be sorted out. Shar Aliya was secured by a fence and barbed wire, but it was unguarded. It was dark by now and a steady rain had begun to fall, yet at the entrance of the camp hundreds of Jews waited to see who had arrived from the boat. Sure enough there were a few people from Dzierzoniow who recognized me. 'Skorupa? You are here?' they asked.

In a line, we were given an outfit and food cards. After a nice introduction we were assigned a tent. The organization was spectacular, only the rain had made our tent a sea and our beds became islands. There was a group of Egyptian immigrants in our tent as well, but apart from exchanging smiles and nods we had little contact. I lay there trying to sleep, but I worried too much about Shelly and Esther. I did not know where they were or how my little angel was doing. I noticed that Moishe and my mother were also awake.

I could see they were bewildered by this place, by the strange light that filled the tent, despite the late hour, and the shimmering calm of the water beneath our beds. It was surreal. The strange sound of the Egyptians' language only added to the mystery of our situation. In time the others dosed off, but I remained awake almost the entire night. In the very early hours of the morning, I heard one of the Egyptians relieving himself into the water. I felt sorry for him – what else was he to do?

The next day was beautiful. I walked out of the tent and saw an orange sun rising over a blue sea, its waves rolling peacefully into the shore. In my white, shortsleeved shirt I enjoyed the warmth and the pleasant ocean breeze. I did what came naturally to me – I explored the camp. I also wanted to find Shelly and Esther.

I wondered where all the people waiting at the gates had come from and soon discovered a compound of barracks left over from the British occupation. The gate, I now saw in the light, had been made to resemble a Union Jack. I spoke to a few people by the barracks and asked them where I could find the hospital for children. Someone told me it was a small wooden building on stilts behind the main medical center. Extremely anxious to see Shelly and Esther, I rushed over to the building, climbed the walls and banged on the windows. Shelly came right over, knowing it had to be me. When she saw me she cried. I asked her how Esther was doing and she told me she was fine. She brought her to the window and I saw her sweet face smiling down at me. The happiness I felt brought me to tears.

Shelly told me that in all likelihood she would be working as a nurse in that hospital. She had met a woman there from Lodz, not a nurse but someone on the staff of the hospital who had connections in the camp. She was a very good friend of the camp director's wife, who was also from Lodz. Getting Shelly a position would not be a problem, but she would have to wait a few days for her paperwork to clear. I was always so impressed by my wife, for someone who resembled a delicate flower, she had the strength of an oak tree.

Again, the organization of that camp was incredible. Later that day, Shelly and Esther left the hospital and joined the family as we moved out of the tents and into the barracks. We were assigned to barrack No. 14, by now my family's official lucky number. There were some 120 people living in that barrack, which was not luxurious but clean. The group fascinated me, I had never seen such a collection of different peoples. How could all of these strange-looking people be Jewish like me?

There were Jews from India, Persia, Morocco, Yemen, Algeria, Tunisia and almost every European country. I could not help staring at the Middle Eastern Jews, who looked like Arabs to me. The men seemed warlike, sporting crooked knives and turbans, and the women, decorated with face paint and long jewelry, were bewitching. The North African Jews dressed much like the Europeans, in collared shirts and suit coats, but their skin was so dark, so weathered. We were all so different, yet we had shared the burden of carrying the teachings of our forefathers throughout the centuries. Now that we had returned to our homeland, what kind of society would we make together?

We settled into the barrack and then we ate. There was plenty of bread and plenty of food, in fact, we had more food cards than we could use. The shortages we had heard about were grossly exaggerated. After eating we went to the medical center for a more thorough physical examination. The medical facilities were modern and well staffed, and we were told that we would have free care for the next six months. If there were terrible hardships in Israel, the government did its best to keep them hidden from the newly arrived immigrants.

That night the Israelis performed a concert for our benefit filled with modern Hebrew songs and music. Yemenite Jews, with wild hair, carried torches and danced in a ceremony heralding the coming harvest. Soon a speaker approached the podium surrounded by an entourage that included Israeli soldiers. It was David Ben-Gurion. We could hardly believe it. As refugees it was impossible to think that our arrival could warrant a visit from the head of the nation. In Russia and Poland we were merely seen as a nuisance. What he said we could not comprehend, but we understood everything with our hearts. To conclude the concert a Yemenite woman sang, 'David Ben-Gurion is the king of Israel.' These were some of the only Hebrew words we knew.

On Sunday my sister arrived. She had not received the telegram I had sent from the boat, but she had been periodically checking with the Israeli officials. What a reunion we had! I could see how happy she was in Israel and I could see that she was pregnant.

She and Oskar were living in temporary housing in Etlit, which was not far from Haifa, still waiting for an apartment from the government. I thought it was strange that they continued to wait for a home after having been here for over a year, but she assured me they were happy and healthy. This was the way it had to be in Israel as hundreds of thousands of immigrants were arriving every month.

Later that day two of my cousins from my mother's side of

the family, the Boms, found us in the camp. They had a carpentry business in Jaffa, using very modern German machinery sent to them by their brother Josef in Berlin. They were officially living in temporary housing because by doing so the government was obligated to build them a permanent home. In reality they rented beds in Tel Aviv and rode rented bikes to Jaffa every day.

There we were, by some miracle, two days in Israel and already surrounded by family. Their presence allowed us to make plans, to be optimistic. Hearing about the government's obligation to provide housing was a relief, it meant that they would find an apartment for us and I would not lament the useless sugar or the missed opportunity to purchase a Swedish house.

Shelly had found work, but I needed some method of making money. I did not want to impose too much on my cousins, but I thought I might be able to help them at their store. I offered them the radio I purchased in Italy in exchange for employment. They laughed at me and told me to keep the radio – things were not done that way in Israel. I would work for them because I was family, not because I had something to offer. It would take some time before I relinquished the Soviet methods.

I was a carpenter again, something I had not been since 1939. In my youth I left a good apprenticeship to study under Master David Gelbert, a decision that seemed so important to me at the time, like life and death. Now, after living through Moraviny, the slaughter at the cemetery, the cold of the Russian north, the treachery of the Soviets and the disappointment of the new Poland, I was back where I had started.

My youth had been cut short by war, but the prospect of picking up where I left off made me feel young again. It was the circle of life, against all odds we had found the beginning again. I was convinced that it was not by accident that we had survived. By putting family in front of everything else and by keeping my pact with God, we had survived. I was proud of everything that we had accomplished together and I was sure we would thrive in this amazing, unfathomable, Jewish state.

# Author's Note

Throughout my years in Russia and again in Poland, I never met one convinced communist. It is an inorganic system, flawed by its rejection of human nature and its dependence on inapplicable political theory. Since those first days in Israel, I have cherished every moment I have lived within a democracy. Still, despite my conviction that my family has bested the evil that attempted to destroy us, we are damaged people living in foreign lands. In short, we remain refugees.

There are tragedies from that period of time that transcend religion, class and culture, but still the most difficult for me to comprehend is the annihilation of our way of life. Our little Jewish ghetto was not allowed to fail or succeed on its own; instead it was wiped off the face of the earth.

As bizarre and unpredictable as my life has been, my story, and the story of my family, is not unique. Each one of us from that era endured equally as horrific, sensational and sometimes uplifting journeys. It is my hope that this memoir serves as a remembrance for those who were unable to tell their stories.

Books in the
Library of Holocaust Testimonies series
may be bought in groups of 10
at a discount of 25%

For further details contact
Toby Harris
Tel:020 8952 9526   Fax:020 8952 9242
Email: toby.harris@vmbooks.com